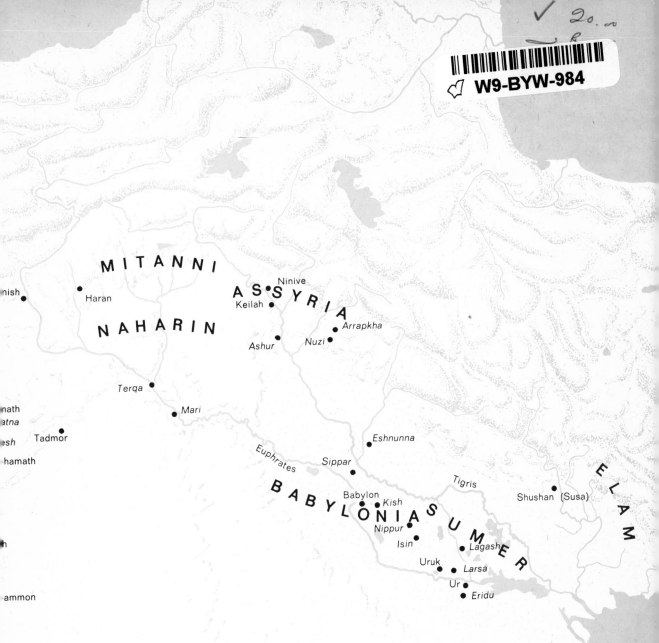

MITANNI

ASSYRIA

NAHARIN

Ninive

Keilah

Arrapkha

Ashur Nuzi

Terqa

Mari

Eshnunna

Euphrates Sippar

Tigris

ELAM

Shushan (Susa)

BABYLONIA SUMER

Babylon Kish

Nippur

Isin Lagaseh

Uruk Larsa

Ur Eridu

Haran

nish

nath

atna

esh Tadmor

hamath

h

ammon

Tema

THE ANCIENT EAST
IN THE SECOND MILLENIUM B.C.E.

Locality mentioned in the Bible . . . . Hazor

Ancient locality mentioned in other sources . . . . *Isin*

Modern name . . . . [Beni Hasan]

JUDGES

THE WORLD HISTORY
OF THE JEWISH PEOPLE

FIRST SERIES: ANCIENT TIMES

VOLUME III: JUDGES

GENERAL EDITOR
BENJAMIN MAZAR

MANAGING EDITOR
ALEXANDER PELI

JEWISH HISTORY PUBLICATIONS LTD.

JUDGES

VOLUME : III

EDITOR

BENJAMIN MAZAR

RUTGERS UNIVERSITY PRESS, 1971

LIBRARY OF CONGRESS CATALOGUE CARD NUMBER 64-15907
ISBN 0–8135–0663–8 look in 1964

PRINTED IN ISRAEL BY PELI PRINTING WORKS LTD., GIVATAYIM

CONTENTS

PART ONE: CANAAN IN THE EGYPTIAN NEW KINGDOM PERIOD

CHAPTER I

CHAPTER II

CHAPTER III

CHAPTER IV

PART TWO: BEGINNING OF THE NATION

CHAPTER V

CHAPTER VI

V

CONTENTS

AUTHORS

PLATES

DRAWINGS

MAPS

PUBLISHER'S NOTE

The present book, Volume III in the First Series of the World History of the Jewish People, is a direct continuation of PATRIARCHS, Volume II of this Series, which appeared recently. The period covered by these two volumes is, in effect, one unit with inter-connected themes throughout.

Professor Mazar's introduction to the previous volume is, therefore, also relevant as an introduction to this volume.

Finally, we want to thank Mrs. Yvonne Eshanu for her editorial assistance in preparing this volume as well as PATRIARCHS.

ABBREVIATIONS FOR BIBLICAL BOOKS

Genesis	Gen.	Habakkuk	Hab.
Exodus	Ex.	Zephaniah	Zeph.
Leviticus	Lev.	Haggai	Hag.
Numbers	Num.	Zechariah	Zech.
Joshua	Josh.	Malachi	Mal.
Judges	Jud.	Psalms	Ps.
I Samuel	I Sam.	Canticles (Song of Songs)	Cant.
II Samuel	II Sam.	Lamentations	Lam.
Isaiah	Isa.	Ecclesiastes	Eccl.
Jeremiah	Jer.	Daniel	Dan.
Ezekiel	Ezek.	Nehemiah	Neh.
Hosea	Hos.	I Chronicles	I Chron.
Obadiah	Ob.	II Chronicles	II Chron.

For quotations from the Bible, the English translation published by the Jewish Publication Society of America has been used. Passages from the Torah were taken from the newly retranslated (1967) version; passages from Prophets and Writings were taken from the standard version (2nd ed., 1955).

ABBREVIATIONS FOR JOURNALS
AND SCIENTIFIC BOOKS

AASOR	— Annual of the American Schools of Oriental Research
AfO	— Archiv für Orientforschung
AJSL	— American Journal of Semitic Languages and Literatures
Alt, Kleine Schriften	— A. Alt, Kleine Schriften zur Geschichte des Volkes Israel, Israel, I–III, München 1953–1959
ANEP	— J. B. Pritchard, The Ancient Near East in Pictures Relating to the Old Testament, Princeton 1954
ANET	— J. B. Pritchard (ed.), Ancient Near Eastern Texts Relating to the Old Testament^2, Princeton 1955
AO	— Der Alte Orient
ARE	— J. H. Breasted, Ancient Records of Egypt, I–V, Chicago 1906–1907
ARM	— Archives royales de Mari
BAr	— Biblical Archaeologist
BASOR	— Bulletin of the American Schools of Oriental Research
BWAT	— Beiträge zur Wissenschaft des Alten und Neuen Testaments
BZAW	— Beihefte zur Zeitschrift für die alttestamentliche Wissenschaft
CAD	— The Chicago Assyrian Dictionary
CAH	— Cambridge Ancient History
CBQ	— Catholic Biblical Quarterly
CRAI	— Comptes rendus, Academie des inscriptions et belles-lettres
Goetze, AM	— A. Goetze, Die Annalen des Muršiliš, MVAG, 38 (1933)
Gordon, UH	— C. H. Gordon, Ugaritic Handbook, Roma 1947
Gordon, UM	— C. H. Gordon, Ugaritic Manual, Roma 1955
HTR	— Harvard Theological Review
HUCA	— Hebrew Union College Annual
IEJ	— Israel Exploration Journal
JAOS	— Journal of the American Oriental Society
JBL	— Journal of Biblical Literature
JCS	— Journal of Cuneiform Studies
JEA	— Journal of Egyptian Archaeology
JNES	— Journal of Near Eastern Studies
JPOS	— Journal of the Palestine Oriental Society
JQR	— Jewish Quarterly Review
JSS	— Journal of Semitic Studies
KAV	— Keilschrifttexte aus Assur verschiedenen Inhalts
Kittel, GVI	— R. Kittel, Geschichte des Volkes Israel, I–III, Stuttgart 1922–1928

Knudtzon, EA	— J. A. Knudtzon, Die El-Amarna Tafeln, Leipzig 1915
Maisler,	— B. Maisler, Untersuchungen zur alten Geschichte und
Untersuchungen	Ethnographie Syriens und Palästina, Giessen 1930
MDOG	— Mitteilungen der deutschen orientalischen Gesellschaft
Mercer, AT	— S. A. B. Mercer, The Tell el-Amarna Tablets, Toronto 1939
MVAG	— Mitteilungen der vorderasiatisch-ägyptischen Gesellschaft
OLZ	— Orientalische Literaturzeitung
OTS	— Oudtestamentische Studien
PEFQS	— Palestine Exploration Fund, Quarterly Statement
PEQ	— Palestine Exploration Quarterly
PJB	— Palästina — Jahrbuch
PRU	— Palais royal d'Ugarit
RA	— Revue d'Assyrologie et d'Archéologie Orientale
RB	— Revue biblique
RHR	— Revue de l'histoire des religions
RSO	— Rivista degli studi orientali
VT	— Vetus Testamentum
VTS	— Supplements to Vetus Testamentum
Wiseman, Alalakh	— D. J. Wiseman, The Alalakh Tablets, London 1953
WZKM	— Wiener Zeitschrift für die Kunde des Morgenlandes
ZA 1–44	— Zeitschrift für Assyriologie und verwandte Gebiete
45 et seq	— Zeitschrift für Assyriologie und Vorderasiatische Archäologie
ZAW	— Zeitschrift für die alttestamentliche Wissenschaft
ZDMG	— Zeitschrift der deutschen morgenländischen Geselschaft
ZDPV	— Zeitschrift des deutschen Palästina-Vereins

HEBREW-ENGLISH TRANSLITERATION

1. All Hebrew names found in the Bible are given as they appear in the English translation of the Holy Scriptures by the Jewish Publication Society of America, Philadelphia, 1955.

2. Those names that are familiar to the English reader are rendered in their customary, accepted spelling (e. g. Caesarea).

3. All other Hebrew names and words are transliterated as follows:

א	Not noted at beginning or end of word; otherwise by ', e. g. pᵉ'ēr or pē'ēr (פְּאֵר), mē'ïr (מֵאִיר).
ב	b
ב	v
ג	g
ג	g
ד	d
ד	d
ה	h (unless consonantal, ה at the end of the word is not transliterated)
ו	w
ז	z
ח	ḥ
ט	ṭ
י	y
כ	k
כ	ḵ
ל	l
מ	m
נ	n
ס	s
ע	'
פ	p
פ	f
צ	ẓ
ק	q
ר	r
שׁ	sh, š
שׂ	s
ת	t
ת	t (Except in the word בית – *beth*)

a) The *dagesh lene* is not indicated, save in the letters ב and פ. *Dagesh forte* is indicated by doubling the letter.

b) The Hebrew definite article is indicated by *ha* or *he* followed by a hyphen, but without the next letter doubled, e. g. *ha-shānā*, not *ha-shshānā*.

ˉ	a	ְּֽ	e
ˉ:	ă		ĕ
ָ	ā	וּ	ū
ָ	o	וֹ	ō
ָ:	ŏ		u
״	ē		i
״	ē, ēi		ī

Sheva mobile (שוא נע) is indicated thus: ᵉ or ĕ. Neither long vowels nor *sheva mobile* are indicated in proper names.

ARABIC-ENGLISH TRANSLITERATION

ء — ' (not indicated at the beginning of a word)		ض — ḍ
		ط — ṭ
ب — b		ظ — ẓ
ت — t		ع — '
ث — th		غ — gh
ج — j		ف — f
ح — ḥ		ق — q
خ — kh		ك — k
د — d		ل — l
ذ — dh		
ر — r		م — m
ز — z		ن — n
س — s		ه — h
ش — sh		و — w
ص — ṣ		ى — y

The Lām of the definite article ال is assimilated before a solar letter. Proper names familiar to the English reader are rendered in their customary spelling.

PART ONE: CANAAN IN THE EGYPTIAN NEW KINGDOM PERIOD

CHAPTER I

THE HISTORICAL DEVELOPMENT

by B. Mazar

THE FIRST QUARTER of the 16th century B.C.E. witnessed the beginning decline of the Hyksos kingdom in Egypt. The long offensive war which the native rulers of Thebes fought to eject the foreign masters ended close to the middle of the 15th century B.C.E. It was Pharaoh Ah-mose, the founder of the Eighteenth Dynasty, who defeated the Hyksos, conquered their capital, Avaris, and laid the foundations of a national-military rule on Egyptian soil, namely, the New Kingdom. Ah-mose did not content himself with the liberation and unification of Egypt, but marched with his troops to southern Palestine where he attacked Sharuhen. This fortress, the full strength and extent of whose defensive works were revealed in Petrie's excavations at Tell el-Far'ah on the Gaza brook, was conquered after a three-year siege.[1] Ah-mose's action paved the way for the extension of Egypt's borders eastwards, and his successors Amen-hotep I (1551/49–1531/29) and Thut-mose I (1531/29 — ca. 1518) followed his example. These two latter Egyptian kings conducted daring military expeditions to Palestine and Syria, apparently without meeting much resistance on their northward progress, for the decline of the Hyksos power had left these countries without any unifying factor or military force able to withstand Pharaoh's armies. Only in Northern Syria did Thut-mose I come up against a strong political factor, namely the Hurrian-Indo-Iranian kingdom of Mitanni, which, from its center in the Khabur Valley in north-western Mesopotamia, had extended its influence beyond Assyria in the east, and across Syria in the west. Though Thut-mose I's campaigns took him as far as the banks of the Euphrates, where he erected a stele commemorating his victories, the Egyptian aim of subduing the Western Fertile Crescent did not materialize. The military campaigns did not end in permanent conquests, Egyptian control of the vital traffic arteries was precarious, while the kings of Mitanni could not be hindered in the consolidation of their position in Syria.[2]

A decisive turning-point was reached in the time of Thut-mose III

(1504–1450) who was the first king to succeed in controlling most of Syria-Palestine and turning it into an Egyptian province, called at first by the ancient Egyptian name of Reṭenu. However, in the course of time the Egyptians used generally the name Hurru, no doubt due to the important position the Hurrian element occupied among the Syrian-Palestinian population of that period. Parallel to these names, the name Canaan makes its first appearance in cuneiform written documents, in the beginning as the name of the Phoenician coast and later, in the Amarna period, as the name of the entire Egyptian province. The latter name became familiar in Egypt during the Nineteenth Dynasty, while in the Bible it usually denotes the region which included the Land of Israel.[3]

At the beginning of Thut-mose III's single rule (1490) the Canaanite kings led by the king of Kadesh on the Orontes, and certainly supported by the king of Mitanni, concluded an alliance against Egypt. Thut-mose's annals contain a detailed description of the campaign during which he inflicted a crushing defeat on the confederates and subjected the country to Egyptian domination. The king left Egypt at the head of a large force, and began his campaign by taking Gaza which he turned into a military base called "That-which-the-ruler-seized." From Gaza he continued along the *Via maris* and encamped at Yaḥam (modern Khirbet-Yemma) in the Sharon. As for the confederates, they encamped their forces at Megiddo, the strongly fortified royal city situated at the spot where the Wadi 'Āra opens into the Plain of Jezreel. Against the advice of his commanders, Thut-mose did not lead his army by either of the easier routes from the Sharon to the Plain of Jezreel, via Zephath, so as to reach the Valley north of Megiddo, or via Taanach, but by the short and narrow central road along the Wadi 'Āra ('Arûna), "his order of march, horse following horse," and surprised the enemy at the Qina brook (Wadi Lājūn). In the decisive battle that followed the confederates were defeated and a great deal of booty including many war-chariots fell into the hands of the Egyptians, though Megiddo, whither the confederates retired, was conquered only after a seven-month siege.[4] In the wake of the Megiddo campaign and the conquest of several other fortified towns, including Jaffa (the siege and conquest of which form the subject of an Egyptian story)[5], large parts of the country surrendered to the Egyptian king. However, Thut-mose was compelled to conduct another sixteen campaigns in Syria in order to establish and consolidate his rule, thereby extending his conquests as far as the northern border of Syria and the Middle Euphrates region, which had been under Mitannian domination.

A pretty clear picture of the position prevailing in Canaan emerges from

Thut-mose III's inscriptions and in particular from the lists of conquered towns.[6] His topographical list mentions no less than a hundred and nineteen towns in Palestine and southern Syria, probably the same towns he had conquered in his first campaign. This list is incomplete since it does not include all those towns and provinces which had not participated in the alliance against Egypt, such as the Phoenician coastal towns and the royal cities in the country's interior. An analysis of this document and of a few additional pieces of evidence leads to the conclusion that at Thut-mose's time the country was already divided into several districts, no doubt a legacy of the past. Another long list contains a further two hundred and thirty-one names of towns in central and northern Syria. All these lists constitute reliable evidence of the political division persisting from the quasi feudal regime of the preceding period. A "Canaanite kingdom" was generally little more than a fortified city which together with the smaller towns and villages surrounding it was governed by a local ruler (in the Amarna Letters — ḫazānu, and occasionally šarru — a "king", and in the Bible: kings of Canaan), assisted by the nobles and owners of large estates members of the military caste, i.e. the Maryannu.[7] Such royal cities were concentrated mainly in fertile areas, or in the districts along the important communication arteries, especially along the Via maris and its ramifications, viz. in the coastal area, in the plains of northern Palestine, southern Syria and in Bashan.

Thut-mose III made great efforts to weld the conquered regions into a single administrative unit, so as to realize his colonial plan of exploiting the economic sources of the province and extend Egypt's defence line beyond Syria. In the course of time the regular administration set up by Thut-mose was adapted to the prevailing local conditions, so that the Egyptians succeeded in maintaining themselves in the conquered country for three hundred years, despite the political, social, and economic changes that took place in their own, and in other countries. Thut-mose's administrative methods, which crystallized in the days of his successors, can be summarized as follows:

1. The entire region was turned into Pharaoh country and governed as an Egyptian province. In most administrative centers Pharaoh retained the local ruler or, in case he revolted, replaced him with a brother or some other member of his family. In some instances, however, Pharaoh appointed a governor from among his own reliable men or Egyptian army officers. In various places we find a kind of oligarchy — government by the notables of the town[8]—which seems to apply to Gibeon and the Hivite cities in the center of the country on the eve of the Israelite Conquest.

2. The sons of Canaanite rulers were dispatched as hostages to Egypt. At the Egyptian court the "royal seed" absorbed the atmosphere of reverence and esteem for Pharaoh.

3. In the Land of Hurru, i.e., Canaan, was set up a complex Egyptian administration supported by regiments from the standing army — which included conscripts from among the local inhabitants as well as foreign mercenaries, — and by garrisons stationed in the royal cities and fortified towns. Next to the colonial heads of government, a vital position was occupied by high Egyptian officials who acted on behalf of the pharaohs and bore the title *rābiṣu* in Akkadian, *sūkinu* in Canaanite (*sōḵēn* in Hebrew). They maintained contact with the local rulers, watched over the balance of power in the province, and supervised the collection of taxes and the corvée. They were responsible for the state of the roads along which Pharaoh's caravans travelled, as well as for the political and economic interests of the Egyptian government as a whole.

4. Various towns of strategic importance as well as vital stations on trade and maritime routes were turned into fortresses garrisoned with Egyptian troops. Gaza, the most important administrative and military center and key position on the way to Egypt, never ceased to serve as such during the whole time Egypt ruled Canaan. Jaffa — also an Egyptian fortress — contained royal depots.[9] Such fortresses were also found along the Phoenician coast, as far north as Ṣumur. It appears that at the beginning Megiddo was also under direct Egyptian rule, but in the course of time it reverted to its status of a royal city, the residence of a Canaanite dynast loyal to Pharaoh.[10] Beth-shean became a stronghold of the Egyptian government during the reign of one of Thut-mose III's successors, and since then it played an important part in the defence system of the Egyptian province.[11]

5. In a number of towns the Egyptian authorities set up sanctuaries dedicated to local as well as Egyptian divinities. The remains of a sanctuary discovered at Lachish, possibly built at the beginning of Egyptian rule, appear to have been the product of the local ruler's initiative, as were, no doubt, the sanctuaries of Megiddo, Hazor and Shechem.[12] In contrast, the cultic center in the Beth-shean fortress, erected in the first half of the 14th century B.C.E., should be attributed to the Egyptians who kept it in use until the end of their rule. In the temenos of the earliest sanctuary of Beth-shean was discovered the Egyptian dedication stele to Mekal, the god of the city. The Egyptian inscriptions found in the successive sanctuaries dating from the 14th to the 12th centuries prove that the Egyptians were interested in fostering Mekal's cult, probably to emphasize their sovereignty

over the locality by patronizing the local cult. Egyptian sources from the time of the Nineteenth and Twentieth Dynasties provide evidence of the existence of Egyptian sanctuaries in Canaanite towns.[13]

6. During the period of Egyptian rule the Akkadian language and cuneiform writing, which had been used in the Western Fertile Crescent for a long time, continued to be used as the international language, especially in trade and diplomacy. Even the correspondence between the Canaanite rulers and Pharaoh's court was conducted in Akkadian, a fact which proves that the Egyptians had adapted themselves to the conditions and traditions of the country.

Although Thut-mose and his successors established a long-lasting regime, they were obliged to undertake from time to time military campaigns to consolidate their rule in Palestine and Syria. Amen-hotep II's (1450–1424) own inscriptions provide detailed information of his campaigns.[14] During one of these campaigns he got as far as northern Syria, whence he returned by way of Kadesh on the Orontes and the Valley of Lebanon (the Beqa'). On reaching the Sharon plain he caught a messenger of the king of Naharin (Mitanni) who had apparently been sent to instigate a revolt of the Canaanite kings.

Another campaign was directed against the rebellious cities along the *Via maris*. Amen-hotep subdued an alliance of rulers at the northern end of the Sharon, and on his northward progress conquered the city of Anaharath (Tell el-Mukharkhash), situated in the north of the Plain of Jezreel, which seems to have been the center of the revolt. Also worth noting is the list of prisoners Amen-hotep II brought to Egypt, which included several hundred rulers, their brothers and sons, as well as *maryannu* and "Canaanites" (Kn'nw, probably meaning merchants) — all members of the upper classes — besides thousands of prisoners from the lower classes, including 36,300 Hurru (inhabitants of the Hurru, i.e. Canaanite province), 15,200 Shasu and 3,600 'Apiru. In addition to other sources, this document provides a cross-section of the ethnic and social composition of Canaan's population. The permanent population was mixed: West Semites ("Canaanites") who constituted the bulk of the country's population, and Hurrians, including an Indo-Iranian element which was specially prominent among the aristocracy, but in the course of time was absorbed by the West-Semitic speaking population. Next to the aristocracy — a legacy of the quasi-feudalistic regime of the Hyksos period — the majority of the population consisted of small farmers, called *ḥupšu* (cf. *ḥofshi*, I Sam. 17:25), who were lower class freemen attached to the soil.

In that period the Habiru ('Apiru in Egyptian sources, or Hapiru in

Fig. 1. Jericho. Plan and section view of a tomb of the Middle Bronze II period.
Prof. K. M. Kenyon, London.

Fig. 2. Beth-shean. Reconstruction and section view of the Late Bronze period temple.
A. Rowe, *The four Canaanite Temples of Beth-Shan*, Philadelphia, 1940, fig. 4

cuneiform writing) of whom we shall discuss later, constituted a distinct class. In the life of the country's border districts the nomadic and semi-nomadic tribes, called *Shasu* in the Egyptian sources, occupied an important place. We also know of various kinds of dependents, servants and slaves, including the *ḥanīkim* (Gen. 14:14; in a document from Taanach–*ḥanaku*) soldiers who served in the ruler's army, and the *asīrū*, i.e., prisoners of war. From the above emerges the picture of an ethnically and socially heterogeneous and divided population.

It appears that the time of Amen-hotep II's successors — Thut-mose IV and Amen-hotep III — was a period of security and stability in Egyptian ruled Canaan, despite administrative weakness and oppressively high taxation. It is a fact that in this time, and particularly during the rule of Amen-hotep III, shipping and trade prospered on the eastern Mediterranean sea-board, new harbors were founded (e.g. Dor, Zalmonah — now Tell Abū Huwām) and commercial relations with Egypt, Cyprus and the lands of the Aegean Sea developed considerably. The imports from these countries into Canaan rose considerably, as proved by the large amounts of Cypriot and Mycenaean vessels, as well as Egyptian products, discovered in the excavations carried out in this country.[15]

At the same time trading caravans plied the overland routes between Egypt, Syria and Mesopotamia, the safety of which was ensured by the Canaanite rulers who shared in the benefits of that traffic.

Much information about the political and social regime and culture of the country during the Eighteenth Dynasty is to be found in the Taanach Tablets[16] and a few other tablets discovered in different parts of the country, and in particular in the Tell el-Amarna Letters, from the royal archives of Amen-hotep IV — Akh-en-Aton (1376–1359), the reformer of the Egyptian religion.[17] To these documents must be added the rich epigraphical material from Ugarit (cf. the chapter "The Ugaritic Writings" in the volume *The Patriarchs* in the same series) which proved itself a true mine of information about the political, social, economic and especially the spiritual life of this important North Syrian harbor-town. Except a number of letters written by the kings of states bordering on Egypt, the majority of the Tell el-Amarna Letters represent the correspondence of Canaanite rulers with their suzerains Amen-hotep III — at the end of his reign — and Amen-hotep IV; a few letters are from Pharaoh to these rulers. Nearly all the documents are written in Akkadian which displays the influence of West Asiatic languages; particularly in the letters from Canaan, spoken "Canaanite" (Northwest Semitic) is discernible through the cuneiform written Akkadian.

Already at the beginning of the Amarna period — toward the end of
Amen-hotep III's reign and the beginning of the reign of Amen-hotep IV—
the situation in Canaan began to deteriorate as a result of Egypt's weakness
and the shortcomings of its rule. That process was especially affected by
the apparition on the political arena of a new power, the Hittite empire,
which challenged both Egypt and Mitanni's positions. The Hittite king
Shuppiluliuma won a decisive victory over Mitanni (in ca. 1370), and
pursued his campaign right into the heart of the defeated kingdom, a
large part of which he annexed; in the east, Assyria, freed of Mitannian
pressure, was also growing stronger. This alteration in the balance of power
brought changes in Syria in its wake. The Hittites established themselves
in the north of that country, extended their influence over central Syria,
but came into collision with Egypt by competing for the rule of Canaan.[18]
In this conflict special importance was attached to the character of Amurru,
a buffer state located in the Lebanon and Mt. Hermon region. Its founder,
'Abd-Ashirti, hewed it out for himself in the days of Amen-hotep III, and
his son Aziru — who betrayed Egypt and was for some time a vassal of the
Hittite king — succeeded in gaining control over extensive areas between
the Phoenician coast and the Syrian desert. The part which these two
rulers played in the struggle between Hatti and Egypt is clearly reflected
in the Amarna Letters, as well as in other Egyptian sources, and later in the
Hittite royal archives. Information about the Amurru state continues until
the time of its destruction at the beginning of the 12th century.[19] Proof of
its existence is also preserved in a biblical source: ". . . , all the land of the
Canaanites, and Mearah that belongeth to the Sidonians, unto Aphek, to
the borders of the Amorites" (Josh. 13:4). From this we learn that already
in the middle of the 14th century the area dominated by Egypt had shrunk
and its influence in western Asia was declining. This development had
repercussions in the Egyptian province proper, sometimes called Canaan
(Kinaḫna, Kinaḫḫi), in the Tell el-Amarna Letters.

In the general restlessness the Habiru bands ('Apiru in Egyptian) which
used to rove across the whole country played an active part. They perpetrated hostile actions or committed robberies, usually in the service of
local dynasts or in alliance with them. The latter undermined the Egyptian
government and strove to extend the limits of their own rule and increase
their political and economic power. Bands of Habiru were also hired by
rulers loyal to Pharaoh. One of the faithful rulers, Rib-Addi, King of
Byblos, complains in his letters to Amen-hotep III: "Since your father has
returned from Sidon, and from that time on the countries have made
league with the Habiru people." He also points out that 'Abd-Ashirti and

his sons were their allies. Biridiya of Megiddo writes as follows: "Behold I guard Megiddo, the city of my lord the King, day and night. With chariots and with soldiers I guard the walls of the King, for mighty is the enmity of the Habiru." He refers to those Habiru bands which had joined up with his enemy Lab'ayu, a powerful ruler from the region of Shechem. The latter, who was trying to gain a measure of independence through alliances with other rulers and by means of various intrigues, had extended his rule and influence far beyond the territory of Shechem, and even destroyed cities in the Plain of Jezreel, among them Shunem. 'Abdu-Heba, ruler of Jerusalem, who was faithful to Pharaoh, denounces "Lab'ayu, who gave the land of Shechem to the 'Apiru." Despite his actions, Lab'ayu never ceased to proclaim his loyalty in his letters to Pharaoh. Although well aware of Lab'ayu's agressivity and influence, Pharaoh nevertheless entrusted him with the protection of the royal caravans travelling to Mitanni and Babylonia. When caught by his enemies, and about to be dispatched by boat from Acco to Egypt and be handed over to Pharaoh, Lab'ayu freed himself by means of bribery. His sons continued their father's policy; one of them — Mut-ba'lu — is mentioned as the ruler of Peḥel (Pella) in the Jordan Valley, and as one of the few to bear the title of king (*šarru*). Mut-ba'lu maintained friendly relations with the governor of Ashtaroth in Bashan, and was appointed by Pharaoh to supervise the caravan trade with Mesopotamia.

The complicated relationship among the rulers themselves and with the Egyptians can also be inferred from the letters that deal with the period when Shechem concluded an alliance with Gezer, an important center in the northern coastal plain, as well as from the information that Beth-shean was garrisoned with people of Gath-carmel, whose ruler was the father-in-law of the governor of Gezer. The allies were, no doubt, mainly interested in watching the principal trade routes.

The same picture of Egypt's waning power and Pharaoh's inability to keep order in the province of Canaan emerges in other parts of the country also. Thus, we hear that the "king" of Hazor — one of the most powerful rulers in the north of the country — had brought under his control the whole area between the land of Geshur in Golan and the coastal strip; Abimelech of Tyre complained about him to Pharaoh to the effect that he had left his own city and joined the Habiru. There must have been good reason to say of this city (Josh. 11:10), "For Hazor beforetime was the head of all those kingdoms" (the royal cities in Galilee).

At that time Jerusalem was an important political center in the south of the country, where Pharaoh had stationed a garrison of Nubians.[20]

Fig. 3.
Rabbath-Ammon. Plan of the Late Bronze temple.
J. B. Hennessy, *PEQ*, 98 (1966), 158 fig. 2.

'Abdu-Heba, the loyal ruler of that city, frequently described in his long letters the difficult situation prevailing in the country, imploring Pharaoh to punish the hostile princes and curb the Habiru. He was on particularly bad terms with the ruler of Gezer and with another ruler from the south of the country who bore the Indo-Iranian name Shuwardata. Things came to such a pass that his two enemies concluded an alliance, invaded the Jerusalem region, and threatened the city's very existence. On the other hand, at an earlier time, perhaps in the days of Amen-hotep III, 'Abdu-Heba and Shuwardata fought together against the Habiru. During that action the rulers of Acco and Achshaph in the Acco plain rushed to their aid with their war-chariots, no doubt at Pharaoh's orders.[21]

From several instances mentioned in the Tell el-Amarna Letters it transpires that the general lack of security affected particularly the traffic on the roads. In one of his letters, 'Abdu-Heba complains that a caravan he had sent to Egypt was plundered in the Valley of Aijalon. More serious is the complaint of Burnaburiash, the Kassite king of Babylonia, that the caravan of the Babylonian merchant Ahutab had been attacked at Hannathon in Lower Galilee, the merchant killed, and the caravan plundered. Burnaburiash accuses of this crime the governors of Acco and Shamhūna (Tell Samuniye near Nahalal) and demands their punishment.

In this period of ebb the principal concern of the Egyptian administration was to hold on to Canaan by any possible means. Complicated diplomatic intrigues, reinforcement of garrisons in the various fortresses and cities, and the dispatch of punitive forces, when necessary, were employed, while further efforts were made to collect taxes and to safeguard the overland and maritime trade routes. Only the ominous advance of the Hittites and the general restlessness in Canaan were able to stir Egypt from its torpor and compel Pharaoh to dispatch a large force to consolidate his rule and suppress the rebellious elements. The campaign was undertaken by Tut-ankh-Amon's military commander, Hor-em-heb, who later usurped the throne of Egypt (1345–1319/7).[22]

The rise to the throne of Ramses I, the founder of the Nineteenth Dynasty, represented a political turning-point in Egypt's relations with the province of Canaan. Seti I (1315–1304), Ramses' son and successor, undertook a series of military campaigns to suppress rebellion in Canaan and consolidate Egypt's position vis-à-vis the Hittites. Since he intended to use the caravan route running through the desert to Canaan, he had fortresses built and wells dug along it and punished severely the nomads (Egyptian: Shasu) who threatened the safety of that traffic. The inscription on one of Seti's stelae, discovered in the sanctuary of Beth-shean, is very

The borders of Canaan in the New Kingdom period.

instructive in that it relates the suppression of a rebellion in his first regnal year.[23] The rebel was the governor of Hammath (Tell el-Hammeh in the south of the Beth-shean valley) who attacked the loyal ruler of Rehob (Tell eṣ-Ṣarem south of Beth-shean) and tried to conquer the fortress of Beth-shean. He was apparently assisted in his design by the ruler of Peḥel. Pharaoh replied by dispatching to Hammath, Beth-shean and Yanoam (apparently Tell el-'Ubeydiye near a Jordan ford) Egyptian units which defeated the rebels in a single day. Even more interesting is another Seti stele from the sanctuary of Beth-shean. The inscription mentions a factor which was to bring about a decisive change in the life of the country.[24] It refers to the activities of the Habiru of a mountain named Yarmuta (Jarmuth - Kaukab el-Hawa) who, together with the *Ta-ya-ru* tribe attacked a group of nomads called Rehem. Pharaoh sent an expeditionary force to this mountainous region situated north of Beth-shean, and put a speedy end to the disturbances. The document indicates that already then nomadic and semi-nomadic tribes represented an important proportion among the inhabitants of the Galilean highlands, and that at times of Egyptian administrative weakness it was they who threatened the peace in the Plain of Jezreel. Further, the Egyptian documents report that at Seti's time the Egyptian government was forced to engage in a difficult war against the Shosu tribes in the country's interior, in the border districts, and especially in the Negev.[25] It seems reasonable to assume that in this period the Semitic tribes of Transjordania, who were ethnically close to the Israelites, had already reached a certain degree of national cohesion and settled in the land to a considerable extent. This development resulted in the emergence of three kingdoms: Edom at Mount Seir, Moab on both sides of the Arnon river, and Ammon on the upper course of the Jabbok river. However, all three kingdoms being established in areas outside the boundaries of the province of Canaan proper, Seti's activities were not directed in their quarter but mainly toward consolidating Egypt's position on the Phoenician coast and in southern Syria, which were threatened by the increasing power and influence of the Hittite king. His campaigns restored Egyptian rule in such important centers as Hazor and Tyre, and extended it as far as the Valley of Lebanon (Beqa') and the Land of Amurru, the vulnerable spot in the Egyptian defence system vis-à-vis the Hittite empire.[26]

Seti I left his son Ramses II (1304–1237) a greatly consolidated and strengthened empire, and fully restored authority over the province of Hurru (Canaan). According to one of the documents, the province of Hurru extended then from Sile (a fortress near Qanṭara) to Upi (the

Damascus area). The change in Egypt's policy towards the East found its expression in the shift of the Egyptian capital from Memphis to the north-eastern Delta, namely to Tanis (Avaris), the old Hyksos capital. This is the royal city the Egyptians called Per-Ra'mses (House of Ramses) and which according to the generally accepted view is the store-city Ramses of the Israelite tradition. No doubt this action emphasized the fact that the Nineteenth Dynasty continued the policies of the Hyksos rulers, hence its encouragement of the cult of Seth, who was identified with Baal, and the strengthening of relations between Egypt and Canaan. Under the Nineteenth Dynasty the Canaanite element and the influence of Canaanite cultic practices increased in Egypt proper, while the Egyptians reinforced their position in Canaan by restoring and building fortresses, by erecting cities in honor of Pharaoh, and by developing overland and maritime trade connections.[27]

The initial period of Ramses II's reign is marked by the hard struggle with the Hittite empire and with the Canaanite elements hostile to Egypt, while the nomadic and semi-nomadic tribes continued to penetrate in growing numbers in the border districts and the interior of the country. This complex situation, which foreshadowed the decline of Egyptian rule in Canaan, forced Ramses to build up his army and reinforce it with Canaanite auxiliary units and mercenary troops, mainly from among the Sea-Peoples. Conspicuous among these were the Lycians (Lukka), the Danuna (Denyen) and the Sherden, which are the first foreign groups on Canaanite soil mentioned already in the Tell el-Amarna Letters.

The wars waged against the Hittites in central Syria lasted for a great many years. The famous battle near Kadesh on the Orontes, described in detail in both Egyptian and Hittite sources, was fought in Ramses's fifth regnal year. We tend to imagine it as a major conflict in which both sides concentrated tremendous forces, including auxiliaries and much chariotry, and employed the best tactics of those days. Though Ramses describes the campaign as an Egyptian victory, the sources show that actually it did not end in a decisive manner and that, in fact, he was forced to withdraw and return to Egypt, probably because of the heavy losses suffered and the increasing weakness of his army.[28] The Hittite king, who knew how to exploit the newly created situation, subjected the king of Amurru and undertook a military expedition to the Land of Upi, the center of which was the Damascus oasis, but which apparently included also areas in northern Transjordan. This was certainly a heavy blow to Pharaoh's prestige, who felt compelled to prepare for a resumption of the struggle. Quite possibly this expedition to the north-east of the Canaan province had also another historical significance. It could have had some connection with the events taking place in Transjordan on the eve of the war of the Israelite tribes against the Amorite kingdoms in Gilead and in Bashan. According to the Bible the Amorites controlled northern Moabite areas in the period between the establishment of the Moabite kingdom and the penetration of the Israelite tribes into Transjordan (Num. 21 : 26). It would seem that the kingdom of Jaazer in Gilead and the Amorite kingdom in the Bashan were established at the same time. From the reports of various sources one might assume that the Hittite invasion, in which the Amorites took apparently an active part, brought about the far-reaching upheavals in Transjordan which the Israelites exploited. According to this argument the momentous events which took place at the beginning of Ramses's reign projected the Israelites into the mainstream of historical events with all the struggles and consequences implied.[29]

At least until his tenth regnal year, Ramses was obliged to engage in fierce battles with the Hittites in the north of the province of Canaan, and suppress at the same time rebellions in Canaan itself, fight the Shosu tribes of Mount Seir and the Moabites as well. The extent to which Pharaoh's hold on the country hung in balance is best illustrated by the fact that, despite its proximity to the Egyptian base at Gaza, the large coastal city of Ashkelon rebelled and was reconquered in an assault. Ramses's topographical lists lead to the conclusion that he was particularly concerned in restoring order along the coastal roads, on the sea-board and along the roads leading to northern Canaan, toward the positions held by his great enemy — the Hittite empire, — while in the interior Egyptian rule had in fact grown lax or ceased altogether.

The continuous wars between Egypt and Hatti weakened both these mighty kingdoms at a time when new political and national forces, which were destined to replace them in Syria and in Palestine, were looming at the horizon. In face of these dangers Egypt and Hatti engaged in negotiations which resulted in the peace and friendship treaty signed in the twenty-first regnal year of Ramses II (ca. 1280 B.C.E.). This treaty, which has been preserved in both the Egyptian and Hittite formulations, remained in force until the end of the Hittite empire.[30] It was in this period that the borders of the province of Canaan were clearly defined, i.e. "The Land of Canaan according to its borders," which is identical with the area ruled by the Egyptians in western Asia, and whose northernmost limit is Lebo'-ḥamath (Lebweh in the Beqaʻ [Valley of Lebanon], Num. 34 :8).[31]

Papyrus Anastasi I, which is written in the form of a satirical letter sent by Hori, an Egyptian official, to the military scribe Amen-em-Opet, sheds

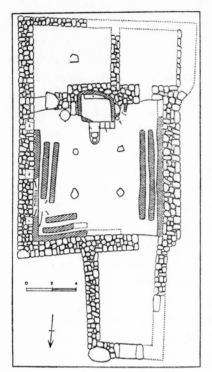

Fig. 4.
Lachish. Plan of the Late Bronze temple (phase III).
Encyclopaedia Biblica, pl. 509.
Design "Carta", Jerusalem.

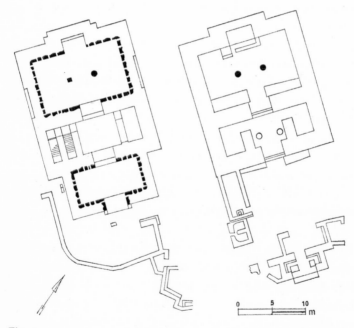

Fig. 5.
Hazor, Lower City. Plan of the Late Bronze temples from stratum II (right),
stratum IB (left).

Prof. Y. Yadin, Director of the Hazor excavations.
Design "Carta", Jerusalem.

some light on this period. Hori derides his friend and proves that his knowledge of Canaan is scant. The letter comprises a kind of guide to Canaan, listing the roads and towns which the Egyptian officials were in the habit of touring. The entire coast with its rich towns as far as Ṣumur in the north, as well as northern Canaan and southern Syria were under Egyptian control. However, in various parts of Canaan, especially in the Lebanon, there roved bands of Shosu who robbed terrified wayfarers of their possessions. Danger threatened the man who travelled along the Wadi 'Āra from Megiddo to the Sharon for there "the Shasu hide behind the bushes." Incidentally he mentions an event which befell the chieftain of Asar (Asher?). On the basis of this source and the mention of the name Asar in other sources some scholars are of the opinion that at that time the tribe of Asher was already living in the north of the country.[32]

The rebellion which broke out in Canaan after Ramses II's death was forcefully suppressed by his son and successor Mer-ne-Ptah (1237–1229). The hymn commemorating this victory of the pharaoh mentions among other things:

> "Plundered is Canaan with every evil;
> Carried off is Ashkelon, seized upon is Gezer;
> Yanoam is made as that which does not exist;
> Israel is laid waste, his seed is not;
> Hurru is become a widow for Egypt."[33]

The text proves that important Canaanite centers — from Ashkelon on the south coast to Yanoam near the Jordan fords south of Lake Chinnereth — as well as Israelites participated actively in this attempt to shake off the Egyptian yoke.

Further, we have to assume that the Israelite tribes and those who had joined them constituted already an important factor in the struggle against Egypt, since their expansion, which was preceded by a slow penetration, ended in an offensive war and the destruction of Canaanite cities, the latter fact supported by archeological evidence. The presence of the Israelites was destined to change the componence of the population, mainly in the interior of the country. However, the Egyptian rule was not threatened by the constant upheavals in Canaan only, or, the mere rise of Israelite tribes, but mainly by the migration of the Sea-Peoples who were leaving their homelands around the Aegean and erupting in increasing masses into the countries on the eastern board of the Mediterranean.

Though Mer-ne-Ptah succeeded in defeating the Libyans and the Sea-Peoples who had advanced as far as the Delta, new waves surged continuously upon the eastern coast of the Mediterranean and at the gates

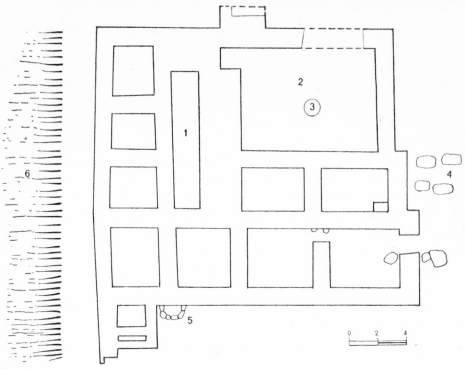

Fig. 6.
Taanach. Plan of the western palace during the Middle and Late Bronze periods.
G. Watzinger, *Denkmäler Palästinas* I, Leipzig, 1933, fig. 6.

Fig. 7.
Beth-shean.Plan of the Late Bronze citadel and reconstruction of the citadel's façade (bottom lef
A. Rowe, *The Topography of Beth-Shan*, Philadelphia, 1930, fig. 2.

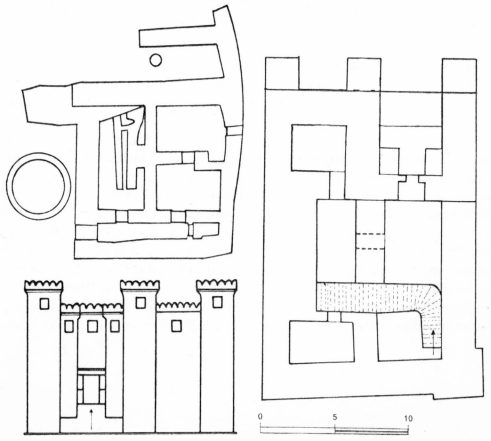

of the Egyptian kingdom. At the beginning of the 12th century the tremendous assault of the Philistines and other Sea-Peoples brought in its wake far-reaching changes in the Western Fertile Crescent, such as the destruction of the Hittite Empire,[34] and later on the total collapse of Egyptian rule in Canaan.

Canaanite civilization at the time under discussion — the Late Bronze Period — is well reflected in the archeological discoveries from the many tells of Palestine and Syria. Remains of city fortifications and the Egyptian illustrations of Canaanite towns show that the governors were able to recruit many people for the corvée. In general the fortification techniques remained the same as in the previous period, namely the last phase of the Middle Bronze II Period. But the strength and dimensions of the fortifications and buildings are much inferior when compared to the achievements of the latter period. Only in respect to sanctuaries new types were introduced, and in some of the temples — such as those of Lachish, Hazor and Amman — a vast amount of local and foreign objects was discovered. The comparative wealth of the ruling class of that time, particularly during its initial phase, is reflected in the palaces, sanctuaries and residences. The culture of the country at that time was much influenced by Egypt and the countries of Western Asia, while the contact with the Aegean and Cyprus was so close that the products of Mycenaean culture had become usual in the country since the beginning of the 14th century B.C.E. Epigraphic sources as well as archeological finds prove the close links of Canaan with its neighbors. Among these the important harbor cities along the East Mediterranean coast, especially Ugarit, had become prosperous centers of international trade.

In this period Canaan proper was a predominantly agricultural and pastoral country. Its main exports were agricultural products such as oil, wine, honey, spices and timber from the Lebanon; the imports consisted mainly of metals, precious objects and manufactured goods. But at the same time various crafts such as the dyeing of purple and blue cloth, the production of metal ware, and even ivory carvings continued to develop in Canaan. This prosperity in all the economic spheres was accompanied by a cultural development in religion and in literature. Its concrete expression is found in the Ugaritic literature, echoes of which can be found in epigraphic Akkadian and Egyptian sources as well as in the biblical literature. During this period several kinds of script were in use in Canaan. Akkadian, written in cuneiform characters, was the international language for diplomatic and trade purposes. On the other hand, Egyptian inscriptions found in Canaan were in the main official documents — particularly those carved on stelae put up by Egyptian rulers and their officials — or inscriptions on objects brought from Egypt. Further, the Ugaritic alphabetic cuneiform writing had been adopted also outside that city, as proved by three documents discovered in Palestine.

The so-called Proto-Canaanite alphabetic script was already widely used in the country in this period. Various excavations have brought to light alphabetic documents, of which three inscriptions were found in Lachish. We have also evidence, particularly from excavations in Byblos, of pictographic writings, so far undeciphered, which clearly show the influence of Egyptian hieroglyphic writing.[35]

The archeological finds in Canaan point to an economic decline in the second half of the 13th century. The outward signs of this process are: the destruction of cities, the weakening in the fortification system, the poorness of the houses, and a low standard of life as compared with the preceding period. The oppressive Egyptian rule, heavy taxation, the lack of security on the roads and the waves of nomadic and semi-nomadic tribes that swept over large parts of the country and settled there, all these were no doubt the main factors which rocked the foundations of the Canaanite regime under Egyptian suzerainty and led to momentous changes in the political and cultural life, as well as in the ethnical character of Canaan.

CHAPTER II

THE EGYPTIAN DECLINE IN CANAAN AND
THE SEA–PEOPLES

by A. Malamat

A. THE DAYS OF MER-NE-PTAH

THE PERIOD OF THE Israelite Settlement extended over some two hundred years, from the later part of the 13th century to the last quarter of the 11th century, with the establishment of the Monarchy. This period is marked by the decline of the great powers in the Ancient East, which facilitated the rise of small nations in Syria-Palestine. These conditions aided the political consolidation and settlement of the Israelite tribes in Canaan, of the Arameans in Syria, and of the nations of Transjordan. Egypt's waning influence on the Phoenician coast led to the political and economic independence of the Phoenician harbor towns.

The peace treaty between Egypt and Hatti, concluded in the twenty-first year of Ramses II, shaped international politics in Hither Asia until his death and Egypt's dominion over Canaan never came into dispute. Papyrus Anastasi I presents a vivid picture of Canaan in this period, of the country's landscape, inhabitants, major cities, and network of roads.[1] This document attests to Egypt's general rule over Canaan, from Gaza in the south to Ṣumur in the north and Damascus (the Land of Upi) in the east, all of which were under the direct jurisdiction of the king. At the same time, it indicates a lack of security along the country's roads and the spread of the Shosu-Bedouin and other unruly elements, no doubt including already the Israelite tribes, in the country's hill-regions. Interesting in this connection is the allusion to a heroic deed by the head of a tribe named ʾisr, apparently identical with the name of the Israelite tribe of Asher; this is reminiscent of the heroic characters described in the Book of Judges.

With the death of Ramses II, the Canaanite city-states attempted to shake off the yoke of Egyptian rule. Mer-ne-Ptah (1237–1228 — higher chronology; 1223–1214 — lower chronology) was thus forced early in his reign to undertake campaigns to Canaan, *inter alia* also against the Israelites. From journals of Egyptian officials stationed on Egypt's eastern frontier

(Papyrus Anastasi III, dating from Mer-ne-Ptah's third year)[2] we learn a great deal of this pharaoh's rule in Canaan and the control over such centers as Gaza and Tyre on the coast, and even over a few places in the hill-country. We know that Egypt ruled the interior from the mention of Gezer[3] and Yanoam (on the Jordan, south of the Sea of Galilee) on Mer-ne-Ptah's Victory Stele (the so-called "Israel Stele"). Also apparently from the time of Mer-ne-Ptah, from his "fourth year", is an Egyptian hieratic inscription on a bowl found at Lachish.[4] This gives a list of produce delivered as tribute to an Egyptian official by the local inhabitants. Shortly after this, the city was apparently conquered and destroyed by the Israelites.[5]

The major threat to Egypt and its rule in Canaan, however, came from an entirely different quarter. The migratory movements of the Sea-Peoples involved extensive dislocations of populations in the Eastern Mediterranean, and may have been connected with the downfall of Mycenae, the Dorian invasion, and the penetration of new ethnic elements into Italy and the neighboring islands. In any event, the Sea-Peoples brought in their wake the overthrow of the Hittite empire and caused the near collapse of Egypt.

The origin of the Sea-Peoples is one of the most complex problems of history, philology and archeology (cf. below the chapter on the Philistines). Ethno-linguistically the Sea-Peoples are Indo-European, and have been defined variously as Illyrians, Pelasgians or Luwians, etc. As for their geographic origin, from whence they invaded Egypt and the Palestinian coast, there are two seemingly conflicting views: the Anatolian hypothesis, placing them on the western and southern seaboard of Asia Minor; and the Aegean hypothesis, tracing them to the islands and Greece.[6] Such clear-cut geographical distinctions, however, seem too rigid. Indeed, for sea-faring people such as these, the coasts of Anatolia and Greece, together with the Aegean Islands, were a single organic sphere interconnected by sea.

The Sea-Peoples, who made themselves felt already in the days of Ramses II, truly reached Egypt in the 5th year of Mer-ne-Ptah. Five confederated "Peoples of the Sea" joined Libyan tribes in attacking Egypt's western flank. This first alliance, according to the Egyptian sources, comprised: the Aqaywasha or Aqawasha (most likely to be identified with the Acheans and the Aḫḫiyāwa of the Hittite sources); the Teresh (the Tyrsēnoi or Tyrrhenians of classical sources, possibly the ancestors of the Etruscans); the Lukka (the Lycians of classical times); the Sherden (who lent their name to the island of Sardinia) and finally the Shekelesh (the Sikeloi of classical records, for whom the island of Sicily was named).[7]

Of these (a) the Lukka and Sherden were known already generations earlier; (b) the Teresh and especially the Shekelesh participated in the onslaught on Egypt also during the reign of Ramses III; and (c) the Aqawasha were mentioned only in Mer-ne-Ptah's inscriptions. Mer-ne-Ptah succeeded in stemming the Sea-Peoples, but could not break their power. New waves of Sea-Peoples subjected Egypt to even stronger assaults in the days of Ramses III (cf. below, D).

In the face of the common danger represented by the Sea-Peoples, the longstanding rivalry between the Egyptian and Hittite empires gave way to more cooperative relations. Mer-ne-Ptah's Victory Stele merely states that "Hatti is pacified," and this probably reflects the new situation. In this context we may see the sending of grain ships by this pharaoh, early in his reign, to the king of Hatti (apparently Tudhaliya "IV"), during a severe famine there[8] — probably the result of incursions by the Sea-Peoples. The Hittites also requested aid from Ugarit (cf. below, C). Indeed, finds at Boghazköy (Hattusa, the Hittite capital)[9] and Ugarit[10] (at this time still a Hittite vassal) indicate positive relations between Hatti and Egypt.

B. The Close of the Nineteenth Dynasty and the Biblical Episode of Cushan-Rishathaim

The power of Egypt declined after the death of Mer-ne-Ptah, and till the ascendency of the Twentieth Dynasty, a period of about 20 years passed during which no Egyptian king was able to keep the throne for more than a few years.[11] Archeological evidence from Palestine indicates the continuation of contacts between Egypt and Canaan even in this period. Thus, sherds of a jar were found at Tell el-Far'ah (Sharuhen, in the western Negev), inscribed with the name of Seti II; and at Tell Deir 'Allā (probably Succoth, near the confluence of the Jabbok and Jordan rivers) a faience jar was found bearing the cartouche of Ta-Usert, Seti's wife, who later reigned as Queen of Egypt in her own right.[12] On the other hand, intercourse with Canaan at about this time is reflected, for instance, in Papyrus Anastasi IV which refers inter alia to ships "loaded with all manner of good things" returning to Egypt from Haru (i.e. Syria-Palestine), as well as in the fact that Mer-ne-Ptah-Siptah, one of Seti II's successors, dispatched an emissary to Haru.[13]

Papyri Anastasi V and VI[14] — containing an account of the pursuit of runaway slaves and that of the entrance of a nomadic tribe into Egypt, respectively — apparently also date from the time of Seti II. The latter papyrus tells that "we have finished letting the Shosu-Bedouin of Edom pass the Fortress of Mer-ne-Ptah which is in Tjeku, to the pools of Per-Atum of Mer-ne-Ptah, which are in Tjeku, to keep them alive and to keep their cattle alive." These reports by Egyptian frontier officials make it evident that, even during this period of decline, Egypt retained tight control over its eastern border — a fact which sheds significant light on the biblical tradition of the Exodus.

At the very end of the Nineteenth Dynasty, however, Egypt reached a state of anarchy and rule apparently fell into the hands of a foreign usurper known only from a later source. Papyrus Harris I, written at the end of Ramses III's reign, or perhaps even after his death, describes the chaotic conditions prevailing in Egypt: "Other times came afterwards in the empty years, and Irsu, a Horite [Ḥȝrw] was with them as prince. He set the entire land as a tributary before him. One joined his companion that their property [of the Egyptians] might be plundered. They treated the gods like people, and no offerings were presented in the temples."[15]

Despite the propagandistic tendency to emphasize the state of chaos in Egypt on the eve of Ramses III's ascent, this document nevertheless preserves the historical nucleus of a foreign subjugation of Egypt. The identity of this foreign ruler is controversial; his designation as a "Horite" refers to "Haru-Hurru, "i.e. Syria-Canaan. It has been suggested recently that he was one Bay, the top official in the days of Mer-ne-Ptah-Siptah (the last king of the Nineteenth Dynasty), or even the king himself. Bay was apparently of Canaanite extraction as possibly, was the above king's mother.[16] In such case there would have been no foreign interregnum between the Nineteenth and Twentieth Dynasties. But this entirely over-looks the mention of Irsu (or Arsu), as well as of the offences he is accused of having committed against the Egyptian cult, which hardly seem compatible with the behavior of a local official, even if of foreign origin.

On the other hand, it is possible that the foreign domination of Egypt is connected in some manner with events in Canaan, reflected in biblical tradition: Cushan-Rishathaim, King of Aram Naharaim, the first "oppressor" of Israel in the period of the Judges (Jud. 3:3–10).[17] This enigmatic period should be regarded against the broader background of events in the Ancient East, rather then merely within the limited framework of Israelite history so closely adhered to in the Bible.[18] It is difficult to assume that a ruler from Aram Naharaim (i.e. from the Euphrates region) should undertake such a large-scale campaign to southern Canaan for the mere subjugation of a single tribe (Judah, or rather Kenaz or Caleb) or even several tribes. Would it not seem more likely that it was directed against

Egypt, the war against Israel being ephemeral? Further, it would appear that Israel's deliverance by Othniel the son of Kenaz is to be linked with the general defeat of this foreign invader of Egypt, at the hands of Set-nakht, the founder of the Twentieth Dynasty.

The linking of the biblical episode with events in Egypt is chronologically compatible. The usurpation in Egypt took place in ca. 1200 B.C.E., which could easily coincide with the first "oppression" of Israel in the time of the Judges. Moreover, Israel's deliverer Othniel also appears in the biblical accounts of the conquest of southern Canaan (Josh. 15:17; Jud. 1:12 ff.), which would also tend to indicate his early date. Thus, the Cushan-Rishathaim episode may well have taken place at the end of the 13th century B.C.E.

Whether Cushan-Rishathaim is to be identified with the foreign ruler in Egypt or not — we cannot ignore the contemporaneity of Egypt's decline at the end of the Nineteenth Dynasty and the possibility of a ruler from Aram Naharaim overrunning Canaan (and even penetrating into Egypt). The latter events are, in any case, hardly conceivable under Ramses II and Mer-ne-Ptah, or Ramses III, all of whom maintained Egypt's dominion of Canaan.[19]

C. The End of the Hittite Empire and the Destruction of the Levantine Coastal Cities by the Sea-Peoples

The fate which befell the Hittite empire and its vassals in Syria in the second half of the 13th century is still known only in outline, in spite of much new epigraphical and archeological material. The last Hittite king of stature was Tudhaliya "IV" — actually III — "the Great King, King of the Universe" (ca. 1250–1220 B.C.E.), son of Hattusilis III who made the peace treaty with Ramses II. The so-called "Annals of Tudhaliya IV" are now considered to date actually from the time of Tudhaliya I or II (who reigned in the 15th century), and cannot be used unreservedly to recon-struct the period of the later king.[20] Even so, Tudhaliya "IV" was still able to marshal forces strong enough to overpower the enemies threatening his empire from several quarters. He succeeded in checking the nations to the west, on the coasts of Asia Minor, who were in turn stirred by pressure of the Sea-Peoples. New documents from the Hattusa archives reveal that he realized a long standing aim of the Hittites, to conquer Alashiya (Cyprus) and to exact tribute from it.[21]

Tudhaliya "IV" still maintained his domination in northern Syria, as is proven by a relief discovered at Alalakh, by documents found in the diplomatic archives of Ugarit (which include a treaty between Hatti and 'Ammishtamru II), and by a vassal treaty dictated to Shaushgamuwa, King of Amurru.[22] This latter treaty shows that as late as the middle of the 13th century Amurru was still a key buffer country in Syria, between Hatti and Mesopotamia; it also sheds light on international relations and diplomatic usage of that time. The treaty denotes the major powers of the day besides Hatti, as Egypt, Babylonia, Assyria, and Aḫḫiyā (the latter name erased at a later date). Of particular interest is a stipulation in the treaty, alongside the clauses concerning military assistance, compelling the Hittite king's vassal to impose a total economic boycott on Assyria. It appears that the Hittites considered the aggressive Assyrian ruler, Tukulti-Ninurta I (1243–1207 B.C.E.), their most dangerous enemy. His hostile attitude toward the Hittites is evident in his campaign against Amurru, as well as in the mention, in his inscriptions, of "28,800" Hittites deported to Assyria, most likely inhabitants of the Hittite protectorates in northern Syria.[23] However, domestic conflicts within Assyria, during which Tukulti-Ninurta was murdered, brought this danger to an end.

The Hittite empire was already on the decline at the end of Tudhaliya "IV"'s reign, but his death brought it toward the very brink of destruction. During the troubled and brief reign of Tudhaliya's son Arnuwanda III (last quarter of the 13th century), the Hittite grip on Syria certainly weakened. The greatest danger still threatened from western Anatolia where various states had joined up with the Sea-Peoples. Shuppiluliuma (Shuppiluliama) II, who succeeded his brother Arnuwanda upon his death, is the last Hittite king mentioned in the sources. The many documents discovered in recent years in the Hittite capital reveal a last brief flicker of glory, prior to the end.[24] Even at this crucial hour the Hittite king concluded treaties with several countries and succeeded in inflicting defeats, such as his triple victory over the fleet of Alashiya (Cyprus), which country may or may not have come under the control of the Sea-Peoples in the meantime.

Around 1200 B.C.E., Hatti met its destruction apparently at the hand, of people which (as we have seen above) had lurked on the northern, western and southern coasts of Anatolia.[25] Traces of this catastrophe have been discovered at many Hittite sites in Anatolia, first and foremost at Hattusa the capital, and at such coastal towns as Tarsus and Mersin. Following this, south Anatolian population groups, mainly Luwian elements, spread over northern and central Syria, reaching Palestine as well, and determining the future ethnic make-up of the region. Many neo-Hittite kingdoms, such as at Carchemish in the north and Hamath in the south, arose at this time. From now on, "Hatti" became the designation in Assyrian terminology, as well as in the Bible, for these latter kingdoms and for Syria in general.

In Syria and Palestine, too, there is much evidence of violent destruction at the coastal towns, which is evidently to be attributed to the Sea-Peoples. This is found wherever excavations have been made in this area; and even at such inland sites as Megiddo (stratum VIIB). The archeological findings do not, however, permit a precise dating of these events.[26] Some of these ravaged cities, such as Alalakh [27] and Ugarit (see below) in the north, and Tell Abu Huwām near Haifa,[28] were never rebuilt, or at least never regained their former status. Other towns, such as the Canaanite settlements along the southern coast — Jaffa, Tel Mor, Ashdod and Ashkelon — were resettled by the Sea-Peoples shortly after. In the south, however, the historical picture is somewhat more complicated, since intermediate settlements have been found at certain sites, between the Late Bronze Period strata and those of the Philistines. Such localities as Jaffa, Ashdod, Tel Mor and even Gezer show evidence of having been destroyed twice — first apparently in the time of Mer-ne-Ptah, in hit-and-run raids from the sea;[29] and the second, a more massive action in the time of Ramses III, involving settlement on the conquered sites.

The destruction of Phoenician harbor-towns, for which as yet there is no archeological evidence, is alluded to in a tradition quoted much later by Justin (XVIII, iii, 5): the king of Ashkelon defeated the inhabitants of Sidon, who "founded" the city of Tyre "one year before the conquest of Troy." This may refer to the destruction of Sidon by the Sea-Peoples, who presumably had already conquered Ashkelon, making it one of their main centers.[30] We learn, moreover, that at that time Tyre lay in ruins and was then rebuilt by the Sidonian refugees (as was the city of Arvad, according to Strabo, XVI, ii, 13), a tradition reflected in Josephus and in the legends of Phoenician coins.[31] Tyre, too, appears to have been destroyed by the Sea-Peoples, since we know from Papyrus Anastasi III that it was still an important center as late as the days of Mer-ne-Ptah. Tyre's stature at about this time is also indicated in a letter sent by its ruler to the king of Ugarit, whom he addresses as "my brother", thus stressing their equal status.[32] (The letter relates that a ship sent from Ugarit to Egypt had already passed Tyre and was at present lying at Acco). But the cities of Phoenicia were not settled by the Sea-Peoples, in contrast to the harbor-towns of Palestine; upon the decline of Egyptian rule they became independent kingdoms.

The archives of Ugarit are a primary source of information concerning the approaching menace of the Sea-Peoples; in recent years they have yielded the only extant sources stemming directly from these dramatic events, the like of which must have been repeated over and over in that period at numerous Mediterranean harbor cities. Thus, several relevant letters written in Ugaritic were found within a kiln for baking clay tablets which was destroyed during the fall of the city; another group of tablets written in Akkadian and found elsewhere in the destruction layer, comprises a correspondance in part or entirely between 'Ammurapi, the last known king of Ugarit, and the Hittite and Cypriot courts.[33] These documents deal, principally, with a famine plaguing the Hittite empire, and with an enemy common to Ugarit and Hatti — most certainly the Sea-Peoples (and their allies).

In one of the letters (*PRU V*, no. 60), the Hittite king urges 'Ammurapi to send him food supplies to relieve the famine; the advance of an enemy is also mentioned. Similar events are related in another letter (*Ugaritica V*, no. 33), ordering the king of Ugarit to send a large quantity (some 450 tons!) of grain by sea to the Cilician coast, the matter being one of "death and life". Another (*Ugaritica* V, no. 171), with its superscription missing, but from a most crucial point in the crisis, orders the total mobilization of the fleet of Ugarit so as to ensure the transport of a supply of grain to the Cilician coast (cf. also *Ugaritica* V, no. 34). A further letter (*PRU* V, no. 63), written to the king of Ugarit by one of his generals in the field, possibly relates of the retreat of combined Hittite and Ugarit forces in southern Anatolia or northern Syria, in the face of an unidentified enemy.

Even more dramatic is the correspondence between Ugarit and Alashiya (Cyprus). In one letter (*Ugaritica* V, no. 22), the "Grand Supervisor" of Alashiya reports that enemy ships made a surprise attack on a fleet from Ugarit off the coast of Cyprus or Anatolia apparently forcing them to surrender. On another occasion (*Ugaritica* V, no. 23), the king of Cyprus warns 'Ammurapi of the approach of sea-raiders, and urges him to place his country on the alert. The king of Ugarit on his part — perhaps in reply to this last letter — reports the first landings of a "commando" of the Sea-Peoples (*Ugaritica* V no. 24): "My father, now the ships of the enemy are coming [here]. He has burned my cities with fire and has done evil things in the midst of the country . . . All my troops [. . .] are stationed in the land of Hatti and all my ships are stationed in the land of Lukka. Until now they have not arrived [back] and thus the country is abandoned to itself . . . Now, seven ships of the enemy that have come here have done to us evil things. Now, if further enemy ships appear please do report to me so that I shall know."

The Eastern Mediterranean in New Kingdom times.

The importance of the last-mentioned letter is that it reveals that Ugarit's helplessness was due to the city's army being away in Hatti and its fleet having sailed off to the land of Lukka (Lycia), on the southern coast of Anatolia. This fits in well with the general politico-military alignment which first emerged in the days of Mer-ne-Ptah, when Egypt and Hatti apparently presented a unified defensive front in the face of the Sea-Peoples, together with their Syrian vassal states such as Ugarit and even Alashiya (which was subjected already by Tudhaliya "IV"; see C, above). These allies embarked on widespread actions, as did their enemies in the latter case, when the Lukkians and several Sea-Peoples joined the Libyans in attacking Egypt from the west, as related in the inscription from Mer-ne-Ptah's 5th year. Ugarit's role in this period seems to have been to bolster the Hittite army, especially at sea, and to meet specific threats such as that which evidently emerged in Lukka.[34] The scope of the fleet of Ugarit may be inferred from one of the letters from the tablet-kiln (*PRU* V, no. 62), in which the king is advised to prepare 150 ships for sea (in addition to his regular fleet?).

The precise date of Ugarit's fall eludes us: one view holds that it occurred already in the days of Mer-ne-Ptah, an assumption based in part on a supposed synchronism between the famines in Hatti mentioned on the one hand in Mer-ne-Ptah's inscription and, on the other hand, in the letters from Ugarit (see pp. 28–30, above).[35] Since, however, famine and other calamities were certainly not rare during the final years of the Hittite empire, such a synchronism is not decisive. Actually Ugarit may have been destroyed within a generation later, for, indeed, the context of the documents could very well fit the period shortly before the final destruction (ca. 1200 B.C.E.) of the Hittite empire (see p. 28, above).[36]

D. Ramses III — Conflict with the Sea-Peoples and Rule in Canaan

The only documentary evidence of the actual destruction of the Hittite empire and the Syrian states is the Medinet Habu inscription of Ramses III's 8th year (ca. 1198, 1187 or 1162 B.C.E., according to the higher, middle [to be preferred] or lower chronology, respectively). This presents an eloquent description of the Sea-Peoples' invasion:[37] "The foreign countries made a conspiracy in their islands. All at once the lands were removed and scattered in the fray. No land could stand before their arms, from Hatti, Kode, Carchemish, Arzawa and Alashiya on, being cut off at [one time]. A camp [was set up] in one place in Amurru. They desolated its people, and its land was like that which has never come into being. They were coming forward toward Egypt, while the flame was prepared before them . . ."

The invaders had penetrated not only Asia Minor but also northern Syria, whence one group conquered Carchemish and another continued southward to the land of Amurru, ravaging it and setting up a base there. This brought to an end the mighty and longlived state of Amurru, whose name is mentioned henceforth only as a geographical term. In their sweep, the Sea-Peoples seized Alashiya (Cyprus), or at least part of the island, as transpires perhaps also from Hittite documents of Shuppiluliuma II (see above, p. 28), as well as from the excavations at several sites on that island, first and foremost Enkomi (revealing two destruction levels at this latter site like at the cities on the southern coast of Palestine).[38]

Within one generation of the death of Mer-ne-Ptah, the political and ethnic map of the Eastern Mediterranean changed radically. Even the names of the Sea-Peoples specified in Ramses III's inscriptions differ (with the exception of the Shekelesh) from those mentioned by Mer-ne-Ptah; the confederation of Sea-Peoples now comprised: the Philistines, Tjeker (most likely to be identified with the Teucrians of the Greek sources), Shekelesh, Denye or Denen (Danuna, Dnnym or Danaoi of the Akkadian, Phoenician and Greek sources, respectively), and Weshesh (mentioned only here).[39]

This is the first mention of the Philistines in an extra-biblical source; their special status is indicated by their usual appearance at the head of the list of Sea-Peoples in Ramses' inscriptions. The Tjeker, several times mentioned together with the Philistines, also settled on the coast of Canaan, north of the Philistines, as is known from the story of Wen-Amon who, a century later, mentions their kingdom at Dor and their maritime activities along the Phoenician coast and Cyprus. It is almost certain that it was this same group that settled also in Cyprus, as is indicated by a Greek tradition according to which Teucros, the ancestor of the Teucroi — to be identified with the Tjeker — founded the city of Salamis, the port of ancient Enkomi (and cf. note 38, above).

The date of Ramses III's first clash with the Sea-Peoples is by no means certain. According to one inscription, Ramses undertook a campaign to Amurru as early as his fifth year, conquering the country, slaying its ruler and carrying away many of its inhabitants. The inscription, however, does not mean that Amurru was captured from the Sea-Peoples. On the contrary, the accompanying relief portrays the captive ruler of Amurru as a typical Syrian and the inscription enlarges upon the victory over

Syrians "who were [formerly] ruining Egypt . . . while they persecuted the gods . . .", possibly referring to the earlier subjugation of Egypt at the end of the Nineteenth Dynasty (cf. above, B). Only at the end of the inscription is there any mention of a victory over Sea-Peoples (Philistines and Tjeker, and possibly a third group).[40] The fifth year would seem, thus, to be the earliest date for the war against the Sea-Peoples; however, this could be a mere anticipatory spill-over from the great battles with the Sea-Peoples in Ramses' eighth year. Whatever the case, in his eighth year Ramses set out to check the southward movement of the Sea-Peoples toward Egypt, engaging them both by land (in Djahi — the Canaanite coast) and by sea (in the Nile Delta, in a second phase of the battle?), as is evident from his reliefs and inscriptions (and see below, the chapter on the Philistines).

Ramses III successfully prevented the penetration of the Sea-Peoples into Egypt, and their attacks subsided. Indeed, in the conflict in Ramses' eleventh year they no longer appear as *allies* of the Libyans; he even settled them in military colonies in his kingdom, and employed them as mercenaries in his army.[41] Still, Pharaoh could not prevent settlement of the Sea-Peoples in Canaan — particularly the Philistines and the Tjeker — and may even have encouraged it, as a measure to avert the threat to Egypt. In fact, the Bible places the Philistines in precisely those areas which had previously been under effective Egyptian rule, namely the southern coastal plain of Palestine, the Plain of Jezreel and the Beth-shean region. At the Egyptian administrative centers in Canaan, such as Gaza, Tell el-Far'ah (south) and Beth-shean (see below), the Philistines or other Sea-Peoples were doubtlessly employed as mercenary forces, useful in quelling Canaanite and other unrest in the countryside.

Apart from the above campaigns another, undated campaign was undertaken by Ramses III, against nomadic tribes in southern Palestine: "I destroyed the people of Seir among the Bedouin tribes. I razed their tents; their people, their property, and their cattle as well, without number, pinioned and carried away in captivity, as the tribute of Egypt."[42] It is not known whether this was concurrent with the greater events which took place to the north or was a separate operation, directed toward the Negev and the Arabah. Most interesting in this context is the recent discovery of an Egyptian temple of the Nineteenth-Twentieth Dynasties in a copper mining center at Timna (Wadi Meinei'yeh), some 25 km north of the Gulf of Elath. Finds in the earlier stratum here bore cartouches of Seti I, Ramses II, Mer-ne-Ptah and Seti II, and in the later stratum, of Ramses III-V. Mining activities in this area under Ramses III may even be referred to in Papyrus Harris I, where the king states that he sent an expedition by sea and then by land to a locality named 'Atika.[43]

Nothing of Ramses III's campaigns to Asia is entirely clear, for no definitive historical sources — such as annals — are extant. Indeed, Papyrus Harris I, the Medinet Habu reliefs and inscriptions, and the archeological evidence from Palestine, altogether yield a rather sketchy picture. The inscriptions and reliefs are, in no small part, pompous and unreliable, particularly the depictions of conquests of North Syrian cities (perhaps with the exception "the city" of Amurru), and no less those of cities in Anatolia (in the land of Arzawa).[44] Ramses III's topographical lists in the sanctuaries at Medinet Habu and Karnak, purporting the conquest of more than 120 cities in North Syria and even trans-Euphratean and trans-Tigridian regions, are equally of no value.[45] These lists, like the reliefs of the sieges of the northern cities, are little more than a plagiarism of those of Ramses II.

The data on Canaan proper in Ramses III's inscriptions and reliefs seem more solidly based, as we have seen. The depictions of typical Canaanite (as well as Shosu-Bedouin) captives — alongside Libyans and Sea-Peoples — complement Ramses's inscriptions mentioning hundreds of captives from the land of Haru (i.e. Canaan–Syria) serving in the sanctuaries of Amon at Thebes and Memphis.[46]

Ramses III, in his several expeditions to Canaan, revitalized Egyptian rule there, establishing centers — such as "Migdol of Ramses III"[47] — along the major highways, especially along the Via maris, to ensure his control. This last brief period of Egyptian grandeur in Canaan is reflected in the archeological evidence at several of these sites, including numerous scarabs bearing the name of Ramses III[48] and other objects inscribed with his name, from such places as Gezer and Megiddo.[49] The finds at Beth-shean (stratum VI) are particularly indicative of this renewed Egyptian activity; Ramses III apparently fortified the city and he refurbished its temple placing his statue there. Egyptian inscriptions found there in the same stratum mention two Egyptian commanders of the local garrison.[50] This garrison undoubtedly included mercenaries from among the Sea-Peoples, for several anthropoid coffins found there are characteristic of them.

The archeological finds in Canaan, including epigraphical material, demonstrate Egypt's positive attitude towards the local gods, evidently to lend an air of legitimacy to its rule there. Egyptian stelae dedicated to various Canaanite deities have been found in Beth-shean and other places, and numerous temples are known to have been maintained by the Egyptians in Canaan.[51] Thus, on the basis of an inscribed ivory from Megiddo, we know of a probable temple dedicated to Ptah at Ashkelon,[52] and Papyrus Harris I mentions "the House of Ramses III in Pa-Canaan" — apparently at Gaza — and that "the foreigners of Reṭenu come to it bearing their tribute before it."[53] This latter papyrus also notes that the Temple of Amon at Thebes possessed nine estates in Haru, indicating that Egyptian priestly interests in Canaan were not limited solely to the religious sphere, but were also economic. Such estates are reminiscent of the later, Israelite priestly and levitic cities.[54] Furthermore the inventories of the same papyrus attest to the fact that the temple estates in Egypt proper drew considerable numbers of serfs, cattle and produce from Canaan.

E. The Disintegration of Egyptian Rule in Canaan and the Intrusion of Assyria into Phoenicia

The Egyptian hold over Canaan under Ramses III was rapidly lost after his death, not to be recovered during the remainder of the Twentieth Dynasty (till ca. 1075 B.C.E.) or during the Twenty-First Dynasty (till ca. 945 B.C.E.).[55] In the time of the feeble Twenty-First Dynasty, Egypt became divided, with a hierocratic state in the south, based on Thebes, and the kingdom of |Tanis in the north. Only towards the end of this latter dynasty, in the mid-10th century, was an attempt made to regain a foothold in Egypt's former territories in Asia, as is recorded in the Bible (I Kings 9:16; and cf. 11:14–22).[56] The latest definite evidence for Egyptian presence in Canaan appears to be a statue-base of Ramses VI (mid. 12th century), discovered at Megiddo.[57] This king was also the last known to have exploited the copper mines in the Sinai Peninsula.[58] Though excavations in southern Palestine have yielded scarabs of Ramses IV (at Tell el-Far'ah, Tell eṣ-Ṣafi, Tell Zakariyya and Gezer), Ramses VIII and IX (at Gezer), and an inscribed ring apparently with the name of the last pharaoh, such finds are insufficient to indicate actual Egyptian rule over Canaan.[59]

Egypt's plight, and especially the decline of its prestige in Phoenicia, is clearly evident in the story of Wen-Amon, who travelled to Phoenicia in the 5th year of Heri-Hor, the priestly ruler of Upper Egypt and a contemporary of the Lower Egyptian Smendes, founder of the Twenty-First Dynasty.[60] Here we see that even at Byblos — where Egyptian influence had prevailed for most of the previous 2000 years — Egypt was given little consideration. A causative factor of a new nature can also be seen in this ebbing of Egyptian power — the rise of Assyria and its intrusion into Phoenicia around the year 1100 B.C.E.

As already discussed (see C, above), in the second half of the 13th century Assyria under Tukulti-Ninurta I had penetrated into the west and even invaded Amurru. The murder of this king, and the re-establishment of a strong local dynasty at Babylon, lowered Assyria's fortunes for close to a century. For a brief period, Tiglath-pileser I (1115–1077 B.C.E.) restored Assyrian power, extending its borders on all flanks and anticipating the rise of the mighty Assyrian empire in the 9th century.[61] Realizing a long-cherished Mesopotamian aspiration, he reached the Mediterranean Sea along the Phoenician coast. Though short-lived and followed by another period of decline, Tiglath-pileser's exploits in the west set an example for the kings of the Assyrian empire in the 9th to 7th centuries.

The main obstacle blocking Tiglath-pileser's drive toward the west were the Arameans, whom he mentions in the annals of his 4th year. This is the first definite mention of that people in any extra biblical source. The annals relate his pursuit of the Arameans beyond the Euphrates and his sacking of six of their "cities" in the Bishri mountains, southeast of the Great Bend of the river, the perennial breeding ground of nomadic tribes. The Assyrian frustration in attempting to subdue the Arameans is evident in the fact that Tiglath-pileser crossed the Euphrates 28 times in the course of repeated campaigns and pursued them as far as the oasis of Tadmor (Palmyra) and even the Lebanon range.[62] He records that he also cut cedars in the Lebanon to build his temples in Assyria; a recently discovered inscription (from the time of Shalmaneser III) reveals that he had his image placed there to commemorate this feat.[63] Upon reaching the Mediterranean, Tiglath-pileser levied tribute from the maritime cities of Arvad, Byblos and Sidon, and he proudly records that he sailed from Arvad to Ṣumur, catching a whale on the way. The silence concerning Tyre may indicate that it was at that time under the hegemony of its sister city, Sidon.

The brief penetration of Assyria to the Phoenician coast served to offset the traditional influence of Egypt there. Further, it paved the way for Assyrian contact with Egypt — through the intermediate of the Phoenician coastal cities. This Assyrian inroad explains the background of Wen-Amon's hostile reception by the king of Byblos and, even more so, the fate of Egyptian emissaries dispatched there a few years earlier (also described in Wen-Ammon's tale). That Egypt attempted to establish relations with Assyria, which had now become a political factor along the Phoenician coast — may be inferred from inscriptions of Tiglath-pileser I and his son Ashur-bel-kala, describing various exotic animals sent by Pharaoh as gifts of good will. Assyria may well have replied to these advances, for a lapis lazuli ornament bearing an Assyrian inscription was found in the tomb of King Psusennes I (successor of Smendes) at Tanis.[64]

. . . .

Upon the wane of Egyptian rule in Canaan, and prior to the rise of Assyria as an effective political power in the west, the local contest for control in Canaan came to a head. The Israelite role in this struggle was decisive, their overcoming the authochtonous Canaanite population, stemming the Transjordanian nations and nomadic raiders on the east, and entering into a fierce and bitter conflict with the Philistines, who saw themselves as heirs to Egyptian rule in the land.[65]

CHAPTER III

SOCIETY AND ECONOMIC CONDITIONS

by I. Mendelsohn

A. The Institutions of Government

AFTER THE CAMPAIGNS of Thut-mose III, Egypt gained complete control over Palestine and large parts of Syria. In conquered Canaan, Egypt introduced no marked change. It inherited the "feudal" Hyksos legacy of numerous independent small city-states and left that situation intact without ever attempting to reorganize the country into larger administrative or political units.[1] Economically, as we shall see below, the dismemberment of Canaan into tiny political city-states wrought great hardship upon the people, since very few such "states" were self-sufficient even in their supply of food and other requirements. Thus, for example, Abimilki of Tyre, which was situated on an island, sent a "gift" to the pharaoh and in return asked that the nearby mainland town of Uzu be joined to Tyre so that his people could use its wood, straw, clay, and drinking water to save their lives.[2] The Egyptian policy of maintaining the political *status quo* was undoubtedly motivated by the intention to keep the subjugated peoples in utter disunity and thus prevent any organized revolt.

The local city-state ruler was usually of native stock whose position as "king" was confirmed by the Egyptian government. 'Abdu-Heba of Jerusalem succinctly expressed his dependence on the pharaoh by stating, in the common obsequious style of the Amarna age, that: "[It was] not my father [and] not my mother [who] gave [Jerusalem] to me, [but] the arm of the mighty king [which] gave [Jerusalem] to me."[3] Such a chieftain was ordinarily called by the title *ḫazānu* "prefect," but those who ruled over large and powerful territories often assumed the title *šarru* "king" or *awīlu* "prince" (literally "man" in Akkadian, i.e. a member of the aristocracy). To maintain his authority the local king had at his disposal a small standing force of charioteers, recruited from the ranks of the *maryannu* class, and a limited number of foot-soldiers conscripted from the *ḫupšu* class. The king was assisted by a group of administrative, judicial and military officials who made up his cabinet. In the immediate entourage of the king of Ugarit were also high officials who bore the title *mūdū*,[4] a

designation which may be translated as "councilor" (cf. the biblical term
m·yudda‘, II Kings 10:11). High military dignitaries close to the king
were called his "brethren," that is, his immediate and trusted aides.[5] It
does not appear that the Canaanite king was an absolute ruler responsible
for his acts only to the Egyptian overlord. From many references in the
Amarna letters as well as from other sources it is quite clear that his authority was circumscribed by a council whose members were chosen from the
ranks of the rich agricultural and commercial families of the city-state.
These councilors were called bēlī-āli "the city lords." In Byblos, the city
lords are mentioned twice in the letters of Rib-Addi[6] and in the 11th
century the legislative and administrative body of the same city is referred
to as the mo‘ed "assembly."[7] In the Keret Epic we are told that the king
once invited his seventy "bulls" and his eighty "gazelles" to a feast.[8] The
text does not inform us about the function of these people who are euphe-
mistically called bulls and gazelles, but from similar references in the
Bible to "the chiefs [lit. "the oxen"] of Edom" (Ex. 15:15), "the mighty
men [lit. "the rams"] of Moab" (ibid.), "the chief ones [lit. "the he-
goats"] of the earth" (Isa. 14:9; cf. Ezek. 34:17; Zech. 10:3), "the
mighty [lit. "the rams"] of the land" (Ezek. 17:13), it is obvious that
Keret's "bulls" and "gazelles" were the representatives of the aristocracy
who in some way shared in the government of the kingdom of Ugarit. The
same situation prevailed in Israel where "the city elders" still retained,
even under the monarchy, their old position as judges and administrators
in the respective communities (cf. I Kings 21:8 ff.; II Kings 10:1 ff.).
There is evidence that not all cities were ruled by kings or prefects. Some
cities seem to have "republics" governed by the local oligarchies without
the benefit of a ḥazānu. In two letters addressed to the pharaoh by the
cities of Tunip and Irqata in Syria the greeting formulas read: "To the
king of the land of Egypt, our lord, thus say the inhabitants of Tunip,
your servants"; or: "This tablet is a tablet from the city of Irqata. To the
king, our lord, thus says Irqata."[9]

In order to maintain themselves the city-states imposed taxes and duties
upon their inhabitants. If the evidence on taxation supplied by the cuneiform texts from the royal palace in Ugarit is to be taken as standard for all
Canaan in the middle of the 2nd millennium B.C.E., the fiscal burden
was indeed heavy. These texts mention, among other levies, the tithe
(ma’šaru, cf. biblical ma‘asēr) on grain, oil, and wine; a grazing tax called
maqqadu; and an import duty called miksu (cf. biblical mekes).[10] From the
Alalakh documents of the 15th century B.C.E. we gather that the local
king charged a toll (miksu) on goods in transit, [11] and that the king was also
the beneficiary of fines paid in cases of breach of contract.[12] The most

exacting tax of all, however, was the obligation of the inhabitants to perform corvée labor. The task, consisting of the construction of roads, the erection of fortresses, the building of temples, and the tilling of the crown lands, was universally practiced in the Ancient Near East. The technical term for corvée labor used in Canaan at this period was the same as that later employed in Israel, namely, *mas*. It is mentioned in the Ugaritic texts as *msm*[13] and the Amarna letters refer to the corvée gangs as *awēlūti massa* "the men of the corvée." The city governments often found it extremely difficult to enforce obedience to this oppressive duty. The high Egyptian official Ahiyami had to order Rewashsha, King of Taanach, to call out the people of his towns "and let them do their work."[14] Biridiya of Megiddo prided himself in a letter to the pharaoh that he had succeeded in assembling "the men of the corvée" of his city and that they were now tilling the soil of the royal domains of Shunem. But he pointedly added that he alone had fulfilled the quota of forced labor, while the rulers of the other cities had failed to do likewise.[15] It is highly doubtful whether members of the aristocracy were liable to corvée labor. In normal times the burden rested exclusively on the shoulders of the common people. In order to facilitate the collection of taxes, the imposition of corvée labor, and military service, a census of the population, with detailed reference to the property and slaves owned by each household, was undertaken at certain intervals. We possess such census-lists from Alalakh and Ugarit.[16]

B. The Social Classes

The population of Palestine and southern Syria was since time immemorial Semitic in origin and in speech. This situation is reflected in the names of the earliest cities in the area which are almost without exception Canaanite. At a late stage during the Middle Bronze Age foreign elements, particularly Hurrians but also Indo-Aryans and Anatolians, entered the country. Because of their superior war techniques these invaders were able to seize power and establish themselves as the ruling class in a number of important cities. It is however erroneous to maintain that the Syro-Palestinian aristocracy of this period was exclusively of non-Semitic stock, or that all non-Semites were members of the ruling class. First, several city-kings and high officials bore good Semitic names, and secondly, the Alalakhian documents from the 18th century prove conclusively that many non-Semitic individuals belonged to the lower classes.[17]

Canaanite society in the middle of the 2nd millennium B.C.E. was semi-feudal in character and consisted of three main classes: 1) the so-called aristocracy, embracing the large land-owners, the big merchants, and the professional warriors, particularly the *maryannu;* 2) the middle class, embracing the small landowners, tenant-farmers, craftsmen, and unskilled laborers; and 3) slaves.

The recently published Akkadian written documents from the royal palace in Ugarit provide us with a fair picture of the semi-feudal conditions existing in that prosperous kingdom. Crown lands, often containing whole villages together with their tenant-farmers, were granted "for ever" by the king to the prominent individuals, usually members of the *maryannu* class. In return, the recipients of such grants were duty-bound to pay certain taxes and to perform a variety of services for the benefit of the king. In case the fief-holder was unable to perform his feudal obligations or was in default of his duties, the land was taken away from him and transferred to another holder. The exact feudal services incumbent upon a fief-holder are nowhere stated explicitly, but from the numerous grants of land in which some obligations are mentioned, and from those grants in which some exemptions of these are specified, it is clear that the taxes (in money and kind) and the duties (corvée labor and military service) were onerous.[18] A fief-holder could free himself from all, or some, of the normal obligations by paying outright a certain sum of money to the king.[19] In such a case he was declared by the king to be *zakū* "free,"[20] that is, he did not have to pay taxes on grain, oil, beverages, large cattle, sheep and mules, and in addition his tenant-farmers were exempted from performing corvée labor.[21] In this connection it should be emphasized that only a certain part of the arable land was under the control of the king, the rest being held as private property by individuals and considered as a commodity that could be sold and bought.

The *maryannu* were a professional warrior class who, due to their superior military equipment — the horse-drawn chariot and the composite bow — occupied a highly privileged position in the Canaanite semi-feudal society. In the Alalakh census lists of the 15th century B.C.E. the *maryannu* are distinguished from the other classes of the population by having after their names the statement "possesses a chariot."[22] The term *maryannu* is most probably related to the Vedic *márya* "young man, warrior," and most of the bearers of this title in the period under discussion were the descendants of the northern peoples who had invaded Canaan in the 18th century B.C.E. As a military class the *maryannu* were the main defensive and offensive force in the respective city-states. For their services to the king they received crown land "in perpetuity" and the income derived from these estates provided them with the means of maintaining themselves and their expensive equipment. The *maryannu* status was hereditary, and not unlike the case in modern monarchies only the king could elevate a commoner to the rank of a "knight." The king Niqmepa of Alalakh bestowed a *maryannu*-ship upon a certain Qabia, with a solemn declaration that none may take that privilege from his hand forever.[23] Similarly, the king of Ugarit granted to a commoner a tax-exempted fief and conferred upon him the title of *maryannu*, in return for which the "knighted" recipient promised that "he would work very hard for the king."[24]

Closely linked to the *maryannu* were the military sub-classes of the *ḥanakū* "retainers"[25] (cf. biblical *ḥanikim*, Gen. 14 : 14), and the *naʿarūnu* "attendants"[26] (cf. biblical *nᵉʿarim*, particularly II Sam. 2 : 14 ff.). As a land-owning class upon whom heavy taxes and restrictions were imposed by Egypt, the *maryannu* exploited every sign of weakness displayed by the occupational power to revolt against it, in the hope of recapturing the position which they had held under the Hyksos rule. They are frequently mentioned in the Egyptian records among the prisoners of war.[27] In one of his campaigns Amen-hotep II lists 550 *maryannu* and 240 of their wives as part of the booty which he had brought back to Thebes from a war in Syria.[28]

The backbone of Canaanite society and its main economic basis were the class of people called in the Alalakh, Ugaritic, and Amarna records *awēlūti ḥupši*. They constituted the bulk of the population and according to the census-lists of the 15th century B.C.E. the ratio of the *ḥupšu* to the *maryannu* class in the kingdom of Alalakh was about 5 : 1.[29] It is quite possible, though documentary evidence is lacking, that the numerical relation between the aristocracy and the toiling masses was substantially the same also in southern Syria and in Palestine during the Amarna age. The term *ḥupšu* (probably derived from the root *ḥpṯ* "be base, vile")[30] was a class designation applied generally, though not exclusively, to the free-born tenant-farmers who constituted the majority of the agricultural population. Like modern share-croppers, the *ḥupšu* possessed small parcels of land, their own houses, and other property, but were on the whole economically dependent on the big landowners on whose estates they were settled. They were subject to the corvée and served in the army as foot-soldiers. In the chaotic and war-torn Amarna period the attitude of the *ḥupšu* in the political struggle was of decisive importance. Because of their numerical and economic strength they were in a position to swing the scales of victory in either direction. This fact is best illustrated in the correspondence of Rib-Addi of Byblos. In his letters to the pharaoh he repeatedly complains that the *ḥupšu* have departed from his dominion for other cities "where there is grain for their sustenance";[31] that because of the desertion of the *ḥupšu* the SA. GAZ people have conquered a city;[32] and finally, in an answer to a letter by the Egyptian king, he asks in despair: "From whom shall I protect myself, from my *ḫupšu?*[33] Indeed, Rib-Addi is so terror-stricken by the mood of his *ḫupšu* that he is afraid lest they would slay him if military aid from Egypt did not reach him soon.[34] Having been reduced to semi-serfdom by the big landowners and to near-starvation by the high taxes extorted from them by Egypt, most of the *ḫupšu* sided with the invading Habiru to the detriment of Egypt and the ruling classes of Syria and Palestine.

The counterpart of the agricultural *ḫupšu* were the freeborn artisans and laborers in the cities. Though Canaan lacked the raw materials necessary for the development of large-scale manufacturing plants, the textile and pottery industries employed sizable numbers of hired workers. In Ugarit some of the artisans, especially those who worked in the royal establishments, were banded together in corporations,[35] and in Israelite Palestine craftsmen were organized in guilds.[36]

It is difficult to assess the number of slaves and their role in the economic life of this period because of the paucity of legal and business documents. The large imperial states of Babylonia, Assyria, and Egypt, and their big temple establishments possessed considerable numbers of unfree personnel, but the small Canaanite city-states and their local shrines could boast only of a relatively small number of state and temple slaves. The bases for the profitable employment of unfree labor were mining industries and latifundia, but both of these prerequisites were lacking in Canaan. There were, of course, big private landowners, and the petty kings possessed large tracts of arable land, but both preferred the employment of the free tenant-farmers and share-croppers to that of slave labor; the former system of working the land proved itself to be safer and cheaper. The same situation also prevailed in industry were we find free-born craftsmen dominating the labor market.[37] The Alalakhian and Ugaritic documents attest to the fact that the number of privately owned slaves was very small, even in those prosperous kingdoms. According to the Alalakhian census-lists the slave population in a number of towns and villages ranged from one to twenty-six, and the largest number of slaves in the possession of one master was three.[38] Only few slaves are mentioned in the entire collection of about 250 documents from the royal palace in Ugarit. It should also be stressed that in comparison with the large masses of free-born people who were taken as war prisoners by Egypt, the number of slaves among them was negligible. In the numerous campaigns conducted by Thut-mose III only about 3,000 slaves were counted as part of the booty,[39] while in the campaigns of Amen-hotep II, who claimed to have carried off as many as

Fig. 8.
Canaanite traders unloading their merchandise in an Egyptian harbor.
Fresco from a tomb at Thebes, 15th century B.C.E.
N. de Garis-Davies — Faulkner, *JEA*, 33 (1947), pl. VIII.

Fig. 9.
Syrians bringing tribute to Egypt.
Fresco from the tomb of Rekh-Mi-Re' at Thebes, 15th century B.C.E.
N. de Garis-Davies, *The Tomb of Rekh-Mi-Re' at Thebes*, New York, 1953, pl. XXII.

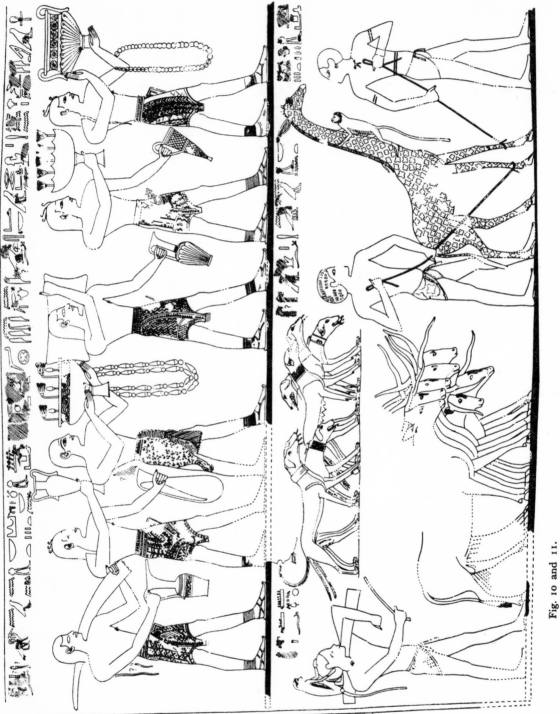

Fig. 10 and 11.
Cretans (above) and Nubians (below) bringing tribute to Egypt. Fresco from the tomb of
Rekh-Mi-Re' at Thebes, 15th century B.C.E.

N. de Garis-Davies, *The Tomb of Rekh-Mi-Re' at Thebes*, New York, 1953. pl. XX.

90,000 captives, not a single slave is mentioned among them.[40] The largest consignment of slave-girls ever sent by a Canaanite ruler as a "gift" to a pharaoh was that of 'Abdu-Heba of Jerusalem, and it consisted of twenty-one girls.[41] Poverty or debts surely caused some people to sell their children into slavery. Thus Rib-Addi of Byblos reported in his letters that because of the constant wars people were forced to sell their sons and daughters in order to save themselves from starvation.[42] But those were exceptional cases in difficult times. It is therefore fair to conclude, on the basis of the available data, that in Canaan slavery played an insignificant role in agriculture as well as in industry.

C. AGRICULTURE, INDUSTRY, AND TRADE

The Egyptian war records unroll before us a detailed picture of the booty carried off from Canaan by the kings of the Eighteenth and Nineteenth Dynasties. These entries contain large numbers of captives, enormous quantities of agricultural products, such as grain, oil, incense, wine, and cattle; manufactured goods, such as chariots, bronze armor, jewelry, and "every pleasing thing of the country"; and also materials which Canaan had to import from abroad, such as precious stones, gold, and silver.[43] In addition to the plunder, the conquered city-states were required to pay regular tribute (*biltu*) and occasional "gifts" (*šulmānu, qīštu, tāmārtu*),[44] and to provide for the Egyptian garrisons stationed in the country. As one Egyptian scribe put it aptly in a report of the fifth campaign of Thut-mose III: "Behold, the army of his majesty was drunk and anointed with oil every day as at a feast in Egypt."[45] The wealth and manpower of Syria and Palestine filled the Nile Valley and made possible the splendor that was Egypt in the period of the New Kingdom. Yet, in spite of the systematic spoliation of their country, the industrious people of Canaan were able to maintain a high level of material well-being for a long time, until they finally reached the point of economic decline in the 13th century B.C.E.

The north coast of Canaan was famous for its wood (that of the Lebanon) and its purple dye. The Canaanites discovered the murex shellfish from which were obtained a purple and a blue that became the most renowned and coveted textile dyes in the ancient world. With this product as its monopoly, Phoenicia became in the Late Bronze Period the center of the manufacture of the purple dyed textile. In fact, it is quite possible that the very name Canaan (*Kinaḫḫi* in cuneiform spelling) meant "land of purple," that is, the country was named after its famous merchandise.[46] Because of the prevalence of purple dye and the abundance of wool in the many

Fig. 11.

Different types of ceramic ware from the Late Bronze period.

After N. Avigad in *Encyclopaedia Biblica* IV, pls. 169–170.
Design "Carta", Jerusalem.

sheep-raising areas, the manufacture of colored textiles was Canaan's most active and prosperous industry through the centuries. Large plants for weaving and dyeing of woolen cloth were in existence in various cities in the country. There were rich copper mines in the Lebanon and throughout the greater part of the length of the Arabah in southern Palestine. It does not appear, however, that these mines were fully exploited in the Late Bronze Period. The reference in Deut. 8:9 describing Palestine as "a land whose stones are iron, and out of whose hills thou mayest dig copper" undoubtedly reflects the conditions under Solomon and his successors who worked the mines in the Arabah.[47] Whatever the case may have been, Canaan produced its own copper tools, manufactured from native, but mostly from imported ore, and it could pride itself on possessing a large and diverse metal industry. The Alalakh tablets show that that city had metallurgical plants in the 15th century B.C.E., some of which produced weapons.[48] The Egyptian war records list considerable quantities of suits of armor, bronze armor, and chariots (that is, wooden chariots plated or strengthened with metal) as part of the booty from Canaan[49] (there are various sources which testify to the manufacture of chariots in the country). Indeed, the numerous local metallurgical factories bear witness to the great technological skill displayed by the ancient Canaanite smiths.[50] As attested by excavations and contemporary inscriptions, jewelry shops were to be found in many towns, and some cities were especially known for their excellent artistic work. The Egyptian records list gold and silver dishes, vessels, and golden bracelets "the workmanship of the country" as part of the booty from Canaan.[51] The existence of forests, especially in the Lebanon and in Amanus, was instrumental in the establishment of a wood industry. From an Alalakhian document we may infer that the carpenter shops in that city employed considerable numbers of skilled workers who produced tables, seats, stools, couches, and carts, both for the local market and for export.[52] Pottery for domestic use was produced in practically every community. But as was the case in many another trade, the pottery industry was concentrated in localities where suitable raw materials were in abundance, and there articles of a high standard were produced.

Canaan, lying at the crossroads between Egypt, Mesopotamia, and Asia Minor, and facing the Mediterranean with its great Minoan and Mycenaean civilizations, served since the Early Bronze Period as a transit center through which goods moved by sea and by land from one country to another. Its seaports, such as Ashkelon, Jaffa, Dor, Tyre, Sidon, Byblos, and Ugarit were open to traffic. These cities carried on an extensive international trade which reached its climax in the 14th century B.C.E. Canaan's main

Fig. 12.
Carved-ivory handle found at Megiddo, Late Bronze.
G. Loud, *Megiddo* II, Chicago, 1948, pl. 204.

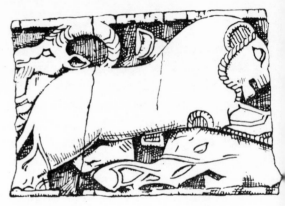

Fig. 13.
Carved ivory plaque found at Megiddo, Stratum **XIV**.
G. Loud, *op. cit.*, pl. 204.

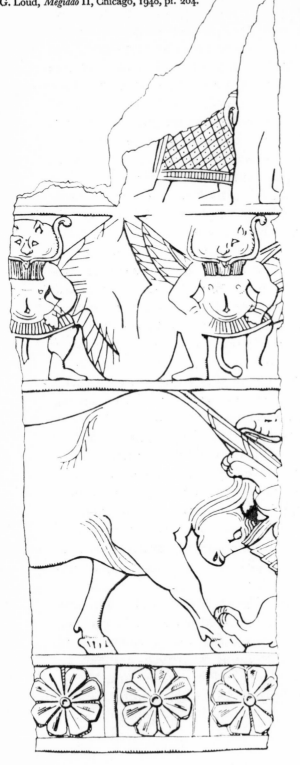

Fig. 14.
Ivory tablet used for a game, Late Bronze.

export articles consisted of woods, colored textiles, and agricultural products, such as grain, wine, oil, and spices.[53] That there was a surplus in
agricultural goods in the country is proven by the Egyptian war records
which list large quantities of grain, fruits, oil, honey, and myrrh.[54] These
as well as manufactured goods were given in exchange for the raw materials
which Canaan imported from abroad, consisting of copper, lead, tin, silver,
gold, ivory, and precious stones. To judge from the Egyptian records and
the Amarna letters there must have been considerable amount of these
materials in the country. Thus Rib-Addi of Byblos mentions in one of his
letters the lump sum of one hundred minas of gold.[55] Furthermore, the
wealthy classes could afford to pay high prices for imported luxury articles
ranging from fine linen, faience, alabaster, and scarabs, imported from
Egypt, to Mycenaean decorated vases.[56]

Local trade was largely in the hands of private merchants, while inter-
state trade seems to have been, with few exceptions, a monopoly of the
kings. International commerce, even in the period of *pax Aegyptiaca* when
the land-routes and the seaports were safe for the traffic, required a large
capital outlay, a condition which practically excluded private initiative.
The situation during the perilous Amarna period was even less conducive
to individual enterprise. No single merchant possessed the means to build
a trade fleet or to outfit a large caravan; only kings were in a position to
do so. There were, of course, exceptions to the rule. In prosperous cities a
number of private merchants sometimes banded together for the purpose
of a joint undertaking. They pooled their resources and formed a company
for specific transactions.[57] The Alalakhian kings bought and sold land and
slaves, lent money on interest, and engaged in industrial enterprises.[58]
The cuneiform documents from the royal palace in Ugarit present the same
picture. The kings not only personally administered the distribution of the
crown lands but also took an active part in all kinds of industrial and
business dealings.[59] Rib-Addi of Byblos complained in his letters that his
enemies had seized two of his ships and were about to capture all his other
vessels.[60] International trade in Egypt was largely concentrated in the
hands of the state. The king sent out special emissaries who acted as pur-
chasing agents for the palace. In the Amarna letters we find references to
the *awēlūti māt miṣri* "Egyptians," that is, royal commercial agents stationed
in various cities in Canaan.[61] In a letter to Milkilu of Gezer the pharaoh
writes that he had sent to him his commissioner of archers with various
products consisting of silver, gold, garments, precious stones, etc., in order
to procure in exchange for these goods forty fine concubines, that is,
weaving slave-girls, "in whom there is no blemish."[62]

CHAPTER IV

CULTURAL AND RELIGIOUS LIFE

by Cyrus H. Gordon

A. The Period and its Sources

THE PERIOD UNDER consideration is roughly the second half of the 2nd millennium B.C.E. More precisely we may take as its beginning the expulsion of the Hyksos from Egypt by Ah-mose, the founder of the Eighteenth Dynasty, and as its close the end of the Twentieth Dynasty with its last king Ramses XI. During this time Israel went through its formative period as reflected in the patriarchal narratives, the Exodus, the Conquest, and the period of the Judges, and leading up to the establishment of the Davidic monarchy.

The Near East in New Kingdom times was very cosmopolitan, and Canaan the most international hub of that cosmopolitan world. Mesopotamian, Indo-European (notably Hittite), Mediterranean and Egyptian cultures mingled in Canaan. Moreover, the Hurrian element was so strong that the Egyptians often referred to Canaan as Hurruland. The native West Semitic Canaanites remained the principal factor linguistically, but culturally they were subject to a plethora of influences in many aspects of their society and institutions.

The sources for the period are remarkably good. The Tell el-Amarna Letters from the reigns of Amen-hotep III and Amen-hotep IV (Akh-en-Aton) are a precious source for Egypto-Canaanite relations at the highest diplomatic level. The Nuzi tablets of the Amarna age provide a full picture of law and custom in a Hurrian community, elucidating the customs depicted in narratives of the Hebrew and Greek heroic ages contained in Genesis and Homer respectively. Legal, historical, diplomatic, literary, and religious evidence of great interest are preserved in Hittite tablets. Ugarit has yielded a corpus of legendary, mythological, religious, epistolary, and administrative tablets in the native Semitic language of the north coast of Canaan.[1] From Ugarit comes also an extensive body of Akkadian texts dealing with law and diplomacy.[2] The Linear B tablets of Crete and Greece are economic and administrative records in Greek.[3]

Egyptian texts of the period are many and varied, of value primarily in the military, diplomatic, literary, and religious fields. And however late the final redaction of the Greek epic and of the biblical accounts down through David's reign, they to a considerable extent preserve an authentic picture of the Levant in New Kingdom times. These literary sources by no means exhaust the list of extant texts. There is, in addition, a mass of artistic and other archeological data. So much of the material has recently been excavated or deciphered, and so much material continues to be discovered from year to year, that the subject before us cannot be stabilized at present. And yet its importance is enormous, because the two main-springs of Western civilization (the ancient Hebrew and Greek) are products of the same East Mediterranean *milieu* during the New Kingdom period.

B. The Major Channels of Cultural Transmission

The enterprising nations of the Near East were given to founding commercial colonies abroad, the best known of these being the Assyrian ones in Cappadocia, which go back to the dawn of the 2nd millennium. But Assyria had them also in other locales, and other nations, too, established commercial colonies abroad. Indeed, several of them might have such colonies in the same city, as was the case at Ugarit, where there were Egyptian and Assyrian colonists.[4] At a great international port like Ugarit other nations doubtless had colonies too, notably the Caphtorians and the Hittites.

Since the early part of the millennium, Babylonia had a type of commercial and financial *entrepreneur* who often engaged in foreign trade. Either he or his agents operated in foreign lands. His activities are delineated with characteristic clarity in Hammurabi's Code, in which he is called *tamkārum*. He served as a kind of minister without portfolio, or ambassador at large, in the interests of his homeland. Thus he was expected to ransom captive Babylonians abroad, and the Babylonian crown guaranteed his reimbursement if the captive or the captive's hometown could not reimburse him. The role of the *tamkārum* was historically significant. Babylonia had developed expert business methods and law (both private and commercial), and in very early times the Assyro-Babylonian *tamkārū* (the plural of *tamkārum*) and commercial colonies carried business and legal institutions from Mesopotamia all through the Near East into Europe and Egypt. These Mesopotamians introduced the clay tablet far and wide: into Canaan, Anatolia, Egypt, and the Mediterranean, and even into Greece itself.

The more mature and efficient legal and economic institutions and methods of the *tamkārum* fell like seeds on fresh and fertile soil. Thus when Hebrew civilization started on the modest beginnings of its career, it absorbed in Canaan not only a mature literary but also a mature legal tradition. The latter is the key to the parallels between the Old Babylonian and Middle Assyrian laws and the oldest strata of Hebrew laws. As for business usage, Hebrew terminology reflects the Babylonian in such words as *rō'sh* "head" in the sense of "principal" (Lev. 5:24; Num. 5:7) as against "interest": an exact reflex of Babylonian *qaqqadum* "head" in the sense of "principal." That the foreign Babylonian *tamkārum* exacted oppressive rates of interest from the Hebrew made the concept of interest odious to the Hebrew; so much so that the law forbids him to exact it of his Hebrew brother. In other words, the prohibition against interest in the Bible is a reaction against the Babylonian system that laid the foundation for the financial structure of a capitalistic economy.

The Babylonian and Assyrian *tamkārū* carried with them their scribal personnel, and used them in a way that established an international postal system. These merchants had to correspond with other similar merchants throughout the Near East. Thus their couriers constituted a postal system that could be used for other purposes, political or personal; and their scribes made of Babylonian the *lingua franca*. Before the Babylonian-writing scribes at Tell el-Amarna, there probably existed in Egypt offices of Mesopotamian *tamkārū* with scribal staffs. If pre-Amarna cuneiform tablets of an economic and epistolary character were to be discovered in Egypt, they should come as no surprise. Be it also noted that cuneiform scribes such as those at Tell el-Amarna conveyed literary and religious texts from land to land. In addition to the epistles, Mesopotamian myths such as *Adapa* and *Nergal and Ereshkigal* were found at Tell el-Amarna, and part of the Gilgamesh Epic at Megiddo; other Mesopotamian literary tablets can be expected to turn up in Israel from time to time.

Another major channel of cultural transmission was the guild system. Society was stratified into many groups. Large segments of the population were farmers and herdsmen. The trend (as always in the Near East) was for the nomadic herdsmen to shift gradually to farming. Whereas the Patriarchs were herdsmen, Isaac is pictured as trying his hand at farming (Gen. 26:12). Eventually such semi-nomadism converts the tribesmen into peasants. In the tablets from Ugarit, much of the population is handled administratively by the state through the tribal units in the case of nomads and semi-nomads, and through the localities in the case of the farmers. But the rest of the population is handled mainly through guild organizations. Scribes, priests, soldiers, builders, bakers, butchers, musicians, and so on, are all grouped into their respective guilds. The Odyssey (17 : 381–386) tells us that while most people were not welcome abroad, guild members (δημιοεργοί) were, since they plied useful crafts that were in demand all over. Homer singles out prophets, physicians, builders, and minstrels. This explains the wide distribution of religious texts, literature, architectural forms, and the arts.

Among the Ugaritic guilds were both the *khnm* (*kohanīm*) and *qdšm* (*qᵉdēshīm*). That both these guilds of priests appear in ancient Israel is a reminder that religious practices spread, from district to district and from people to people, with the priests of specific guilds who moved about with the mobility of Homeric δημιοεργοί.

The highly stratified society that we find at Ugarit is strongly reminiscent of the caste system of India. The upper classes of priests and of warriors are each subdivided in the Near East of New Kingdom times (and into a host of sub-castes in India). The elite warriors were *maryannu* "charioteer(s)." But there are many other classifications of soldiers, some of international distribution such as the *šnn* (Ugaritic *ṯnn;* Late Egyptian *snn*).

The connections of royalty are, as in India, with the priestly and the warrior classes. This is borne out by the tribal connections of the kings at Ugarit with the *Ṯʿ* tribe, to which priests, officials and presumably military officers belong as well as the line of kings celebrated in the Keret Epic.[5]

Every advanced society needs occupational stratification because of the diverse specializations in the arts, crafts, and professional services. But the social picture in Canaan during New Kingdom times is far more complicated with guild stratification than society actually requires. That various occupations should exist is a foregone conclusion; but that a huge proportion of the people should be administratively controlled through a host of guilds confronts us with a situation radically different from that in the Mari tablets or in Egypt. In Mari, people are either residents of towns or members of tribes. In Egypt, people belong to their nome; and to this day the loyalty of the Egyptian peasant is to his village. But in Ugarit (and doubtless in other parts of contemporary Canaan) occupational stratification takes on the form of a class system, approaching (though not actually becoming) a caste system. This development cannot be divorced from the Indo-European migrations into the Near East which, commencing at the beginning of the 2nd millennium B.C.E., continued throughout most of that millennium. It was these waves that brought the Hittites, the Indo-European ruling class of the Mitannians, the Greeks whose language first appears in Linear B, and other ethnic groups speaking Indo-European

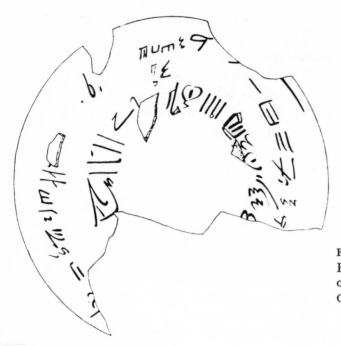

Fig. 15.
Egyptian hieratic inscription incised
on a bow found at Lachish.
O. Tufnell, *Lachish* IV, London, 1958, pl. 44.

Fig. 16.
Inscription in an unknown language found at
Tell Deir 'Ālla.
Prof. H. J. Franken, Leiden.

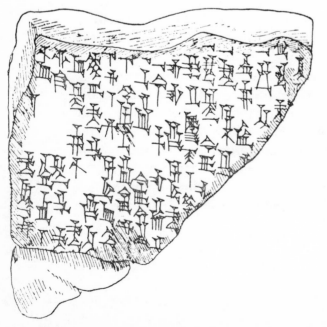

Fig. 17.
Akkadian inscription in which a fragment of the
Gilgamesh epic is rendered, found at Megiddo.
Atiqot II (1958), 109.

languages from the east with many Indoid features, such as quite a few Mitannian names of persons and gods, and the virtually Sanskrit numerals in the Kikkuli hippological text. The introduction of the horse-drawn chariot by the Indo-Europeans revolutionized the art of war and deeply affected the history of the ancient world. Thus during the first half of the 2nd millennium hordes that included Indo-Europeans and their horse-drawn war chariots swept all through Canaan, from north to south, and invaded Egypt, terminating the Middle Kingdom. The invaders, commonly called Hyksos, were expelled from the Delta sometime between 1580 and 1570 B.C.E. But Egypt had learned from the Hyksos the valuable lesson of chariot warfare. It was this lesson that made possible Egypt's Empire Period (as the New Kingdom is often called), culminating in the conquests of Thut-mose III. The Empire gave such an impetus to Egypt's reputation abroad that long after it was little more than a memory, Egypt continued to enjoy diplomatic, commercial, and cultural prestige, with the result that the Valley of the Nile contributed heavily to the synthesis in the East Mediterranean that produced the birth of Western civilization.

C. The Heroic Tale and its Literature

The New Kingdom period constituted for much of the world an heroic age characterized by dislocation, war, and, above all, migrations. The Greek epics and early Hebrew sagas depict heroic societies operating according to rules, and under conditions, different from those of classical Greece and Israel. The formula to express this is: "In those days there was no king in Israel; every man did that which was right in his own eyes" (Jud. 21:25). If we examine the narratives, we find that they mirror social institutions that go strikingly with those in the Hurrian community of Nuzi during the Amarna age, as, for example, in inheritance rights, as reflected in the Book of Genesis. In the Nuzi tablets, oral last wills and testaments by aged parents expecting death are binding; they dovetail with the oral last wills and testaments of Isaac and Jacob.[6]

The standard of what is worthy of saga in Israel in New Kingdom times is of a piece with the standard of the Ugaritic epics. Preoccupation with the continuity of the line (specifically with the birth of a son by the destined bride in accordance with a divine promise) appears in both the Keret and Aqhat Epics uncovered at Ugarit, even as in the Hebraic traditions from Abraham through to the birth of Samuel, never again to appear in the historical books of the Hebrew Bible. Just as the promised son must be from Hurriya in the Epic of Keret, so must he be from Sarai in Genesis. A son from any but the destined bride is not the fulfilment of the divine promise; thus Ishmael born of Hagar is not to carry on the main line from which Israel's kings are to spring.

Heroic epic, in the East Mediterranean, features an Indo-European motif which is totally lacking in the earlier literatures or the Near East, namely, the Helen of Troy motif. The king (Menelaus or Keret) loses his bride (Helen or Hurriya) and must win her back. David's regaining of Michal may be a truncated version of this theme. Furthermore, a hero other than the king can lose his beautiful woman so that the interest in the story is in hearing how he got her back. Thus in the Iliad not only has Menelaus lost Helen, but Achilles loses Briseis. The theme was so much in vogue that the public could not get enough of it and it was worked into the same as well as different compositions again and again. We therefore need not regard the seizure of Sarah successively by Pharaoh and Abimelech (Gen. 12 : 11 ff.; 20 : 1 ff.) and the near-seizure of Rebekah by Abimelech (Gen. 26 : 7–10) as the result of careless editing (that is, as repetitions of the same incident). The threefold appearance of the motif is rather a genuinely recurrent theme of East Mediterranean literature during New Kingdom days. The rage of Samson over the loss of his Philistine bride results in calamities for the Philistines including many slain (Jud. 15: 1–8). However folkloristic this tale is in the Book of Judges, it is a reflex of the same motif, exemplified by the wrath of Achilles over Briseis that sent many brave Achaeans to Hades. Such motifs are completely lacking in the older literatures of Egypt (for example, the Romance of Si-nuhe) and Mesopotamia (for example, the Gilgamesh Epic). And after the Davidic narratives, the historical books of Israel show no interest in the amours of the kings of Israel or Judah, no matter how inevitable such affairs are in real life. Before and after the period in question, the standard of what was worthy of saga was quite different. Such motifs in the East Mediterranean of New Kingdom times were of Indo-European inspiration, as their prominence in the epics of India, Greece, and the Teutonic peoples show.

"Migration" is the key word of the age, migration in fact and migration in story. The narrative of Abraham typifies the theme of migration. He starts from Ur of the Chaldees; proceeds to Haran in north Mesopotamia; moves south to Canaan; wanders to Egypt; returns to Canaan; has dealings with Philistines around Gerar and Beer-sheba, and with Hittites around Hebron. His Egyptian counterpart in story is Si-nuhe, an Egyptian who wanders through Canaan where he has many an adventure and a glamorous career, but the only happy ending for him is to return to his own land.

This type of story (episodic wanderings culminating in homecoming) is part and parcel of the Gilgamesh Epic, which however deals also with the hopeless quest for immortality or rejuvenation. Hebrew epic more realistically provides immortality through progeny. Egypt succeeded in producing the world's first written literature for sheer entertainment without the burden of ponderous problems such as immortality, either of the individual or of the line. After all, the cult of the dead in Egypt offered eternal bliss to the satisfaction of those who could pay for it. Released from the need of solving so grim a problem (or of solving any problem connected with nationalism), the Egyptians were free to create a purely enjoyable written literature without the heartache and frustrations inherent in the Gilgamesh Epic.

The overseas interests of the Egyptians produced also wondrous sea yarns in Middle Kingdom times. The tale of the Shipwrecked Sailor tells of an Egyptian's harrowing experiences on a magic isle in the Red Sea. But the sailor managed to reach home in Egypt, laden with gifts. In late Egyptian literature, the episodic wanderings of Si-nuhe and the tall sea-stories of the Shipwrecked Sailor type are combined.[7] The tale of Wen-Amon, of the beginning of the 11th century, tells of how an Egyptian got into one scrape after another, at sea, in the ports of the Levant, and on isles such as Cyprus, before fulfilling his mission and returning home. To this extent, Wen-Amon is the forerunner of the Odyssey (which is also an East Mediterranean tale for entertainment, about a hero who wanders for years from isle to isle and coast to coast, with many a narrow escape before his happy homecoming), even as the Epic of Keret is the forerunner of the Iliad.[8]

D. THE PHILISTINE INFLUENCE

The influence of the Caphtorians, to whom the Philistines belonged, was considerable long before the New Kingdom. "The Jordan" bears the name for "river" in Old Crete (Ἰάρδανος). In Hebrew, "Jordan" appears not as a pure proper name (like "Israel" or "Jerusalem") but usually with the article, like ha-nāhār "the River" which designates the Euphrates, or as "this Jordan" or "the Jordan of Jericho." The Mandeans still use "jordan" to signify any river. When the Philistines consolidated their position in the coastal region and the Shefela, the pressure they exerted pushed the tribe of Dan out of its area, as Jud. 18 relates. The Samson cycle reflects Philistine domination over the Danites and other local segments of the Hebrews. It was Philistine oppression that evoked the formation of the monarchy, haltingly under Saul, and successfully under David. Philistine supremacy was based on a higher technological civilization than the Hebrews possessed until David's time. That the Philistines kept the Hebrews disarmed by controlling metallurgy (I Sam. 13:19–22) shows that Philistine power had technology behind it.

Once we recognize the fact that the rise of the United Monarchy was in large measure the Hebrew response to the Philistine stimulus, we shall be able to evaluate Israel's debt to the Philistines. Their artistic contribution lives on in the word *kaftōrīm*; while *kōva'* "war helmet" (long recognized as a Philistine loan) reflects their military pre-eminence. The significant thing is that the Philistines were Caphtorian linguistically, so that Hebrew and Greek cultures had linguistic, literary, and historical contacts with each other from the dawn of Hebrew and of Greek civilization. The plainest index is the corpus of early Hebrew words with Greek counterparts, for example, *mᵉkērā* (Gen. 49:5) "sword" — μάχαιρα; *lishkā* "chamber" — λέοχη; *lappīd* "torch" — (λάμπας pl. λαμπάδες), the antiquity of which is reflected by its occurrence in the name of Deborah's husband, Lappidoth.[9]

The Caphtorian impact on the institutions of Israel was great. Crete was famous for its laws, reputedly revealed to Minos in a mountain cave by Zeus. The revelation of the law to Moses on Mount Sinai goes with East Mediterranean rather than with Babylonian traditions. Moreover, Minos is aided by his master craftsman Daedalus: a necessity in so artistic a tradition as the Cretan. Israel's national life could have dispensed with its "Daedalus," but yet, in keeping with the East Mediterranean scheme, Daedalus has his counterpart in Bezalel, master craftsman of the lawgiver Moses.

The pattern of migrations gave rise to parallel national epics of the exodus type. Nations would celebrate in song their advent from their original land to the new promised land under divine guidance. Amos (9:7) knew of such epics and states: that God brought not only Israel out of Egypt, but the Philistines out of Caphtor and the Arameans out of Kir.

The concepts, the literature, and the religious institutions of early Israel often go hand in hand with general developments in Canaan of the New Kingdom age. For example, not only is the exodus motif international, but the celebration of the baking of *mazzā* (= "unleavened bread") has East Mediterranean ramifications. The Epic of Keret singles out the baking of bread for the vast host in preparation for its departure. And the probable identity of *mazzā* with μάζα demonstrates the East Mediterranean spread of the word, spanning Semitic Hebrew and Indo-European Greek.

Fig. 18.
Impressions of cylinder seals
in the style of Mitanni, found
at Beth-shean, Late Bronze.

A. Rowe, *The four Canaanite Temples at Beth-Shan*,
Philadelphia, 1940, pl. XL.

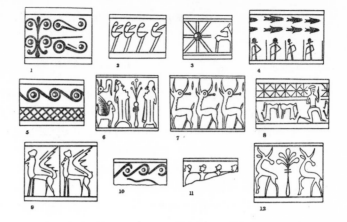

Fig. 19.
Impression of a cylinder
seal found at Beth-shean
on which Ramses II is
depicted shooting at a
target below which are
chained two prisoners
of war.

A. Rowe, *op. cit.*, pl. XXXVIII, 5.
Design "Carta" Jerusalem.

Fig. 20.
Impression of a cylinder
seal bearing the inscription
"Ashtoreth", found at
Beth-el, 13th century B.C.E.

W. F. Albright, *BASOR* 56
(1931) 1 fig. 1.
Design "Carta" Jerusalem.

Fig. 23.
Impression of a seal in
the Hittite style, found
at Hazor, Late Bronze.

Y. Yadin, *IEJ*, 8, (1958), pl. 7d.
Design "Carta" Jerusalem.

Fig. 21.
Impression of a cylinder
seal in the Cypriot style,
found at Tell Abu-
Huwām, beginning of
the Iron Age.

R. W. Hamilton, *Quarterly of the
Department of Antiquities in Pales-
tine*, 4 (1935), pl. 38 no. 217.
Design "Carta" Jerusalem.

Fig. 22.
Seal on which is incised
the inscription *Lava* in
late Proto Canaanite
script. It was found in the
Aijalon Valley; 12th
century B.C.E.

R. Giveon, *PEQ* 93, (1961), 38.

E. KINGSHIP IN CANAAN

For about the first three centuries of our period, the Near East had power-ful states, such as the Egyptian and Hittite empires. Canaan, in between, was composed of city-states and small kingdoms which were often obliged to pay tribute to the great powers. For about the last two centuries of the period, the collapse or decline of the great powers left a power vacuum in Canaan. This gave an opportunity to the smaller Canaanite groups to extend their sway over their neighbors and forge a kingdom of some size. The Philistines had the manpower and the technical skill to dominate Palestine, until, toward the end of the 2nd millennium, David broke the Philistine grip and extended his rule from the Egyptian border to the Euphrates River to form the largest empire in its day.

Kingship in Canaan took on various forms. Melchizedek was both king of Salem and priest of *El 'Elyon*. In Ugarit the king is divine through the fiction of having suckled divine breasts. The common epithet of kings in Homer, διοτρεφής "divinely fed," can hardly refer to anything different. *Shod m'lakim* (= "the breast of kings") in Isa. 60:16 reflects the same concept. Moreover, at Ugarit, both in art and in the texts, the concept of the dual kingship is portrayed. A carved ivory panel from the royal bedstead at Ugarit shows two kings sucking the breasts of a goddess, which ties in with the expression "the two who suck the breast" in the mythological texts.[10] Dual kingship was the rule at Sparta. To be sure, dual kingship may have different typological origins in different localities and periods. In later Judaism the ideal of dual kingship persisted, with one spiritual and one temporal ruler reigning side by side in harmony. In addition to the long-known traditional sources, the Qumran scrolls mention *M'shīḥēy Aharon v'-Yiśra'el* "the two Messiahs: the priestly one of Aaron and the temporal one of Israel" in the *Manual of Discipline*.[11] That this is a diminishing old concept rather than a waxing new one in the Second Temple period is evident. Its existence in early Canaan at Ugarit makes it likely that an-cient Israel knew of it, even if normative Judean ideology rejected it.

The institution of kingship in Israel naturally owes much to its forerun-ners in New Kingdom Canaan. We must content ourselves here with a single specific illustration. In the Legend of Keret it is the eighth daughter ("Octavia") who is elevated to the position of firstborn. The selection of David for anointment by Samuel is told (I Sam. 16:1–13) in a way that also highlights his elevation from youngest and eighth child over his seven elder brothers. That fratriarchy existed in ancient Israel is quite clear from I Chron. 26:10 where *rō'sh* "fratriarch" is distinguished from *b'kōr* "firstborn," for Hosah appointed his son Shimri as fratriarch even though the latter was not the firstborn.

F. Other Pre-Hebraic Antecedents

The rules of fratriarchy operate when "brethren dwell together" (Deut. 25 : 5) ; and when this is the case, levirate marriage was one of the component institutions. Like so much else in the Near East, levirate marriage was brought into the area by the Indo-Europeans in the 2nd millennium B.C.E.[12] It is well attested in India, going back to the heroic age reflected in the Indian epics. Levirate marriage is not considered a new marriage ; it is in theory simply a new stage of the first one. The automatic character of levirate marriage is clear from patriarchal times (Gen. 38) and remains so down through the Babylonian Talmud. This is its nature also in Early India, where widows do not remarry. Indian levirate marriage is also in theory a continuation of the woman's first marriage, with the second husband merely functioning *in loco fratris*.

The pentakontiad system of reckoning pervaded Canaaan and other East Mediterranean areas. Actually it consisted of seven heptads totaling 49, climaxed by 50. Reckoning days in sevens is common in Ugaritic, Greek epic and other kindred literatures, so that there is no question concerning the pre-Hebraic antecedents for the seven-day week. The same goes for the seven-year sabbatical cycle (and Jubilee cycle of 49 or 50 years). This has implications for religion as well as time-reckoning. In Canaan the year is not divided into fertile and sterile seasons. There is a rainy and a rainless season, but even during the rainless months there is normally a harvest of summer fruits with the grape harvest running right to the very end of the rainless months. The risk of famine is not seasonal, but rather one of a dry year, or, worse yet, a series of dry years. Years were grouped in sevens, and there were fertility rituals for securing a good sabbatical cycle. At Ugarit the struggle between the fertile god Baal and the sterile god Mot was envisaged as taking place once in seven years.[13] Baal, like Yahweh, gives the earth water, but those life-giving waters are not limited to the rains ; they include also dew both in Ugarit and in Israel.[14]

G. Monotheism

The monotheistic stamp of Judaism has origins in the patriarchal traditions. This does not imply that the monotheistic purity of Deutero-Isaiah can be found in New Kingdom Canaan. But the fact remains that in

Canaan of that period the monotheistic trend was strong. Some of the Canaanites were devoted to *El 'Elyon*, God the Most High, "Maker of heaven and earth," who was the cosmic world-ruler, and was neither a local deity nor a specialized member of any pantheon. Melchizedek was a priest of that *El 'Elyon* and the Bible (Gen. 14: 18–20) connects Abraham therewith. Since Old Kingdom times in Egypt, Re (or Ra) monotheism was a powerful force, existing side by side with the pattern of local deities. It was the growth of the Egyptian empire that made of Re a world god ruling all the lands, as well as the cosmic force inherent in the Sun. Solar monotheism reached its apex in the Aton-Re religious revolution of Amen-hotep IV (Akh-en-Aton) exactly in the patriarchal period,[15] and it is hard to fancy the biblical Abraham as isolated from Egyptian influence. He migrated to Egypt; the Egyptian woman Hagar was an integral part of his immediate family circle. Patriarchal Canaan and the Egyptian Delta were not only close geographically; they were the scene of frequent shifts of population back and forth. Egyptian art and texts confirm the Bible in representing such shifts. While Akh-en-Aton's monotheism was the most spectacular monotheistic movement of the age, Israel's was the lasting one, no matter how unimpressive it may have seemed to the casual observer in those days.

The aniconic character of Yahwism is not without parallel in New Kingdom times either. Highly idolatrous cultures often have one or more aniconic cults. In Mesopotamia, where idolatry was rife, the god of heaven, Anu, does not seem to have had idols made in his image. And while the image-loving Egyptians sooner or later represented graphically everything they thought about (including Re), yet the ancient Re temples (like that of the Fifth Dynasty pharaoh Neuserre in the 3rd millennium) had no idol of Re; instead the real Sun was worshiped at an altar in the open temple court. The absence of the idol differentiated Re worship from that of the other gods in their temples. Nor have we any reason to suspect that Melchizedek's *El 'Elyon*, "Maker of heaven and earth" (Gen. 14: 19), was represented by any idol.[16] There are several aniconic trends in the Bible world; but it is at least of passing interest that precisely in the Mosaic period even the Assyrian god Nusku is depicted as worshiped in the form of a simple symbol on an altar without any trace of anthropomorphism or idolatry.[17]

The internationalism of New Kingdom Canaan required also a kind of religion that transcended the tribe and the locality. Hebrews and Philistines desired of each other only that they be god-fearing men who could be counted on to act decently. Kindness to the stranger is the prime test of god-fearing men, regardless of whether we read the Odyssey or Genesis (20 :11). Any cult tends to carry with it a code of ethics. Jacob and Laban could swear by their respective ancestral gods (Gen. 31 : 53) to each other's satisfaction. The Patriarchs could make treaties of friendship with the uncircumcised Philistines, as long as both parties believed in *El 'Olam* (= "the Everlasting God") who transcends individual cults (Gen. 21 : 23).

The nature of our task forces us to dwell upon the common elements that link the Hebrews with their contemporary world in New Kingdom times. So many new discoveries are coming to light that one hesitates to claim anything specific in the Bible as unique, lest a forthcoming discovery disprove the claim before the latter gets into print. But there is one claim that will never be disproved. In New Kingdom times, only two nations emerged as continuous forces of major magnitude in world history: the Hebrews and the Greeks.

Historic Judaism may well pride itself on its international grandeur; from its inception it is not a provincial cult. Conventional believers and scholars often make the mistake of viewing the patriarchal origins of the Jewish people as comparable with the life of the tent-dwelling nomad in the Syro-Arabian Desert. Abraham may have lived in tents and owned camels, but that is almost as far as the analogy with the modern Bedouin goes. Abraham is pictured as having contacts from Mesopotamia to Egypt. He deals with Philistines, with Canaanites, and with the Hittites of Hebron. The patriarchal origins of the Hebrew people stem from Canaan — from the cosmopolitan hub of the most cosmopolitan period of remote antiquity.

PART TWO: BEGINNINGS OF THE NATION

CHAPTER V

THE EXODUS AND THE CONQUEST

by B. Mazar

A. THE EXODUS FROM EGYPT, THE WANDERINGS IN THE DESERT,
AND THE CONQUEST OF TRANSJORDAN

IN THE ISRAELITE TRADITION the Exodus is described above all as the emigration of the tribes of Israel from the land of Goshen, which was caused by a national-religious awaking, the aspiration to get away from "the burden of the Egyptians" and to press eastward to the Promised Land where the forefathers of the nation had lived. Intertwined in this tradition are memories from the days of the wanderings which marked deeply the nation's soul, and of Moses the man of God, whose personality pervades the entire historic episode. He is bound up with the emergence of the religion of Israel, which is revealed as the faith in YHWH, the one and only God of the nation, who is also the God and the Creator of the world. It is Moses who leads the nation "out of the iron furnace" of Egypt, from bondage to freedom; he is their leader in war and peace. Moses gives laws to the people and the individual, and it is he who lays the foundations of the national unity of the tribes of Israel and their religious and social organization. This conception, running like a scarlet thread through the biblical literature, is emphasized by the ancient poet:

> When Moses charged us with the Teaching
> As the heritage of the congregation of Jacob.
> Then He became King in Jeshurun,
> When the heads of the people assembled,
> The tribes of Israel together.
>
> (Deut. 33:4–5).

Even at the time of their settlement in Canaan the Israelites were animated by the consciousness that after the exodus from Egypt the God of Israel who revealed Himself to His people in all His splendor and might at Mount Sinai, was coming to the aid of Israel both in the battles fought on the way to the Land of Canaan and in the land itself (Jud. 5:4–5;

Deut. 33:3, Habakkuk 3:3, Ps. 68:8–9). It is not by chance that we find
in the Song of Deborah the parallelism:

יהוה זה סיני¹ – יהוה אלהי ישראל

namely JHWH the Lord of Sinai — JHWH God of Israel (Jud. 5:5),
which emphasize the sanctity of the mountain as the dwelling place of the
God of Israel. Israelite tradition has preserved the view that the God of
Israel first revealed Himself by His real name to Moses in the days when
he was tending the sheep of Jethro (according to another tradition, Reuel)
the priest of Midian who sheltered him while fleeing from Pharaoh, and
whose daughter he married: "I appeared to Abraham, Isaac, and Jacob
as El Shadday, but I did not make Myself known to them by my name יהוה
[YHWH]" (Ex. 6:3); "... Thus shall you speak to the Israelites: The
Lord, the God of your fathers, ... has sent me to you:

> This shall be My name forever,
> This My appellation for all eternity" (Ex. 3:15).

And at the hallowed place on Sinai, Moses was given the mission
of bringing his people out of Egypt, and of serving God upon that
mountain (Ex. 3:12). In spite of the many still obscure details, there
emerges from the epic poetry, and the fund of national memories and
legends of the people, a broad outline of the character of the national
group *Israel* which, followed by a "mixed multitude" (Ex. 12:38), left
Egypt for the Eastern deserts. No doubt, they had for the most part already
established a loose federation of tribes, clans and families whose main
occupation was pasturage. They were linked to one another by origin
and lineage, possessed a tradition of common forefathers and their ties to
the land of Canaan and its southern border district. On the other hand,
complete obscurity surrounds the crystallization process of the tradition
that mentions invariably twelve Israelite tribes. This tradition persisted as
a cardinal idea in the nation's consciousness during the generations that
followed. Even more obscure is the extent of the influence exerted on this
group by the well-developed and continued religious conception bound
up with faith in one God initiated by Moses, and the degree to which it
represents a vital factor in the exodus from Egypt.² Nor can we draw any
conclusion from the biblical sources as to the magnitude of the Exodus
and the number of Israelites who left Egypt and wandered in the desert.
The traditional figure of 600,000, which is mentioned more than once
in the census in the desert, is simply a typological number; what it referred

to is apparently one thousand battalions, intending to express the idea of a large number of people.[3]

From the Egyptian and biblical sources we learn that the land of the Delta had been absorbing during a long time a steady stream of immigrants from the East, including families of shepherds. Many of these clung to their fathers' faith and followed their ways. Since they represented an inferior class among the Egyptian population, the authorities exacted from them a property tax and corvée work. Evidently, the largest concentration of Israelite families, mainly sheep and cattle breeders, was in the land of Goshen; apparently Goshen is simply the Semitic name for the territory between the field of Zoan (Ps. 78:12), which is the land of Ramses (Gen. 47:11), in the north, and Pithom, which should be identified with Tell er-Ruṭāba in Wadi Thumeilāt in the south.[4] This also emerges from the fact that the city Ramses appears as the first stop of the tribes of Israel during the exodus from Egypt, while the second stop and the point of setting out on the journey is Succoth, which apparently is the same as Tjeku in the Egyptian sources (the modern Tell Maskūṭa), an important border fortress east of Wadi Thumeilāt, and its immediate environs, west of the bitter lakes.[5] Indirectly, we can learn something about this matter from a number of Egyptian documents. Thus, Papyrus Anastasi VI (from the end of the 13th century) tells of the permission granted to the nomadic tribes from Edom to cross Tjeku, the fortress of Mer-ne-Ptah, to the pools of Per-Atum (Pithom) in order to refresh themselves and their herds.[6] Particularly instructive are the sources which mention the employment of people from Asia, including 'Apiru, at various types of work required for the king, including such respectable professions like clerical work, but, in particular, at hard work in agriculture (mainly in the vineyards), in the mines, and in public works.[7] This evidence can throw light on what is told of the employment of the Israelites at hard labor: "So they set taskmasters over them to oppress them with forced labor; and they built garrison cities for Pharaoh: Pithom and Raamses" (Ex. 1:11). Particularly interesting is the mention of the building of Ramses, which is certainly to be identified with Per-Ramses (the House of Ramses), the new capital city of the Nineteenth Dynasty, which was founded by Ramses II in the area of Zoan (Tanis), the ancient capital of the Hyksos. This act fits in with the policy of Seti I and his son Ramses II, who sought to move northward the center of gravity of the Egyptian royal government, so as to be nearer to the roads leading to Canaan. This enables us also to date the central event of the exodus from Egypt, which constitutes an important historical landmark in Israelite tradition, to the beginning of the reign of Ramses II (1304–1237) who employed much forced labor in the erection of Per-Ramses, his capital.[8] It is true that there are those who question this date, relying on various biblical sources, such as I Kings 6:1, according to which 480 years elapsed from the exodus of the Israelites from Egypt to the building of the Temple of Jerusalem in the fourth year of Solomon's reign — which would place that event in the 15th century B.C.E.[9] It transpires, however, that the number of years mentioned in this priestly source — no doubt a chronicle of the Jerusalemite Temple — is made so as to fit the twelve generations of priests from Aaron to Azariah of the House of Zadok, the first priest to officiate in the Temple. Each generation was schematically assigned a period of forty years, but if we assign about 27 years for each generation, we arrive at the beginning of the 13th century. As for the length of time the Israelites stayed in Egypt — four hundred and thirty years, according to Ex. 12:40–41 — we should consider Albright's theory that this figure refers to the date of the establishment of Hyksos rule in Zoan (approximately 1725) which is apparently hinted at both in the "Four Hundred Year Stele," erected by Ramses II, and which refers to a ceremony held towards the end of the reign of Hor-em-heb, as well as in a biblical source (Num. 13:22).[10] A similar period — the same round figure of four hundred years — appears also in Genesis 15:23.[11] The same applies to the round and exaggerated figure, three hundred years ("While Israel dwelt in Heshbon and in its towns."), mentioned by Jephthah (Judges 11:26). Although these biblical figures do not enable us to establish the chronology of the exodus from Egypt, they do not conflict either with the assumption that the event that impressed itself so deeply in the nation's consciousness took place during the first regnal years of Ramses II. This was a period characterized by the heavy wars Egypt waged against the Hittites in the land of Amurru, in central Syria, culminating in the great battle near Kadesh on the Orontes river, in the fifth year of Ramses's reign. The outcome of that battle was the retreat of Pharaoh's army and the decline of Egypt's prestige. Moreover, as a result of the battle of Kadesh the state of Amurru became again a subject ally of the Hittite king and immediately thereafter the Hittites, undoubtedly together with their ally, invaded the land of Upi, that is, the regions of Damascus and northern Transjordan.[12] This event, which certainly made a deep impression and was followed by a series of revolts throughout Canaan as far as Ashkelon in the south, and in the border regions of the country, can be linked with the biblical account of the Amorites winning control of Transjordan, and the establishment of the kingdom of Heshbon: "Now Heshbon was the city of Sihon king of the Amorites, who had fought against a former [first] king of Moab and taken all his land from him as far as the Arnon" (Num. 21:26).[13] The memory of this event was preserved in an ancient lament on the fall of Moab, which was well known in Israel (Num. 21:27 ff.) and of which the prophets made use when predicting the fate of Moab.[14] The deterioration of the political situation in Transjordan, following the expansion of the influence of the Hittites and their ally Amurru, certainly disrupted the political alignment of Egypt in Asia, and caused effervescence among the nomadic tribes from Seir to the land of Goshen. Ramses had good reasons to undertake military campaigns and send punitive forces to various districts, including the lands of Edom and Moab. His forces, that apparently reached Transjordan, fought the nomadic tribes in the lands of Moab and Seir[15] to re-establish Pharaoh's prestige and consolidate his rule in those areas and along the vital communication arteries. Among these the "king's highway," was particularly important for Egypt's security and the defence of that country's approaches. It is worth mentioning that the archeological surveys in central and southern Transjordan furnish additional evidence of the great changes that took place in those areas in the course of the 14th–13th centuries B.C.E. The first sign of such change was the renewal of permanent settlement by the peoples of Ammon, Moab and Edom who established themselves there. Evidently they did not found national kingdoms or started establishing a network of cities and border fortresses[16] before the end of the century, a date that fits perfectly with the biblical text which reports that Sihon fought against the *first* king of Moab. This date fits also with the Egyptian sources from the time of Ramses II. The course taken by events at the end of the 14th and the beginning of the 13th century B.C.E. can serve as background for what we read in Exodus 1:8–10: "A new king arose over Egypt... And he said to his people: "Look, the Israelite people are much too numerous for us. Let us deal shrewdly with them, so that they may not increase; otherwise in the event of war they may join our enemies in fighting against us and rise from the ground."

The biblical traditions concerning the wanderings of the Israelites in the desert, the identification of the various camping places in general and of Mount Sinai in particular, and the historical conclusions which emerge from these traditions, are fraught with complicated problems. Not for nothing are the scholars divided concerning both fundamentals, and details. And it is certainly no simple matter to settle the dispute between upholders of the two basic and contradictory theories: the "southern" theory supported by ancient tradition, which holds *Yam Sūf* to be the Gulf of Suez and which locates Mount Sinai in the south of the Sinai Peninsula

(Jebel Catherina or Jebel Mūsā); and the "northern" theory, favored by a number of scholars, which maintains that *Yam Sūf* is the Sirbonian Sea and that Mount Sinai is to be sought closer to Kadesh-barnea, namely Jebel Hilāl.[17] And then there are those who reject both these theories and make other suggestions, such as identifying *Yam Sūf* with Lake Timsah or with Lake Manzala, the latter identification relying on the Anastasi III papyrus, which mentions *pasuf* (= *ḥa-suf*) in the neighborhood of the city of Ramses.[18]

A basis for the beginning of the journey may be found in the account that "God did not lead them by way of the land of the Philistines, although it was nearer . . . The people may have a change of heart when they see war . . . So God led the people roundabout, by way of the wilderness at the Sea of Reeds" (Ex. 13:17–18). And to this may be added the fact that before crossing the Red Sea, the Israelites encamped by Pi-hahiroth, between Migdol and the sea, before Baal-zephon (Ex. 14:2). The anachronistic reference, "by way of the land of the Philistines," no doubt refers to the southern end of the *Via maris*, which was the main road leading to Canaan, and along which there rose at the time of Seti I and Ramses II a long line of fortresses ending with Migdol at the Egyptian border (perhaps Tell el-Ḥeir) and Sile (perhaps Tell Abu Ṣeyfeh near Qanṭara).[19] As for Baal-zephon, it may be assumed that this simply indicates the temple of Baal-zephon (Zeus Kasios of the Greek sources), erected on the bar which separates the Sirbonian Sea from the Mediterranean.[20] Even though it is difficult to decide upon these data, they seem to support the northern theory; and — although the historical background remains obscure — it is not impossible that this is the region where occurred an event forever engraved in the people's memory: the drowning of the Egyptian chariotry.

On the other hand, there exists no basis permitting the location of the site of Mount Sinai, which is also called Mount Horeb, as well as Mount Paran, in different traditions. The various data in the Bible which would point to its location in Mount Seir or in the Wilderness of Paran (Deut. 33:2; Jud. 5:4–5; Habakkuk 3:3), the distance given between Mount Horeb and Kadesh-barnea ("It is eleven days from Horeb to Kadesh-barnea by the Mount Seir route." Deut. 1:2), the list of the camping sites, the similarities when describing the nature of the mountain, do not suffice for a definite identification. Moreover, it is not impossible that even in the biblical period there existed various traditions as to the location of the holy mountain, and that it was the identification of Mount Sinai of the ancient tradition with Mount Horeb already in the pre-exilic period, that led to its being sought in one of the granite mountains of southern Sinai, far from the southern border of Canaan (cf. I Kings 19:8).

The cycle of stories about the hosts of the Israelites in the desert, of how they fared at times of war and peace, and the events connected with Moses, as narrated in the books of Exodus and Numbers, are the fruit of various and occasionally conflicting traditions, handed down in the different tribes, and which add up to a comprehensive chapter composed of an admixture of ancient memories, folk legends, and ideas of later periods. Particularly enlightening is the source preserved in Numbers 33, which gives a detailed list of the camping sites in the desert, together with allusions to important events — a kind of summary of the Israelites' comings and goings.[21] The great majority of the localities mentioned in this detailed list, and in the other sources, as places where the Israelites encamped — no doubt various oases over which they dispersed — cannot be identified; we know only a few places in the southern Negev and the Arabah.

A number of encampments are linked by tradition with events deeply rooted in the people's memory; thus Rephidim is the place where they warred against Amalek, where Moses took his oath to exact vengeance from that people of desert marauders, and where he built an altar which he named *Adonai-nissi* (The Lord is my banner; Ex. 17:18–16). The various traditions mentioning Moses' strong ties with the Midianites and the Kenites, who lived among the Israelites, are connected with the mountain of God. According to one of those traditions Jethro brought Moses his wife, Zipporah, and her two sons, in the vicinity of Mount Sinai. There he praised God for having rescued the Israelites from Egypt, offered Him a sacrifice, and suggested to Moses the establishment of an efficient legal-administrative system (Ex. 18). Another tradition speaks of Hobab son of Reuel the priest, Moses' father-in-law (and there is another view that the reading should be Moses' son-in-law), whom other sources consider as a Kenite. He is described as accompanying the Israelites on their journeys since the time they encamped by the holy mountain, and serving them as a guide: "... inasmuch as you know where we should camp in the wilderness and can be our guide" (Num. 10:29–32).[22] Hazeroth, the second halt of the Israelites on their journey from Mount Sinai, is linked by tradition with the conflict that broke out between Moses and Aaron and Miriam who objected to his marrying a Cushite woman.[23] However, Israel's tradition places at the center of the events that took place during the wanderings through the desert the period spent at Kadesh-barnea, which was doubtlessly an especially important event in the history of the tribes. Indeed, many memories are connected with

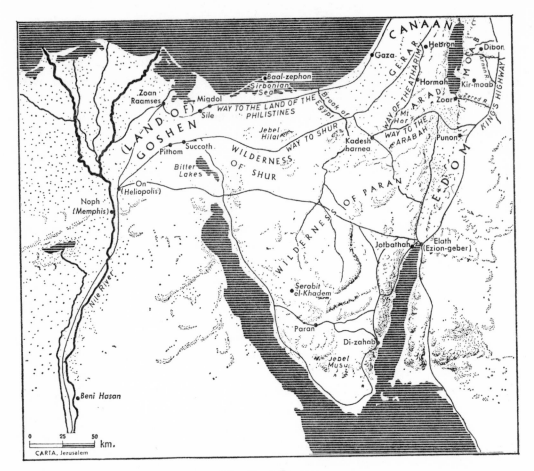

The Sinai Desert.

Kadesh-barnea, the large oasis at the southern end of the Negev ('Ain el-Qudeyrāt) which was also known by the name En-mishpat (Gen. 14:7), and its immediate neighborhood, where the Israelites stayed "many days" (Deut. 1:46). This place functioned as a national-religious center around which the tribes of Israel under Moses' leadership united.[24] According to tradition Kadesh is the place where Miriam was buried (Num. 20:1), just as Mount Hor, which is close to the oasis, was regarded as the burial place of Aaron (Num. 20:22–29). It is from Kadesh that spies were sent out to reconnoiter the land, from there started the unsuccessful attempts to enter the land of Canaan (Num. 14:40 ff.) and to go up to the Negev "by way of Atharim" to do battle with the king of Arad, "who dwelt in the Negeb". This attempt ended in defeat at Hormah (apparently Tell el-Milḥ), as may be concluded from the analysis of the conflicting testimony provided by the various scriptural sources (Num. 14:45; 12:1 ff.; 33:37 ff.; Deut. 1:44).[25] From Kadesh did the Israelites set out on their journey to the Arabah and to the eastern side of the Jordan.

There were apparently two distinct traditions with respect to the progress of the Israelites from Kadesh to the eastern side of the Jordan, and they reflect no doubt two waves of migration which occurred at different times, but which were fused in the biblical narrative into a single journey. The list preserved in Numbers 33 mentions immediately after Mount Hor, which was in the vicinity of Kadesh, Zalmonah, Punon (Pinon) and Oboth in the northern Arabah, whence they continued their journey to Ije-abarim on the border of Moab and to Dibon-gad, and thence by way of Almon-diblathaim to the plains of Moab, opposite Jericho: "... they encamped by the Jordan, from Beth-jeshimoth as far as Abel-shittim in the steppes of Moab" (Num. 33:49). According to this source, the Israelites crossed in a straight line Edom and the heart of Moab, and there is no hint of any opposition met as they came up "the king's highway" and reached the plains of Moab.[26] There are arguments in support of the suggestion that these were the tribes of the Rachel group (the House of Joseph)[27] which separated from the rest of the tribes during the sojourn at Kadesh. They preceded them in Transjordan taking advantage of the special circumstances created by the tremendous events which had shaken these areas: the war of the Amorites against Moab, and the campaigns of Ramses II. It is also assumable that after the stay in the plains of Moab (at Shittim) the journey was continued under the leadership of Joshua the Ephraimite, who crossed the Jordan and invaded the plain of Jericho on the western bank of the river.

As against this tradition, the other traditions refer to the later and principal migration wave of the Israelite tribes, which came after the kingdoms of Edom and Moab had grown stronger and fortified their countries' borders, a fact that enabled them to reject the Israelites' request to pass along "the king's highway" (Num. 20:14 ff.; Jud. 11:15 ff.). Consequently the Israelites were obliged to leave Kadesh by "the road to the Sea of Reeds" — to circumvent Edom and Moab — and to continue their journey through the wilderness as far as the desert of Kedemoth, east of Arnon, "but the people grew restive on the journey." Here, on the approaches of the Amorite kingdom, in the area of the Arnon's springs — connected by tradition with the Israelite tribes' sojourn — was to take place an event fraught with decisive geo-political consequences: the Israelites under the leadership of Moses defeated Sihon, King of the Amorites, at Jahaz (perhaps Khirbet el-Medeiyineh).

As a result of this battle the tribes of Israel conquered the kingdom of Heshbon (Num. 21:23–24) and Amorite Jaazer (Num. 21:32), and in the course of time they extended their rule over the expanses of Gilead, "from the Arnon unto Jabbok, even unto the children of Ammon; for the border of the children of Ammon was strong" (Num. 21:24). The biblical tradition even tells of the expansion towards the Jordan Valley, as far as the important urban centers Succoth and Zaphon, which were conquered later,[29] and towards the expanses of northern Gilead, an area for the most part afforested and unpopulated. This tradition also tells of the defeat inflicted on Og, King of Bashan, at Edrei, as a result of which the Israelites gained dominion over northern Transjordan. In spite of the fact that the biblical sources do not enable us to draw definite conclusions as to the course of events and the undoubtedly complicated and internally difficult progress of settlement and expansion of the tribes of Israel on the eastern side of the Jordan, there emerges, nevertheless, quite a plausible picture of a number of developments which determined the fate of these areas. According to the biblical tradition the senior tribe of Israel, Reuben, and the tribe of Gad, both considered as belonging to the Leah group — of which they had absorbed other families — settled in the excellent grazing sections of Gilead and the plain between Heshbon and the Arnon. They turned these areas into Israelite territory and adjusted to the conditions prevailing in the places where they settled. Reuben remained essentially a semi-nomadic tribe, while Gad went over to permanent settlement, absorbed the various ethnic elements in Gilead, turned wide areas into farmland, and in the course of time settled even in the fertile areas of the Jordan Valley. The Israelites inherited, no doubt, besides a spacious land, also its political differends with the bordering kingdoms, in particular with Moab which could not renounce its aspirations of recuperating the territory north of the Arnon. It is not mere chance that various memories of conflicts with Moab have been preserved — "... Moab was alarmed because that people was so numerous." These quarrels involved also Moab's allies and dependents the nomadic Midianites, who were scattered over wide areas, and who were famous not only as camel breeders and shepherds but also as caravan traders. It may be assumed that after the Israelite invasion of Transjordan the Moabites and the Midianites attempted to frustrate the efforts of the Israelite tribes to settle in that land and its grazing grounds (Num. 22:25–31; Josh. 13, etc.). In the course of time the Israelites consolidated the irsettlement and spread over wide expanses while carrying on a continual struggle with their neighbors and the nomadic tribes. That struggle was put an end to only in the days of the United Kingdom.

The traditions of that time mention places considered holy by all the inhabitants of the land, whether Moabites or Israelites, including Beth-peor and Mount Nebo from whose peak Moses gazed at the Promised Land before his death, and in whose vicinity, "in the valley in the land of Moab near Beth-peor," he was buried, "and no one knows his burial place to this day" (Deut. 34:6). It may not be amiss to recall the verses of Moses' blessing:

And of Gad he said:
Blessed be He who enlarges Gad!
Poised is he like a lion
To tear off arm and scalp.
He chose for himself the best,
For there is the portion of the revered chieftain,
Where the heads of the people come.
He executed the LORD'S judgments
And His decisions in Israel.

(Deut. 33:20–21).

The events pertaining to the colonization of this area in the period that followed have considerably blurred the character of the beginnings of the settlement of the tribes of Israel. For during the period of Settlement proper the land of Gilead and the adjacent areas became a kind of territorial reserve for the settlement of Israelite families from the western side of the Jordan, who came there impelled by an excess of population and the hunger for suitable farming and grazing land available in sparsely settled areas. It thus transpires that the colonizing and cultural value of the land of Gilead, both as a supplementary area for internal colonization and as a haven in times of external defeat or domestic disorders, became fully apparent only at the time of the emergence of the Israelite area of settlement on the western side of the Jordan. Further, it appears that the settlement in Transjordan of national groups belonging to the House of Joseph, including Machir, and the connection of the concept "the half-tribe of Manasseh" with northern Transjordan, belong to a later stage of the Settlement period.[30]

B. THE CONQUEST OF THE LAND OF CANAAN

The conquest of the Land of Canaan is understood by the historiographer, the author of the Book of Joshua, as a rather complete and uniform action carried out in one time, and which determined the fate of the people and the country. The Bible links this chapter indissolubly with the figure of

Joshua son of Nun, who led the people after the conquest of the eastern bank of the Jordan and the death of Moses. He crossed the Jordan at the head of the tribes of Israel, conquered first Jericho and Ai, and, after defeating the alliance of the kings of the south headed by the king of Jerusalem, he took the royal cities in the mountains and lowlands of Judah; "and Joshua smote them from Kadesh-barnea even unto Gaza . . . even unto Gibeon" (Josh. 10:31). Finally he also defeated the alliance of the kings of the north headed by the king of Hazor in the battle at the waters of Merom. "So Joshua took all that land . . . from the bare mountain, that goeth up to Seir, even unto Baal-gad in the valley of the Lebanon under mount Hermon; and all their kings he took, and smote them, and put them to death" (Josh. 11:16–17). The list of the kings of Canaan whom Joshua defeated (Josh. 12), gives the names of 31 cities and territories (according to the Septuagint only 29), including some which are not mentioned in the description of Joshua's wars. It is true that even according to what is related in the Book of Joshua "there remaineth yet very much land to be possessed," and there is even a list of the districts of "the land that yet remaineth" along the borders of Canaan, which had yet to be conquered (Josh. 13:1–6; and see Jud. 3:1–4). Nevertheless most of the land passed under Israelite rule in the time of Joshua, and the author of the book attributes to him the division of the country into tribal lots, and the delimitation of the boundaries of their respective territories. It was he who set aside the cities of the priests and the Levites and the cities of refuge, and established the various rules and regulations governing the Israelites' conduct in the conquered land, which were issued in various sanctified places.

The Book of Joshua is supplemented by the Book of Judges, in which are related the deeds of the Israelites and the course of events after Joshua's death, their struggle with the Canaanites, with the neighbors of Israel and with invaders from without, as well as their wanderings within the land, and their domestic quarrels before a king rose in Israel. It is worth mentioning that in contrast to the Book of Joshua, the Book of Judges implies, particularly in Chapters 1, 4 and 5, that the conquest and the wars of Canaan were not a uniform, national action, but a composite process in which unions of tribes, or individual tribes, were involved.

This historiographic tissue, the fruit of a long and complicated process of literary creativity and the crystallization of a uniform, national-religious historiosophic conception that reflects a reality rich in incidents and events which found expression in various traditions, fragments of ancient chronicles, epic poems, folk tales and legends drawn from different sources — all Israelite, tribal, or local — were combined and blended into one great

and continuous chapter. Not for nothing do the scholars struggle manfully
to give a proper interpretation to the events which left their mark in the
memory of the people, to separate the early sources from the later ones,
to throw light on the process of the Conquest and the beginnings of the
Settlement of the tribes of Israel in the land — all this against the background of the period in which the event took place, and taking into account
the epigraphic documents and the directly, or indirectly, relevant archeological discoveries. As a matter of fact the opinions of scholars today are
divided both on fundamental questions and details. Various efforts, occasionally conflicting ones, have been made to analyze the sources and to
weld them into a single chapter, so as to provide a logical and reasonable
picture of the conquest of the land at its various stages.[31]

The victory monument from the fifth regnal year of Mer-ne-Ptah (ca.
1233 B.C.E.), known as the "Israel Stele" provides a point of departure
for the discussion of the Conquest and Settlement of Canaan since it
states, *inter alia*:

> ... Plundered is Canaan with every evil;
> Carried off is Ashkelon; seized upon is Gezer;
> Yanoam is made as that which does not exist;
> Israel is laid waste, his seed is not;
> Hurru is become a widow for Egypt!
> All lands together, they are pacified.[32]

From this single Egyptian document which mentions Israel as an ethnic
group we can conclude that a group of Israelite tribes had already settled
in Canaan at the time of Mer-ne-Ptah, and had even clashed with an
Egyptian army sent to punish those who had rebelled against Pharaoh's
authority. Other Egyptian documents from the time of the Nineteenth
Dynasty mention marauders, nomadic and semi-nomadic tribes, who were
roving within the borders of Canaan and endangered the peace of the
land; from time to time the Egyptian authorities would dispatch punitive
battalions to suppress them. It is not impossible that they included Israelite
clans and ethnic groups close to them.[33] Particularly instructive in this
respect is Papyrus Anastasi I, dating apparently from the end of Ramses II's
reign which describes, *inter alia*, the danger represented by the plunderers
who stalk the travellers in Canaan, and in particular on the road from
Megiddo to the Sharon; and which mentions in this description the chief
of an ethnic group who is called Aser.[34] It has been suggested that the name
'sr, which apparently was previously mentioned in documents of Seti I,
be identified with the tribe of Asher, and there are scholars who have

drawn the conlusion that this ethnic group had reached western Palestine in the 14th century.[35]

As for the archeological testimony, it proved as a fact that in the second half of the 13th century B.C.E. many "Canaanite" settlements were destroyed, including royal cities familiar to us from the Egyptian documents, from the letters of Tell el-Amarna, and from biblical sources. On the ruins of those cities were generally erected sparsely populated settlements or even temporary settlements of semi-nomads. Such was the fate of the important urban center of Hazor, which according to the testimony of the Bible was "the head of all those kingdoms" (i.e. the Canaanite kingdoms in the north of the country). It was destroyed by the Israelites and burned down (Josh. 11) following the fateful battles at the waters of Merom and the brook of Kishon. The excavations at the site have revealed that after the decline of the city, in the latest stage of the Late Bronze Period (cf. Jud, 4:24), Hazor — including the king's fortress and the large lower city adjoining it — was utterly destroyed at the close of the period mentioned (the end of the 13th century) and on its ruins there arose a settlement of semi-nomads, evidently the tribe of Naphtali.[36] It should also be noted that the archeological survey in the hills of central Galilee revealed many traces of small permanent settlements, which were established by new settlers in the transition period between the 13th and the 12th centuries. The new settlers cultivated virgin land in this hilly and afforested area.[37] Here was undoubtedly the center of the early settlement of the tribes of the north (Harosheth-goiim[38] of Jud. 4), whence they spread out the to Canaanite cities in the north of Galilee, and to the thickly populated valleys held by the Canaanites. A similar phenomenon was revealed in a number of other sections of the country, such as the southern part of the hills of Ephraim, in the land of Benjamin and in the *Lowland* (Shefela). Nevertheless, archeological research raises sometimes difficult and complicated questions, or occasionally even astonishing ones. The excavations at the village of Bītīn have revealed that the Canaanite Beth-el, which according to the testimony of the Book of Judges was conquered by the House of Joseph (1:22–26), was destroyed close to the end of the Late Bronze Period; most likely in the third quarter of the 13th century B.C.E.[39] On the other hand, the excavations at et-Tell, east of Beth-el,— which is certainly none other than the site of the biblical Ai, — show that the ancient city was destroyed in a late stage of the Early Bronze Period (approximately in the 23rd century), and that it remained desolate until about 1200, when a small Israelite settlement arose on the site.[40] Great interest is also aroused by the results of the excavations at Tell es-Sulṭān, the site of the biblical

Jericho. It is an instructive fact that no walls from the Late Bronze Period have been found on the site. The remains of buildings and graves from the period are few, neither are there numerous finds including implements from the last stage of the Late Bronze Period.[41] This situation has resulted in various attempts to give a proper interpretation to the archeological evidence found at Ai and Jericho, which would seem to conflict with the account given in the Book of Joshua of the Israelite conquest of these two royal cities under that leader. According to one of the hypotheses, the stories of the conquest of Jericho and Ai belong to the category of etiological legends, prevalent in Joshua 2–10, which explained various local phenomena, such as the crumbling walls of ruined Jericho, the heap of stones in the valley of Achor, "a heap for ever" named Ai (= the ruin), the gate of destroyed Ai where a great heap of stones stood "to this day", or the dwelling of a Canaanite family related to Rahab, the harlot of Jericho, among the Israelites.[42] As against this hypothesis, other suggestions have been put forward, such as the one which assumes that the Late Bronze wall of Jericho disappeared through erosion and exposure over a period of many generations, or that its inhabitants used the Middle Bronze Period glacis for the defence of the small town.[43] As for Ai, there are scholars who assumed that the mound served as a temporary military outpost for the inhabitants of Beth-el, or that the conquest of Beth-el was confused with the conquest of Ai; there are also those who reject the identification of Ai with et-Tell.[44] In any case, up to now the problem has not been satisfactorily solved. On the other hand, the excavations and surveys in the hills of Ephraim and Benjamin have yielded a picture similar to that which emerges from the surveys in Gilead and the hills of Galilee, as well as in Judea, namely, that many settlements were established in the period of transition from the Bronze Age to the Iron Age and in the course of the 12th century, which would indicate the beginnings of Israelite colonization. Some of these settlements arose on the ruins of the Canaanite cities after a short (e.g. Beth-el), or a long (e.g. Mizpeh, Ai, Shiloh) interruption in the settlement of the place, while most of them were founded in new locations which had not been settled previously (e.g. Gibeah of Benjamin, Ramah, Bethlehem and others). It should be added that remains yielded by the excavations at el-Jīb testify to a considerable settlement in that place from the Middle and Late Bronze Periods but particularly in the Iron Age.[45] They support the identification of the place with Gibeon, which according to the testimony of the Book of Joshua was "a great city, as one of the royal cities" (10:2) and the center of the Hivite cities which made peace with Joshua and accepted his authority.

Turning to the Lowland (Shefela), it should be noted that a number of mounds have yielded definite evidence of the destruction of Canaanite cities at the end of the Late Bronze Period. The fact is particularly striking at Tell Beth Mirsim (according to Albright perhaps Debir), Tell el-Ḥēsī (perhaps the biblical Eglon), and Beth-shemesh.[46] It is instructive that on the ruins of the fortified Canaanite city at Tell Beth Mirsim (Layer C2) only a camp of semi-nomads was found (Layer B1). The situation of Lachish, however, has not been cleared up beyond all doubt. On the one hand, it transpires that the Canaanite temple at the foot of the western slope of the tell was destroyed at the end of the Late Bronze Period; on the other hand, it can be concluded from a number of finds discovered at the summit of the mound, and from the discovery of anthropoid coffins, that in the days of Ramses III Lachish was a fortress manned by a garrison of Sea-Peoples. It is possible that in the brief interval between the reigns of Mer-ne-Ptah and Ramses III the place had accommodated a small settlement of semi-nomads.[47] To sum up it can be affirmed that in the final stage of the Late Bronze Period, and especially at the very end, i.e. in the second half of the 13th century B.C.E., various Canaanite cities, including royal cities and fortresses, were destroyed. Testimony to their conquest by the tribes of Israel is provided by the Books of Joshua and Judges. It also transpires that at the end of the 13th century, and doubtlessly in the 12th century, the settlement of the Israelites progressed at an increasing rate, particularly in the highlands and on the hill slopes, that is, in "the hill-country of Israel, and the Lowland of the same," on the western side of the Jordan, and among the mountains of Gilead as well. According to archeological finds we may conclude almost certainly that the Israelite conquest, with the attendant wars and destruction of Canaanite cities, and the beginning of the Settlement of the Israelite tribes, can be dated mainly to the second half of the 13th century B.C.E.

Since we have reached the stage of discussing the course of the Israelite conquest — insofar it is possible to reach conclusions on this subject from the analysis of the early traditions which are included in the biblical sources, as well as from epigraphic and archeological data — our hypothesis, alluded to in the previous section, must be mentioned. According to that hypothesis a distinction must be made between two waves of Israelite migration and those who accompanied them. They followed close on one another in the 13th century B.C.E.: the first, the group of "the Rachel tribes" (the House of Joseph), and the second, the group of "the Leah tribes" and those attached to them. Of the first migration we have testimony in Numbers 33, in the description of the journey of the Israelite camp from Kadesh via the northern Arabah and along "the king's highway" — which ran through the center of Moab — to the plains of Moab. During this journey the Israelites encountered no opposition and were not obliged to bypass Edom and Moab from the east; "They encamped by the Jordan, from Beth-jeshimoth as far as Abel-shittim, in the steppes of Moab" (Num. 33:49). The description of this journey is well complemented by the account in the first chapters of the Book of Joshua narrating the progress of the tribes of Israel under the leadership of Joshua son of Nun, from the camp at Shittim, their crossing the Jordan, their arrival in the plains of Jericho, and the pitching of their camp in Gilgal.

It seems that the House of Joseph group and their followers (consisting of the tribes which appear in the genealogical lists as the children of Rachel and Bilhah) separated from the other tribes of Israel at Kadesh and reached the plains of Moab before the destruction of the kingdom of Sihon. It is not impossible that this massive group of tribes abandoned the fertile plains of Moab and crossed into western Palestine when the second wave of migration arrived, and decided the question by settling in the areas captured from Sihon of Heshbon, or perhaps because of some events unknown to us which took place while the Israelites were camped at Shittim, of which various pieces of information have been preserved in the biblical sources (Num. 25:1 ff; 31:16; Micah 6:5).[48]

The tradition connected with the name of Joshua son of Nun, whose memory is engraved deep in the heart of people as the first leader of the conquerors of the western side of the Jordan, testify to the fact that he belonged to the House of Joseph, and specifically to the tribe of Ephraim. There has even been preserved the genealogical list which links him to the family of Beriah son of Ephraim (I Chron. 7:23–27). It is told of Joshua that he was at first the servant of Moses (who changed his name from Hosea to Joshua), that he excelled as a commander in the war with Amalek at Rephidim, and that as one of the leaders of the tribe of Ephraim he was among those sent from Kadesh to spy out the land of Canaan and who, like Caleb the son of Jephunneh, did not bring back evil reports. Connected with the name of Joshua are various traditions about battles, conquests of cities, and miscellaneous events, some of which appear to be reliable and are connected mainly with the regions where the House of Joseph and those who accompanied them settled; areas which were at a later period divided up into the inheritances of the tribes of Benjamin, Ephraim, Manasseh and Dan. Other traditions stem from the general conception that Joshua took the entire land. No less illuminating is the fact that the various memories of Joshua's activity are linked particularly with places of assembly, holy places of the Rachel tribes — Gilgal, Shiloh, and the vicinity of Shechem (Mount Ebal, the Israelite sanctuary outside the city, and the tomb of Joseph whose remains were brought out from Egypt). The tradition that Joshua's inheritance was Timnath-serah in the hill-country of Ephraim (Josh. 19:49–50; 24:30; Jud. 2:9) — where he built a city and in the vicinity of which his grave is shown — is also of historical value.[49]

Ancient traditions testify that Joshua's first camping place was at Gilgal east of Jericho, and that this camp served as a bridgehead for an assault on the mountain district north of the kingdom of Jerusalem, namely the hills of Benjamin and Ephraim.[50] The web of stories about Joshua's deeds while he stayed at Gilgal includes a description of the battle he fought together with his allies, the Gibeonites, against Adoni-zedek, King of Jerusalem. This event stayed engraved in the memory of the people and was also rendered in poetic fashion in the Book of Jashar (Josh. 9; 10; 1–15). No doubt there is a kernel of historical truth in the story of the four Hivite cities — Gibeon, Chephirah, Beeroth and Kiriath-jearim — which made peace with Joshua, an event which impelled the king of Jerusalem, who surely claimed the overlordship of this region, to establish an alliance with the kings of the neighboring cities in the south of the country and go out to fight Gibeon. This gave Joshua an excuse to hasten from his camp at Gilgal to the aid of Gibeon, and to strike a resounding blow against the allied armies. According to the biblical description, Joshua pursued them by way of the descent of Beth-horon as far as the valley of Aijalon, reached Azekah, and returned crowned with victory to his camp at Gilgal. The author of the Book of Joshua tied up with this battle a web of stories about conquests of cities in the lowland and in the hill-country, which were actually accomplished at a later date by the tribe of Judah and various clans which had joined it (Kenaz and Caleb).[51] It would appear that in the wake of these victories the House of Joseph did indeed become an important political factor in the central mountains of the country, and the way was cleared for them to proceed even to the northern lowland; but Joshua was unable to conquer important fortified cities, such as Jerusalem, or the cities of the lowland. Moreover, we learn from the sources in Judges that Beth-el was captured by the House of Joseph only after Joshua's death (Jud. 1:22–26), that the "Amorite" cities in the valley of Aijalon area continued to exist, "yet the hand of the house of Joseph prevailed, so that they became tributary" (Jud. 1:35), whereas the Danites, who were attached to the House of Joseph, and who settled at the western edge of the area of expansion, particularly the region of Eshtaol and Zorah, were forced by the Amorites into the mountains (evidently the vicinity of Kiriath-jearim; cf. Jud. 18:12), "for they would not suffer them to come down to the valley" (Jud. 1:34). And perhaps there is some connection between these data and the hazy tradition about the bloody clashes between the sons of Ephraim and the men of Gath "that were born in the land" because "they came down to take away their cattle," and the Israelite settlement in the vicinity of Beth-horon (I Chron. 7:20 ff.) and Timnath-serah (Josh. 19:49). In any case, it transpires that in "the time of the elders that outlived Joshua" (Jud. 2:7), that is, in the course of the third quarter of the 13th century, the tribes of Joseph and their followers had already settled in the hills of Ephraim and Benjamin and along their western slopes, wherefrom they expanded northward to the regions of the country that were later included in the tribal lot of Manasseh. This process was accompanied by the establishment of new settlements and the preparation of virgin land and afforested districts for agriculture (Josh. 17:14–18),[52] the destruction of Canaanite cities, the establishment of treaty relations with the cities that could not be taken (e.g. Shechem, Tirzah and Tappuah), and the expansion of those families of the House of Joseph and their followers, who were seeking an inheritance in which to dwell (cf. Judges 18:1), over wide areas, westward to the Sharon,[53] and northward to the hills of Galilee. It is possible that even at an early stage of this chain of developments the tribe of Naphtali penetrated Harosheth-goiim (in central Galilee) and settled that mountainous and afforested region which became the base from which they advanced towards the Canaanite cities in northern Galilee, captured Kedesh in Galilee, and threatened the peace of the kingdom of Hazor.[54] On the other hand, every attempt to expand into the valleys met with powerful resistance: "And the children of Joseph said [to Joshua]: 'The hill-country will not be enough for us; and all the Canaanites that dwell in the land of the valley have chariots of iron'" (Josh. 17:16). They therefore settled — as nomadic families had done before them[55] — among the hills on the borders of the Canaanite kingdoms, concluding treaties with them and also taking active part in the latter's domestic quarrels and in their attempt to throw off the Egyptian yoke. Against this background it becomes clear why in his expedition to Canaan Pharaoh Mer-ne-Ptah punished heavily not only the rebellious cities, including Yanoam (apparently Tell el-'Ubeydiye near one of the important fords of the Jordan south of Lake Chinnereth), but also the Israelites. It is also possible that this event caused the weakening of the group of the tribes of Joseph, and made it easier for the second wave of the tribes of Israel to penetrate western Palestine from the land of Gilead, via the fords of the Jordan (see below). In the course of time the tribal organization of the House of Joseph and its appendages, which at the time of Joshua apparently constituted a united entity, was disintegrating. There began a process of self-isolation of large blocks of families, incidental to the absorption of foreign elements, resulting in independent tribal-territorial frameworks such as Benjamin and Ephraim. Nevertheless, this did not spell an end of the ties between them, which were expressed in the fostering of common national and religious traditions, in resort to the sanctified places, and in the preservation of their common interests in times of war and peace. At the same time, they continued to expand from their center in western Palestine; a mass immigration eventually flooded northern Gilead and the Bashan as a result of the land hunger of the surplus population, the invasions from without, the domestic quarrels among settlers, and to no small degree also because of the pressure of the "Leah tribes," which settled in the country and even drove the House of Joseph out of various regions. Based on an analysis of the sources contained in the Book of Numbers, in the previous section was mentioned the hypothesis that the second wave of the tribes of Israel, which reached Transjordan coming up from Kadesh by way of the desert after forcing their way through the kingdom of Sihon and gaining control of the area between the Arnon and the Jabbok — included the tribes mentioned in the genealogical lists of the Bible as the tribes of Leah and Zilpah. Attuned to this is the ancient and reliable tradition that the Israelites who settled in these areas after the conquest of the Amorite kingdom were the clans of Reuben and Gad. It is in this context that attention should be paid to the allusions that ancient families who belonged to Judah and perhaps also to Simeon[56] attached themselves to Reuben and its inheritance.

We learn about the beginning immigration of the "Leah tribes" into western Palestine from the opening passages of the Book of Judges, namely a description of the journey of the tribes of Judah and Simeon after Joshua's death, and their wars with the Canaanites. From the verse, "And Judah went up; and the Lord delivered the Canaanites and the Perizzites into their hand; and they smote of them in Bezek ten thousand men," which is followed by the story of the capture of Adoni-bezek, King of Bezek (Judges 1:4 ff.), it can be concluded that the tribe of Judah and those who accompanied them came up from the Jordan Valley, following the roads travelled from the earliest times by "them that dwelt in tents." After the victory of Bezek, which is one of the important approaches from the plain of the Jordan to the hills of Ephraim (cf. I Sam. 11:8; the modern Khirbet Ibziq?),[57] they crossed the hills (as the children of Dan had done, going in the opposite direction; Jud. 18:13) and, as related afterwards, they captured Jerusalem[58] and pressed southward to the land of Judah and to the Negev. Although there still are many obscure points in the short description of this journey, in which are intertwined various traditions of conquests of cities, it reflects nevertheless in its essentials an important chapter in the history of the Israelite conquest which can be dated to the last quarter of the 13th century B.C.E.[59]

The situation in Canaan at that time undoubtedly helped the group of tribes to storm wide areas even outside the hill region, and to influence the fate of the country to a far greater extent than the House of Joseph had done. For already in the days of Mer-ne-Ptah, Egypt had reached the limits of her military and political power, and it could anticipate danger not only from the agitation in Canaan and the pressure of the Libyans, but also from the wave of Sea-Peoples who were advancing toward the borders of the kingdom. After the death of Mer-ne-Ptah, Pharaoh's rule in Asia was waning, and the foundations of government and the defence network of the Canaanite kingdoms crumbling. As a result of this turn of events insecurity and economic depression prevailed, enabling nomadic and semi-nomadic tribes to raid populated areas and even to conquer centers of government and fortified cities.

Very little information has been preserved regarding the course of the conquests and the settlement in western Palestine of the second wave of the Israelite tribes, that of the "Leah tribes" and their followers, and even the little that was preserved has been partly woven into the stories of Joshua's conquest. In Judges I we read of the destruction of Jerusalem and the conquests in the south of the country: "And afterward the children of Judah went down to fight against the Canaanites that dwelt in the hill-country, in the South, and in the Lowland;" and the episode ends with the interesting tradition that Judah and Simeon smote "the Canaanites that inhabited Zephath, and utterly destroyed it. And the name of the city was called Hormah." This refers to the same city of Hormah, apparently the center of the region of Arad, which the Israelites were unable to conquer when they camped at Kadesh and attempted a breakthrough into Canaan. This description is supplemented by a hazy tradition that Judah also took Gaza, Ashkelon, and Ekron, but it transpires from the Septuagint ("and he did not drive them out" instead of "and he took") that the text is garbled, as confirmed by what follows: "And the Lord was with Judah; and he drove out the inhabitants of the hill-country; for he could not drive out the inhabitants of the valley, because they had chariots of iron." In this episode are likewise merged traditions about the conquest and settlement of various tribes and families who accompanied Judah, some of which had joined in on the journey from the north, while others had come up from the desert, along the roads of the Negev, upon the breaching of the defence network of Canaan. The latter had settled in the south of the country and were eventually incorporated to the tribal organization of Judah. There is an instructive tradition which relates that the family of Hobab the Kenite, Moses' father-in-law, went up out of the city of palm trees with the children of Judah to the Negev of Arad and settled there, and that a branch of this family—Heber the Kenite—severed itself from the rest "and had pitched his tent as far as Allon-bezaanannim which is by Kadesh" on the border of Naphtali, under the protection of the king of Hazor (Jud. 1:15; 4:11, 17).[60] Of great interest are the traditions about Caleb, who conquered Hebron, and about Othniel son of Kenaz, who conquered Debir, or Kiriat-sepher (Josh., 14:13; 15:13 ff.; Jud. 1:10 ff.). They are no doubt drawn from the cycle of stories about Caleb, who settled in Hebron and on wide expanses in the hills of Judah and in the Negev (South) of Caleb, and of the Kenizzites who were related to them.[61] This cycle included also an account of the deeds of Othniel the Kenizzite, who apparently lived at the end of the 13th century (Jud. 3:8 ff.).[62] The stories of the conquest of Hebron and Debir were included in the descriptions of the wars of the period, which relate the destruction of various royal cities and fortified towns attributed to Joshua (Josh. 10:16 ff.), while in fact they reflect the conquests of the tribe of Judah and its followers. The cities captured, according to those descriptions, included the lowland cities of Makkedah, Libnah, Lachish, and Eglon, which are described as royal cities; and we can rely on the information that: ". . . Horam, King of Gezer came up to help Lachish" (Josh. 10:33), and suffered a defeat. As we have seen, archeological excavations of the mounds in the Shefela (Lowland) testify not only to the burning of fortified cities at the end of the Late Bronze Period, but also to the settlement of semi-nomads on their ruins. We also learn of the founding of an increasing number of new permanent settlements in various parts of the Shefela and the hill-country, at an early stage of the Iron Age. Various sources in the Bible, including the chapter on the lineage of Judah (particularly I Chron. 2–4), refer to this chain of events, and contain ancient memories of the difficulties encountered by the settlers who had to adjust to the conditions of the country, go over to permanent settlement and struggle with external forces. We learn about the settlement of the children of Judah in the Shefela (Lowland) and in the northern part of the hills of Judah, the center of which was in Bethlehem; about the expansion of the Calebites and other ethnic units in the central and southern part of the hill-country, about the assimilation of these elements and of the remnant of the Canaanite population into the tribal organization of Judah, and about the nomadic and semi-nomadic tribes, including the Simeonites, and their expansion in the Negev.[63] At the same time there arise various problems concerning the developments in Judah and the relations with the House of Joseph during the early period of the settlement of that tribe and their followers, even before the Philistines became a political and colonizing factor in the lowland area. From the few available sources we can conclude that Jerusalem was held by the Jebusites, who may have settled there during a Hittite penetration of the country following the destruction of the Hittite empire,[64] and that west of that city, as far as Gezer, the still very compact Gentile settlement area that separated the territory of Judah from the House of Joseph proved itself a thorn in the side of the tribes.

Even more difficult problems arise around the "Leah tribes" group, which settled in other areas of western Palestine. From the progress of events in the period of settlement it can be concluded that the tribes of Issachar and Zebulun, who were apparently accompanied by the Asherites, separated from the second wave which came from Transjordan. Most of them went up to Lower Galilee, and from there spread westward toward the Phoenician seacoast. Others turned southwards and settled in the west and south of the Ephraim hills, on the border of the inheritance of the tribes of Joseph. From various allusions in the Book of Judges and in the genealogical lists it transpires that early Issacharite families lived in the Shamir (or Shimron) area in the hills of Ephraim (Jud. 10:1; Chron. 7:1), and families of Asher lived south-west of the mountains (I Chron. 7:30 ff.).[65] As for the main block of the tribes of Zebulun and Issachar, who certainly constituted at first a united group, no definite information has been preserved of the circumstances under which they penetrated the Canaanite-held areas of Lower Galilee situated south and southwest of the area settled by the families of Naphtali with whom they concluded treaties. It may be assumed that the political conditions prevailing after the death of Mer-ne-Ptah prepared the ground for their quick settlement and expansion, for the incorporation of the Canaanite settlements in Lower Galilee into their tribal framework, and for the alternating relations of war and peace with the Canaanite kings in the valleys who, owing to their politico-military and economic superiority, were still the decisive factor in the north of the country. As for the tribe of Asher, that settled in the coastal area and its hinterland, they dwelt "among the Canaanites, the inhabitants of the land; for they did not drive them out" (Jud. 1:32). The events described in

Joshua 11 and in Judges 3:31 and in Chapters 4–5 undoubtedly refer to
the early period of settlement of the tribes of Issachar and Zebulun.
These events took place against a background of struggle between the
tribes of Israelite settlers and the kingdoms of Canaan, under the leadership
of the kingdom of Hazor, and the beginning penetration of the Sea-Peoples
(especially the Philistines; Jud. 3:31) into the north of the country.[66] The
two victories the Israelites won in the north during their wars with the
kings of Canaan — the one at the waters of Merom in northern Galilee,
which is ascribed to Joshua (Josh. 11:1–15), and the other in the Plain of
Jezreel (the brook of Kishon), which is linked with the names of Barak the
son of Abinoam of Kedesh-naphtali and Deborah the prophetess from the
hill-country of Ephraim (Jud. 4–5) — undoubtedly constitute a single historical episode which continues to be vague insofar as date and order of
events are concerned.[67] In any case, the victory resulted from a deterioration
of the security conditions and an attempt of the king of Hazor to exert his
authority over the tribes of Israel at Haroshet-goiim. This attempt served
to enforce the unity of the three tribes — Naphtali, Issachar and Zebulun —
and arouse their spirit so as to launch an offensive war. In that conflict the
tribes of Joseph, from the center of the country, who had hastened to their
aid, played a very important role (see the chapter, "The Period of the
Judges," below). No doubt in the wake of the battle in the Valley of Jezreel
the power of the kingdoms of Canaan diminished, the network of fortified
cities which separated the center of the country from the Plain of Jezreel and
Galilee was breached, and perhaps the Egyptian fortress at Beth-shean
(Level VII) was destroyed. The battle at the waters of Merom, in which
Jabin, King of Hazor, was joined by the kings of Shimeon (thus rather
than Shimron, the modern Tell Samuniye, near Nahalal), Achshaph
(apparently, Tell Qeysan in the plain of Acco), and Maron (thus rather
than Madon, apparently located in Upper Galilee), ended in the conquest
of Hazor. This chain of events is alluded to in the verse: "And the hand of
the children of Israel prevailed more and more against Jabin the king of
Canaan, until they had destroyed Jabin, king of Canaan" (Jud. 4:24),
which is reflected in the last stage of Canaanite Hazor (Level XIII), where
there are clear indications that decay and decline had set in just before the
destruction and burning of the king's fortress and the lower city (see above).
Here is provided certain foundation for the biblical statement that "as for
the cities that stood on their mounds, Israel burned none of them, save
Hazor only" (Josh. 11:13). But it is obvious that with the conquest and
destruction of Hazor there began an influx of the clans of Naphtali and
related groups into the heart of the former kingdom of Hazor, the valleys

of upper Jordan, and Chinneroth, and that they dominated these fertile regions where Canaanite cities abounded, and which represented especially important centers on the caravan routes that linked Syria and northern Transjordan with western Palestine and the Phoenician coast. This wave of immigration included also the Danites, who had separated from their brethren who remained in their previous area of settlement, and came to live among the "quiet and secure" people living in Laish and its vicinity under the protection of the kingdom of Sidon. After destroying the city of Laish the Danites founded in its place their own city, Dan (Jud. 17–18; Josh. 17:47).[68]

At the end of the wars in Canaan (Jud. 3:1) and before the Philistines began to assume an important place in the history of the country, the various tribes of Israel had already settled and established themselves in areas "from Dan unto Beer-sheba," while "Canaanite" city-states still existed in the valleys of the north and in the heart of the country, and the seacoast as well as the areas north of Galilee continued to be "the land that yet remaineth." The author of the Book of Joshua had good reasons to observe: "and there remaineth yet very much of the land to be possessed" (Jud. 13:1).

CHAPTER VI

THE SETTLEMENT OF CANAAN

by Y. Aharoni

A. The Area and Character of the Israelite Settlement

THE ISRAELITE SETTLEMENT concentrated mainly in the hilly areas of Canaan. There were two reasons for this phenomenon: a) These regions were sparsely populated at that time and entire wood covered areas were completely uninhabited.[1] Forests covered a considerable part of Galilee, part of the mountains of Ephraim and Judah, particularly their western slopes, and much of Gilead, especially to the north of the Jabbok, where extensive forests still existed at the time of the Israelite Kingdom, b) the Canaanite cities had developed mainly in the densely populated plains. The Bible repeatedly stresses the fact that the tribes of Israel were unable to pit themselves against the strong cities of the plain, "though they have chariots of iron, and though they be strong" (Josh. 17: 18). In the hill country, on the other hand, though there existed royal cities, the distance between towns was larger, the population was sparse, and a part of it was represented by semi-nomadic elements called Habiru. The kings of the weaker and more isolated hill cities did not possess great numbers of iron war chariots, the principal weapon which the settling tribes really feared, nor could they employ them as effectively as in the valleys and plains. As early as the Amarna period we hear of daring rulers who seized control of extensive areas in the hill country, as for example Lab'ayu the ruler of Shechem, who extended his sway over the entire hill country of Ephraim. Egyptian sources from time of the Nineteenth Dynasty mention that mountain areas were seized by various tribes named *Shosim* (*Shasu* by the Egyptians), while the valleys remained under Egyptian rule. The Victory Stele of Seti I (ca. 1300 B.C.E.) discovered in the excavations of Beth-shean, mentions that in the vicinity of that town some nomadic tribes revolted and were suppressed by the Egyptians. Among the tribes mentioned were the *'Pru* from the mountain of *Yrmt*.[2] From the list of Issachar's towns we know Jarmuth (Josh. 21:29; Remeth-Josh. 19:21; Ramoth-I Chr. 6:73), which was situated in the hill-country north of Beth-shean.[3] Hence, this area was already occupied by nomadic tribes at the end of the 14th century and it was only on account of its proximity to vital roads and its being located on rolling plain that the Egyptians paid more attention to it than to the mountain area. Interesting information is contained in the letter of the Egyptian scribe Ḥwry, written in the 13th century, in the reign of Ramses II.[4] In that part of the papyrus which deals with the geography of Canaan, the writer describes the main roads, particularly the various branches of the *Via maris*, from Ṣumur on the northern coast of Canaan down to Sile on the Egyptian border, and the eastern branches that led via the Plain of Jezreel and the Jordan Valley to Damascus and to the Beqaʿ (Valley of Lebanon). As long as the Egyptian traveller passes the towns in the plains we hear nothing of specific security problems, but the moment he is forced to cross into the hilly area he finds himself in *Shasu* country which Egypt was unable to control. The same situation prevailed on the vital pass of the Wadi ʿĀra, the main branch of the *Via maris* that linked the Plain of Jezreel to the coastal plain. This is what the writer has to say: "The wadi is dangerous, full of Shasu who hide themselves amongst the bushes. Some of them are as tall as four or five cubits from heel to nose. Their faces are fierce and their heart is pitiless and they do not listen to entreaties. You are lonely, there is no messenger with you, there is no army behind you, you do not find a guide to show you a passage ... your path is full of rocks and stones, there is no foothold, the way is full of reeds and thorns..."

The Bible usually calls the kings of the hill-country — Amorite kings, as against the Canaanite kings of the plain. This distinction, as far as we know, is not due to any ethnic difference, but is based on the geographical situation and on the resulting social and political differences.[5] The first stages of the Israelite Settlement as well as the early battles of the Conquest took place in the Amorite hill-country, and it is no mere coincidence that the majority of the kings of the highland with whom they came into conflict or contact are called Amorites in the Bible.[6]

This situation is clearly expressed in Josh. 17:14 ff.: "And the children of Joseph spoke unto Joshua, saying: 'Why hast thou given me but one lot and one part for an inheritance, seeing I am a great people, forasmuch as the Lord hath blessed me thus?' And Joshua said unto them: 'If thou be a great people, get thee up to the forest, and cut down for thyself there in the land of the Perizzites and of the Rephaim; since the hill-country of Ephraim is too narrow for thee.' And the children of Joseph said: 'The hill-country will not be enough for us; and all the Canaanites that dwell in the land of the valley have chariots of iron, both they who are in Beth-shean and its towns, and they who are in the valley of Jezreel'. And Joshua spoke unto the house of Joseph, even to Ephraim and to Manasseh, saying: 'Thou art a great people, and hast great power; thou shalt not have one lot only; but the hill-country shall be thine; for though it is a forest, thou shalt cut it down, and the goings out thereof shall be thine . . ."

Opinions differ as to whether this description refers to the expansion of the House of Joseph in Transjordan or to their settling in the afforested parts of the actual hill-country of Ephraim,[7] but this picture reflects the Israelites' inability to penetrate the Canaanite valleys and the necessity to settle among the mountains there to cultivate virgin land and to cut down the original forests.

This and other passages of the Bible reflect also the desire and the vital necessity to switch over from a semi-nomadic existence based mainly on the breeding and grazing of flocks to agriculture and permanent settlement. The sources testify to the existence of such a general aspiration and to a main phase of settlement which ended within a short span of time. Nevertheless, various tribes lagged behind in their settlement, while some did not succeed to settle in the areas allotted them, usually for objective reasons which made the transition to permanent settlement difficult (cf. below).

This fact is stressed in the biblical accounts and has been confirmed by archeological research. As against the accounts from the period of the Patriarchs, which describe a life of pasturing flocks and living in huts or tents,[8] nearly all the stories from the period of the Judges allude to agriculture and mention permanent habitations in towns and villages. This applies, for example, to the Song of Deborah and the story of Gideon. The exception is represented by a few tribes — Dan, Simeon, and Reuben — who, as we already said, lagged behind in the process of settlement. In Jacob's blessing, which describes the position of the tribes in the period of the Judges, the economy was already characterized by agriculture and husbandry of various fruit trees such as olives and vines. Of particular significance is the production of wine which was foreign to nomads and semi-nomads.[9] Various settlements that had been founded by the Israelite tribes in the hill-country of Ephraim, Benjamin and Judah have been investigated. Several of them were new settlements, others were rebuilt on a layer of complete destruction or on sites that had been deserted for a long time. At Beth-el and Debir (Khirbet Rabud) the Canaanite town was destroyed and after a brief interval Israelite settlements rose on their ruins. At Ai and at Mizpeh (Tell en-Naṣbeh) in Judah an Israelite settlement was established after the place had been forsaken for a long time. A shorter gap, but still several hundred years long, has been detected at

Shiloh and at Beth-zur. The Israelites founded Gibeath Benjamin (Tell el-Fūl) and other places in the same neighborhood, such as Ramah and Geba, which have not been excavated yet. In all these places the remains clearly prove the general and rapid transition from a semi-nomadic life to permanent settlement at the end of the 13th or the beginning of the 12th century.

Archeological surveys in Transjordan and in Galilee revealed the same picture. Nelson Glueck, in particular, discovered in southern Transjordan numerous settlements founded at the end of the 14th and particularly in the course of the 13th century, after an almost complete interruption of permanent settlement in that area which had lasted hundreds of years. The settlement discovered belonged in part to the tribes of Ammon, Moab and Edom who were close to the Israelite tribes (within two or three generations they achieved actual and continuous settlement and established organized kingdoms in their respective areas) and partly, no doubt, to the settling Israelite tribes, particularly the tribe of Gad.

A process of vigorous and concentrated settlement, in spite of the very difficult terrain, emerged clearly also from the survey carried out in Upper Galilee. A continuous chain of tiny settlements from the beginning of the Iron Age, and which had been established in about the 13th century, were discovered in an area extending from Peqi'in to the Kezib brook (Wadi Qurn). These are the first permanent settlements established on virgin soil in one of the highest districts of Upper Galilee, and which had been completely covered by forest until then. Some of them are located on the mountain tops, some on slopes or in valleys; the distances between them do not exceed 2–3 km on the average, sometimes even less. A decisive consideration in the selection of a settlement site was the convenient access to the tiny and scattered plots of cultivable land in this difficult, rocky terrain. In most of the cases they were, no doubt, open, unfortified settlements. We have before us a typical picture of the establishment of clans in small, closely placed settlements in the craggy, afforested mountain areas. What caused this vigorous process of transition from a semi-nomadic life which had lasted hundreds of years to agriculture and the establishment of permanent settlements in spite of exceptionally difficult conditions?

There seem to have been three economic and security factors which fostered the settlement in the hilly areas. Two of these factors were technical inventions, widespread in Canaan in the 13th century, and though not made by the children of Israel, they were soon adopted by the settling tribes.

1. *Introduction of Iron Implements.* In the 13th century Palestine saw the

transition from the Bronze Age to the Iron Age. This metal was brought into the country from the north. The art of smelting iron had been mastered as early as the 14th century by the Hittites who guarded it as a kind of precious monopoly.[10] When the Hittite kingdom was finally defeated and collapsed under the strong assault of the Sea Peoples, at the beginning of the 12th century, the use of iron implements spread over the whole of the Ancient East. The Philistines tried to inherit this monopoly and control the iron production as we see from I Sam. 13:19 ff. The passage proves at the same time that the use of iron tools was already common in Palestine. The Philistines prevented their smiths from working in Israel "Lest the Hebrews make them swords or spears; but the Israelites went down to the Philistines to sharpen every man his plowshare, and his coulter . . . and his axe, and his hack." This shows that the Philistines did not prevent the Israelites from using iron tools for agricultural purposes, but forced them to obtain these implements and to repair them in their territory, against stiff payment of course (I Sam. 13:21).

The iron tools, which were stronger and more efficient than the bronze ones, eased the arduous work of cutting down forests and preparing the rocky soil for agriculture.

2. *The Invention of the Plastered Cistern.* In the layers from the Late Bronze Period, especially from its last stages, were discovered plastered whitewashed cisterns which permitted the collection and storage of water the year round.[11] This invention freed the settlers of their dependence upon springs — until then the proximity of a water source having been a primary condition for the establishment of any permanent settlement. This invention permitted the establishment of settlements based on the collection of rain-water and its storage throughout the year in plastered cisterns. Neither was this an Israelite invention. It appears for the first time in the Canaanite cities which had to make tremendous efforts to secure water supplies for times of siege. This invention was also quickly adopted by the settling tribes and it enabled them to found many small, independent and scattered settlements, even in places that were far from springs.

3. *The Security Factor.* The defence of the settlements and their inhabitants was not based, like that of the Canaanite cities, on the heavy armament and strong fortification of every individual place, but mainly on collective defence based on the family and the tribe. In the accounts from the period of the Judges there are few instances of an Israelite town being besieged; instead we are frequently told of enemies invading Israelite territory, the muster of a clan's or tribe's warriors and the final repulsion of the foe. To begin with, most of the Israelite concentrations were small,

some being open settlements and others having poor fortifications as compared to the mighty walls of the Canaanite towns. This was due partly to a lack of technical ability at the beginning of the settlement and partly to the tribal rule which prevented the recruitment of large labour forces for collective defensive works. However, these tribal security arrangements were well suited to the settlements scattered over craggy mountain areas. The poor roads and the difficult approach were also taken into account in safeguarding that type of settlement.

All these factors explain how a dense settlement in the hilly areas was possible in that period. But they do not explain what was the strong incentive for this rapid settlement. In the stories in Genesis the fathers of the Israelite tribes appear in those same areas, namely among the hills of western Canaan, and in Gilead; they move from place to place, particularly in the suitable grazing seasons (cf. for example the wanderings of Jacob's sons with their flocks from Hebron to the valley of Dothan in the north of the hill country of Ephraim. See also the story of Joseph, in Gen. 37:13 ff.). It is therefore possible that part of the tribes reached the mountains of Canaan in the first stage of the settlement by the natural process of transhumance customary in the life of semi-nomads.[12] At the same time, one cannot accept the view held by a number of scholars that the entire process of the Settlement was a natural and slow transition from grazing to settlement in the summer pastures. This theory is contradicted by the biblical accounts, by the destruction layers found in the excavated Canaanite towns, as well as by the indications of the rapid settlement of the majority of the tribes within a short span of time. At least a part of the Israelite tribes used force to break into Transjordan and the hilly areas of Canaan where they destroyed various towns, mainly in isolated districts.

Such an invasion is not a unique phenomenon but the result of the expansion of Hebrew and Aramean tribes over all the countries of the Fertile Crescent, from the Euphrates to the Jordan. At that very time the Ammonites, Moabites and Edomites settled in Transjordan, and various Aramean tribes occupied extensive areas in northern Transjordan, in the Valley of Lebanon and in the upper Euphrates regions. The Israelite tribes were a segment of this extensive migration which came from the eastern deserts, and the pressure of this wave was probably the decisive factor which necessitated their speedy settlement in the sparsely populated areas of Canaan. The desert areas and the border districts being speedily occupied by various tribes who followed in their footsteps, and prevented them from returning and using the winter pastures in the desert, the Israelite tribes were forced to seek their livelihood in rapid and vigorous settlement. Their strength proved insufficient to give them control of the developed Canaanite districts, but it sufficed to ensure their settlement in the difficult mountain areas.

The Ammonites, Moabites and Edomites settled in contingent uninhabited areas and soon after their settlement set up well organized monarchies.[13] As against this, the Israelite tribes could not settle in a continuous area, and even within the various tribal territories there remained concentrations of the former inhabitants, some of which withstood the pressure of the Israelites, while others were absorbed by the Israelites in the course of time. This appears to be the main reason why in spite of the rapidity of their settlement even the Israelite tribes in the center of the country preserved their tribal and family organization for more than two hundred years, until the rise of the Israelite Monarchy.

The settlement of the Israelites was a complicated and by no means smooth process in which not all the tribes were equally successful. The picture which emerges from the Bible gives us the results of this process at a later stage of the period of the Judges. At that time the tribal framework had already crystallized and most of the tribes lived in their permanent territories. However, fragments of information included in various stories and genealogical lists point to two basic facts which marked the beginnings of the settlement:

1. Some of the tribes or clans left their original areas, where they had been unable to settle, and moved to other places.

2. The tribal framework in its final form crystallized only during the time of the Judges. At the beginning of that period certain families still moved from one tribe to another according to the particular circumstances of their settlement. Occasionally various families belonging to the same clan joined different tribes so that the name of their family appears with several tribes.

The only case of a tribe migrating after failing to take possession of a certain area to be clearly described in the Bible is the migration of Dan. This should not lead us to the conclusion that this event took place later than similar movements of other tribes. The main migration of Machir seems on all accounts to have taken place after it, but the story of Dan was preserved because of its end. It describes the circumstances under which Moses' grandson established the important sanctuary at Dan[14] at which his descendents ministered until the day of exile from the country (Jud. 18:30) Hence, the information is not an incidental and supplementary episode of the story, but constitutes its essential part. We find no reason to dispute the date of the migration it gives, since it seems reasonable to assume that Moses' grandson could not have lived after the end of the 13th century.[15] This date also fits in with the circumstances of the migration. The tribe was still semi-nomadic, living in a camp and travelling with its flocks and possessions. The attempt to settle in the coastal plain of Zorah and Eshtaol and their neighborhood met with the vigorous opposition of the Amorite cities (Jud. 1:34–35), led most probably by Gezer. There is as yet no mention of Philistine oppression which reached its climax in this area several generations later.[16] The Song of Deborah, according to all appearances, already counted Dan among the northern tribes (Jud. 5:17); and there might be in it an allusion to a degree of servitude to Sidon (cf. below).[17] At the same time there is sufficient ground to assume that only a part of the tribe migrated to the north while another part of its families remained in the south and in the course of time were absorbed by other tribes. In fact we are not told that the whole tribe of Dan migrated: "And there set forth thence of the family of the Danites, out of Zorah and Eshtaol, six hundred men girt with weapons of war" (Jud. 18:11). The family of Hushim from Dan (Gen. 46:23) is also mentioned among the families of Benjamin (I Chron. 8:8). Samson belonged to a Danite family which lived in Zorah (Jud. 13:2), at the very earliest in the beginning of the 11th century, when the Philistines already ruled Judah; but the Danite migration cannot be dated as late as this period.

There is reason to believe that also other tribes migrated, though no story concerning them was preserved.[18] That families of Manasseh migrated to Gilead is proved by the fact that the Song of Deborah still mentions Machir, the father of Gilead, as a western tribe. A passage about one of the judges ". . . Tola the son of Puah, the son of Dodo, a man of Issachar; and he dwelt in Shamir in the hill-country of Ephraim" (Jud. 10:1) — alludes to the migration of families of Issachar from the mountains of Ephraim to its inheritance in the north of the plain of Jezreel, Puah being known as one of the chief families of Issachar (Gen. 46:13 etc.).[19] Concerning the migration of Asherite families from the hill-country of Ephraim to Galilee we possess clear evidence in the genealogical lists of this tribe (Gen. 46:17 ff., Num. 26:44 ff., I Chron. 7:30 ff.).[19] Three of its families lived on the border of Benjamin and Ephraim: Japhlet — the Japhletites (Josh. 16:3), Shual and Shalisha — the land of Shual (I Sam. 13:17; the land of Shalisha and the land of Shaalim, I Sam. 9:4). The family of Malchiel is settled in Birzaith,[20] Βηρ ζαιθ according to the Septuagint (it is apparently Βαρ ζυθα, Βαρ ςυτω of Josephus, Antiq. XII, 11:1, now Khirbet Bīr Zayt to the north of Beth-el).[21] Two Asherite families are also found with families of the House of Joseph: Beriah in Ephraim and in Benjamin (I Chron. 7:23,

30–31; 8:13) and Shemer (Shomer) in Benjamin (I Chron. 8:12 — according to the Septuagint). It is possible to supply further, though less certain examples,[22] but the names which we mentioned suffice to prove that at least part of the families of Asher first lived in the hill-country of Ephraim, and that a part of the clans which remained in this area were finally absorbed by Ephraim and Benjamin.

There are many examples of the same family being mentioned with several tribes, which proves that various clans of the same family separated and were absorbed by different tribes. The families of Becher and Beriah are mentioned with Ephraim and Benjamin;[23] the family of Shema is mentioned in Judah and Benjamin; the family of Zerah is mentioned in Judah, Simeon and also among the families (chiefs) of Edom. Similarly, various families that are common to the southern tribes and to the settlements of Mount Seir (cf. below the paragraph on the southern tribes), testify to the migration of clans in these areas.

B. Stages in the Settlement of the Different Tribes

The settlement of the Israelite tribes was concentrated in four separate areas: 1) Judah and the Negev; 2) the hill-country of Ephraim; 3) Galilee; 4) Transjordan. The first three areas were separated by Gentile enclaves: Jebusite Jerusalem and Amorite Gezer in the south, the Canaanite Plain of Jezreel in the north — and the deep Jordan Valley which separated them from the tribes in Transjordan. Since each of these areas underwent an individual process of settlement due to specific conditions and circumstances, they require separate treatment.

1. *The Southern Tribes.* Only Judah and Simeon are considered southern tribes. The account of the tribal inheritances actually assigns the whole territory to the tribe of Judah alone and emphasizes that the lot of the sons of Simeon was "in the midst of the inheritance of the children of Judah" (Josh. 19:1). Judah's southern border (Josh. 15:1–4) was identical with the southern border of Canaan (Num. 34:3–5), which ran in a wide bend from the eastern end of the Dead Sea through the Wilderness of Zin to Kadesh-Barnea and followed the Brook of Egypt down to the Mediterranean Sea. The northern border went as far as the southern limit of Jebusite Jerusalem, whence it ran on to Kiriat-jearim (Baalath, Baalah) the Gibeonite city, then continued westwards with the brook of Sorek (Wadi eṣ-Ṣarār) to the sea.[24]

This general framework of the tribe of Judah included not only Simeon, but also closely related ethnic elements such as the sons of Caleb, Jerahmeel.

Kenaz and Cain. The accounts in Joshua, Judges and particularly the genealogical lists in I Chronicles give us the general lines of the various areas of settlement.[25] The sons of Caleb were a strong and widespread group which took possession of the southern half of the Judean mountains, from the neighborhood of Hebron in the north to the boundaries of the Negev in the south. Hebron itself was conquered by Caleb the son of Jephunneh (Josh. 14:13–14; 15:13–14). The same story is also told about Judah (Jud. 1:10), furnishing an interesting example of how, after a time, the actions of various tribes that became attached to Judah were attributed to it.[26] The families of Kenaz, who were related to Caleb, lived in Debir (Kiriath-sepher) and its surroundings (Josh. 15:15–17; Jud. 1:11–13).[27] According to I Chron. 2–4 families of the sons of Caleb lived in Beth-zur, in Tekoa, in (Beth-) tappuah and Ziph near Hebron, and more to the south in Maon and Eshtemoa, in Socoh, Goshen (Geshan), Madmannah and (Beth-)pelet. The two last named which were in the South of Caleb (1 Sam. 30:14) are also mentioned among the towns of the Negev district of Judah (Josh. 15:27, 31). At the time of David parts of this area were still called by the names of the families and tribes which had lived there, namely, the South of Caleb, the South of the Jerahmeelites and the South of the Kenites. The Kenites lived in the neighborhood of Arad, to which place they went up "with the children of Judah" (Jud. 1:16)[28], and the children of Jerahmeel apparently occupied the southernmost districts in the neighborhood of Bir Rekhmeh.[29] Those who lived in these southern, semi-desert areas lagged behind in their settlement so that these districts developed only at the time of the Kingdom of Judah.

The children of Simeon occupied the central Negev, from the neighborhood of Beer-sheba to Hormah, ancient Zephath.[30] As late as the time of the monarchy most of them still lived in temporary settlements, grazing their flocks (cf. particularly I Chron. 4:32, 41). Simeon's special connection with Judah was responsible for this district being called "The South of Judah," at the time of David. This name occurs together with the South of Caleb, the South of the Kenites, the South of the Jerahmeelites, etc. (I Sam. 27:10; cf. also 30:14).

The connections between the southern tribes and the Arabah and Mount Seir stand out in the genealogical lists. Of the four Hebron families of the children of Caleb (I Chr. 2:43) at least two clearly originated in the south. The name of Korah which occurs with the chiefs of Edom (Gen. 36:16), is also connected with the district of Zoar and the Arabah[31]; Rekem is one of the chiefs of Midian (Josh. 13:21); according to one view this family gave its name to the Edomite city of Rekem, which is the ancient name of Petra.

Also the family of Shema appears to be connected with the Arabah and Edom. In an inscription of Ramses II from 'Amara "Shm't in the Land of Shasu" is mentioned together with Seir.[32] This name recalls the Kenite family of the Shimeathites (I Chr. 2:55), and Shimei — one of the sons of Simeon — an extensive family (I Chron. 4:24–27) for whom the Negev settlement Shema is apparently called (Josh. 15:26). Similarly Kenaz appears as one of the chiefs of Edom (Gen. 36:9–15).

The connections between the southern tribes and the ancient Hurrian elements of Mount Seir, recognized from the genealogical lists, clearly point to that neighborhood as the origin of those families. These connections cannot be explained according to any later data. Among the Mount Seir Hurrians (Gen. 36:20 ff.; I Chron. 1:38 ff.), there is the Shobal family which lived in Kiriath-jearim and which is related to Hur, Ephratah and Caleb (I Chron. 2:50–52) and the family of Manahath, of the families of Judah, which is related to Shobal (I Chron. 2:52), and whose name seems to be connected with the town of Manahath, south-west of Jerusalem. Hurrian elements are particularly prominent with the families of Jerahmeel (I Chron. 2:25 ff.): Onam, Jether (Jithran). Oren also occurs with the Hurrian children of Seir (Gen. 36:20 ff.; I Chron. 1:38 ff.); Onam's descendants: Sheshan, Ahlai, Peleth and Zaza (I Chron. 2:31–33) also seem to bear Hurrian names.[33]

The connections of the Kenites — the ancient metal workers — with the Arabah and Edom, with their copper and iron mines, cannot be doubted[34] and the people of the Kenite house of Rechab (I Chron. 2:55), are on the one hand connected with the families of Caleb and Kenaz, and on the other, with Ir-nahash and Ge-harashim in Edom (I Chron. 4:12–14).[35] There is also evidence of connections between the Kenites and the Amalekites who inhabited the southern deserts (I Sam. 15:6; Jud. 1:16 — according to the version of the Septuagint Mss.).[36]

The genealogical lists of Simeon and even Judah supply connections with Mount Seir. The Zerah family of Judah is mentioned among the sons of Simeon (Num. 26:13; I Chron. 4:24) and also among the sons of Edom (Gen. 36:13,17; I Chron. 1:37). However, the Zerah family of Judah which apparently inhabited the eastern district in the vicinity of the Judean desert,[37] lost its importance as against the family of Perez and the rest of Judah's families. In Simeon's genealogies it is only mentioned in the above mentioned lists; and it is missing altogether from the lists in Gen. 46 and Ex. 6 where its place is taken by the family of Zohar.

The numerous connections between the families of Caleb, Kenaz, Jerahmeel and the Kenites with the ancient elements of Mount Seir and the

Arabah are hardly accidental. They point to a number of circumstances in the settlement of the tribes of Judah and Simeon. Apart from these connections of origin that speak for themselves, we also possess direct information and allusions to the penetration of these families from the south. At the beginning the story of the spies sent out from Kadesh referred only to the Hebron area (Num. 13:22) and in the original account Caleb was the only one who gave an encouraging account and recommended going up there (Num. 13:30). As a reward he was given the Hebron area (Josh. 14:14), a fact which seems to reflect an early tradition of Caleb's migration from the south, unconnected with the rest of the Israelite tribes. Another tradition preserved relates that the Kenites came up to the neighborhood of Arad from the City of palm-trees (Jud. 1:16), which in this case probably does not refer to Jericho, but Zoar which is also called the city of palm-trees (Mishnah Yᵉvamoth 16:7) or to Tamar which is close to the northern edge of the Arabah.[38] The ancient road which went up from the mountain of Sodom to the neighborhood of Arad runs along a deep brook, which to this day bears the name of Wadi el-Qeini.[39]

The genealogical lists supply scraps of information which prove that even after their settlement in new places the southern tribes continued practising to some extent crafts and trades which had certainly been specific of a family or tribe since the days of their wandering. Thus we find mentioned in them families "that wrought fine linen" (I Chron. 4:21) — i.e. cloth weaving and dyeing — which were descended from the house of Ashbea. This circumstance is clearly demonstrated by the excavations of Tell Beth Mirsim where a concentration of looms and cloth dyeing installations was found in the houses dug up.[40] At Jabez, the location of which is not known, lived families of scribes who were descended from the Kenites (I Chron. 2:55) and who were greatly revered on account of their profession (I Chron. 4:9). Similarly, the instance that the name of Debir was changed to Kiriath-sefer[41] appears to attest that a much respected concentration of scribe families lived there. In Netaim and Gederah, the location of which is not certain either, lived families of potters, some of whom became in the course of time the king's own potters (I Chron. 4:23). We have already mentioned the Kenites' traditional metal work, and among the families of Caleb we find "Joab the father of Ge-harashim; for they were craftsmen" (I Chron. 4:14), whose family was no doubt related to both the Kenites and to Caleb.

The center of Judah's inheritance was in the neighborhood of Bethlehem, between Jerusalem in the north and Hebron in the south. Among the settlements of the children of Perez, the chief family of Judah, are mentioned:

The Tribal Lots.

Etam, Gederah (Gedor), Hushah, Tekoa, and Bethlehem (I Chron. 4:3–5), all of which are situated between Bethlehem and Beth-zur. This is Judah's ancient area of settlement among the mountains (Jud. 1:19) and most of these localities were apparently founded by the settling families. The only place excavated in the Judean mountains and where remains of a town from the period of the Settlement were found is Beth-zur,[42] where Calebite families lived (I Chron. 2:45). It transpires that though the town had been inhabited during the Middle Bronze Period, it was virtually abandoned during the entire Late Bronze Period — ca. three hundred years — and was rebuilt only at the beginning of the Iron Age. On the other hand, it is possible that Bethlehem existed in the Late Bronze Period, if the argument is correct that it is mentioned in the Tell el-Amarna Letters as a town in the land of Jerusalem.[43] The Bible frequently mentions the name Ephrath or Ephratah which is Bethlehem, and one of the leading families of Judah, Hur, which lived in Bethlehem is related to Ephratah: ". . . Hur the first-born of Ephratah, the father of Bethlehem" (I Chron. 4:4). It is possible that Ephratah is an ancient Canaanite family of Bethlehem which was absorbed by the tribe of Judah, and for this reason the Bible mentions no tradition of the conquest of Bethlehem by the sword.

In any case it is obvious that in the early stages of its settlement Judah absorbed Canaanite families living in the Shefela, into which families of Judah moved from the settlement areas in the hill-country. In Gen. 38 we find an interesting description of this phenomenon; it is an outstanding example of tribal traditions assuming the character of the story of the eponymous hero of the tribe. The story describes neighborly relations and intermarriage with Canaanite families in the form of family relationships and the marriage of the tribe's father. Judah is a shepherd who married women from among the Canaanites of Adullam, Chezib (Achzib) and Timnath. These localities are in the Shefela (Lowland), on the way from the Judean Mountains to the northern coastal plain, west of the Beth-lehem area which was Judah's early tribal lot in the mountains. The fact that this area is not mentioned in the stories of the Conquest in the Book of Joshua (Joshua 10), which deal only with the settlers further south and southwest is not a mere accident.[44] According to I Chron. 4:21–22 the Shelah family, of the sons of Judah, extended from Lachish,[45] and Mareshah in the Coastal Plain to Bethlehem among the mountains. The absorption of the various Canaanite elements contributed, no doubt, toward Judah's speedy settlement. This phenomenon, as well as its wide expansion over the Shefela, have to be reckoned among the factors which raised and placed Judah at the head of the southern tribes. In the course of time the families of Caleb were also absorbed among the families of Judah, as proved by the example of Hur the father of Bethlehem, who was also considered Caleb's son. In final analysis, most southern groups were turned into sons of Judah so that all the southern tribes were included in the term "The House of Judah" (II Sam. 2:4, 11; I Kings 12:21–23, etc.).

The southern tribes were separated from the Joseph tribes by an enclave of Gentile cities which extended from Jerusalem to Gezer. Despite the fact that the conquest of Jerusalem by Judah is related to an early phase of the Conquest (Jud. 1:8) they apparently did not manage to maintain their position there, and until the time of David the city was held by the Jebusites whose origin and nature have not been clarified yet. The border between Benjamin and Judah running south of Jerusalem along the Valley of the son of Hinnom (Josh. 15:8; 18:16), and the fact that Jerusalem remained a Gentile town made each of the two tribes claim it for itself (Jud. 1:21; Josh. 15:63). Gezer, the key city that dominated the way to Jerusalem at the western end of the Valley of Aijalon, remained Canaanite until Solomon's days (I Kings 9:16) — since the tribe of Ephraim had proved unable to take it. Further, at the eastern end of the Coastal Plain, the tribe of Dan had tried to settle but could not resist the Amorites, being forced to give up at least part of the area: "But the Amorites were resolved to dwell in Har-heres, in Aijalon and in Shaalbim" (Jud. 1:35). Har-heres is apparently identical with Beth-shemesh on the brook of Sorek, on the northern border of Judah; Aijalon, Shaalbim commanded the passes in the neighborhood of the Valley of Aijalon. The mountain slopes between these localities and Jerusalem were partly occupied by the Gibeonite towns, and partly covered by forests. The description of Judah's northern border does not mention here any settlements, but only two wooded mountain ranges: Mount Seir and Mount Jearim (Josh. 15:10).

Even though the entire area between Jerusalem and Gezer was not Canaanite throughout, the main mountain passes as well as the Coastal Plain were in the possession of the Gentile cities. All that was left here for the southern Israelite tribes were difficult, circuitous passes on the mountain slopes which were forest-land in the west and desert in the east. This situation is clearly reflected in the story of the concubine in Gibeah (Jud. 19). The Levite who went to take his concubine from Bethlehem in Judah to his home in the Ephraim mountains did not want to spend the night in the Jebusite "city of a foreigner, that is to say, not of the children of Israel." In spite of the late hour he continued on his way in order to reach one of the Benjamite towns, Gibeah or Ramah. This story illustrates the fact that foreign Jerusalem controlled the main passes which connected the territory of Judah to that of the tribes of Joseph. At the same time it emphasizes the feeling of relationship that linked the separated groups of tribes as opposed to the foreign city that was not of the children of Israel.

The towns which separated the southern tribes from the tribes belonging to the House of Joseph constituted a real barrier for more than two hundred years and this gap was not bridged even after David had conquered them. During the entire period of the Judges we do not hear of the southern tribes taking part in a common action with the northern tribes; and in the Song of Deborah the names of the southern tribes are altogether absent — they are not even blamed for non-participation in the war. This led some scholars to the conclusion that at the beginning the southern tribes were not considered as belonging among the Israelite tribes, but only joined the tribal covenant with the establishment of the monarchy, and that Judah came into the country directly from the Negev and the Arabah, together with the rest of the southern tribes.[46] But this view has to be rejected since it cannot explain the connection existing between the Israelite tribes in spite of their being cut off, an example of which is given in Judges 19. The preservation of early traditions about these very tribes, dealing with their activities in the hill-country of Ephraim, namely, the incident with Simeon and Levi in Shechem (Gen. 34) and Judah's campaign southwards by way of Bezek (Jud. 1:2 ff.) cannot be due to mere chance. Only Judah and Simeon's ancient connections with the rest of the Israelite tribes can explain why their full genealogy is given and both are mentioned as tribes from among the other southern tribes. This community of origin possibly helped Judah in gaining ascendancy over all the rest of the southern tribes.

2. *The "House of Joseph."* Three tribes settled in the central mountain district of Canaan. Beginning from the south they are: Benjamin, Ephraim and Manasseh.

According to the genealogical scheme only the latter two are sons of Joseph, but at times the term "House of Joseph" includes all the central tribes, including Benjamin, Joseph's younger brother (Josh. 18:5 ff.). This area is the house of the tribes of the hill-country of Ephraim parallel to the House of Judah. The connection between Benjamin and the tribes of the House of Joseph was natural on account of Jebusite Jerusalem which, as we said, separated Benjamin and Judah, and it apparently also found expression in the name of the tribe of *Ben-jamin* which means "Son of the South."[47]

The view that Ephraim is basically a geographical name seems reasonable. Its ending, which is customary with place-names,[48] points to this, as well as the fact that the name of Mount Ephraim usually refers to the whole of the central hill-country (Josh. 17:15, 20:21; Jud. 7:24; I Sam. 1:1; I Kings 4:8). It appears that to begin with this name referred to the high mountain range north of Beth-el, which was the center of Ephraim's tribal lot,[49] and with this tribe's rise in importance it spread over a wider area.

Thus, the uneven development of the tribes of the House of Joseph was not due to any difference of origin, but to the different circumstances of their settlement, and particularly to their specific relationship with the autochthonous population of the hill-country. The tribe of Manasseh, which settled mainly north of the Shechem region, maintained at first amicable relations and concluded covenants with the Canaanite towns within its borders. The Bible contains no tradition of conquests or battles in this area, in spite of the fact that at the beginning the tribal center was in the neighborhood of Shechem (Jos. 24:1 ff.).[50] There are grounds for assuming that even before that time there existed Hebrew tribes in these areas, though this is no proof that armed conflicts had then taken place. Quite the contrary, as early as the Amarna period Hebrew tribes had penetrated into this region with the agreement of the local population which used them for their own purposes and did not apparently fear the results of the presence of foreign elements in the uninhabited hill-country. However, the penetration of the House of Joseph altered the balance of power, and the Canaanite cities felt soon enough the superior power of the new settlers. The difference did not, however, find expression in a change of attitude toward them, but in a reversal of the legal status. The Canaanite cities were absorbed by the Israelite tribe. This fact is reflected in the genealogical lists which included the names of the different Canaanite towns as sons and daughters of Manasseh, for example Shechem, Tirzah, Hepher (Num. 26:31 ff.; 27:1; Josh. 17:2 ff.). From the story of Abimelech the results clearly show that Shechem remained Canaanite, but its inclusion in the genealogical lists of the Israelite tribe granted it equal rights with the rest of the sons of the tribal father, namely with the Israelite families and clans.

Manasseh's settlement and expansion is marked by the absorption of the Canaanite elements within the framework of the Israelite tribe. This was conditioned by the character of the region. In the Judean mountains and in the southern part of the hill-country of Ephraim the early population had mainly settled along the watershed line where the highway ran along the mountains (cf. Jud. 20:31; 21:19). North of Shechem the mountains

Ibsha "the ruler of a foreign country" leads a caravan of "thirty-seven Asiatics bringing stilium to Egypt. Wall painting in the tomb of Khnum-hotep III at Beni-Hasan; Middle Kingdom period.

Mari. People offering sacrifice.
Prof. A. Parrot, Paris.

Canaanite nobleman.
Bronze plaque from Hazor,
Late Bronze period.
Prof. Y. Yadin, Jerusalem.

Middle Bronze I Age pottery vessels from Megiddo.
IDA and YMCA, Jerusalem.

Two anthropomorphic vessels; above; from Jericho (Middle Bronze Age): below: from Lachish (Late Bronze Age);

IDA, Jerusalem.

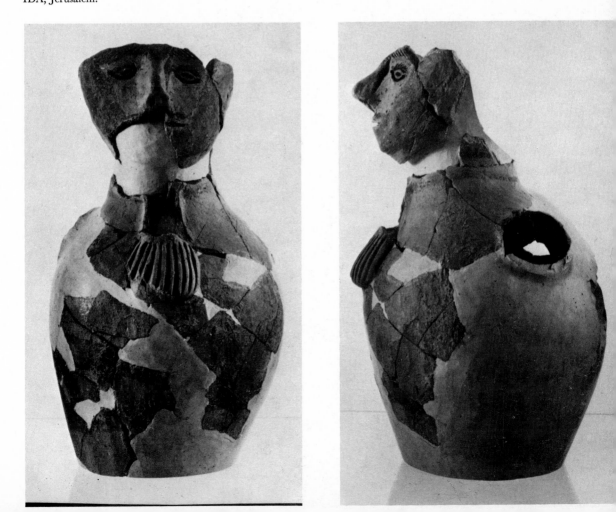

Two zoomorphic pottery vessels;
above: from Jericho,
Middle Bronze Age;
below: from Beth-shean,
Late Bronze Age.

Prof. Kathleen M. Kenyon, London;
IDA, Jerusalem.

Late Bronze I Age
Mycenaean kylix found
at Lachish.
IDA, Jerusalem.

Late Bronze I Age
krater of Bichrome ware
from Tel-Nagila.
Mrs. Ruth Amiran, Jerusalem.

Late Bronze Age
faience vessels from
Tell Abu-Huwam.
IDA, Jerusalem

Middle Bronze Age carved ivory
incrustations from Jericho (above)
and el-Jisr (below).
Prof. Kathleen M. Kenyon, London;
IDA, Jerusalem.

One side of Late Bronze Age ivory box from Tell el-Far'ah-south: Scene in the ruler's court. IDA, Jerusalem.

Incised ivory plaques from Megiddo, Late Bronze Age. Above: two prisoners brought before a ruler; middle: Canaanite war chariots engaged in battle; below: people at a banquet.

Oriental Institute, University of Chicago.

Late Bronze carved ivory box decorated roundabout with high reliefs of lions and sphinxes, from Megiddo.
IDA, Jerusalem.

Late Bronze Age ivory carvings
from Megiddo:
above: representation
of a noblewoman;
right: the god Bass.
Oriental Institute, University of Chicago.

Late Bronze A
carved ivory
combs from
Megiddo.
IDA, Jerusalem.

Late Bronze Age carved ivory
handle representing
a woman's head
found in Beth-el.
IDA, Jerusalem.

Late Bronze Age ivory bottle
in the shape of a woman,
from Lachish.
IDA, Jerusalem.

Late Bronze Age carved
ivory plaques from
Megiddo;
above: griffon in
Mycenaean style;
below: mythological scene,
Hittite style.

Oriental Institute, University of
Chicago.

were lower, the road forked out into two main branches and the population was divided along with it. The fertile valleys sheltered a stronger and denser Canaanite population, though even here there existed woody and un-inhabited areas, which provided an extensive stretch of land for the settle-ment of the Israelite tribes alongside the Canaanite towns. The roads permitting access into the valleys of this area were better than in the other parts of the hill-country and helped in strengthening the links between the plains and the hill-country. The Tell el-Amarna Letters mentioned the attempts of Lab'ayu, King of Shechem, to extend his dominion to the Sharon in the west and to the Plain of Jezreel in the north. The tribe of Manasseh did the same in the following period. The latter's early expansion to the Sharon is proved by the inclusion of Canaanite Hepher (Josh. 17:2) among the children of Manasseh (Num. 26:32–33; 27:1; Josh. 17:2–3). The fact that Hepher was in the Sharon is proved by its being mentioned among the towns of Solomon's third district (I Kings 4:10), which lay between the towns of the Coastal Plain in the south and between the district of Dor and the Plain of Jezreel in the north. All of these had been basically Canaanite regions, the majority of which were conquered only relatively late.[51] The all-important *Via maris* ran along the eastern part of the Sharon because its central section was covered with forests and swampy. The continuous chain of Canaanite towns strung along that road were not conquered by the Israelite settlers and, in course of time, they came under the rule of the Philistines and other Sea-Peoples.[52] Further west were only isolated towns which lay by the estuaries of the rivers, e.g. Tell Zarur on the Haderah river.[53] Already in the Late Bronze Period various nomadic tribes entered the area and used the clearings in the Sharon forest and swamps. This situation is indicated in the description of an expedition of Amen-hotep II in the 15th century: he made two raids into the eastern Sharon, westwards of Socoh and Yaḥam and returned with booty which included large flocks and herds. It transpires that Manasseh also penetrated into that region, which lay west of the main branch of the *Via maris*, hence, Hepher's inclusion among the children of Manasseh. This also explains the border line between Ephraim and Manasseh which followed the westward course of the Kanah brook (Josh. 16:8;17:9). The name of the Kanah brook has been preserved to this day in Wadi Qanah which flows southwest of Shechem and joins the Jarkon west of Aphek, on the northern border of the tribe of Dan (Josh. 19:46). The entire Sharon was thus included in Manasseh's territory reflecting the process of settlement in this region. The chain of towns along the *Via maris* could not be con-quered during the first phases of the Settlement, but the area west of them was penetrated by Manassehite families who absorbed the isolated Canaanite settlements.

The eastern section of the border between Ephraim and Manasseh exhibits a similar phenomenon in the Jordan Valley. From the neighborhood of Shechem the border runs south-east to Naarah and Jericho (Josh. 16:7) where it joins Benjamin's border (Josh. 18:12). Hence the western Jordan Valley was also considered Manasseh's territory, while Ephraim's early tribal inheritance was confined to the hill-country.

The northward expansion of the clans of Manasseh to the Plain of Jezreel and beyond it, apparently took place at about the same time.[54] The story of Gideon attests to the penetration of part of Abiezer the Menassehite into Issachar's area north of the Plain of Jezreel, in the neighborhood of Gibeath-hamoreh and Mount Tabor. The tribe of Manasseh claimed for itself the Canaanite towns in the Plain of Jezreel: Beth-shean, Ibleam, Taanach and Megiddo (Josh. 7:11; Jud. 1:27), which had not been conquered by the Israelite tribes. At the beginning these regions were considered as belonging to the Galilean tribes, therefore the remark: "And Manasseh had in Issachar and in Asher Beth-shean and its towns" (Josh. 17:11).

The absorption of the Canaanite towns and the tribe's expansion in extensive and fertile regions gave Manasseh the supremacy in the hill-country of Ephraim. The tribe bore at first the name of its chief clan which was Machir. The Song of Deborah does not mention yet Manasseh, but counts Machir along with Ephraim and Benjamin (Jud. 5:14).[55] Manasseh, Joseph's firstborn — and Machir, Manasseh's firstborn — had the prerogative over the entire tribal inheritance of the House of Joseph, which explains the distinction "For the children of Ephraim in the midst of the inheritance of the children of Manasseh" (Josh. 16:9) and the position of the towns of Ephraim "among the cities of Manasseh" (Josh. 17:9).[56] However, in the course of time Manasseh's diverse composition resulted in its splitting up and weakening, and following the migration of parts of the tribe to nearby areas — particularly Machir's emigration to Transjordan — the seniority passed to Ephraim. Already in Gideon's story (Jud. 6–8) the family of Abiezer belongs to Manasseh and not to Machir, and Ephraim appears as the tribe enjoying supreme authority. Their position is illustrated by the fact that they blamed sharply Gideon for having undertaken a military operation without consulting them.

Ephraim's process of settlement was quite different from that of Manasseh. Their tribal inheritance extended over the southern and higher section of the Ephraim mountains (in the wider sense). The region had but a few unimportant Canaanite towns which were conquered and destroyed and

Israelite settlements built on their ruins. The Bible relates that the House of Joseph destroyed Canaanite Beth-el (Jud. 1:22 ff.) which was confirmed by the excavations made there. After a short while a typical Israelite settlement rose on the site.[57] At Shiloh an Israelite settlement had been built during the early stages of the Settlement on débris of early Middle Bronze II Period habitation.[58] The town of Tappuah at the northern boundary of Ephraim's inheritance was not conquered at the beginning, neither did it assimilate to the tribal framework as we know from the fate of its land: "The land of Tappuah belonged to Manasseh; but Tappuah on the border of Manasseh belonged to the children of Ephraim" (Josh. 17:8). It appears that the town held out a while although the lands belonging to it had already been occupied by the children of Manasseh on their southward expansion; in the end, the town itself fell into the hands of the tribe of Ephraim.

Ephraim's tribal lot therefore included only the mountain region and had a continuous and uniform Israelite population. It was this fact which raised it to a superior position among the Israelite tribes at the time of the Judges.

Benjamin, the southernmost tribe of the House of Joseph, occupied at the beginning the cramped area between Beth-el in the north and Jebusite Jerusalem in the south. The south-western district of this area was owned by the Horite cities of the Gibeonites,[59] which had accepted Israelite rule. This region was considered Benjamin's inheritance, but the Gibeonite cities had not been accepted into the tribal framework so that their inhabitants had an inferior status (Josh. 9:23). The Israelite tribe settled in their vicinity and dominated the highway going up from Jerusalem to Beth-el and particularly the passes to the Judean Wilderness in the east and the area beyond, down to the neighborhood of Jericho and the Jordan. In this place were excavated two tells which had first been settled in the 13th–12th centuries: Gibeah (Gibeath Benjamin) and Tell en-Naṣbeh (apparently Mizpeh), and the pottery found there was characteristic of the beginning of the Israelite Settlement.[60] The archeological survey proved that in this period a continuous chain of small settlements had been set up between them, such as Ramah, Geba, Michmash, etc. This area of settlement was crowded into the space between Jerusalem in the south, the Gibeonite cities in the south-west and Ephraim in the north. For that reason the Benjamite clans spread westwards — in the northern Coastal Plain to the surroundings of Aijalon, Gath-Gittaim,[61] Ono and Lod (I Chron. 8:12–13), as well as migrated to Gilead (cf. below the discussion of the Transjordan tribes). As a result of its central position, its connections with various tribes and its military and colonizing importance, this small tribe was destined to play a decisive role in the establishment of the United Israelite Monarchy.

3. *The Galilean Tribes.* Five of the Israelite tribes settled in Galilee: Zebulun in the south-west of Lower Galilee; Issachar — in the south-east of Lower Galilee and in part of the Plain of Jezreel; Asher — in the west of both Lower and Upper Galilee; Naphtali — to the east of it; Dan — at the foot of Mount Hermon, at the northern end of the Jordan Valley.

The Galilean tribes were separated from the tribes inhabiting the hill-country of Ephraim by the enclave of Canaanite towns in the Plain of Jezreel. These towns were considered as belonging to Manasseh, but as we have already noted, most of them: Beth-shean, Ibleam, Taanach, Megiddo, etc. as far as Dor on the Carmel coast were not conquered in the early stages of the Settlement. This chain of large and well established Canaanite cities bordered on the towns of the Plain of Acco in the west, and the towns of the northern Jordan Valley in the east. It was in these towns that the main Canaanite power was concentrated at the time of the Judges, as we read: "The Canaanite on the east and to the west" (Josh. 11:3) or more precisely "And the Canaanite dwelleth by the sea, and along by the side of the Jordan" (Num. 13:29). In Deborah's war the Canaanite army with its nine hundred chariots, concentrated in this area, where it could rely on fortified cities. After the Israelite victory we do not hear of their being conquered either, but recent excavations at Taanach have established that the city was completely destroyed in about 1125 B.C.E.[62]

The Canaanite plain cut off the Galilean tribes from the other tribes and the isolation seems to have been very real at the beginning of the Settlement, but with the passage of time and the increased Israelite penetration of the Plain of Jezreel this situation changed. Lower Galilee, a region of extensive and fertile valleys became a center of Israelite settlement. Most of it was uninhabited forest land until the Israelite period, with the exception of the strips along the important highways which ran through Lower Galilee: a) One of the main branches of the international *Via maris* coming from Megiddo passed between Gibeath-hamoreh and Mount Tabor and went through the Horns of Hittin (Qarn Ḥaṭṭin) to the north of the Sea of Galilee. On this route we find two important Canaanite towns: Anaharath (Tell el-Murkharkhash) and the tell of Qarn Ḥaṭṭin which might be Shemesh Adam of the Egyptian sources — the biblical Adamah; b) The road that cuts across the width of Lower Galilee and connects the Jordan Valley with the Plain of Acco. This is the Darb el-Ḥawarnah that passes between the valley of Jabneel and the valley of Beth-nethophah.[63] Along this line we know also a few tells from the Canaanite period, e.g. Jabneel (Tell en-Na'am), and Adamim[64] (et-Tell, above Khirbet ed-Dāmya) in the valley of Jabneel and Hannathon (Tell el-Baydawiyya) in the valley of Beth-nethophah.

The Galilean tribes also began by settling in uninhabited regions separated by Canaanite strips. Of the tribes discussed, Issachar dwelt between the valley of Jabneel and the valley of Beth-shean, and between the Jordan Valley and the valley of Chesulloth at the foot of Mount Tabor. Zebulun's settlements extended from here to the Plain of Acco in the west and to the valley of Beth-nethophah in the north. Naphtali got as far south as the valley of Jabneel and the valley of Beth-nethophah, which is also Asher's south-eastern border. It results that the tribes first occupied the empty regions between the Canaanite strips which they conquered in the course of time and annexed to their tribal lots. That is the reason why the borders between the tribes pass just through the valleys. Thus, the southern border of Naphtali runs through the valley of Jabneel. The border between Issachar and Zebulun ran along the Plain of Jezreel and the valley of Chesulloth. Places in the Beth-nethophah valley appear at the border between Zebulun and Asher.

The borders of three of the Galilean tribes Naphtali, Zebulun and Issachar met at Mount Tabor. Holy Mount Tabor apparently served as a kind of border sanctuary, perhaps as a common amphictionic center. Moses' blessing to Zebulun and Issachar may be an allusion to it: "They shall invite their kin to the mountain, where they offer sacrifices of success" (Deut. 33:19). These tribes were powerful at the beginning of the Settlement, a fact proved by Deborah's war. Of the Galilean tribes only Naphtali, Zebulun and Issachar fought in it, and they concentrated their forces before the battle on Mount Tabor.

The development of the tribes and their relationship to the neighboring Canaanite inhabitants were to a large extent governed by the specific circumstances of each tribal area.

Asher seems to have been the first to occupy his inheritance. Asher's name appears in Egyptian topographical lists of the north of the country from the time of Seti I (ca. 1300).[65] From the time of Ramses II we have evidence not only of Asher's existence, but even of the establishment of a town in Galilee called Gath-Asher, apparently J/Gath, to the north-east of Acco. It also appears that Asher dwelt a certain time in the hill-country of Ephraim, before going up to his permanent inheritance (cf. above). Asher's towns which can be identified with certainty are: Kabul, the above-mentioned Gath-Asher, Abdon,[66] Kanah, all of which are situated on the western slopes of Lower and Upper Galilee. It appears that the tribe's early inheritance was situated in the hinterland of the Canaanite towns of the Plain of Acco and Tyre. It is not surprising that the tribe failed to conquer the large and well established Canaanite cities in this region (Jud. 1:31), but that it fell under their influence very soon and its residence on the sea-coast was bought at the price of a certain degree of servitude (Jud. 5:17). This explains the remark: "But the Asherites dwelt among the Canaanites." Neither does the Bible mention that in the course of time the Canaanites became Asher's tributaries, a development related about most of the other tribes. Only after Deborah's war, the weakening of the Canaanite cities, and the rise in importance of the Israelite tribal league does Asher consolidate and its name is favorably mentioned in Gideon's war (Jud. 6:35).

Issachar shared a similar fate. This tribe was compressed within the limits of a small district surrounded and isolated by powerful Canaanite towns. Here too we have evidence from the end of the 14th century, relating that at the time of Seti I different tribes, among them "*'Prw* from the mountain of *Yrmt*" which is near Beth-shean, penetrated the district (cf. above). The convenient ridge of hills between the valley of Beth-shean and the valley of Jabneel was, apparently, the first settlement center of the tribe. Various settlements such as Jarmuth (Remeth), En-haddah, Hapharaim, Shahazim, Beth-shemesh, etc. (Josh. 19:19–22) were founded in that area.

Several towns in the Plain of Jezreel counted as belonging to Issachar, e.g.: Shunem, Chesulloth, Jezreel and perhaps Kishion (Josh. 19:18–20). Jacob's blessing relates the circumstances governing the settlement in this region: "Issachar is a strong-boned ass, crouching among the sheepfolds. When he saw how good was security, and how pleasant was the country, he bent his shoulder to the burden, and became a toiling serf" (Gen. 49:14–15). It results that this tribe acquired its settlements in a section of the Plain of Jezreel under conditions of bondage to the Canaanite cities, and it seems that the origins of its name is *īsh sakār* (hired man-labourer). Issachar penetrated into the plain in the area Jezreel-Shunem in a narrow section, between Gibeath-hamoreh and Gilboa. Information concerning the bringing of Hebrew tribes to this area appears already in the Tell el-Amarna Letters.[67] In one of his letters Biridiya, King of Megiddo, writes: ... Let the king be informed concerning his servant and concerning his city. Behold, I am working in the town of Shunama, and I bring men of the corvée, but behold, the governors who are with me do not as I [do]: they do not work in the town of Shunama, and they do not bring men for the corvée, but I alone bring men for the corvée from the town of Yapu . . ." From another letter we know that Shunem was destroyed sometime earlier by Lab'ayu, King of Shechem, and at Pharaoh's command the vacuum created in that place was filled by corvées so that the soil did not remain fallow and the Egyptian treasury deficitary. Part of this corvée was brought from the town of Yapu, which is apparently Josephus' Yafa near Nazareth, ἰαφα (Wars, ii, 20:6; iii, 7:3), i.e., Japhia on the border of Zebulun and Issachar (Josh. 19:12).

Zebulun settled between the north-western end of the Plain of Jezreel and the valley of Beth-nethophah. This district of wooded hills, where part of the forests stands to this day in the vicinity of Bethlehem-Alonim, became the center of the tribe. One of the "lesser" judges, Ibzan, lived in Bethlehem (Jud. 12:8 ff.). The absorption of the Canaanite cities within its borders — Shimron (Simeon) and Jokneam in the Plain of Jezreel on one hand, and Hannathon in the valley of Beth-nethophah on the other — represented no doubt a second stage in its settlement. From the words of Jacob's blessing ("Zebulun shall dwell by the seashore; he shall be a haven for ships, and his flank shall rest on Sidon," Gen. 49:13) and Moses' blessing ("For they draw from the riches of the sea, and the hidden hoards of the sand," Deut. 33:19) it appears that at a certain time the tribe had expanded also westwards in the Plain of Acco, and according to that view this is the place where to seek the two cities of Kitron and Nahalol which were not conquered by the children of Zebulun (Jud. 1:30) and which have not been identified to this day.

Naphtali,[68] the largest and strongest of the Galilean tribes, settled in central Galilee[69] and on the eastern slopes of its hills. In the south its territory extended as far as the valley of Jabneel, Mount Tabor and the valley of Beth-nethophah. In the north the tribe extended its area as far as the Upper Galilee at the very beginning of its settlement. Archeological survey[70] has shed here an interesting light on the development of the settlement.

The highest mountains of Upper Galilee are to be found in the south where they reach a height of more than 3500 feet. They slope northwards forming a mountainous tableland with an average height of 1500–2000 feet which is crossed by several deep rivers. The northern part of Upper Galilee is more fertile, being blessed with wider stretches of arable land and plenty of springs. Even at present the population is much denser there than in the southern part of the district. These conditions determined the character of the early settlement as the archeological survey has proved. It transpires that only the northern part was quite densely populated in the Canaanite period, while the southern part was covered with forest till the Iron Age when it began to be settled. The border between these two parts ran approximately along the brook of Kezib (Wadi Qurn).

In the southern part of Upper Galilee was discovered a dense network of small settlements which had been established at the beginning of the Iron Age, in ca. the 13th and 12th centuries. A distinct type of pottery was found in these settlements, different from the contemporary pottery in the southern parts of the country. All these facts have led to the following two conclusions:

(a) The settlement in the forest covered and difficult area of southern Upper Galilee shows that at the beginning of the settlement, the Israelites were unable to penetrate into the Canaanite regions of northern Upper Galilee. Therefore the Israelite and the Canaanite population lived here also side by side for some time. Only when the Israelite population grew stronger did it spread northwards, which necessarily led to armed conflicts with the Canaanite population living there.

(b) The tradition of the distinct pottery, which apparently originated in the north, proves that at least a part of these tribes had started living in the north at an earlier date, imitating the craftmanship of the neighboring Canaanite areas.[71]

Thus, to begin with, the tribe of Naphtali settled in the afforested land that included the central and eastern part of Lower Galilee and the southern part of Upper Galilee. Only after heavy fighting with the Canaanites — Deborah's war and the war at the Waters of Merom — did it expand north and east conquering the rich Canaanite districts of Upper Galilee and the northern Jordan Valley. The tribe gained control of the north-eastern branch of the international *Via maris* and occupied extensive, densely populated areas. From the long list of fortified cities situated in Naphtali's tribal lot (Josh. 19:35 ff.) it looks as if nearly all of them were former Canaanite cities, e.g. Chinnereth (Tell el-'Oreimeh), Adamah (Qarn Ḥaṭṭin?) Hazor (Tell Waqāṣ) and Kedesh (Tell Qades). Beth-shemesh and Beth-anath, which were conquered at a later stage (Jud. 1:33; Josh. 19:38), were apparently situated in the heart of Canaanite Upper Galilee.[72]

Dan's settlement in the north, after its failure to settle in the Coastal Plain in the south, was altogether different. This is the only clear case in which we know of a settlement that began with the conquest of Laish, a Canaanite town which was given the name of the tribe. This city of Dan became the center of the settling tribe,[73] and Laish-Dan was identified with Tell el-Qaḍi, in the north of the Huleh Valley, at the foot of Mount Hermon, near one of the sources of the Jordan. The tribe succeeded in gaining control of this area blessed with fertile soil, plenty of water and a pleasant climate, ". . . And behold, it is very good . . . the land is large . . . a place where there is no want, it hath every thing that is in the earth" (Jud. 18:9–10). This conquest was seemingly facilitated by specific political circumstances to which the Bible alludes when relating that Danites ". . . came to Laish, and saw the people that were therein, how they dwelt in security, after the manner of the Sidonians, quiet and secure . . . and they were far from the Sidonians" (Jud. 18:7), as well as in another passage which says that the Danites ". . . came unto Laish, unto a people quiet and secure, and smote them with the edge of the sword; and they burnt the city with fire. And there was no deliverer, because it was far from Zidon . . ." (Jud. 18:27–28). This verse alludes to connections between Canaanite Laish and Sidon which could not come to its aid on account of the distance. According to one view, this tribe became also attached to the Sidonian cities after a short time, and it was due to this circumstance that it maintained itself in its small but rich tribal lot; it seems to be in this spirit that must be understood the censure expressed in the Song of Deborah: "And Dan, why doth he sojourn by the ships?" (Jud. 5:17).[74]

In spite of the separate development of the Galilean tribes and the existence of a Canaanite enclave in the Plain of Jezreel the barrier existing between them and the House of Joseph was neither so deep nor so full of consequences as was the case with the southern tribes. This was due to a number of reasons: a) The continuous northwards expansion of the population of the hill-country of Ephraim which began with the ascent of the children of Asher. It has been suggested that at least part of the tribe of Issachar also came from the hill-country of Ephraim. The northward expansion of the families of Manasseh, from beyond the Plain of Jezreel, and the Danites' migration from the south have been discussed already. This continuous stream certainly helped to preserve the connection between the blocks of tribes; b) The already mentioned succession of settlements in the narrow part of the Plain of Jezreel, in the neighborhood of Jezreel-Shunem. Even though the Issacharites dwelt there at first under the protection of the Canaanites, they doubtlessly acted as a bridge between the tribes, and this link grew stronger as the Canaanite cities declined. There existed apparently a second bridge in the neighborhood of Jokneam, in the narrow space between the hills of Lower Galilee and the Carmel range, where the borders of Zebulun, Asher and Manasseh met. The fact that Jokneam is not mentioned among the unconquered cities of the Plain of Jezreel (Josh. 17:11; Jud. 1:27) seems to prove that it had fallen into the hands of the settling tribes at an early stage; c) The Galilean tribes as well as the Joseph tribes had to resist the pressure of the Canaanite cities of the Plain of Jezreel, so that they united in fighting them. In the decisive battle of Deborah's war three Galilean tribes and three tribes from the hill-country of Ephraim fought side by side. The common dangers and war no doubt strengthened the ties between the two groups of tribes.

4. *The Tribes across the Jordan.* The process of the settlement of the Israelite tribes in Transjordan[75] has grown clearer in the light of the special function this region filled in the history of the country as explained by archeological survey[76] and the Egyptian sources.

Transjordan has two contradictory characteristics which played a decisive part in its history:

(a) It is a spacious land, rich in comparison with Canaan to the west. The Jordan Valley, especially its eastern side, is a plain well irrigated by the many brooks which run into the river making it adequate for agriculture. ". . . how well watered was the whole plain of the Jordan, . . . like the garden of the Lord, like the land of Egypt" (Gen. 13:10). The Transjordanian ridge which rises high above the deep Jordan Valley forms an extensive and convenient tableland which is blessed with abundant rainfall due to its altitude and inclination. Moreover, an important international road, called "The King's highway" in the Bible (Num. 20:17; 21:22), ran the whole length of Transjordan from the south to the north.

(b) Transjordan is a district bordering on the Arabian-Syrian Desert, the biblical land of the *Children of Kedem*, which has since times immemorial suffered under the frequent invasions of the desert marauders. This is why the history of Transjordan displays extreme and sudden changes of fortune never witnessed in western Canaan. Periods when a network of dense settlements covered the mountain heights and the Jordan Valley prospered greatly alternated with century-long periods of destruction and absence of permanent settlement in most of the country, turning Transjordan into an abode of nomad shepherds.

Such a change took place in Transjordan about the 13th century, in the transitional period from the Bronze to the Iron Age. In the 20th century B.C.E. the Canaanite population, which had flourished in most of Transjordan in the later centuries of the third millennium B.C.E., was overtaken by a sudden calamity that caused its destruction. The destruction did not include the Bashan nor the northern Jordan Valley where permanent settlements continued to exist in the south, as far as the neighborhood of Irbid, some 15 km south of the Jarmuk. Recent excavations carried out at Zaphon, some 50 km south of Lake Chinnereth, at Tell Deir 'Ālla, probably Succoth in the Jabbok valley, and near Rabbath Ammon revealed habitation of the Late Bronze Period. Yet these finds do not change basically the fact that extensive areas of central and southern Transjordan were on the whole uninhabited during the centuries which preceded the Israelite's settlement and only on the eve of their penetration did various Hebrew tribes enter this region, establishing the kingdoms of Ammon, Moab and Edom. Politically the whole of central and southern Transjordan was considered an uninhabited region that was not included within the boundaries of Canaan, which had been an Egyptian province since the 15th century B.C.E. This situation is clearly expressed in the outline of Canaan's borders (Num. 34), and in many other passages in the Bible.

The history of the Israelite penetration in Transjordan bears also the characteristics of a process of settlement in a border district. When the Israelite tribes first penetrated there they found extensive tracts of land fit for settlement and expansion; nevertheless the area always remained a border district, incidental to Canaan, the final goal of the tribes. This view is emphatically expressed in the story of the altar built by the Transjordan tribes (Josh. 22:9 ff.) ". . . In the forefront of the land of Canaan in the region about the Jordan."[77] In answer to the protest of the tribes settled in western Canaan, the Reubenites and Gadites[78] pointed out that their intention had been to erect an altar to the Lord as evidence of the connection existing between them and the rest of the tribes, in spite of their dwelling outside the land of Canaan; ". . . In time to come your children might speak unto our children, saying: What have ye to do with the Lord, the God of Israel? for the Lord hath made the Jordan a border between us and you, ye children of Reuben and children of Gad . . ." (Josh. 22:24–25).[79]

In spite of the fact that their settlement included large areas, the Transjordan tribes did not establish a separate unit, but remained border tribes which needed the protection of their western brethern. Yet, they filled the vital function of an economic, political and spiritual hinterland for the western tribes, and northern Gilead in particular served as an extensive area for the settlement of the excess population from the west.

According to the Bible the three tribes, Reuben, Gad and the half tribe of Manasseh settled in Transjordan at the beginning of the Conquest. This view actually reflected the situation of the settlement in Transjordan at the end of the period of the Judges; however, in its beginning the process of settling was more complicated and not restricted to a single uniform stage.

The first tribes to settle in Transjordan were Gad and Reuben. The settlement of the half tribe of Manasseh in northern Gilead belongs to a later stage, being the result of the unification of various clans that moved from western Canaan[80] to this region. The biblical passages which tell of early negotiations with the Transjordan tribes mention frequently only Gad and Reuben (e.g. Num. 32:1 ff.; Josh. 22:25); hence the half tribe of Manasseh joined them as a late addition. Decisive evidence for this process is brought by the Song of Deborah which mentions Machir among the tribes of the House of Joseph in the hill-country of Ephraim (Jud. 5:14). Here is proof that the migration of the tribe to Transjordan and Machir's becoming the father of Gilead belong to a later stage.

The description of Gad's inheritance can be understood only in the light of that tribe's settlement before the settling of northern Gilead. In the north, Gad's inheritance extended as far as Mahanaim on the Jabbok,[81] but did not include the Gilead regions ('Ajlun) to the north of the Jabbok. However, in the Jordan Valley Gad's territory extended northwards along the entire eastern bank of the river ". . . Unto the uttermost part of the sea of Chinnereth" (Josh. 13:27). This situation originated in the period when most of the forest-covered 'Ajlun area was still uninhabited, and the whole inhabited Jordan Valley was considered Gad territory despite the fact that the center of its inheritance lay south of the Jabbok. We know that in the Tell Amarna period there existed several Canaanite towns in northern Transjordan among which figured Zaphon and Peḥel. Zaphon which is mentioned among the cities of Gad (Josh. 13:27) appears also as one of the families of this tribe (Gen. 46:16 [Ziphion]; Num. 26:15). This fact implies the absorption of the Canaanite city into the framework of Gad[82] which was the strongest tribe in Transjordan at the beginning of the settlement.

The relations between Reuben and Gad were rather complicated and it is doubtful if they both settled at the same time. Gad was the chief tribe in southern Transjordan before the terms Gad and Gilead began to overlap to some extent.[83] According to Josh. 13:15 ff. the tribe of Reuben dwelt in an area between the Arnon which is in Moab's territory in the south, and Heshbon in the north, while Gad occupied the region north of Heshbon. Yet, according to Num. 32:33 ff. the Gadites lived in the whole of southern Gilead and Reuben occupied only a certain part of it which consisted mainly of Heshbon and its surrounding towns. For example, Dibon, which Josh. 13:17 mentions among Reuben's cities, is here enumerated among Gad's cities (Num. 32:34), and in another verse it is even called Dibon-Gad (Num. 33:45). Also Ataroth, 14 km north-west of Dibon and which apparently has to be identified with Khirbet 'Aṭṭarus, is here mentioned among Gad's town's (Num. 32:34), a fact which is confirmed by the Mesha stele where we read: "And the men of Gad dwelt in the country of Ataroth from times immemorial."

In contrast to Gad about whose dwelling in western Canaan we find no allusion at all, there exists clear evidence of connections between Reuben, Judah and Benjamin. On the border between Judah and Benjamin, west of Jericho stands ". . . the Stone of Bohan the son of Reuben," in the vicinity of the valley of Achor (Josh. 15:6; 18:17). This is the place where Achan the son of Carmi of the tribe of Judah was stoned (Josh. 7), but Carmi is also one of Reuben's chief families (Gen. 46:9; Num. 26:5–6; I Chron. 5:3).

According to one view Reuben originally tried to settle in western Canaan and migrated to Transjordan after failing in this attempt. Since most areas there were already occupied by Gad, Reuben was pushed to the periphery of the land, remaining a semi-nomadic tribe living on the fringe of the desert. It is therefore surprising that Heshbon and its surrounding towns are expressly reckoned among Reuben's cities, the conquest of this area having constituted the Israelites' principal expedition of the Conquest (cf. above). Hence it seems more likely that Reuben settled in this area at the time of the Conquest,[84] but that its expansion was restricted by the Gadites who had occupied the neighboring areas earlier, particularly the land of Jaazer north of Heshbon. Gad apparently belongs to the early wave of migration which arrived in the 14th century and that is why he and his brother Asher are reckoned among the sons of Leah's handmaids.[85] It may be that the "three hundred years" of Israelite settlement prior to Jephthah the Gileadite (Jud. 11:26) which bring us to the 14th century refer to Gad's settlement. Perhaps the tradition concerning the tribe's route of migration along the "King's highway" in the heart of Edom and Moab, a route which also passed through Dibon-Gad (Num. 33:44 ff.), is a reference to that tribe's penetration. The tribe of Gad did not migrate from its early inheritance as did the tribe of Asher in the west, but succeeded in establishing itself in this region in spite of the penetration of new elements. This is, apparently, the reason why one part of Reuben's families was forced to migrate to western Canaan, and another part to the eastern border of the district.[86]

The settlement of various clans from among the tribes in northern Gilead was a slow and prolonged process.[87] As we said, this region served mainly as a place of settlement for the excess population of the western tribes, except for the Galilean tribes who expanded northwards.

All this evidence is naturally fragmentary and incidental, pointing merely to the general process, but without enabling us to establish a precise and complete picture of the circumstances. The passages mentioning the destruction of the "fugitives of Ephraim" in the story of Jephthah (Jud. 12:1, 4–5) seem to prove that Ephraimite families did settle in Gilead; possibly the forest of Ephraim, north of Mahanaim (II Sam. 18:6), also represents an allusion to this settlement. We have evidence of the close relations between Benjamin and the neighborhood of Jabesh-gilead in the story of the Benjamite men who kidnapped women of Jabesh-gilead (Jud. 21) and Saul's connection with this city (I Sam. 11:1–13).[88]

Most of the information in this matter is contained in the genealogical lists which relate marriages, family connections, and in which certain family names occur with both western and eastern tribes. The families of Benjamin, Shuppim (Shephupham) Huppim (Huphamites) (Num. 26:39; I Chron. 7:12) are also mentioned in connection with Machir, the father of Gilead (I Chron. 7:15). Similarly we find there existed family relations between Benjamin and Gad: Ezbon the son of Bela the son of Benjamin (I Chron. 7:7) is also mentioned among the Gadites (Gen. 46:16).

We know of the family connections between Judah and Gilead from I Chron. 2:21: "And afterward Hezron went in to the daughter of Machir the father of Gilead; whom he took to wife when he was three score years old; and she bore him Segub. And Segub begot Jair, who had three and twenty cities in the land of Gilead."[89] Jair is generally considered Manasseh's son (Num. 32:41; Deut. 3:14) and a large district in northern Gilead was called by his name Havvoth-jair.[90] This refers apparently to settlements of semi-nomads who lived at the beginning in camps of tents and huts which developed gradually into towns. Assyrian inscriptions from the 13th–11th centuries mention an extensive tribal association called Ya'uri or Ya'ri which reached the neighborhood of the Euphrates[91] during its wanderings and it is quite possible that part of their clans settled in Gilead. It is assumable that these are the earliest elements which penetrated and occupied this region and that at a later time, following the migration of various Israelite families to northern Gilead, they intermarried and were finally absorbed among the Israelite tribes so that Jair came to be considered Manasseh's son.

Machir's children represent the weightiest settlement in Gilead. The Song of Deborah still mentions Machir's name instead of Manasseh's among the tribes of the hill-country of Ephraim (Jud. 5:14). Therefore the tribe's main migration to Transjordan could not have taken place before the 12th century. At the beginning Machir was the strongest clan in the northern hill-country of Ephraim and it was only after the migration of most of it to Transjordan that Manasseh rose to the leadership of the western tribe. Machir became the father of Gilead and since his was the strongest family, the rest of the families and clans living in Gilead were attributed to him after a certain lapse of time. However, this process took place at a late stage of the period of the Judges, after the crystallization of the Covenant of the Twelve Tribes, which prevented the formation of any additional tribe. Since the center of influence continued to be represented by the western tribes, Manasseh became in the course of time the father of the tribe and Machir, the father of Gilead, became his son. Among the various families which were attributed to them, some lived in western Canaan (Abiezer, Helek, Asriel, Shechem, Shemida, Hepher, Tirzah, etc.) and some in Gilead (Huppim, Shuppim, Peresh, Sheresh, Ulam, Rekem and Bedan). This is an interesting example of the formation of a genealogical list from the complicated process of the various stages of the Settlement. We generally learn only the final results, but are unaware of the early stages.

The Israelite settlement in northern Transjordan reached the zenith of its expansion with Nobah's conquest of Kenath (Num. 32:42) which has apparently to be identified with Qanawāt on the slopes of the Hauran mountains. However, Nobah's genealogy is not clear, in spite of his being included in the description of the final conquests of Manasseh, neither are the circumstances of its expension known. This is probably also the stage at which the border of the Israelite settlement in northern Transjordan extended as far as Hermon and Salcha, which is apparently Salkhad south of Qanawāt (Deut. 3:8 ff.; Josh. 12:5; 13:11; I Chron. 5:11), but the areas north and east of the Jarmuk fell very soon into the hand of the Arameans (I Chron. 2:23).

C. The Outcome of the Settlement

The biblical scheme of the tribal lots reflects the territorial picture which had emerged at the end of the main process of the Settlement.[92] From all that has been said so far the results clearly show that this scheme is based on actual achievements on the one hand, and on still unrealized territorial aspirations of the tribes, on the other. This is particularly noticeable in the description of Judah's southern border (Josh. 15:2–4) which is identical with Canaan's southern border (Num. 34:3–5), but which claimed a desert region in the south outside the tribe's territory. In the east the tribal lots extended to the Jordan, this being the eastern border of Canaan (Num. 34:12), in the west to the sea — Canaan's western border (Num. 34:6), though, in actual fact, not a single tribe achieved continuous settlement on the coast, and large areas of Canaan were considered "land that yet remaineth," i.e. to be conquered. For example, Judah's northern border extended westwards toward the sea as far as the Philistine area, but actually there was no Israelite settlement in that region. Only the northern border of Canaan was indefinite because it ran far north at the end of the Lebanon range, and through the Lebanon Valley, (Beqa'), a fact which might account for Naphtali and Asher's northern borders not being outlined.

The Transjordan tribes are not included in the border scheme of the tribal inheritances, since that region lay beyond the borders of Canaan. Their places of settlement are mentioned first (Josh. 13) and the division of the Land of Canaan among the rest of the tribes is dealt with after.

Regarding the areas which were actually settled, the description of the tribal territories reflects therefore the reality as it was at the end of the main phase of the Settlement, while the changes which took place later are not taken into account. Dan's tribal lot is located in the south, but we saw that part of the tribe migrated to the north. Following the wars with the Canaanites in the north, a certain shifting of positions seems to have taken place: families of Manasseh pressed northward and seized areas in Issachar and Asher (Josh. 17:11); while Zebulun apparently spread into the Plain of Acco as far as the coast (Gen. 49:13; Deut. 33:18–19). This development proves that the tribal areas had crystallized in an earlier period and we see that in the 12th and 11th centuries the borders of the various tribal territories did not undergo any far reaching changes except for an increasing migration to northern Gilead.

On the other hand, we have clear evidence of various territories which withstood the pressure of the settling tribes. These districts are mentioned in the description of the different tribal lots and they are also concentrated in Judges 1. Judah did not conquer the Jebusites who inhabited Jerusalem (Josh. 15:63); but according to Judges 1:21 it was Benjamin who did not succeed in conquering the city according to the border scheme which placed Jerusalem in Benjamin. Ephraim did not conquer Gezer (Josh. 16: 10; Jud. 1:29). Dan did not inherit the towns of the coastal plain; Har-heres (Beth-shemesh?), Aijalon and Shaalbim (Jud. 1:34–35). Manasseh did not inherit Bet-shean, Ibleam, Taanach and Megiddo in the Plain of Jezreel,[93] nor Dor on the Carmel coast (Josh. 17:11–12; Jud. 1:27); neither did Zebulun inherit Kitron and Nahalol (Jud. 1:30). However, since these cities have not yet been identified it is not clear what region is referred to. Asher did not inherit Acco, Achzib, Aphek and Rehob[94] in the Plain of Acco, nor Sidon and Ahlab (Mahalab) on the Phoenician coast (Jud. 1:31), while Naphtali did not inherit Beth-shemesh and Beth-anath (Jud. 1:33), which apparently have to be looked for in the north of Canaanite Upper Galilee.

The Bible prefaces the lists of towns and the delimitation of the tribal territories with a general sketch and summary of the "land that yet re-

THE SETTLEMENT OF CANAAN   127

maineth" (Josh. 13:1–6; cf. also Jud. 3:3). The text of this passage is somewhat fragmentary and various attempts have been made to reconstruct it,[95] but its general content is quite clear. The description enumerates all the Philistine territories in the south; the whole of the Canaanite coastal area "unto Aphek to the border of the Amorites." This most probably refers to the Amurru kingdom in the Lebanon region (cf. above), and the Aphek mentioned here is therefore identical with Aphka near the source of the river Ibrahim between Byblos and Lebo-hamath. The passage goes on to mention Gebal (Byblos) the northern frontier of the Canaan which was not conquered and to the east of it:... "All Lebanon, towards the sun-rising, from Baal-gad under Mount Hermon as far as Lebo-hamath," that is to say, the entire eastern part of Lebanon as far as the Valley of Lebanon (Beqaʻ), from Mount Hermon, which is the settlement border of the Transjordan tribes (Deut. 3:8; 4:48; Josh. 11:17; 12:1, 5; 13:11; Jud. 3:3; I Chron. 5:23), to Lebo-hamath which is on the border of Canaan.

We have already discussed the circumstances which prevented the Israelites from penetrating to these areas in the early stages of their settlement. These were extremely fertile, developed, and densely inhabited regions crossed by international trade routes which enriched Canaan and its culture. The Israelite tribes were forced to content themselves mainly with distant and very difficult districts among the mountains. In the absence of land propitious to the creation of settlements they were forced to cut down natural forests and break virgin soil in order to farm.

It is not to be assumed that the Israelite tribes chose to settle the hard way, but the military reality and the local population did not leave them any other alternative (Josh. 17:14 ff.). The task being difficult, their settlement was accompanied by setbacks and trouble. Not all the tribes and clans were able to make such a tremendous effort, though most tribes succeeded in settling in their limited tribal lots.

This process led to far-reaching results in the history of the nation and the country. For the first time in the history of Canaan settlement got the better of many uninhabited areas scattered among the populated districts in the Canaanite period. It is true that during the achievement of the settlement process the blocks of tribes became separated and non-Israelite elements existed in various localities. But in final analysis, there emerged a continuous settlement over the entire country, in the plains as well as in the hill-country, and the conditions so created made for the political and demographical unity of the Land of Israel.

Against this background there developed an original and independent Israelite life and culture. It is doubtful whether such a development would have come about if the Israelites had conquered the rich Canaanite districts right at the beginning. We have one analogy, the Philistines whose settlement began with the conquest of a rich Canaanite area in the southern central plain, and who adopted very quickly the culture and way of life of the conquered whose material culture was superior. It is needless to say that the difference between the settling Israelite tribes and the Canaanites was even bigger. The fact that the Israelites acquired the technical achievements of the Canaanites within a short time, while preserving almost unimpaired their independent way of life and the spiritual values which they had brought with them from the desert, is to be explained in large measure by the compact and separate nature of their settlement.[96]

The necessity to settle in the mountain areas was responsible for the fact that the Israelite occupation became more than a conquest. For the first time the center of gravity of the country moved to the mountain districts creating conditions propitious for the establishment of an independent and strong monarchy.

The conquest of the whole country during the period of the monarchy brought about the establishment of a united state which disposed, for the first time, of a continuous territory buttressed by the strong hinterland of the hilly districts and Transjordan. The result was an increase and strengthening of the country's economic and military resources. The conditions in which the tribes occupied and settled in their respective districts have to be considered one of the decisive factors in the territorial and historical revolution that took place when the land of Canaan became the Land of Israel.

CHAPTER VII

THE PERIOD OF THE JUDGES

by A. Malamat

A. JUDGESHIP AND THE BOOK OF JUDGES

THE COMPLETE LACK of extra-biblical sources directly pertaining to the historical events of the period of the judges compels any survey of this period to be based almost exclusively on the collection of narratives contained in the Book of Judges. Assessment of this book as a historical source is determined by the evaluation of its composition, structure and particularly the manner of its recension.[1] A sharp distinction must be drawn between the actual stories of the judges, which are based on ancient, often tribal traditions, and the historiosophical and pragmatic framework into which they were integrated.[2] The pragmatic-theological (the so-called "deuteronomic") editing of these individual stories is based on two doctrines which largely contradict the historical reality of this period: a) the pan-Israelite concept which elevates tribal events and the scope of a judge's actions to a national level; b) the concept of historical periodicity, which views the events of the period as a series of recurring cycles, each comprising four successive stages: the people's reverting to idolatry and its subsequent oppression, appeal to God and consequent redeliverance, followed by a period of quiescence.[3]

Current Bible criticism has, however, gone too far in considering the background of the events of the period as entirely tribal and local, and the deliverer-judge as the mere leader of a single tribe or even clan. Yet, the historical reality of the time was that generally several tribes were simultaneously affected by foreign pressure, and that relief from it required a common action, the scope of which was beyond the ability of any individual tribe. The authority of the deliverer-judge undoubtedly extended beyond the confines of a single tribe, and thence the relation of a group, or confederation of tribes, to any particular set of events should not be considered as a later amplification under tendentious pan-Israelite influence. Admittedly, this is still far from the biblical image of the judge as an actual pan-Israelite ruler. Furthermore, the periodic appearance of the judges cannot be accepted at face value — excluding *a priori* the simultaneous activity of two or more judges — and certainly not the chronological sequence as arranged by the editor of the Book of Judges.

Following Max Weber, the regime of the judges has been defined as a charismatic leadership, distinct from the other types of legitimate rule — both the traditional (i.e. the patriarchal-tribal) authority and the rational-legal (i.e. bureaucratic) authority.[4] This regime was based on the people's belief in the appearance in time of crisis of a divinely appointed deliverer. Thus the long-recognized theological-psychological nature of charisma finds its sociological-political manifestation as well. The charismatic personality enjoyed an especially close relationship with God, expressed in divine revelations and occasionally accompanied by public performances of miracles. This leadership is characteristically spontaneous and personal, the authority being neither hereditary nor dependent upon social status within the tribe, and it was certainly not supported by any kind of bureaucratic apparatus. A national religious awakening would cause the people to gather around a leader upon whom it became entirely dependent. Hence, government in the period of the judges was characterized by a rather sporadic leadership, stability being achieved only upon the establishment of a monarchy in Israel.

The following are the charismatic deliverer-judges: Othniel, Ehud, Gideon, Deborah, Jephthah and Samson (despite his lack of a popular following), and probably also Shamgar son of Anath (see p. 137). However, the Book of Judges attests to a different sort of judge, to whom no acts of deliverance are attributed and consequently does not possess any charismatic traits. These, today called "minor judges", are five in number: Tola, Jair, Ibzan, Elon and Abdon (Jud. 10:1–5; 12:8–15). Following Klostermann and Alt, biblical criticism has generally assumed that these minor judges were powerful tribal leaders, holding a permanent, pan-Israelite office, and serving as actual jurists and dispensers of law in the period preceding the monarchy. Their terms of office were even thought to have been used in chronological reckoning.[5]

The assertion that while the major judges did not achieve national recognition—notwithstanding their acts of deliverance—it was specifically the minor judges who enjoyed pan-Israelite recognition and authority, is difficult to accept. No easier to accept is the assumption that the deuteronomic editor made the original stories of the deliverer-judge conform with the pattern of the minor judges by attributing to the former pan-Israelite authority, and assuming them to have simply filled the charge of a *shōfēṭ*, i.e. allegedly a mere dispenser of the law. That this concept of a "judge" replaced that of a supposedly archaic "deliverer" (*mōshī'a*) in a late editorial stage of the Book of Judges[6] is equally untenable. Indeed, it is proved by the Mari Texts that as early as the 18th century B.C.E. the West Semitic term *šāpiṭum* (as well as its verbal form) indicated a person of prominent rank within the tribal organization, whose authority exceeded that of a mere justice.[7] The Phoenician (and possibly Ugaritic) *šft* and the Punic "*suffetes*" are also used in the sense of a ruler or magistrate. This is certainly also the case in the Book of Judges, where the term *shōfēṭ* and the verb *shāfāṭ* both refer to a leader of the people, whether a major judge or a minor judge, and such activity indeed included the office of arbitrator and judge in the legal sense of the word.

Actually, the modern sharp distinction between minor and major judges in the Bible should probably be toned down to a mere difference in literary sources drawn upon. While the periodic deeds of the deliverer-judges are presented as folk narrative, the data on the minor judges were drawn from strictly factual sources, e.g. family chronicles containing only such details as the tribal affinity of the judge, his seat of office, the exact duration of his charge, his burial-place and notes on his descendants. An intermediate type is found in Jephthah: the end of his story (Jud. 12:7) gives the details generally associated with the minor judges, yet he was certainly a deliverer-judge. His is not a hybrid historical figure, as some would have it,[8] but simply the outcome of the use of several different literary sources. However, the affinity between the two supposed types of judge is best evidenced in the person of Deborah: as a prophetess she was definitely a charismatic figure, able to rouse the people to war; yet even before that war she was renowned as a judge amongst the Israelites in the mountains of Ephraim (Jud. 4:4–5). The same applies to Joshua: along with his wartime leadership he served as an arbitrator among the tribes, as proved by the case of the House of Joseph complaining about their inheritance (Josh. 17:14 ff.).[9] It is quite possible, on the other hand, that the minor judges also engaged as leaders in actual battle, but no information of their deeds has come down to us.[10] The mention that the first minor judge, Tola son of Puah, "arose to save [*lehōshī'a*] Israel" (Jud. 10:1) is not necessarily a late editorial interpolation: it might even be the original heading of the entire list of minor judges. The case of Jair the Gileadite may support this assumption for several traditions preserved in books of the Bible other than Judges mention his warlike activities in northern Transjordan (Num. 32:41; I Chr. 2:22). It would thus appear that there was no essential difference between major and minor judges, except for the above mentioned variant manner in which they are portrayed in the Book of Judges.

Both types represented the sort of political regime prevailing prior to the monarchy.

While Judges 1, as a chapter, properly belongs to the Conquest cycle (cf. above, the chapter on "The Exodus and Conquest"), the appendixes to the Book of Judges, dealing with Micah's images and the migration of the tribe of Dan (Jud. 17–18), and the episode of the outrage at Gibeah (Jud. 19–21), are of quite a different order. In these chapters there are no judges upon the scene; they were later appended to the book and underwent a redaction oriented on the monarchy, as can be seen from the repeated statement: "In those days there was no king in Israel; every man did that which was right in his own eyes" (Jud. 17:6; 18:1; 19:1; 21:25). These facts, however, still leave us in the dark as to the precise dating of the events related. Arguments have been brought forth to place them at the beginning of the period of the judges, and others to support a date much later in this period, which seems preferable. The Gibeah incident and the subsequent inter-tribal war may be ascribed to the span of time somewhat prior to Saul's kingship, as will be shown below (pp. 161–163 f.). The dating of the Danite migration, culminating in the conquest of the city of Laish, however, remains uncertain, as do the precise factors leading up to this uprooting, whether under Amorite pressure (Jud. 1:34) or because of Philistine oppression, or both (see also p. 136). Without denying the historical substance of this account, it seems to have been a sort of literary copy of a biblical narrative pattern evolved for portraying campaigns of inheritance (which pattern was followed on a much larger, pan-tribal scale, in the Exodus-Conquest cycle).[11] In any event the occurrence of Jonathan the son of Gershom the son of Moses (read thus instead of "Manasseh" in Jud. 18:30), as well as that of Phinehas the son of Elazar the son of Aaron in the subsequent story of the outrage at Gibeah (both, interestingly enough *third* generation priests), do not seem to carry any particular chronological significance, as several scholars have sought (cf. also below note 87).

It transpires from all the above mentioned that the value of the Book of Judges as the framework for an historical and chronological survey is problematic, and some scholars go so far as to doubt the very possibility of exploiting this source for a continuous historical description.[12] Before accepting that the sequence of the stories, as transmitted in the Book of Judges, reflects the actual historical process, additional arguments should be adduced. Due to the shortcomings of this book as a historical source, all other biblical references to this period are of special interest, particularly where such data are independent of the traditions contained in Judges. We shall first mention the citations in other biblical books of events already known from Judges which provide a historical perspective of their evaluation at a later time:

a) Israel's defeat of the Midianites in the days of Gideon, which became a symbol of God's might, is echoed in Isa. 9:3 — "the day of Midian" and 10:26 — "As in the slaughter of Midian at the Rock of Oreb."

b) Abimelech's death at the "tower of Thebez" is referred to by Joab while fighting the Ammonites — "Who smote Abimelech the son of Jerubbesheth? did not a woman cast an upper millstone upon him from the wall, that he died at Thebez? why went ye so nigh the wall?" (II Sam. 11:21). Thus, the manner of Abimelech's death served, in later days, as a classical warning against the dangers of siege warfare.[13]

c) Israel's sin at Gibeah is referred to in Hos. 9:9 — "They have deeply corrupted themselves. As in the days of Gibeah"; and 10:9 — "From the days of Gibeah thou hast sinned, O Israel."
Of particular interest are the data independent of the stories related in Judges which allude to additional details:

d) The prophet Hosea (6:7–9) may allude to the fratricidal war between Gilead and Ephraim in the time of Jephthah. Here, in contrast to the tradition in Judges (which is biased in favor of Gilead), the Ephraimite prophet Hosea takes a clear anti-Gileadite line:[14] "But they at [the city of] Adam [AV: like men] have transgressed the covenant; There they have dealt treacherously against Me. Gilead is a city of them that work iniquity, it is covered with footprints of blood [i.e. the massacre of the Ephraimites]. And as troops of robbers wait for a man, so doth the company of priests; They murder in the way toward Shechem [i.e. the route of flight taken by the Ephraimites], Yea they commit enormity."

e) Samuel in his farewell speech (I Sam. 12:9–11), which is formulated in the same spirit as the pragmatic framework of Judges, lists Israel's oppressors on the one hand and its deliverers on the other, as complementing each other, thus recapitulating the major events of the period of the judges. Unlike the order in Judges, however, the sequence of oppressors is given as: Sisera, the Philistines and Moab; while the deliverers are Jerubbaal (and not Gideon; cf. above, (b), Jerubbesheth), the otherwise unknown Bedan,[15] Jephthah and Samuel himself.

f) Ps. 68:8–15 may contain an allusion to the war of Deborah and the episode of Abimelech:[16] first, the theophany parallel to the Song of Deborah, followed by the victory over the Canaanite kings ("kings of armies flee, they flee"), and mentioning the passive stand of a part of the Israelites ("When ye lie among the sheepfolds", etc.; cf. Jud. 5:16), finally, the mention of Zalmon where Abimelech mustered his army for the attack on Shechem (Jud. 9:48).

g) The most comprehensive survey of the period of the judges is contained in Ps. 83, composed probably in the time of the judges or somewhat later.[17] It first gives a list of Israel's oppressors: "Edom and the Ishmaelites; Moab and the Hagrites; Gebal[18] and Ammon, and Amalek; Philistia with the inhabitants of Tyre" (vv. 7–8). The twinning of these peoples suits the historical reality of the period, since on the one hand nomadic tribes joined at times in the incursions of the Transjordanian nations (cf. below, paragraph C), while on the other hand there were special ties between the Phoenician coast and Philistia. It may be that the continuation: "Assyria [Ashur], also is joined with them" alludes to the campaigns of Tiglath-pileser I to the Lebanon and Phoenicia, and to the initial Assyrian appearance on the horizon of Israel (cf. above, in the chapter "The Egyptian Decline in Canaan . . .," paragraph E). This is followed by mention of the victories over the Canaanites and the Midianites in the days of Deborah and Gideon, adducing additional details about the Midianite defeat at En-dor and Adamah (i.e. the city of Adamah; cf. below, p. 146).

Despite all the shortcomings of the Book of Judges as a historical source, the narratives therein are of great typological value, as a true portrayal of the mode of life and the historical phenomena distinguishing the period under discussion. The same applies to the Book of Ruth, which reflects the situation "in the days when the judges judged" (Ruth 1:1), and throws some light on the relations between Moab and Judah at that time. The original position of the Book of Ruth as an appendix to Judges is still upheld by the canon of the Septuagint, by the writings of Josephus and in the talmudic literature.

Moreover, each episode of the judges describes an encounter with an enemy of particular type: the war against the Canaanites, the country's indigenous population (Deborah and Barak), the conflicts with the nations of Transjordan–Moab and Ammon (Ehud and Jephthah); the inroads of the nomads from the eastern desert (Gideon); and finally the ever-increasing Philistine challenge on the west (the Samson cycle, for which see below the chapter on "The Philistines and their Wars with Israel"). It is interesting to note the absence of any reference to a conflict with the Arameans, who were in the process of settling in Syria and northern Transjordan in the 12th and 11th centuries B.C.E. It is only at the end of the 11th century, with their consolidation in states, that they became Israel's sworn enemy at the time of kings Saul and David.

B. The War of Deborah and Barak Against the Canaanites

The consolidation of the Israelites' power, and their numerical growth at the expense of the indigenous Canaanite population, in increasingly broader areas, led to the greatest and most decisive confrontation during the period of the judges — the war of Deborah and Barak. In contrast to the other wars of the judges, it was against the autochthonous element in Canaan they were pitted in this encounter (the Sea-Peoples may already have participated in it; cf. below), in which the strongly fortified cities, as well as the chariotry of the enemy, played a determinant role. This episode raises serious historical and chronological problems, due to the double tradition, prose and poem, preserved in Chapters 4 and 5 of the Book of Judges and its apparent contradiction with the description of the battle at the waters of Merom, and the utter destruction of Hazor, as related in Joshua, Chapter 11.

The difficulty in the relationship between the war of Deborah and the battle at the waters of Merom "in the days of Joshua" is that both were fought against a wide Canaanite alliance which covered large areas in Galilee and in the adjacent valleys, both headed by Jabin, King of Hazor. It is not the name of this king which presents the difficulty, since this might have been a sort of dynastic name at Hazor.[19] It is inconceivable, however, that Hazor — which was utterly destroyed at the time of Joshua (Josh. 11:10 ff.) as confirmed by archeological evidence — should have played a primary and decisive role in a Canaanite league several generations later. Moreover, the archeological finds indicate that the huge lower city at Hazor was permanently laid waste, and the upper city was not rebuilt until the time of Solomon. In the period of the judges only a poor, open settlement, appears to have been established there by the Israelites (strata XII–XI).[20]

Several suggestions have been made to account for the difficulties raised by these two contradictory traditions. Of these, two warrant special attention:

1) The battle at the waters of Merom and Deborah's war are no more than two closely linked phases of a single armed conflict which proved decisive in the struggle between the Canaanites and the Israelites in the northern part of the country. Quite opposite to the chronological order in the Bible, the war of Deborah represents the first stage in this chain of events, when the kingdom of Hazor was still at the height of its power. The initial defeat of the Canaanite forces in this war was followed by the second and concluding stage — the battle at the waters of Merom which finished

Hazor off and ended Canaanite resistance in the north.[21] In this case, Deborah's war must be considered an integral part of the Conquest cycle and should be dated as early as the second half of the 13th century, since Hazor was destroyed at this time according to the archeological evidence. For the improbability of so high a dating, see below.

2) If the traditional chronological sequence is accepted, we must consider the appearance of Hazor in the story of Deborah, and probably also the name Jabin, as a later interpolation, inspired by the somewhat similar events in the Book of Joshua.[22] Actually, Hazor is only incidentally mentioned together with King Jabin (Jud. 4:2, 17; and cf. I. Sam. 12:9; Ps. 83:10, where either one or the other is mentioned but not both together), whose title in this episode is given as "king of Canaan" (Jud. 4:2, 23–24). This title may have been attributed to Jabin either because Hazor was considered "the head of all those kingdoms" (Josh. 11:10) or because a later King Jabin assumed hegemony over the north of the country. Moreover, neither Hazor nor Jabin fit into the topographical or military picture as it emerges from the story of Deborah. Indeed, at that time the enemies of the Israelites were led by Sisera, an army commander (and only he is mentioned in the Song of Deborah) who dwelt in Harosheth-goiim[23]; also the battle-scene differs here completely from that described in Joshua. It might thus be assumed that the introduction of Jabin and Hazor into the Deborah episode was a tendentious scribal move, telescoping the two fateful battles in the north of the country.

It appears that the war of Deborah should be placed in the middle or the second half of the 12th century B.C.E. It has been argued that the words in the Song of Deborah: "Then fought the kings of Canaan, in Taanach by the *waters* of Megiddo" (Jud. 5:19), imply that Megiddo itself lay in ruins at this time and for this reason the less important Taanach was referred to. In this case, the war of Deborah should best be dated within the occupational gap between the destruction of Megiddo stratum VIIA and the establishment of stratum VIB, i.e. within the third quarter of the 12th century.[24] Whether this archeological-literary correlation is accepted or not, the date itself is also in accord with the results of the recent excavations at Taanach, which prove that the Canaanite town still existed as late as ca. 1125 B.C.E. (cf. Jud. 1:27), after which date there followed a lengthy occupational gap.[25]

Perhaps such a late dating would also fit in well with certain conclusions arrived at from the Song of Deborah. Thus, the song mentions the tribe of Dan between Gilead and Asher (Jud. 5:17), indicating the previous migration of this tribe to its northern habitat. Secondly, there is a reference in the song to Shamgar son of Anath (v. 6) who defeated a band of 600 Philistine warriors (Jud. 3:31).[26] It is not known for sure whether Shamgar was an Israelite or a foreigner.[27] His name as well as his patronymic, and the fact that he is mentioned in the song together with Jael, who was the wife of Heber the Kenite, would suggest his having been a non-Israelite. Even if he was Canaanite, the Israelites seem to have considered him as a God-sent deliverer, since he averted a Philistine threat to them. Had his deed taken place at an early stage of the Settlement, it could be dated no earlier than the beginning of the 12th century, as the Philistines made their appearance in Canaan only in the days of Ramses III (cf. the chapter "The Egyptian Decline in Canaan", paragraph D). Consequently the war of Deborah must be dated later than this.

It would seem that the encounter with the Philistines at that time took place in the northern part of the country, for the Song of Deborah ignores completely the south of the land — including the Philistine area — and because Shamgar's "patronymic" may signify no more than his having originated from Beth-anath, a Canaanite town in Galilee (Jud. 1:33). It has also been suggested that Sisera's name could indicate a relation to the Sea-Peoples.[28] In such a case we would have to assume that already in Deborah's war the Canaanites were led by a new element — the Sea-Peoples, who had penetrated into the north of the country.

As already mentioned, in analyzing the Deborah episode we have two versions before us: the narrative account (Jud. 4) and the Song of Victory (Jud. 5). Such double accounts, prose and poetry, of military victories are found also elsewhere in the Bible (cf. Ex. 14 and 15) and in the Ancient Near East.[29] Deborah's Song is much older than the narrative version and was composed soon after the events related, but the reliability of the prose source cannot be ignored especially since poetic licence plays no part in it, as it does in the song. The prose — despite its present form — still preserves an authentic historical kernel. Though the two sources do not correspond, and seem contradictory at first sight, they may actually complement one another.[30] The outstanding discrepancies between the two — the tribes participating in the battle and the scene of the actual battlefield — are not indicative of two separate, disconnected battles. On the contrary, they are rather depictions of different stages of one and the same battle.

The brunt of the Israelite war of liberation was borne by the tribes of Naphtali and Zebulun, who alone are mentioned in the narrative. They mustered 10,000 warriors, and their commander, Barak son of Abinoam, was himself of the tribe of Naphtali. Also the Song of Deborah attributes special military prowess to these two tribes; "Zebulun is a people that jeoparded their lives unto the death, and Naphtali, upon the high places of the field" (Jud. 5:18). It is no mere accident that just the tribes who dwelt in the hilly districts were particularly disposed toward an uprising. They were less affected by Canaanite pressure since the latter's chariotry could not take the offensive in the hill-country. This indeed is the reason why they attained a certain measure of sovereignty, and tribes such as Zebulun, Naphtali and Ephraim, respectively the House of Joseph, could even exact tribute from the Canaanites living in their midst (cf. Josh. 16:10; Jud. 1:30, 33, 35, as against vv. 27, 31, concerning the lowland districts of Manasseh and Asher; while Issachar is conspicuously absent from the lists).

However, the rather precarious position of the Israelite tribes dwelling in the lowlands, particularly the Plain of Jezreel — such as Issachar — obliged them to succumb to the Canaanites (cf. Gen. 49:14–15). These tribes, were, therefore, less able to initiate resistance, though the war was waged in their very territory. (For the absence of Issachar in Gideon's war see below p. 143). Even if it were assumed that Deborah was of the tribe of Issachar, which is doubtful, the initiative of the war was taken at her center of activity in the hill-country of Ephraim, between Ramah and Beth-el (Jud. 4:4–5). Thus, also, Tola son of Puah, "a man of Issachar" actually lived in Shamir, in the hill-country of Ephraim (Jud. 10:1). The tribe of Manasseh, as such, is not mentioned in Deborah's war. It appears, however, that Machir — mentioned in the song as one of the participating tribes — represented those branches of the tribe that still dwelt in the upland districts west of the Jordan (prior to their migration to the east) thus explaining the emphasis in Deborah's song: "Out of Machir *came down* governors" (Jud. 5:14).

This difference in disposition between the highland and the lowland tribes may explain the military cooperation evolved in Deborah's war between the tribes of Galilee and those of the central hill-country mentioned only in the song, i.e. Machir, Ephraim and Benjamin. At any rate, the Song of Deborah reflects the maximal unity achieved by the Israelites in the face of foreign oppression in the period of the judges. This solidarity encompassed tribes from Benjamin in the south to Naphtali in the north, lending support to Deborah's image as "a mother in Israel" (Jud. 5:7). But progress from this situation to actual concerted action of *all* the Israelite tribes was still far off. Indeed, in the song, Deborah censures several of the tribes (Reuben, Gilead [= Gad], Dan and Asher) for having adopted a passive role rather than coming "to the help of the Lord against the mighty." The song mentions only ten tribes, since Judah and Simeon in the south were apparently beyond the poet's horizon. Hence, the Song of Deborah cannot be adduced as evidence for the existence of an Israelite amphictyony, as has been held. The distinctive trait of such an amphictyionic league is a confederation of twelve (or six) tribes focused upon a single religious center; such a situation is lacking in the reality of the period of the judges.[31]

As for the military events as such[32], the two armies facing each other were ill-matched in strength and organization. The Israelite force, comprising only light infantry, was a poorly armed militia (Jud. 5:8) pitted against a professional, well-trained Canaanite army whose punch lay in its chariotry. According to the Bible, Sisera had nine-hundred "iron chariots." However exaggerated the number may be, it still implies a considerable force that was apparently recruited from a number of Canaanite city-states which had leagued up for this war. The main problem facing the Israelite command was, therefore, how to overcome the formidable Canaanite chariotry.

The actual battle, unlike the preparations leading up to it and the depiction of Sisera's murder, is only sketchily related. Moreover, since in accord with the historiographical tendency of the Book of Judges, military leadership and victory were described to the Providence[33] the course of the battle itself is not always clear. An analysis of the biblical text, however, is likely to shed light on the Israelite plan of operations which was based on an "indirect military approach," as usual in the stategy of the wars of the Conquest and of the judges. It seems that the Israelites aimed at neutralizing the Canaanite chariotry by exploiting local topographic and weather conditions. If we consider Chapters 4 and 5 in Judges as two phases of the same war, as we have done above, the chain of events can be reconstructed as follows: Barak summoned 10,000 warriors of the tribes of Naphtali and Zebulun to Kedesh, probably Kedesh-Naphtali, Barak's birthplace in southern Naphtali.[34] Thence he led them to Mount Tabor which possessed several obvious advantages as his operational base: a commanding position overlooking the plain and providing a perfect means of observing even distant enemy movements; further, that position among the wooded mountain slopes — which initially concealed the Israelite force — was beyond the reach of the Canaanite chariotry. This base gave the Israelite command the advantage in timing the attack to suit their needs — certainly a major factor in their operational plan.

The enemy, to whom the Israelite position must have purposely been "leaked" (Jud. 4:12), apparently concentrated forces at the foot of Tabor, in a secondary valley opening into the Jezreel plain (later known as the valley of Chesulloth) — which was far from providing the wide expanse suitable for the deployment of chariotry. Moreover, the Israelites seem to have delayed their uprising till the rainy season which often turns the low lying valleys into quagmires, thus altogether depriving the Canaanite chariots of their mobility.[35] The Israelite light infantry could then successfully attack the chariotry, a great part of which was certainly bogged down, while others seem to have been able to retreat to their bases in the southwest, i.e. in the vicinity of Megiddo and Taanach. This flight route was, however, blocked by another obstacle — the rain swollen Kishon brook (Jud. 5:21). The final engagement which sealed the enemy's fate must have been fought in the latter locale. Perhaps it was only then that the Israelite tribes dwelling in the central hill-country joined their brother-tribes, similarly to what happened in Gideon's war when the Ephraimites joined in the defeat of the enemy who had already been put to flight.

Even Sisera, the enemy commander, was forced to abandon his chariot and flee on foot to the tent-encampment of Heber the Kenite, who had left his tribe in the Negev and moved to the Plain of Jezreel. Here "Heber" may not be an actual personal name, but rather a personification of a nomadic family unit which had severed itself from its parent tribe.[36] The Kenite clan had cultivated friendly relations with both the Canaanites and the Israelites with whom it concluded later familial ties (Jud. 4:11, 17). Sisera met his death at the hands of Jael, the wife of the head of the clan, who seems to have been a charismatic personality in her own right, similar to Deborah and who — like her — dwelt near a sacred tree, i.e. "Elon [= oak]-bezaanannim which is by Kedesh." The killing of Sisera may have been an obligatory act in accord with a possible covenant concluded between the Kenites and Israel.[37]

Following the defeat of the Canaanites in Deborah's war, and despite the fact that their main centers do not seem to have been conquered at that time, the Israelite tribes settled in Galilee were freed of their yoke. In the Plain of Jezreel and its environs in particular, the Israelite position was consolidated, and the tribes of Manasseh, Issachar and Zebulun were able to expand their territories, the latter even to the sea-coast (Gen. 19:13). Further, this victory secured for the first time territorial continuity between the tribes in the northern and central parts of the country — just as this was the first occasion on which these tribes had engaged in a joint military operation of major proportions.

C. GIDEON AND THE MIDIANITE INCURSION

Deborah's Canaanite victory paradoxically brought about new dangers for the Israelites settled in the north. The weakening of the Canaanite power structure, which came on top of the collapse of Egyptian rule in Canaan in the second half of the 12th century (cf. above the chapter, "The Egyptian Decline in Canaan") left the eastern frontier open to nomadic incursions. The Israelites had not yet attained a position to insure the country's security through replacing the highly developed Canaanite defence system. The eastern desert tribes exploited this situation by invading the cultivated areas, a phenomenon common in Palestine in times of political instability — such as the period of the Israelite Settlement. This is well reflected in Psalm 83 which mentions the Ishmaelites, Hagrites, Amalekites and Midianites who harassed the Israelite tribes. As late as Saul's time, fierce battles were fought with Amalek (I Sam. 15) and with the Hagrites (I Chr. 5:10). It was only after the establishment of David's stable regime that these incursions were curbed. The proximity of the story of Gideon to that of Deborah in Judges seems, therefore, to follow the actual course of historical events, and not to be due to the arbitrariness of some late editor.

The mass raids into the cultivated areas usually involved several nomadic tribes acting in concert. Thus, the Midianites who invaded Canaan in Gideon's days were joined by the Amalekites and the "Children of the East" (*bᵉnē Qedem*: Jud. 6:3); later, in the days of Saul, the Hagrites who attacked the Israelite tribes in Transjordan acted in concert with the desert tribes of Jetur, Naphish and Nodab (I Chr. 5:18–19). Fully nomadic tribes would often attach themselves to more settled nations which were setting out on military expeditions (as reflected in Ps. 83; see above, p. 134). Thus, Amalek joined Eglon, the king of Moab, in his war against Israel (Jud. 3:13), Kenite clans joined the tribe of Judah during the campaign of inheritance (Jud. 1:16), and, according to biblical tradition, "a mixed multitude" attached itself to the Israelites during the Exodus from Egypt (Ex. 12:38).

The nomadic wave penetrating into Canaan at the time of Gideon was headed by the Midianites, a loose association of tribes (see below) which appear to have reached their zenith in the 13th–12th centuries.[38] At this time the Midianites concentrated in the fringe regions of southern Transjordan, as is indirectly indicated by their route of flight after their defeat (see below). The Midianites' special ties with southern Transjordan are also revealed by their clash with the Israelites in the time of Moses (Num.

25 and 31) and their close contact with the king of Moab (Num. 22:4 ff.) and the Amorite King Sihon (Josh. 13:21). However, the Midianite area of movement was enormous, extending as far as Egypt (Gen. 37:25 ff.; I Kings 11:17–18) in one direction and the Euphrates in the other (Num. 22:4 ff.), while splinter groups reached as far as Sheba in South Arabia (Isa. 60:6). They played a vital part in the spice and incense trade in western Asia, and this may serve to explain Midian's putative relationship to the children of Abraham's concubine Keturah (note that Hebrew *qᵉṭōret* means "incense") in the genealogical tables of Genesis (25:1–2).

The Midianite prosperity in the 12th century, as well as the rise of the desert tribes in general is the direct result of the large scale domestication of the camel.[39] This animal, of little importance previously, had come then into common use as a means of transport and even as a vehicle of war, thus becoming a prime factor in the very existence of the tribes of the Arabian desert, in both war and peace.

Gideon's story gives characteristic details of the mode of life and tribal organization of the Midianites which can be supplemented by other biblical sources. It transpires that at the time of the Israelite Settlement, the Midianites comprised five sub-tribes — apparently called *ummōt*, i.e. tribal units (Num. 25:15), ruled by five "kings" or "chieftains" (Num. 31:5; Josh. 13:21), a division indicated also in the genealogical tables of Genesis (25:4).[40] In Gideon's story, only two Midianite kings are mentioned — Zebah and Zalmunna — along with two army commanders — Oreb and Zeeb; these four are also designated as "princes" (Ps. 83:10; 12). It appears that the interchange of the several titles — king (*melek*), chieftain (*nāsī*), prince (*nāsīkh*), an appellation also designating heads of the Aramean tribes in southern Babylonia, and commander (*śar*) — merely reflects the various functions of the same tribal heads, i.e. their respective political, administrative, religious and military charges. The Bible mentions also Midianite "elders" (Num. 22:4, 7). Such leadership is characteristic of the tribal associations throughout the Ancient East, particularly the multiplicity of "kings", though their numbers tended to decrease gradually as the result of political consolidation. The restricted number of two Midianite kings in Gideon's account may indicate either an advanced stage of tribal organization or that merely a part of the confederation came into conflict with the Israelites.

The mass incursions of the Midianites and allied desert tribes in Gideon's day apparently took place toward the end of the 12th century B.C.E.[41] Crossing the Jordan into the Beth-shean plain, they aimed at the large and fertile valleys which separated mountainous Galilee from the central hill-country. According to the biblical evidence, they made deep inroads into the south reaching even the area of Gaza (Jud. 6:4), a long-range raid undoubtedly facilitated at that time by the weakness of the Canaanite city-states, and especially the collapse of Egyptian rule along the *Via maris*. As it so often happened, it was during the summer, close to harvest time, that the Midianite hordes broke into the cultivated areas in search of food and pasture. Thus, the Israelite rural population was particularly hardhit, especially in the Jezreel region. Their crops ruined or plundered, and in the absence of proper fortified cities, the Israelites were forced to take to "dens which are in the mountains, and the caves, and the strongholds" (Jud. 7:2). These insecure conditions prevailing in the period of the judges seem to be reflected also in the archeological evidence.[42]

The initiative of effective counter measures was taken by Gideon the son of Joash of the clan of Abiezer, one of the principal branches of the Manasseh tribe. Gideon's family home was at Ophrah, apparently to be located at the present-day village of eṭ-Ṭaiyibeh, north-east of the hill of Moreh. This was probably an enclave of the tribe of Manasseh within the territory of Issachar (cf. Josh 17:11).[43] Thus, Gideon's statement that "my family is the poorest in Manasseh" could be an allusion to the hard-pressed state of his clan as a result of its being cut off from the bulk of the tribe. The Bible describes how Gideon received inspiration for his mission while "beating out wheat in the winepress, to hide it from the Midianites" (Jud. 6:11), that is, while doing his work secretly and personally experiencing the enemy's oppression. As with the other Israelite deliverer-judges, Gideon's military actions were preceded by a national religious re-awakening. But only in Gideon's case is the nature of this religious surge explicitly described — that is, the uprooting of Baal and Asherah's worship in Ophrah — similar to Saul's annihilation of the foreign cult on the eve of his decisive battle with the Philistines (I Sam. 28:3 ff.).

Besides his fellow tribesmen from Manasseh, Gideon summoned to the war against the Midianites elements from the tribes of Asher, Zebulun and Naphtali who had settled north of Manasseh (Jud. 6:35).[44] Most remarkable, however, is the absence of Issachar, for the events described occurred in the territory of this very tribe which — dwelling in the lowlands — was presumably the most seriously affected. Opinions differ as to the precise location of the battle. Judging by the various topographical data, it would seem that the central Midianite camp which Gideon attacked, was "on the north side of them, by Gibeath-moreh [hill of Moreh] in the valley" (Jud. 7:1) or, more precisely, near En-dor (Ps. 83:11),[45] i.e. in the valley between the hill of Moreh and Mount Tabor. Another intimation for such a northern location is the fact that the Midianite kings slew Gideon's brothers at Tabor (Jud. 8:18–19). Gideon and his men encamped beyond the hill of Moreh, on the north-western slopes of the Gilboa range, above the well of Harod. Similar to Barak's base, this camp was sited beyond the enemy's reach and permitted easy retreat into the mountains of Gilboa if the need arose.

The major military problem facing Gideon was the enemy's numerical superiority and, particularly, his skilful use of camel-warfare; meeting the Midianites openly would have placed the Israelites in a situation which might well have ended in disaster. Thus, Gideon resorted to a night attack that served to neutralize the enemy's superiority and extreme mobility. The meticulous planning and precise execution of this attack constitute a classical example in military history of how a small and poorly armed force can overcome a much larger and stronger one. Though the Book of Judges generally tends to diminish the merit of human genius in military exploits in favor of the Divine, a detailed analysis of the text (Jud. 7) can reveal the still-valid tactics employed in this night-manoeuvre, as summarized below:[46]

The difficulties inherent in night operations caused Gideon to limit the size of his force to three hundred men, selected from among 10,000 warriors who remained with him. So as to compensate for the smallness of his force he selected only highly qualified troops by means of a peculiar test — the crux being the manner in which they drank water from the well of Harod; several explanations have been given of this test. It was the prerequisites of night fighting, however, which must have demanded here such a test, to ensure a well-disciplined force, fully capable of silent action. Without resorting to the usual textual emendations or analysis, it seems that Gideon rejected those warriors who proved their unsuitability by drinking noisily. Thus, "everyone that lappeth of the water with his tongue, as a dog lappeth [i.e. in a noisy manner] him shalt thou set by himself; likewise everyone that boweth down upon his knees to drink" [i.e. those who relaxed their vigilance while drinking] (Jud. 7:5). Gideon rather picked those "that lapped putting their hand to their mouth" [i.e. carefully, so as not to make noise and also to be able to keep watch]—who "were three hundred men" (Jud. 7:6).

Gideon's surprise attack relied upon the cover of darkness and the full effects of psychological warfare. His advance reconnaissance revealed that a defeatist attitude was already prevalent in the enemy camp (cf. the dream in Jud. 7:13–15). Dividing his men into three companies, as usual in Israelite practice (cf. Jud. 8:43; I Sam. 11:11, 13, 17 f.), he

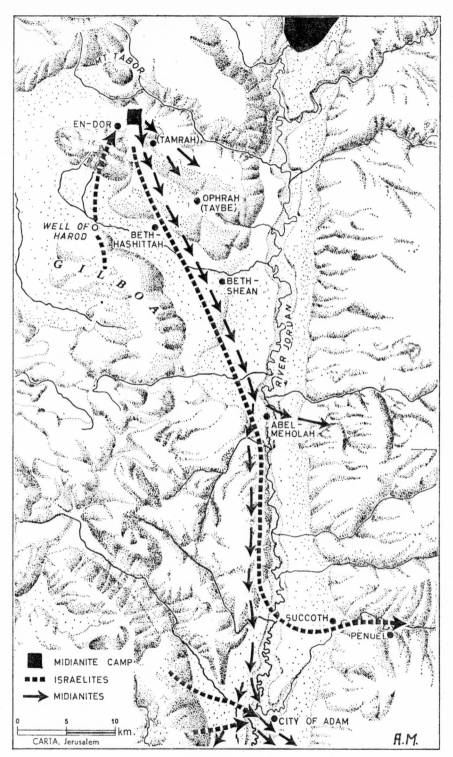

Gideon's Campaign.

encircled the Midianite camp; the actual attack came from three sides simultaneously. The action was timed for the "beginning of the middle watch", that is, close to midnight, just after the changing of the guard ("had but newly set the watch", Jud. 7:19), this being the critical moment in the sentry system. The peculiar "weapons" of Gideon's troops — horns and torches, the latter hidden in jars — proved effective; they were well-suited for signalling the attack and for identification in the dark, and further brought about utter chaos in the enemy camp. The torches were apparently also used to set on fire the tents in the Midianite encampment. The large herds and camels were undoubtedly stampeded by the horn blasts, they being just as unused to night raids as their owners. In the ensuing rout it was impossible to distinguish friend from foe, "and the Lord set every man's sword against his fellow, even throughout all the host" (*ibid.* 22).

Gideon's tactics were a complete success, and his victory lived in the memory of future generations as "the day of Midian" (Isa. 9:4). Gideon's military genius is shown in his following the victory through to the end by pursuing the enemy for some 150 miles beyond the Jordan. The survivors of the Midianite horde fled to the Jordan valley trying to ford the river near Abel-meholah (Jud. 7:22),[47] and apparently also further south at the city of Adamah (Ps. 83:11) (see map p. 145). Using another stratagem, frequently employed in the period of the judges (cf. Jud. 3:28; 12:5), Gideon blocked the enemy's line of retreat by seizing the fords with the aid of the tribe of Ephraim (Jud. 7:20–24). The Ephraimites captured the two Midianite commanders, Oreb and Zeeb, which exploit was also cherished for generations (Isa. 10:26; and cf. below, p. 160).

Gideon crossed the Jordan and moved up the Jabbok in pursuit of the Midianites who, following nomadic practice, tried to slip away into the open desert. During this lengthy campaign, Gideon requested supplies from the cities of Succoth[48] and Penuel (Tell edh-Dhahab); however, their inhabitants, being unsure of the outcome of the war and fearing Midianite reprisals, refused him. Gideon surprised the Midianites a second time by taking a short-cut through nomadic territory — the "way of them that dwelt in tents" (Jud. 8:11) — apparently east of Rabbath-Ammon. This time he dealt them a fatal blow, catching them entirely off guard and "secure" in their camp at Karkor (in Wadi Sirḥan); in this battle the two Midianite kings fell into his hands. Returning from his distant pursuit, Gideon punished the "princes and elders" of Succoth, razed the citadel at Penuel and killed its inhabitants. At Succoth a *na'ar* (Jud. 8:14) had "written down" for Gideon the names of the 77 town leaders (and cf. below note 82). This person was most probably not a mere "youth", but an official of the town-council to whom the identity of its members was well known and who also knew how to write. Hence, this passage should not be adduced as evidence for wide-spread literacy among the Israelites in this period, as so frequently done.

Gideon's victory put an end to the incursions of the desert raiders into Canaan, though their pressure continued in outlying districts and in the populated areas of Transjordan.

D. Premature Attempts to Establish a Monarchy and the Episode of Abimelech

In contrast to the other deliverer-judges, Gideon did not fade subsequently from the historical scene; upon his triumphal return, the Israelites offerred him the kingship, similar to the case of Saul who, at least according to one biblical version, was enthroned by the people in the wake of his victory over the Ammonites (I Sam. 11). This was the first attempt to establish a dynastic regime in Israel, prompted by a desire to stabilize the sporadic rule of the charismatic leadership which arose only in times of crisis. According to the biblical source, Gideon rejected the advance of the "men of Israel" to crown him as king and establish a hereditary monarchy on the grounds that this contravened to the concept of divine kingship: "I will not rule over you, neither shall my son rule over you; the Lord shall rule over you" (Jud. 8:23). This ideological anti-monarchism was not necessarily the expression of a later, theocratic editor, as held by biblical criticism, but is true to the mood prevailing in the period of the judges, as derived from the belief in the freedom of the individual.[49]

An even sharper expression of this anti-monarchism in the same period is found in Jotham's fable which denounces kingship as a futile and arrogant, absolutist institution. Though parable, it was an excellent reflection of Canaanite monarchy and its decorum, such as the ceremonial anointment of the king ("The trees went forth on a time to anoint a king over them" — Jud. 9:8) and the special protection afforded by the king's shadow (cf. the irony contained in the words of the bramble: "Come and take refuge in my shadow" — Jud. 9:15).[50] At the same time, the very offering of the crown to Gideon as well as Jotham's fable indicate that in certain circles there was already a trend to institutionalise charismatic leadership. This also applies to Jephthah and the elders of Gilead who granted his request to be a "head over all the inhabitants of Gilead", that is, a supreme ruler wielding authority in both war and peace (cf. below, p. 158).

Notwithstanding his outward refusal, Gideon did *de facto* retain certain important privileges usually belonging to the ruler, relying no doubt on the support of his band of warriors, which represented a sort of private retinue. Such a troop was several times instrumental in seizing the reins of government, as in the case of Abimelech, of David at Hebron and Rezon son of Eliada at Damascus (I Kings 11:23 ff.). Indeed, the brief biblical account of Gideon's later days provides several elements characteristic of kingly rule, elements quite foreign to true charismatic authority:[51]

(1) The establishment of an ephod at Ophrah — which may have become a cultic-political center — possibly connected with the religious act of Gideon's official appointment.

(2) The name of Gideon's son, Abimelech, i.e. "the father is king," seems to allude to a royal status.

(3) The double name Gideon-Jerubbaal (not necessarily stemming from two different sources) could be a case of a double royal name, a feature common in the Ancient East and the later Israelite Monarchy.

(4) The setting up of a harem on a royal scale, as indicated by his numerous progeny, and especially his marriage to a woman of the Shechem nobility, a sort of political-royal marriage common in the ancient world.[52]

(5) The allusion to the royal status of Gideon and his brothers by Zebah and Zalmunna, "As thou art, so were they; of one form with the children of a king" (Jud. 8:18).

(6) Even more significant is the demand of Gideon's sons to inherit their father's rule: "...that all the sons of Jerubbaal, who are threescore and ten persons, rule over you, or that one rule over you?" (Jud. 9:2).

All these arguments point to the special status and considerable prestige enjoyed by Gideon as a result of his deeds of deliverance. His family and his tribe — Manasseh — grew doubtlessly very influential in the north of the country, even in the Canaanite cities which remained in the hill country of Manasseh, as far as Shechem. The Bible emphasizes that in driving off the Midianites Gideon delivered also Shechem itself (Jud. 9:17), which came under his protection. Untrained in monarchical tradition, Gideon, the originally charismatic leader, did not make proper succession arrangements. Abimelech, the offspring of his marriage into a noble Shechemite family, exploited his maternal connections to rid himself of his brothers and seize power in the foreign city. This city's upper class undoubtedly supported Abimelech, hoping to obtain political and economic advantages under his rule.

The oligarchic "lords of Shechem" (*ba'alē Sh^ekem*) crowned Abimelech king in a public religious ceremony (Jud. 9:6). Not only was Canaanite

Shechem a most suitable site for the establishment of a kingship — it having long harbored monarchist traditions — but it displayed also a remarkable tendency to accept the authority of rulers not native to the town.[53] Thus, it appears that Lab'ayu, Shechem's aggressive ruler in the Amarna period, was an outsider who reigned supported by the Habiru bands in the area; a similar situation is found in Abimelech's time when Gaal the son of Ebed entered Shechem at the head of his kinsmen and seized control for a short while (Jud. 9:26). It seems that the distinctive feature here was that a single authority ruled over both a tribal entity and an urban center. Perhaps such rule is also reflected in the patriarchal tradition in the unique appellation of the eponym Shechem: $n^e \acute{s}i$' $h\bar{a}$'$\bar{a}re\!\chi$ — "prince [actually: chief] of the country" (Gen. 34:2), i.e. personifying both urban and rural elements. Such a political setup is known elsewhere in the ancient Near East, most notably from the Mari documents, which mention kings, each ruling over an urban center and a tribal territory.[54]

The above system of government, based on a covenant between an outsider and the nobility of Shechem, may very well explain the nature of the local deity, "El-berith" or "Baal-berith," i.e. the god of the covenant; that is to say, this deity apparently served as a party to, or rather as the guarantor of, specifically such a treaty. A further allusion to this may be found in the designation of the ruling class of Shechem as the "men of Hamor" (see below), i.e. of a donkey, signifying, as it has been suggested, a party to a covenant, since among the West Semites the donkey was used in the ritual of treaty-making.[55]

Abimelech did not make Shechem his permanent royal residence, but rather appointed Zebul, his minister, as ruler of the city (Jud. 9:28, 30). Supported by mercenary bands, Abimelech himself began to extend his sway over the Israelite and Canaanite inhabitants in the central hill-country, eventually transferring his residence to Arumah, a secure site southeast of Shechem (Jud. 9:41).[56]

The Shechemites envisaged the increasing connections between Abimelech and other towns as contrary to their own interests; this provided the background for the ensuing strife with their king. Gaal, who incited the Shechemites to rebel, seems to have exploited the social tension prevailing in the town and the ethnic difference between the Hivite element (Gen. 34:2) and the truly Canaanite citizens — by appealing to the rooted nobility, i.e. the "men of Hamor the father of Shechem" (Jud. 9:28). The pretext for the conflict with Abimelech was provided by the Shechemite nobles who had seized control of the roads in the area, thus grossly obstructing the former's mercantile operations (Jud. 9:25). This measure misfired and Gaal, who had made his way in the city — as mentioned above — was ejected from Shechem by Zebul and the elements still loyal to Abi-melech.[57] In the end Abimelech himself turned against Shechem and reduced it to rubble.

The archeological evidence from the Late Bronze Period levels unearthed at Tell Balaṭah, the site of ancient Shechem, is particularly illuminating for the story of Abimelech. It transpires that the city was divided into a lower town and, to the north, an acropolis which was built on a 30 foot high foundation of beaten earth. This citadel was apparently the "Beth-millo" mentioned in Jud. 9:6, 20. Here were found massive fortification walls and a large building (ca. 80 x 65 feet) with an entrance flanked by towers. This building complex served as both fortress and temple (such complexes are known as *migdāl* or *migdōl* in Canaanite/Hebrew), evidently the biblical "tower [*migdāl*] of Shechem" to which the "hold [*zᵉrīaḥ*] of the house of El-berith" was attached (Jud. 9:46).[58] In this precinct were found an altar and three stelae (*mazzēvōt*), two of which survived from an earlier sanctuary dating from the Middle Bronze Period. The third stele, erected in the courtyard in the Late Bronze Period, could be the one alluded to at Abimelech's coronation (Jud. 9:6), which probably took place here, and not at a sanctuary outside the city as often held.[59] The archeological finds prove that Shechem was a longstanding cultic center and, as such, was adapted into the Israelite traditions of the Patriarchs and Joshua.

There is also archeological support for Abimelech's utter destruction of the "tower of Shechem" (Jud. 9:45 ff.), i.e. the fortress-temple, at the end of the 12th century B.C.E., and for the fact that it was never rebuilt. Abimelech performed the symbolic act of sowing the ruins with salt, a ritual known also from other occasions in the Ancient East, and which has been explained in several manners.[60] It appears, however, that it was meant as the penalty for the violation of the covenant (hence the biblical expression "covenant of salt") into which the "lords of Shechem" had entered with Abimelech when accepting his sovereignty.

After the destruction of Shechem, Abimelech continued quelling the rebellion which must have spread to other towns in the central hill-country. He besieged Thebez (a textual corruption of Tirzah?)[61] — apparently also an ancient Canaanite stronghold. The course of the siege may have been similar to that of Shechem (Jud. 9:50 ff.): first the lower town was taken and its inhabitants and patrician families (*baʻᵃle hāʻīr*) fled to the "strong tower" (*migdāl ʻōz*) within the city, i.e. to the fortress-temple on the acropolis. Just as the Shechemites sought final refuge in the "hold of the house of El-berith", here the citizens fled to the uppermost part of the fortress (*gag hammigdāl*). In this attempt, however, while trying to set fire to the fortress, Abimelech was fatally wounded, following which his army dispersed (see above, p. 133).

Abimelech's three-year rule — limited in both time and area — may therefore be considered as an abortive attempt at kingship, particularly as it derived its inspiration from a Canaanite conception of monarchy. His gaining control was due only to the support of non-Israelite elements, and this in addition to the wanton slaughter of his own brothers. The absence of all charismatic flavor in his rule is stressed by his emphatic reliance upon mercenaries (Jud. 9:4) — paid from the treasury of the sanctuary of Shechem, — and in Abimelech's indirect rule through Zebul. This is in absolute contrast with the true charismatic leadership of the judges who relied on voluntary forces and needed no bureaucratic apparatus. Hence, it is not at all surprising that biblical tradition presents Abimelech in a negative light, regarding him as neither king nor judge: "And Abimelech held sway [*wayyāsar*, i.e. held dominion] over Israel three years" (Jud. 9:22). This was merely an ephemeral episode, since the time was not yet ripe for the establishment of a monarchy in Israel.

E. ISRAEL AND THE TRANSJORDANIAN STATES

Israelite fortunes in Canaan in the period of the judges are characterized by the struggle against the country's indigenous, Canaanite population, and later with the Philistines. The story of Abimelech is a good example of the ever-changing relations with the Canaanite elements, as is the Samson cycle regarding the Philistines. At times relations were good, neighborly, at others they deteriorated to the point of open conflict. The tension, increasing with the consolidation of Israelite power, led to hostilities in Transjordan as well. In contrast to Cis-Jordania, the Israelite tribes there were faced by nations somewhat akin to themselves (the Bible links the origin of Edom, Moab and Ammon to the Hebrew Patriarchs) and which had but recently undergone the process of settlement the Israelites were experiencing.[62]

In northern Transjordan, Aramean tribes expanded alongside the Israelites, but no major clashes took place between them in the period of the judges, apparently because of the existence, until then, of vast areas suitable for settlement north of the Jabbok river, such as the sparsely inhabited regions of 'Ajlun and Bashan. Between the Jabbok and Jarmuk rivers numerous settlements were founded in the Early Iron Period, as shown in a recent survey (see note 63). The relatively stable relations

between the Arameans and Israelites in the pre-monarchical times appear
to be reflected in the biblical tradition of the covenant concluded by Laban
the Aramean and Jacob the Hebrew in northern Gilead. (Gen. 31:44 ff.).

The situation was different in the region to the south of the Jabbok
where the peoples of Ammon, Moab and Edom had achieved political
consolidation, establishing kingdoms early in the 13th century B.C.E.
More or less stable regimes brought prosperity to these countries and
obviously tended to curtail the expansionism of the Israelite ,tribes. We
hear of open clashes between Israel and Moab (the Ehud episode), as well
as with the Ammonites (the Jephthah episode), but there is no mention
of such a conflict with the Edomites, whose land lay, apparently, beyond
the Israelite sphere of interest in this period. It has been suggested that
the first oppressor of Israel in the period of the Judges — Cushan-
Rishathaim — was a king of Edom, and not of Aram Naharaim (Jud. 3:8 ff.);
but such an emendation of the biblical text is unconvincing (though the
change of *resh* to *dalet* in the word Aram is in itself plausible, the elimination
of the second element — Naharaim — is much more difficult). On Cushan-
Rishathaim as an oppressor coming from the north, see above the chapter
"The Egyptian Decline in Canaan", paragraph B.

The lay of the land in southern Transjordan — the fertile valleys and
the broad tablelands of the interior — with brooks flowing down to the
Jordan river or the Dead Sea, led to intensive cultivation and a proliferation
of settlements at the beginning of the Iron Age.[63] Moreover, Transjordan's
natural wealth attracted the Israelite tribes of Cis-Jordania the surplus
population of which migrated there continually. The Book of Ruth (1:1)
provides a good illustration of such migration brought about by economic
conditions and periods of drought. On the other hand, Moab and Ammon
aspired to extend their dominion over the regions west of the Jordan
(see below).

Events in Transjordan, in the period of the judges developed therefore
in the shadow of the rapid increase of its population, although the habitable
territory there was limited by the desert on the east and the Jordan river
on the west. These factors intensified the struggle among the several forces
which had crystallized in the area — between the Israelite tribes and
the neighboring kingdoms on the one hand, and among these kingdoms
themselves on the other. The strengthening of one of these forces necessarily
involved the weakening of the others, as there was no room for two neighboring parties to prosper together in this limited region. Hence, in the
13th–11th centuries B.C.E. the various political factors here entered upon
a cycle of alternate ups and downs, each exploiting every opportunity of

extending its domain at the expense of the others. This rhythmic process may be sketched as follows:

Moab's ascent under King Eglon meant not only the weakening of its Israelite neighbors but apparently also that of the kingdom of Ammon (see below). And contrariwise, Moab's decline in the 12th–11th centuries, following its defeat by Ehud, restored Israelite strength in Transjordan and paved the way for increased immigration of Israelite elements from the west. These latter entertained neighborly relations with the Moabite population, even intermarrying with them, as evidenced by the Book of Ruth and the genealogical tribal lists of Benjamin and Judah (cf. I. Chr. 8:8; also 4:22). At the same time, Moab's decline doubtlessly led to the ascent of Ammon in the north and Edom in the south.

Whereas earlier the Ammonites had been compelled to render military assistance to the Moabites (Jud. 3:13), they now were able to gain ascendancy over them, as can be inferred from the exchange between Jephthah and the king of the Ammonites (cf. below pp. 000-000). This posed a new and increasing threat to the Israelites. On the other hand, the remark in the Edomite king-list in Gen. 36:35, according to which a king of Edom — Hadad the son of Bedad — defeated the Midianite tribes in the "field of Moab," points to an Edomite domination in the area. In any case, Moab alone was unable to withstand the inroads of the desert raiders. It is noteworthy that none of the three sources — the story of Jephthah, the passing remark in the list of Edomite kings, and the Book of Ruth — presuppose the existence of a monarchy in Moab. The two latter sources, which may deal with approximately the same period (ca. 1100 B.C.E.)[64] speak only of "the field of Moab." This perhaps infers that Moab had actually ceased to be a monarchy, and could regain its position only after Ammon's defeat by Jephthah, and particularly by Saul.

This fluctuation of fortunes in Transjordan is particularly conspicuous in the prosperous region between the Arnon brook in the south and the Jabbok in the north, an area which had been for many generations a true bone of contention between Ammon, Moab and the Israelite tribes. Every now and then there was a major change in control. This buffer region, and particularly its western parts — the Plain of Moab ('arvōt Mōāb) — was known not only for its economic value but also for its considerable strategic importance. The plains of Moab controlled the Jordan fords and, when dominated by hostile forces, could constitute a dire threat to Cis-Jordania, especially the territories of Benjamin and Ephraim. On the other hand, Israelite domination there prevented the expansion of Ammon and Moab west of the Jordan.

At the beginning of the 13th century B.C.E. this area was apparently divided between Ammon and Moab, though it was soon conquered by Sihon the Amorite king who pushed Ammon eastward beyond the upper course of the Jabbok and Moab to the south of the Arnon (cf. Num. 21:26). At that time Egypt had also become a factor to be reckoned with in the power-struggle prevailing in the region, as shown by a recently published inscription of Ramses II according to which this pharaoh dispatched a military expedition to distant Moab, conquering sites even north of the Arnon.[65] In the wake of the Israelite defeat of Sihon and his Amorite kingdom, the tribes of Gad and Reuben settled extensively there (cf. above the chapter "The Exodus and Conquest") while Moab and Ammon were eager to regain control of their lost territories.

1. *Ehud and the Moabites.* Moab's hour struck during the reign of King Eglon, most likely during the 12th century B.C.E. (lack of any chronological data prevents a more precise dating). The Moabites succeeded in expanding northwards beyond the Arnon where they annexed the *mīshōr*, i.e., the northern plateau — and westward to the plains of Moab, becoming due to the domination of these areas a significant political factor.[66] From there the Moabites continued to extend their sway even to the western bank of the Jordan capturing the City of Palms, apparently the site of Jericho (Jud. 3:13).[67] Once in possession of this bridgehead they oppressed the land of Benjamin (for eighteen years) and even threatened the territory of Ephraim.

It was apparently during this period that Moab gained to some extent control over the land of Ammon, as might be inferred from the participation — though only indirectly involved — of Ammonite forces in the Moabite attack on Israel: "And he gathered unto him the children of Ammon and Amalek; and he went and smote Israel" (Jud. 3:13). The Amalekites' joining Moab in this campaign may indicate that the latter also held sway over the desert fringes and the nomadic bands there. The peak of power reached by Moab at that time was matched only in the 9th century during the reign of King Mesha.

There is no information on Edom's political stand at this time, though it was obviously on the defensive against Moab, its flourishing and aggressive neighbor to the north. Moreover, in the first half of the 12th century Edom became involved in a conflict with Egypt when an expedition sent by Ramses III invaded the land of Seir subduing its inhabitants (cf. above the chapter "The Egyptian Decline in Canaan" paragraph D). There may very well have developed closer connections between Edom and Israel during this period of Moab's ascent, since both faced a common danger. This may be indicated by the name of the place to which Ehud fled after killing the king of Moab (provided the odd name "Seirath" actually does refer to the land of Seir [Jud. 3:26]).[68]

Israel's uprising against Moab was initiated by the Benjaminite leader Ehud, son of Gera, the scion of a noble family (Gen. 46:21; I Chr. 8:3,7), which was still famous generations later (Shimei, who lived in David's day, belonged to the same family). Ehud, who was aided in his struggle by the Ephraimites, seems to have occupied a key position in Benjamin even prior to his heroic exploits for he had headed the delegation which brought tribute to the king of Moab. According to the usual practice, it was precisely the heads of vassal states who appeared before their overlord to do homage.

The biblical account of the actual war between Moab and Israel is very brief and the few geographical data recorded are insufficiently clear,[69] nor is the site of King Eglon's residence specified. Seemingly he dwelt then at his summer residence (in the city of Medeba?) since he received Ehud in the "cool upper chamber" (the early Aramaic version, followed by the AV and RV — Jud. 3:20 has already "in a summer parlour"), i.e. the highest and coolest storey in a building.[70] In accordance with its folkloristic character the Book of Judges does, however, give a detailed and quite realistic description of Ehud's heroic deed and the circumstances of Eglon's assassination, enabling us to comprehend the nature of the stratagem employed by the Israelite deliverer.

Ehud acquired a double edged dagger especially designed for stabbing, a weapon still rare in those days.[71] Because of its small size ("of a cubit length"), and especially as he "girded it under his raiment upon the right thigh" and not upon the left as usual, he was able to approach the king without the weapon being noticed. The manner in which he carried his dagger, and that of his drawing it with an unexpected motion of the left hand to thrust it into the king's flabby belly (Jud. 3:21), prove that Ehud was left-handed or probably ambidextrous, for like the rest of his tribe he was evidently skilled in using both hands to wield weapons (cf. I Chr. 12:2).

After this courageous deed Ehud spread the revolt throughout the mountains of Ephraim where Moabite domination was less strong; from there he began driving the enemy out of western Palestine. The Israelites blocked the crossings of the Jordan to cut off the Moabites' line of retreat (Jud. 3:28; and cf. 7:24; 12:5-7; as well as pp. 146-147). The Bible however does not relate of a pursuit across the river into Moab proper, nor do we learn anything of the tribes of Gad and Reuben who must have been the principal victims of Moab's expansion. This may reflect the fact that the Book of Judges gives only a Benjaminite tradition of the events, or that these two Transjordanian tribes stood aside, as in Deborah's war, because the continuous oppression of the kingdoms of Moab and Ammon had rendered them too weak to join in the struggle.

Ehud scored a decisive victory over Moab resulting — according to the Book of Judges — in the longest period of peace ensured to Israel by an act of deliverance, i.e. some eighty years (Jud. 3:30) — which may simply denote a time span of two generations. Moab did not recover during the period of the judges and even under the early Israelite Monarchy continued to be the weakest of the southern Transjordanian states, Israel's principal enemies on this flank being then Ammon and Edom.

2. *Jephthah and the Ammonites.* As mentioned, Moab's decline and the crushing blow dealt by Gideon to the Midianite tribes allowed Ammon to consolidate and rise to power. The Ammonites had been especially sensitive to the desert raiders because of their front-line position. That kingdom, centered around Rabbath-Ammon (present-day Amman), consisted of a small strip of land on the upper Jabbok which flows to the north. Despite its small size and its location on the fringe of the desert, Ammon was in a strategic and geopolitical position of the first order, due to its command of a section of the "King's highway," i.e. the international artery linking Syria with southern Transjordan, whence it continued to the Gulf of Elath and the Arabian peninsula, while another branch ran across the Jordan river into western Palestine. This domination of an intersection of roads lent Ammon considerable political power and unusual economic prosperity, especially in periods when it could bring under its control the caravan trade of the desert tribes.[72]

On the other hand because of its precarious geographical position, a lack of "strategic depth," and because of the frequent pressure exerted by the marauding desert tribes to the east as well as by the sedentary populations to the west and south, the Ammonites were compelled to fortify their borders far more thoroughly than their neighbors who were able to rely partly on natural defense lines. The great organizational and technical ability of the Ammonites is clearly evidenced in the establishment of the chain of border fortresses surrounding Rabbath-Ammon on the west and south (cf. Num. 21:24), which were discovered during the archeological surveys of the thirties and, again, the fifties and sixties of the present century.[73] These massive forts, some built on a square or rectangular plan, but most of them of a distinct circular type (known as Rujm el-Malfuf), were apparently constructed in the Early Iron Age and continued in use throughout the existence of the Ammonite kingdom. This close network of forts offered an efficient means of communication, vital in foiling attempts of penetration into the heart of the country.

The biblical account of the defeat Jephthah inflicted upon the Ammonites "from Aroer until thou come to Minnith even twenty cities and unto Abel-keramim" (Jud. 11:33) apparently refers to an onslaught against the western line of defence. The twenty "cities" were doubtlessly mere border forts, while Aroer was not the well known city on the Arnon river but "Aroer that is before Rabbah" (Josh. 13:25), located southwest of Amman. South of this Aroer, on the way to Heshbon, are Minnith (ca. 5 km south of Amman) and Abel-keramim which may be located at the village of Naʿur (13 km southwest of Amman).[74] However, unlike David, Jephthah failed to break through to Rabbath-Ammon proper and gain a decisive victory over the Ammonites.

As Ammon grew stronger it expanded far beyond its borders, both in the southwest, into Moab, and northwestwards into the fertile region of el-Buqeiaʿ which is encompassed by the bend of the Jabbok and Waddi Umm ed-Dananir. This western part of "Greater Ammon" may have been referred to in the Bible as "half the land of the children of Ammon" (Josh. 13:25). The Ammonites expanded also further westward into the land of Gilead, then crossed the Jordan attempting to subdue the territories of Ephraim, Benjamin and even Judah. This offensive against the Israelites was contemporaneous with the increased Philistine pressure from the west (Jud. 10:7–9) and may have even been encouraged by the latter. The Israelites retaliated once the Ammonites had gone up against Gilead (Jud. 10:17; the reference here seems to be to the town of Gilead, located at Khirbet Jelʿad 9 km south of the Jabbok, between el-Buqeiaʿ and the plateau of Arḍ el-Arḍa),[75] since their action endangered the densely populated area in the fertile land of Gilead and the lower Jabbok region. This region was settled principally by the tribe of Gad supplemented by immigrants from the tribes of Manasseh and Ephraim.

In this hour of peril the elders of Gilead turned to Jephthah, the outcast whom his brothers had expelled from his father's patrimony since he was the son of a harlot (Jud. 11:1–3).[76] Jephthah had fled to the land of Tob, probably in the region of the Jarmuk, where no firm regime was established even in much later times (cf. 2 Sam. 10:6 referring merely to the "men" and not to a king of Tob). There he gathered a band of freebooters which, in the opinion of the elders of Gilead, could enable him to lead successfully in a war against the Ammonites. It was the existence of this band which invested Jephthah with bargaining power concerning his future status (Jud. 11:6 ff.). Indeed he declined the initial offer to become the "commander" (*qāzīn*) of Gilead, that is a leadership limited to the duration of the war. He consented only when the elders offered to elect him "head [*rō'sh*] over all the inhabitants of Gilead" i.e. supreme ruler over the entire Israelite region, maintaining his authority in peace time as well (cf. the parallel expression concerning Saul's leadership, I Sam. 15:17). Jephthah's appointment as both "head and commander"[77] was similar to the coronation ceremony of a king — involving the conclusion of a covenant with the people's representatives, namely, the council of elders, and solemnized in a religious act "before the Lord in Mizpah" (Jud. 11:11; cf. the crowning of Abimelech and, in particular, of Saul and David).

The town of Mizpah, apparently called Mizpeh of Gilead later in this story, was the religious and political center of that region, hallowed already in the tradition of the Patriarchs (Gen. 31:49). Opinions differ concerning the site of this town which served as a base for the Israelite army under Jephthah. According to one view it should be located north of the Jabbok, but the biblical context would rather suggest a place south of the Jabbok close to the city of Gilead, for it is stated that the Israelites encamped just opposite the Ammonite army.[78] Before Jephthah decided to attack he took the diplomatic step of attempting to negotiate with the Ammonite king (Jud. 11:12–28). Though the literary form of the diplomatic negotiations is late and raises various difficulties, it still remains an important historical source reflecting the seemingly authentic claims of both parties to the possession of the contended area between the Jabbok and the Arnon.[79] Jephthah based Israel's claim on the fact that their forebears had conquered this area from Sihon, King of the Amorites, and not from Ammon or Moab. A further argument was that the Israelites had right of possession because of their long residence there. The reference to 300 years in this context is not clear, though it may, similarly to other round figures in the Book of Judges, merely indicate so many generations (reckoning 40 years per generation). By applying to the figure a more realistic reckoning (i.e. on the basis of 25 years per generation) we arrive at a period of slightly under 200 years, which would fit perfectly the time-span between the Israelite conquest of Transjordan (i.e. the first half or middle of the 13th century B.C.E.) and Jephthah's time (i.e. the first half of the 11th century B.C.E.).

The Ammonite counter-claim seems to have been based on the assertion that even prior to Sihon's expansion the Ammonites had occupied the northern part of the area in dispute. Moreover, the Ammonite king appears in the negotiations also as the suzerain of the land of Moab, which entitled him to the territorial claims of that country as well, for Moab once occupied the southern part of the contended region (cf. Num. 21:26). Indeed, Ammon's supposed domination of Moab in Jephthah's days and the consequent assumption of its rights and privileges would account more readily than other alternate explanations for the fact that Jephthah refers to Chemosh — actually the national deity of Moab — as the god of Ammon's king (Jud. 11:24).

Upon failure of the negotiations, Jephthah levied Israelite troops from the tribes of Gad and Manasseh, but his appeal to the Ephraimites went unheeded (Jud. 12:2–3). As already mentioned, Jephthah's was not a decisive victory, since it did not take the Ammonites long to recover. However, another event in the aftermath of the war left its mark on Israelite history: the outbreak of the fratricidal strife between the Gileadites and the Ephraimites.

F. Inter-Tribal Wars

The initial cause of the bitter and cruel feud between Jephthah and the Ephraimites (Jud. 12:1–6) can be found in the latter tribe's ambition to dominate the Israelite settlement in Transjordan. They were, no doubt, supported in their aspiration by numerous kindred elements which had infiltrated into Gilead from the west. The very name "forest of Ephraim" north of Mahanaim (II Sam. 18:6) points to a considerable settlement of this tribe in Gilead, while the taunting words in the story of Jephthah: "Ye are fugitives of Ephraim, ye Gileadites in the midst of Ephraim and Manasseh" (Jud. 12:4) point, despite their ambiguity, to the same fact.

The Ephraimites went up to the city of Zaphon, which is probably Tell es-Sa'idiyeh[80] near the eastern bank of the Jordan, north of the Jabbok (known from the Amarna Letters and from the list of Gadite towns in Josh. 13:27), with the probable intention to continue on to Jephthah's residence in Mizpah. Being routed and put to flight, they attempted to steal across the Jordan so as to reach their kindred's territory. The heavy Ephraimite losses (42,000 according to the exaggerated biblical account) may indicate that Jephthah exploited this opportunity to clear Gilead of all the Ephraimites who had settled there. In connection with the Ephraimites' flight to the Jordan fords we are told the interesting detail that their pursuers identified them by their pronunciation of the password

"Shibboleth": "And he said 'Sibboleth'; for he could not frame to pronounce it right" (Jud. 12:6). Whatever the precise meaning of this, it shows that in the 11th century B.C.E. there existed dialectal differences even among the northern Israelite tribes.[81]

The war between Gilead and Ephraim was hardly the only instance of inter-tribal strife in the period of the judges. From the Book of Judges we know of several such conflicts the climax of which was reached in the bitter war described in the story of the outrage at Gibeah (see below). It is worth noting, however, that such feuds were never attributed by the biblical sources to differences over territorial rights or encroachments, but rather to either the refusal of one tribe to come to the aid of other tribes in actions against foreign oppressors or, conversely, to not having been called upon to render such assistance.

Thus, the Ephraimites charged both Gideon and, perhaps unjustifiably, Jephthah of having failed to summon them to war with the enemy (Jud. 8:1; 12:1 — both passages explicitly using the term "men ['îsh] of Ephraim" in specifically referring to warriors). Their exclusion deprived them of both the glory and, more important probably, their fair share in the spoils. Gideon succeeded in appeasing the Ephraimites by inviting them to join in the pursuit of the Midianites, in which they managed even to win a decisive victory, as we have seen. This latter achievement is well reflected in Gideon's address to the Ephraimites: "Is not the gleaning of Ephraim better than the vintage of Abiezer? [i.e. Gideon's own clan]. God hath delivered into your hand the princes of Midian, Oreb and Zeeb; and what was I able to do in comparison with you?" (Jud. 8:2–3). But the conflict in Jephthah's time led to bloodshed and the slaughter of the Ephraimite warriors.

There were occasions, however, when tribal units or even whole tribes would refuse to participate in a campaign they were requested to render assistance. A case in point is Deborah's war with the Canaanites, when several tribes were denounced for shirking their duty (as we have seen above, p. 138). Here also the inhabitants of Meroz, who could easily have taken part in the battle near Taanach, close to their town, were cursed in particular, "because they came not to the help of the Lord" (Jud. 5:23).[82] This reminds of the dire results of the refusal of the people of Succoth and Penuel to provide provisions for Gideon's troops during their pursuit of the Midianites.

Two phenomena stand out in all the above mentioned incidents:

(1) The antagonism or even open rift which frequently appeared between the tribes west of the Jordan and those to the east; there is no extant evi-

dence for a single war of deliverance involving joint action of the tribes on both sides of the river in the period of the judges. This rivalry between the two sections of the Israelites is further manifested in the biblical tradition in Joshua 22, relating the setting up of an aggressive tribal confederacy in the west, with an eye on the Transjordanian tribes who had erected an altar "over against the land of Canaan, in the borders of Jordan" (v. 11).[83]

(2) The principal instigator in the various inter-tribal conflicts, such as the incidents with Gideon and Jephthah, was the tribe of Ephraim; it was also this tribe which was the driving force behind the large-scale operations against Benjamin, the culmination of the episode of Gibeah. Thus, Ephraim became involved with all its neighboring tribes: Manasseh, Gilead (= Gad) and Benjamin. It would appear that the reason for all this strife was the growing power and prestige of these tribes resulting from the victories of Gideon of Manasseh, Jephthah the Gileadite and Ehud of Benjamin and the ever-increasing drive for pre-eminence of Ephraim. The eventual position of superiority of the latter tribe is also reflected in Jacob's blessing of the sons of Joseph, in which the right of primogeniture had been granted to Ephraim instead of Manasseh his elder brother (Gen. 48:17 ff.; and cf. I Chr. 5:1–2), which most likely anticipates the time after Abimelech's failure and the decline of Manasseh.[84]

The Gilead-Ephraim war which broke out just after Jephthah's victory over the Ammonites seems to have facilitated the recovery of the vanquished nation. About two generations later, on the eve of Saul's kingship, the Ammonites again pressed northward, this time as far as Jabesh-gilead north of the Jabbok. Saul, who was a Benjaminite and as such quite likely a blood relation of the inhabitants of Jabesh-gilead,[85] rushed to their aid. The historical circumstances which led up to this action may be better understood through the episode of the outrage at Gibeah, the most conspicuous and far-famed case of Israelite inter-tribal war in the period of the judges (Jud. 19:21). Though many scholars have doubted the historicity of this episode, and despite all the tendentiousness and literary embellishments, it seems to be based on an early historical kernel still echoing in Hosea's prophecies (Hos. 5:8; 9:9).[86]

As for the historical-chronological background, the episode of the outrage at Gibeah fits well within the interval between Jephthah's days (first half of the 11th century B.C.E.) and Saul's accession (ca. 1025 B.C.E.).[87] On the one hand the story reflects the special bonds between Benjamin and Jabesh-gilead: this town, alone in all Israel, refused to join in the punitive action against Benjamin and was severely punished by the other tribes for having violated the Israelite confederation's vow. Further, after most of Benjamin had been annihilated, the nubile maidens (i.e. the specific meaning of *betūlōt*) of Jabesh-gilead were given to the remaining Benjaminites to ensure the survival of the tribe (Jud. 21:8 ff.). These facts, namely the weakening of Jabesh-gilead and that city's special relationship with the tribe of Benjamin, link up very well with the above mentioned circumstances on the eve of Saul's reign: the Ammonite offensive against Jabesh-gilead and its subsequent appeal for help addressed specifically to the tribe of Benjamin, and not to the tribe of Ephraim which lived closer.

On the other hand, the story of the events concerning Gibeah may be considered as a continuation of the conflict between Ephraim and Gilead since the days of Jephthah. The tribe of Ephraim was not only the instigator of the pan-Israelite war against Benjamin, as already noted, but was also behind the punitive expedition against Jabesh-gilead. Admittedly, according to the biblical account the immediate cause of the pan-Israelite action was a gruesome sex crime committed at Gibeah in the territory of Benjamin, the victim of which was the concubine of a Levite from Mount Ephraim. But time and again in biblical historiography such seemingly private, individual family incidents actually reflect historio-political events. The actual background to this story was undoubtedly provided by inter-tribal rivalry for hegemony in Israel, especially that between Ephraim and Benjamin.[88]

Whatever the case, the story of the outrage at Gibeah reveals most instructive details on the religious, social, institutional and military facets of the Israelite confederation, as well as its inter and super-tribal organization in the period of the judges. Thus we learn of the important role played by Beth-el (but not by it alone) as a religious center and even as the seat of the Ark of the Covenant "in those days" (Jud. 20:18, 26–27).[89] The story reflects well the Israelite "primitive democracy" in action, and describes the functioning of its central institutions, the "congregation" (*'ēdā*) and the "general assembly" (Jud. 20:1 ff.).[90] The tribal representatives were summoned to a general assembly at Mizpah, on the border of Benjamin, (vv. 1–2) to hear the Levite's accusation (vv. 3–7); they reached a unanimous decision and passed sentence on the impenitent tribe which had committed the offence (vv. 8 ff.). This assembly was also the supreme authority which declared a general conscription and ordered the tribes to select a tenth of the potential warriors to furnish provisions for the army, probably through the clan apparatus (vv. 10–11; and cf. Jud. 21:10 ff.).

This army was summoned by the drastic method of dispatching parts of the concubine's corpse to each of the tribes (Jud. 19:29) with the clear intent of spreading horror among the people — similar to the summons to Saul's war against the Ammonites (I Sam. 11:7). Such primitive tribal customs are known also from elsewhere in the Ancient East, particularly from Mari.[91] The town of Gibeah or Gibeath-Benjamin was conquered by a stratagem identical to that of the conquest of Ai (Josh. 7–8): warriors were placed in ambush behind the city, while another unit of the attackers feigned flight so as to draw away the defenders of the town thus enabling the ambushing forces to enter without struggle the helpless city.[92] It is of particular interest that in both these instances, at Ai and at Gibeah, the final conquest was preceded by unsuccessful attempts ending in real retreats on the part of the attackers. It may thus be assumed that the stratagem employed in the final attack was based on staging an additional "defeat" to lull the enemy into false confidence (Josh. 8:6–7; Jud. 20:39).

The episode of the outrage at Gibeah is the only instance of a pan-Israelite tribal confederation in the period of the judges acting as a well organized and consolidated body (excluding, of course, the punished tribe) without a judge to lead it, or as yet a king.[93]

CHAPTER VIII

THE PHILISTINES AND THEIR WARS WITH ISRAEL

by B. Mazar

THE MOMENTOUS EVENTS which occurred at the end of the 13th century and the beginning of the 12th century B.C.E. determined the fate of Canaan for many generations. This was the period when the Hittite empire was shaken to its very foundations and subsequently destroyed, when Egypt's political and military power in Asia was beginning to decline, while in the country's interior the Israelite tribes had already succeeded in striking roots on both sides of the Jordan. They occupied large areas in a complicated process of settlement and continuous struggle with the Canaanite city-states, with the neighbors on their borders and the nomads from the desert. This was also the time when the migrations and massive invasions of those whom the Egyptian sources called "Sea-Peoples" resulted in the settlement of Philistines and allied peoples on the country's coasts. This unsettled state of affairs is also indicated by a sudden interruption in the import of Mycenaean vessels on the eastern coast of the Mediterranean.

Concerning the origin of the Philistines and the time they first made their appearance on Canaanite soil opinions differ. From the Egyptian sources we learn that one of the most important Sea-Peoples, the Philistines (Pr/lst) entered the historical scene of the eastern Mediterranean in the days of Ramses III (1206–1174). Hence, the stories in Genesis 20: 21 and 26 about Abimelech, the king of the Philistines in Gerar, should be considered anachronistic, i.e. employing a late concept for early events or, as reflecting the historical reality in Israel on the eve of the Monarchy. The explanation that distinction should be made between early Philistines who lived in the land of Gerar at the time of the Patriarchs and the late Philistines who appeared on the country's coast in the 12th century B.C.E. seems farfetched.[1]

According to biblical tradition the Philistines are descendants of the Caphtorim. The fact that in the table of nations (Gen. 10:14 should be read: "And the Caphtorim, whence the Philistines came forth") the Caphtorim are enumerated among the peoples living in Egypt proper may possibly refer to the presence of settlers and garrisons from among the Sea-Peoples. According to Deut. 2:23 the Caphtorim, who had come from Caphtor, destroyed the Avvim who lived in villages as far as Gaza, and settled subsequently in their places. These are probably the Philistines and those attached to them who settled along the "Way of the land of the Philistines", (Ex. 13:17), as far as Shihor, which is before Egypt (cf. Josh. 13:3). Other sources also point out that the Philistines originate from Caphtor (Amos 9:7) which is the island of Crete (Jer. 47:4; in the Septuagint: the islands of Caphtor). The name Kaptara is already known from the 18th century B.C.E. Akkadian tablets from Mari as that of the land of rich merchandise, while on a late Assyrian tablet, doubtlessly based on an ancient source describing the empire of Sargon the Great, Kaptara appears as a country beyond the Upper Sea. Further, it is significant that in the Ugaritic epic of Anath it is said that the residence of Kothar, the god of artisans, is in Kaptar which is described as a distant place in mid-sea, distinguished for artistic work and for trade relations with the East (i.e., the isle of Crete).[2] Kefti'u, the Egyptian name for Crete and the neighboring islands, is apparently an early Egyptian way of writing the name Caphtor.[3] From the above-mentioned it seems probable that in the East Caphtor (Kaptara) was the old and current name for the island of Crete, the important center of the Minoan civilisation.

The Bible also mentions the name of Crete in connection with the Philistines, but the name Caphtor is earlier and more comprehensive. Settlers called Cretans lived in the western Negev ("Negev of the Cherethites", I Sam. 30:14), which further in the same chapter is called "the land of the Philistines" (I Sam. 30:16). The Cherethites and Pelethites (apparently Philistines) served in David's army as mercenaries and body-guards. The connection between the Cherethites and the Philistines is so close that at times Cherethites is simply a synonym for Philistines (Zeph. 2:4–5, Ezek. 25:16).

The problem of the original Philistine language is most difficult. The names of the Philistine gods mentioned in the Bible are West Semitic: Ashtoreth, Dagon, Baal-zebub (II Kings 1:2, apparently an intentional distortion of Baal-zebul). This is obviously the result of their rapid cultural assimilation during the generations immediately following their settlement in the midst of the Canaanite population. The emphasis laid in the biblical sources upon their being uncircumcised, and mention of several of their religious and cultic usages such as the prohibition to tread on the threshold of Dagon's sanctuary in Ashdod (I Sam. 5:5), or the cultic ceremony in

Dagon's temple in Gaza (Jud. 16:23 ff.) as well as the episode of the plague of emerods and mice (I Sam. 5:6 ff.), must not be considered as peculiar to the Philistines. It can be reasonably assumed that already the first generations of Philistine settlers in Canaan had adopted the language of Canaan as well as many cultural assets of the ancient inhabitants of the country, together with the laws and customs which they had practised since times immemorial.

One might suppose that various elements stemming in the religion and traditions they brought along from their country of origin merged with the Canaanite culture they adopted, a fact which would explain the affinity between different literary motifs in the Bible (such as the stories about Samson) and in Greek legend. As to the personal names peculiar to them — those mentioned in the Bible (Achish, Goliath and also Phicol) as well as those known from the Egyptian Wen-Amon Scroll (War/laktar/l, War/lat, Makamar/l and Beder the Tjeker ruler of Dor, and cf. below) — it was suggested that most of these names are Anatolian or more precisely Luwian.[4]

Similarly, various suggestions were put forward for the term $s(a)ran$, plural: *sarney Pᵉlishtīm* (lord and lords of the Philistines respectively), which appears to be related to *tyrannos*, a Greek loan-word from one of the Anatolian or Aegean languages. Some attempts were made to conclude from the personal names, from several Hebrew words which were perhaps borrowed from the Philistine (such as *'argāz* = box, *qōva'* = helmet, *pilegesh* = concubine, and the place name Ziklag), as well as from other data, that the Philistines originated from south-western Anatolia or from Cilicia; while others went as far as to look for a connection between them and the Illyrians who reached the coasts of the Aegean Sea during the irruption into that area of the Balkan peoples.[5]

Recently even the old idea of a connection between the Philistines and the Pelasgians has been revived. This assumption is based on various Greek traditions, on the fact that the Odyssey mentions the Pelasgians as inhabitants of Crete, and particularly on a linguistic consideration (Pelastikon-Pelasgikon).[6] However, all these attempts appertain for the time being to the domain of pure conjecture. Just as doubtful is the attempt to draw conclusions from the late 13th century inscriptions discovered in the sanctuary of Succoth in the Jordan Valley (Tell Deir 'Allā), which according to one view are related to the Minoan Linear script and presumed to represent one of the scripts of the Sea-Peoples, perhaps even the Philistines.[7]

The rise of the Philistines took place in the transitional period between the 13th and 12th centuries B.C.E., when the Hittite and Egyptian empires were still presenting a united front against the tremendous pressure the Sea-Peoples exercised by land and sea.[8] The first harbingers of the movement of these peoples were the Lycians and Sherden who terrorized the east Mediterranean sea-board in the el-Amarna period. At the time of Ramses II we find Sherden troops serving in the Egyptian army. As a result of the increasing assault on the coastal areas of the Aegean Sea and the east Mediterranean sea-board the great centers of Mycenaean culture were destroyed, sea trade was disrupted and the Hittite bases in Cyprus and on the coasts of southern Anatolia and northern Syria were affected. Documents from the last quarter of the 13th century found at Hattusa, the Hittite capital, and Ugarit, clearly mention the approaching catastrophe. Since the time of Mer-ne-Ptah, who succeeded in defeating a league of Libyans and Sea-Peoples, including the Lycians, Achaeans, and Denyen[9] — an action which saved Egypt from invasion until the time of Ramses III — the movement of the Sea-Peoples from the Aegean Isles by way of Rhodos, Cyprus and the southern coast of Anatolia did not cease. This upheaval which caused the destruction of the Hittite empire, threatened directly Egypt and the province of Canaan within its realm. It transpires that early in the reign of Ramses III, in his fourth (or fifth) regnal year, the Egyptians had already engaged the Sea-Peoples on the borders of Canaan (Djahi) expelling them from their area of influence, but, in the king's 8th year a league of five Sea-Peoples flooded anew the area leaving destruction and ruins in its wake. The inscription of Ramses III gives an eloquent description of the murderous onslaught of these nations. The new tide included the Pelesheth (Pr/lst), Tjekel (Skr/l), Shekelesh (Shkr/lsh), Denyen (Danuna) and Weshesh,[10] who had concluded their alliance while still on their islands, prior to their sudden expansion. All the countries in their path, the land of the Hittites in Anatolia, Carchemish on the Euphrates, and even far Alashiya, viz. Cyprus, succumbed to their assault and were simultaneously destroyed. The invaders broke into Syria and encamped in the land of Amurru which they sacked completely, then moved southward, toward Egypt. However, they were brought up short by Pharaoh Ramses III who defeated them in a brilliant action by land and sea which saved Egypt from disaster.[11] It was probably during these events that Hattusa, the Hittite capital, and Ugarit, the great seaport, were destroyed. Disaster overtook many towns on the coasts of Syria and Palestine, including a city situated in the estuary of the Kishon (Tell Abu Huwām), which had been a prosperous port in the Late Bronze Period. As already mentioned, the battles between Egyptians and invaders, port-

rayed in detail on the reliefs in the sanctuary at Medinet Habu near
Thebes, were fought by land and sea. All the warriors portrayed in the
land battle scene and the majority of those portrayed in the sea battle
are Philistines, or belong to kindred peoples. They are distinguished by
plume-crested helms (cf. below) and braided hair pushed under the helms,
in contrast to a separate group of maritime invaders wearing horned helms,
which are typical of the Sherden and other Sea-Peoples.

It is interesting to note that the plume-crested helm has a long tradition
in Crete, for it appears already as one of the written characters on the
Phaestos clay disc (15th century B.C.E.); and the figure of a warrior with
a similar helm appears on a 13th–12th century ivory carving discovered
at Enkomi in Cyprus. Surprising in the depiction of the land battle is the
presence of chariots and carts conveying the women and children who
accompanied the invader-warriors on their expeditions. As for the portrayal
of the sea battle, the Sea-Peoples' boats, which are depicted advancing
under sail only, have high prow and poop both ending in duck heads.
These features make them quite different from the Egyptian ships. According to these depictions the Philistines and their confederates were tall,
brawny and clean-shaven men, usually armed with spears, longswords and
round shields. They also wore armor that protected the warrior's upper
body.[12]

When the storm subsided, Ramses III summoned all his resources to
maintain Egyptian rule in Canaan and to reinforce its defence system.
He had fortified cities rebuilt and strongholds set up for the Egyptian
forces, manning them with garrisons. Among these belong the fortresses
of Beth-shean (stratum VI) and of Sharuhen (Tell el-Far'ah) in the north-
western Negev, and, as it transpires, also Lachish (to which the excavations merely allude) where graves containing anthropoid coffins slightly
similar to the Egyptian ones were found. The head-gear of the figures
on the coffin lids closely resemble the plume-crested helms of the Philistines
on the Medinet Habu reliefs. These are probably the coffins of the
garrison's soldiers; similar coffins were found in Egypt itself, e.g., at Tell
el-Yahudiyya, Tell Nabasha in the Delta, and at Aniba in Nubia. These
latter date from the 12th–11th centuries B.C.E. It may well be that the
main difference in the ornament of the helms points to the presence of
different ethnic units, or of various Philistine tribes and peoples close to
them. No less instructive than the actual coffins are the other finds from
the graves, which not only point to the common cultural background
of garrison forces in the Egyptian service who had absorbed Egyptian
and Canaanite influences, but also to the very obvious Aegean element

Fig. 24.
Naval battle between the Sea-Peoples and the Egyptians in the days of Ramses III.
Fresco from Medinet Habu, Egypt.

H. Gressmann, *Altorientalische Bilder zum A.T.*, Berlin, 1927, pl. IL.

Fig. 25.
Fragment of a scene depicting a battle between the Egyptians and the Philistines
in the days of Ramses III. Fresco from Medinet Habu, Egypt.

H. Gressmann, *loc. cit.*

stemming from the tradition they had brought along from their homeland.[13]

It emerges that the settlement of the Philistines, the Tjeker and other
Sea-Peoples on the coast of Canaan and on its borders had already begun
in the days of Ramses III. The details of this process are unknown, but it
appears that the Egyptians themselves were interested in absorbing an
ever increasing number of professional soldiers from among the Sea-Peoples,
so as to man their fortresses. These garrison forces included both captives
and mercenaries with the help of which the Egyptians sought to control
the Canaanite population. We even learn from Egyptian sources that
groups from among the Sea-Peoples were permitted to live on royal estates,
to settle under the patronage of Pharaoh and in his service. Of particular
interest is the passage in Papyrus Harris I which mentions Pharaoh's
victory over the Denyen in their own islands, the destruction of the Tjeker
and the Philistines as well as that of the Sherden and Weshesh from the sea.
The passage goes on to describe how many captives were settled in fortresses,
and the provisions they were all apportioned from the royal treasury and
granaries.[14] As Egypt's administrative and military power continued to
decline in the course of the 12th century, the need to enrol foreigners to
maintain its waning authority in Canaan increased. This situation consolidated the hold of the mercenary troops in the fortified cities, while the
stream of invaders from the sea who were settling then in the coastal region
increased. The newcomers established themselves in the Canaanite towns
and even founded new settlements. In the course of time they developed
into a militaristic ruling minority and became also an enterprising economic
factor in trade and in the metal industry.

A significant phenomenon, prominent from the first half of the 12th
century, is the mass of painted pottery attributed to the Philistines, which
was discovered over their entire settlement area in south-western Palestine,
and its diffusion to such distant areas as the mountain region and the
valleys. These vessels clearly recall the tradition of the Late Mycenaean
pottery (Late Helladic II C1) and are related to the pottery of that same
period (the first half of the 12th century) from Sinda in northeast Cyprus,
and from Perati in Atica. Philistine pottery is distinguished by a wide
range of motifs painted in black and red, which in addition to a series
of Mycenaean motifs, displays Cypriot, Egyptian and Canaanite influences.
The eclectic character of this ceramic fits in well with all we know of the
Philistine material culture (weapons, seals, figurines, etc.). It reveals something of their origin — their source of inspiration before they reached the
shores of Canaan — and the influences they absorbed in the course of time

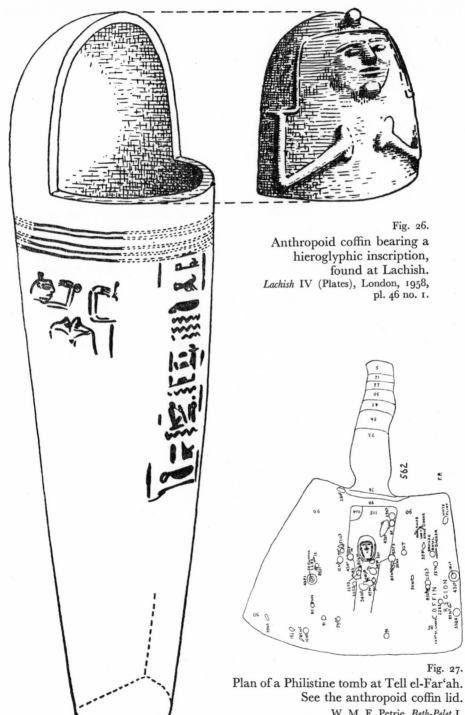

Fig. 26.
Anthropoid coffin bearing a
hieroglyphic inscription,
found at Lachish.
Lachish IV (Plates), London, 1958,
pl. 46 no. 1.

Fig. 27.
Plan of a Philistine tomb at Tell el-Far'ah.
See the anthropoid coffin lid.
W. M. F. Petrie, *Beth-Pelet* I,
London, 1930, pl. XIX.

as mercenaries in the Egyptian army and as settlers in Canaan.[15] It should be noted that in the development of Philistine pottery, three stages can be discerned, beginning with the first half of the 12th century — its floruit — which is remarkable for the quality and richness of decoration, until its decline in the second half of the 11th century.

Presumably, the settlement of the Philistines and the peoples close to them was a process replete with events and conflicts with the native population. The legendary exploit of Shamgar son of Anath (Jud. 3:31) "Who smote of the Philistines six hundred men with on ox-goad; and he also saved Israel," indicates that already in the 12th century Philistine bands collided with the Israelites in the north of the country; nor is it impossible that events of this kind had some bearing on the Philistine control of Megiddo and other Canaanite centers.[16] Different sources, on the other hand, show that the Philistines began by settling on the country's southern coast, along the Philistine Road which leads to Egypt, and on the coast of the Philistine Sea, and only later did they begin to extend their authority toward the interior. They doubtlessly settled first in such important centers as Gaza, Ashkelon and Ashdod, and after penetrating the center of the Coastal Plain — two other cities — Gath (Tell eṣ-Ṣafi)[17] and Ekron (probably Khirbet el-Muqanna') were added; both centers in the proximity of the tribal lots of Judah and Dan. Not for nothing does the Bible point out that the regions of the Philistines which belonged to "the land that yet remaineth" extended from "Shihor, which is before Egypt, even unto the border of Ekron northward." These districts were under the jurisdiction of the five Philistine lords: the Gazite, the Ashkelonite, the Ashdodite, the Gittite and the Ekronite (Josh. 13:3). From this part of the country, which became theirs for many generations, they set forth with increasing forces to conquer the near-by areas in the Negev and the territories of Judah and Dan. The expansionist aspirations of the Philistine lords led to conflicts with the Israelite tribes. In the course of time these clashes turned into a fateful struggle which resulted at the onset in the subjugation of the southern and central tribes, but ended with the formation of the independent Israelite Monarchy and the rejection of the Philistine yoke.

Interesting details about the Philistines and the Tjeker on the Canaanite coast are contained in the Egyptian sources. The Onomasticon of Amen-opet mentions three Sea-Peoples on Canaanite soil: the Sherden, Tjeker, and the Philistines, and three cities: Gaza, Ashkelon and Ashdod which enjoyed a special political as well as commercial status. It is possible that the author actually assigned them to the area ruled by Egypt.[18]

Another important document is the letter of Wen-Amon, a priest at the sanctuary of the god Amon in Thebes, who was dispatched to Byblos to acquire cedar wood for the ceremonial barge of the god.[19] The letter mentions by name four rulers of the coastal cities situated between Egypt and Phoenicia. One of these was Beder (or Bedel) the Tjeker ruler of Dor whose maritime power was such that he could despatch a fleet of eleven warships to Byblos for the purpose of apprehending Wen-Amon. The other three were, no doubt, the rulers of other important Philistine cities. Another of them, Warkatar/l, possibly the ruler of the harbor city of Ashkelon, kept up trade and apparently also political connections with Sidon. The letter of Wen-Amon reads: "As to this Sidon ... aren't there fifty grainships which are in Khabur with Warakat which journey and draw near to his house?" The term *Khabûr* apparently refers to large trading companies headed by the rulers themselves, and whose associates were the mercantile nobility.[20] We might mention that part of the goods Wen-Amon brought from Egypt represented the taxes to be paid to the Philistine princes War/lat, Makamar and Beder, ruler of Dor. In this connection should be mentioned the Greek historical traditions and legends connected with the Troyan war. One of these traditions, preserved by the historian Justin who obtained it probably from the historian Timaeus (4th century B.C.E.), — relates that the Sidonians built (rebuilt) Tyre after being routed by the king of the Ashkelonites. This event which took place as it were, "one year before the destruction of Troy," hints at Ashkelon's great importance in the history of Sidon before the rise to greatness of Tyre. It is not impossible that Sidon's weakness, which is alluded to in the account of the Danite's conquest of Laish (Jud. 18:7, 28), is to be connected with this event.[21] The Danaean heroes of Greek legend are doubtlessly connected with the Denyen (Danuna) mentioned together with the Philistines and Tjeker in Ramses III's inscriptions. Of particular interest is the fact that in the 8th century B.C.E. inscription from Karatepe in Cilicia, Azitawadda, King of the Danuna, appears as a descendant of the house of Mpsh, who is certainly none other than the Danaean Mopsos who occupies such an important place in Greek legend, and who in the course of his wanderings reached not only Cilicia, but also Palestine where — according to one tradition — he even conquered Ashkelon.[22] The same applies to the Danaean Perseus whose life story is interwoven with that of the daughter of the king of Abyssinia, Andromeda, whom he rescued from the rock she had been chained to in the Jaffa sea. This prompted the suggestion that the Danaeans had settled in the neighborhood of Jaffa, between Philistia in the south and the Tjeker principality of Dor, and it was probably they who founded the earliest settlement at Tell Qasileh (stratum XII).[23] The general picture that emerges from the Egyptian sources fits in with the one emerging from the archeological finds and the early biblical literature. Although the gradual assimilation of the Philistines and the groups attached to them to Canaanite culture began with their settlement in the coastal area, in the Shefela, and in various centers along the traffic routes, they did not completely discard their Aegean heritage. Moreover, their maritime trade connections were responsible for the fact that in the course of time the areas under their rule were actually enriched by new influences from the regions of the Aegean Sea and Cyprus. Apart from the obvious phenomena in Philistine civilisation, we might point out some additional features, particularly the development of metallurgy, as it has found expression in different places (Tell Qasileh, Tell el-Ḥesi, Beth-shemesh), and especially the introduction into general use of iron and the beginning of its distribution in the course of the 11th century. This development was doubtlessly a result of the sustained maritime connections with the coast of Anatolia.[24] It might also be argued that this period witnessed the adaptation of the Canaanite alphabetical writing so as to fit the administrative, military and mercantile purposes of the Philistines and Phoenicians, with the Israelites following in their footsteps. Apparently this was also the time when the alphabetical script of twenty-two consonantal signs written horizontally from right to left spread in the Eastern Mediterranean area; this is the prototype of the 10th century Phoenician-Hebrew classical writing.[25]

The biblical sources draw the picture of a mighty national body, an alien element on the soil of Canaan, viz. the league of the five Philistine lords who subdued both the Canaanites and the Israelites by means of an elite of princes and professional warrior champions.

Especially interesting in this connection is the description of Goliath, the heavily armed champion from Gath; "And he had a helmet of brass upon his head, and he was clad with a coat of mail... and he had greaves of brass upon his legs, and a javelin of brass between his shoulders. And the shaft of his spear was like a weaver's beam; and his spear's head weighed six hundred shekels of iron; and his shield bearer went before him" (I Sam. 17:5-7). Due to their excellent organization, superior armament, which included chariots, and military strategy acquired while serving as professional soldiers, the Philistines were able to dominate the mass of Canaanites, to establish an elite class among the population, and to extend their rule over the Israelite areas in the interior of western Palestine. Their conquests were doubtlessly aimed not only at the domination of the native inhabitants and the exaction of corvées and tax, but also at the domination of the overland route just as they controlled the sea routes. To that purpose the Philistines established military posts and garrisons in the towns and fortresses situated at strategic points (I Sam. 13:3; II Sam. 23:14). In the event of rebellion in the conquered areas they dispatched to the assistance of the garrisons (I Sam. 10:17) *ḥamashḥith*, a professional, mobile military unit able to repress any attempt at throwing off their yoke. In this respect the Philistines proved themselves the heirs of the Egyptian political system of the period preceding them, and like the Egyptians they conscripted auxiliary units from among the local population (cf. I Sam. 14:21).

From the stories about Samson we learn that the Philistines oppressed the southern tribes: "Now at that time the Philistines had rule over Israel" (Jud. 14:4); and the men of Judah tell Samson: "Knowest thou not that the Philistines are rulers over us?" (Jud. 15:11). Timnah (Tell Batashi on the Sorek brook), which seems to have been considered a suburb of Ekron, was at that time a Philistine town in the neighborhood of the Danite cities — Zorah and Eshtaol. From the Samson stories can be drawn the conclusion that in times of peace the relations between Philistines and Israelites were good enough to permit occasional intermarriage. It is in times of political and military tension that Samson assumes the character of an Israelite hero dedicated to fighting the alien ruler. The words Samson uttered before his tragic death remained forever engraved in the nation's memory: "Let me die with the Philistines" (Jud. 16:30).

About the middle of the 11th century the ever increasing Philistine pressure on the center of the Israelite tribes in the hill-country of Ephraim led to the decisive military campaign of Eben-ezer, situated close to the main Philistine base of Aphek in the Sharon (Ras el-'Ain). From the description in I Sam. 4 we learn that the hosts of the Philistine lords were faced by a large Israelite volunteer force, apparently made up mainly of Ephraimites. In order to encourage the warriors the Ark of the Covenant was brought from the center at Shiloh to the battlefield. However, the Israelites were routed, the ark taken into captivity, and its bearers, the priests slain in battle. The biblical source does not relate what happened in the aftermath of the war, but it transpires that the Philistines penetrated into the hill-country of Ephraim and destroyed Shiloh and its sanctuary (Ps. 78:60, Jer. 7:12–14; 26:6), a fact which is borne out by the excavations conducted there.[26] The Philistines increased their pressure on the Israelite tribes and succeeded in subjecting to their rule the territories of Ephraim and Benjamin. This victory gave them control over the decisive part of the Israelite area of settlement west of the Jordan. It also ensured their grip on the main caravan routes leading from Philistia to the northern plains, and in particular the *Via maris*, while important centers such as Megiddo and Beth-shean became their strongholds. The warlike spirit alive among the Israelite tribes was no doubt quenched, the inter-tribal connections loosened, while divisions and rifts within the Israelite settlement aided the Philistines in consolidating their rule. The capture of the Ark of the Covenant and the destruction of Shiloh, the site of the ancient sanctuary in the heart of the hill-country of Ephraim, maybe also the federative center of the central tribes, crushed the spirit of the great tribe of Ephraim which had enjoyed a special position among the Israelite tribes during the preceding generations. It seemed as though the independent, national-religious will to try to shake off the foreign yoke was broken, while an organized military force had not yet emerged in the area of Israelite settlement. The Philistines exploited this situation by various methods of sub-jugation which included the stationing of garrisons in important cities ("Gibe'at Elohim, where is the garrison of the Philistines," I Sam. 10:5, appears to be none other than Gibeath Benjamin of I Sam. 13:2–3),[27] the exaction of heavy taxes as well as the monopolization of the metal industry: "Now there was no smith found throughout all the land of Israel; for the Philistines said: 'Lest the Hebrews make them swords or spears'; but all the Israelites went down to the Philistines, to sharpen every man his plowshare, etc.," (I Sam. 13:19 ff.).[28]

The Philistine hegemony over large parts of western Palestine after the battle of Eben-ezer and their control of the land and sea routes led to an extensive development of their material culture. In this period the tradition of the Philistine pottery had already died out, though something of its decorations and shapes still persisted. Its place was taken by ceramic ware locally developed, but displaying external influences, which is distinguished by a large number of new shapes, a mature style, and increasing use of slip and burnish. Along with it the quantity of imports increased, particularly from Egypt, Phoenicia and Cyprus. This is clearly demonstrated at Tell Qasileh, on the northern bank of the Jarkon (level X), which had then reached the height of its prosperity as a sea-trading center. What particularly distinguished this settlement is the planned lay-out with its pleasant houses, rich in storage vessels. Outstanding there is the square three room house from which developed the four room house characteristic of the period of the Israelite Monarchy. Like Tell Qasileh, Megiddo became a prosperous town (stratum VIA), which was probably not only the fastness of the Philistine ruler, but also a caravan trading center. The public building from this period discovered close to the city gate of Megiddo was, apparently, the residence of the Philistine governor.[29] As to Beth-shean, it appears that the two sanctuaries in stratum V with their west-ward looking entrance and their holy of holies placed inside the temple — in its eastern section — must also be attributed to this period.[30] A biblical source also mentions the wall of Beth-shean (I Sam. 31:10), and a temple of Ashtoreth.

In this period, as in the preceding one, the strength of the Philistines lay in their administrative and military organization, in the considerable enterprise they displayed in developing land and sea trade, and probably also in metal work. However, Philistine rule did not endure long. As soon as a movement directed against the oppressors came into being in Israel, with the main purpose of throwing off the foreign yoke and promoting the political establishment of the Israelites, the foreign rule was shaken. This movement, which started in the hill-country of Ephraim and Benjamin, was aided by certain flaws in the Philistine administration. From the distant bases of their settlements in the coastal area and in the Shefela the Philistines were unable to enforce, over a prolonged period, the authority of their governors in the hostile surroundings of the mountainous region, and even less to employ effectively their war chariots, when required. From Samuel's and Saul's stories in the Bible we learn that the movement of rebellion, which was given vigorous expression at large public meetings held in sanctified places, frightened the Philistines and led to military clashes. It is related that Samuel the Seer from Ramathaim-zophim in the southern hill-country of Ephraim, who acted in this period of ebb, made the tour of the holy places in Ephraim and in Benjamin judging the people and conducting religious ceremonies at Beth-el, Mizpah and Gilgal. His activities also included the fostering of the national movement that had started among the people and which crystallized upon the establishment of the monarchy in Israel. Particularly instructive is the story of Israel's war with the Philistines in the days of Samuel. The latter assembled the people at Mizpah, in the south of the hill-country of Ephraim, and there conducted a religious ceremony "before the Lord": "And when the Philistines heard that the children of Israel were gathered together at Mizpah, the lords of Philistines went up against Israel. And when the children of Israel heard it, they were afraid of the Philistines."

The Bible relates further that Samuel and his voluntary forces defeated the Philistines near Mizpah: "And the men of Israel went out of Mizpah and pursued the Philistines, and smote them, until they came under Beth-car" (I Sam. 7:7–12). As to the passage: "And they came no more within the border of Israel ... and the cities which the Philistines had

taken from Israel were restored to Israel from Ekron even unto Gath...
and there was peace between Israel and the Amorites" (I Sam. 7:13–14),
it may possibly refer to the time of Saul. It was, after all, only after Saul's
elevation as King of Israel that the geopolitical situation changed in the
Israelite hill-country and in the lowlands.

According to the biblical tradition it was Samuel the Seer who, in spite
of his essential opposition to the abolition of the tribal regime, acceded
to the demand of the elders of Israel at a time of danger and emergency
and anointed Saul son of Kish, a mighty warrior of the tribe of Benjamin,
as king over Israel (I Sam. 8). Moreover that same biblical source puts in
Samuel's mouth the description of the "manner of the King that shall
reign over you," and interprets the people's plea "that we also may be like
all the nations, and that our king may judge us, and go out before us,
and fight our battles." The people doubtlessly saw in the king a redeemer
from the Philistines.[31] It was the establishment of royal authority based on
a standing army which included professional archers (I Chr. 8:40; 12:2),
and the circumstances which effected the unification of the tribes and re-
kindled their warlike spirit that were responsible for Saul's victories over
the Philistines, and for carrying the war from the hill country down into
the Shefela and to the borders of Philistia.

Possibly at the time the monarchy was established in Israel the political
life of the Philistines underwent a similar change. Worth mentioning is the
fact that it is precisely during Saul's reign that a Philistine king, Achish
King of Gath, is mentioned for the first time (I Sam. 21:11, 27:2). This
begs the question whether the struggle between Israel and Philistia in the
last third of the 11th century was to a large extent the main factor only in
the formation of Saul's monarchy in Benjamin and its establishment inside
the Israelite area of settlement, or, also in the creation of Philistia's monarchy, which had its center at Gath of the Philistines close to Israel's
border.[32] The Hebrew poetry dating from the beginning of the Monarchy
points also to the special importance of the residence of the Philistine king —
Gath—, near Ashkelon, the large harbor and trade center: "Tell it not
in Gath, publish it not in the streets of Ashkelon" (II Sam. 1:20). Not for
nothing is Gath described as a royal city (I Sam. 27:5). The authority
of King Achish was certainly considerable in peace and in war time, thus
explaining why David sought refuge with him while fleeing from Saul.
Achish even appointed him to Ziklag, to guard Philistia's southern border.
The stories of Abraham and Isaac moving at a time of drought from Beer-
sheba to the land of Gerar where they lived under the protection of
Abimelech, King of Philistia (Gen. 20:26), can only by conjecture be

considered a reflection of the historical development of the relations between the southern tribes and the Philistine tribes in the western Negev at the time the monarchy was established in Philistia.

This also transpires from the name given to Achish in the heading of Ps. 34: "[A Psalm] of David, when he changed his demeanour before Abimelech." It is against this background that we must also understand the political organization of Philistia, as it appears in these stories which mention next to the king, Phichol the captain of his host, Ahuzzath his friend, and his servants — a royal set-up which recalls the one existing in Israel at Saul's time.

The stories in the Book of Samuel show that Achish's support of David against Saul represented an attempt to restore Philistia's former glory by employing the stratagem of *divide et impera* besides the use of force. From their base at Aphek in the Sharon the Philistines set out along the coastal road toward the Plain of Jezreel, so as to attack Saul's kingdom from the north. The ensuing war ended in the defeat of Saul, who was slain at Mount Gilboa, and in the strengthening of Megiddo and Beth-shean the Philistine bases in the plain (I Sam. 29:31).

However, in final analysis both the political stratagem and the use of force missed their mark. The crisis between the two currents in the Israelite nation was soon resolved, and the results of the unification of Judah and Israel represented a blow for the Philistines. David ruled over all Israel, consolidated the kingdom founded by Saul, and succeeded in raising the Israelite kingdom to the status of an important political factor. David inflicted the Philistines a number of defeats, first in the Vale of Rephaim and later in the northern Shefela, thus opening the way to the Sharon and the Plain of Jezreel. He was able to break the military, political and economic power of the Philistines by annexing large areas north of the Jarkon and in the regions of the Shefela and the Negev. But he was unable to gain control of the large Philistine cities on the southern coast, and Gath, the object of fierce battles, remained a royal city even in Solomon's time (I Kings. 2:39), though it might possibly have recognized the authority of the Israelite king. It is interesting to note that David employed a troop of mercenaries called Gittites (II Sam. 15:18 ff.). After the decline of Philistia as a paramount political and economic factor, the Egyptians and Israelites took over part of its dominion of the sea and trade routes, while Tyre, the importance of which as the Sidonians' new capital had grown since the time of David, exploited the disturbance in the balance of power due to Israel's rise and Philistia's decline to establish itself in the position of an international trading center.

PART THREE: ISRAELITE SOCIETY AND ITS CULTURE IN THE SETTLEMENT PERIOD

CHAPTER IX

THE ISRAELITE TRIBES

by J. Liver

A. Introduction

BIBLICAL HISTORIOGRAPHY regards the people of Israel as consisting primarily of the twelve Israelite tribes, that is, of an association of tribes bound by ties of kinship and origin, and maintaining institutions stemming from a tribal regime. In the Bible this approach applies to the earlier periods of Israelite history, when the tribe was a well-defined social and political unit, as well as to later times, from the establishment of the monarchy onwards, when the tribe was no longer an organic whole in the social or political structure of Israel and the concepts associated with tribal society had lost most of their actual content. During the entire biblical period the religio-social outlook based on the tribal tradition persisted in Israel, despite the acute antagonism between that tradition and the monarchy, which by its very nature as an hereditary authority imposing its rule on a national-territorial group, tends to destroy the entire fabric of tribal institutions. The tribal concept, which left its imprint on biblical historiography as a whole, is based on the social conditions of the period under discussion in this volume, that is, from the beginning of the history of Israel as a nation to the establishment of the monarchy.

B. The Tribe, the Family, and the Father's House

A discussion of the texts dealing with the structure and way of life of the Israelite tribes is largely dependent upon a clarification of the terms for a tribe and its sub-divisions employed in the Bible.

In the Bible the term *shēvet* (= "tribe") represents a clear and well-defined concept. It denotes one of the twelve tribes of Israel, but not that of other nations, even though the latter may have had a similar tribal structure.[1] Another word for an Israelite tribe is *maṭṭe*. These two terms, which have the similar primary meaning of "a staff, rod," as for example, a shepherd's staff (Micah 7:14; Ps. 23:4), and the scepter of a ruler (Ezek. 19:11; Ps. 45:7; etc.), may refer to situations in which the tribe undertakes action as a united, cohesive body, as in times of war or of wandering in search of new pastures. In a few passages however — and in these the extant text presents difficulties — *shēveṭ* signifies not a tribe but a family, which is a sub-unit of an Israelite tribe (Num. 4:18; Jud. 20:12; I Sam. 9:21). It is however doubtful whether in the original version of these passages *shēveṭ* had this meaning.

While the meaning of *shēveṭ* and of *maṭṭe* is generally clear, confusion exists about the subdivisions of the tribe, i.e. a "family" (*mishpāḥā*) and a "father's house" (*beth'av*). "Family" usually applies to a wider group subdivided into "fathers' houses," as is evident from Josh. 7:14 (cf. Deut. 29:17), but in other passages it also means a tribe (Jud. 17:7; etc.). Then again, while "father's house" is in several instances used in the sense of "family" (Ex. 6:14; Num. 3:24; etc.),[2] "heads of their fathers' houses" denote the princes of the tribes (Num. 7:2; Josh. 22:14; etc.). This confusion is due to the fact that at the time when these historical accounts were put in writing the tribal regime had already been undermined and the Israelites were adapting themselves to life in a settled country. Precise distinctions between terms associated with the tribal structure were no longer in current use, so that one term could designate — in a borrowed or extended sense — some other tribal unit.

Generally a "father's house" denotes a restricted family group, comprising the offspring of one father, the head of the father's house, and including the family dependents, such as slaves and servants, and those who, rejected by their own tribe or family, seek protection, as well as the grown-up sons together with their wives and children. A "father's house" is based on patriarchal rule,[3] all the offspring — including the adults — being subject to the father's authority, and all together forming a compact social unit during his lifetime. Upon his death the "father's house" disintegrates. By contrast, the "family", which comprised several "fathers' houses," is not a mere mechanical combination of the latter, but a permanent group persisting down the generation, and the members of which are called by their patronymic. Thus, for example, Ehud son of Gera, in the days of the Judges, and Shimei son of Gera, a contemporary of David (II Sam. 16:5), were members of the leading Benjaminite family of Gera, which traced its descent to Gera son of Benjamin (cf. Gen. 46:21). "Tribe," "family" and "father's house" denote relationships and not any fixed number of individuals. A family could be comparatively large, a tribe smaller than a large family, as was the case with the tribe of Dan which in the period of the Judges consisted of only one family (Jud. 18). Similarly, a big father's house, numbering scores of souls, could be larger than a declining family and yet only a father's house within a large family.

Another term applied to a tribal body is "thousand" (*'elef*) which, when referring to part of a tribe, is identical with "family" (Jud. 6:15; I Sam. 10:19; 23:23; etc.), though in some passages both refer to a tribe (Num. 1:16; 10:4; Josh. 22:14). The "thousand" is generally associated with the family's military functions, being the family unit equipped for war.[4] The military formation of the tribe is thus expressed in "thousands." The term "thousand" also denotes a military unit consisting of a fixed number of men, subdivided into hundreds and into still smaller units. But the "thousand" as the family's military unit did not comprise exactly that number. Often it undoubtedly consisted of a much smaller number of warriors, as in the case of the family of the Danites, of whom "six hundred men girt with weapons of war" set forth (Jud. 18:11), while according to a widely held view the three hundred men whom Gideon selected for battle (Jud. 7:6) were all members of his family, that of Abiezer. Nonetheless, there appears to be a connection between the two uses of the term "thousand." Although there is no proof of it in the Bible, the military formations of the fathers' houses, which were the sub-units of the family, may have been deployed in hundreds, which were the sub-units of the "thousand."

C. The Tribal Regime Prior to the Conquest

The tribal regime in Israel has its origin in the nomadic period preceding the Conquest. Such a regime existed not only in Israel but also at a particular stage in their social development among other peoples, whether chronologically and regionally close to, or distant from the Hebrew tribes. The picture of the Israelite tribal regime and structure that emerges from the biblical accounts, most of which, in their final form belong to a later stage of social evolution, is fragmentary and indefinite. In order to describe tribal society at the beginning of the Israelite history, it is therefore necessary to have recourse not only to biblical and Ancient Eastern sources, but also to post-biblical material on the tribal regime among other nations, in particular nomadic and semi-nomadic Arab tribes,[5] these being ethnically and linguistically related to the tribes of Israel. The assumption that an analogous regime existed among the Israelites is supported by the basic similarity between the external conditions which led to the formation of the Israelite tribal regime and those of the ancient Arabs, especially such of their tribes as wandered in the border regions of the settled country. That the Bedouin in the Negev and east of the Jordan preserve to this day a tribal regime is due to these very conditions.[6] The tribal regime and concept of life are closely associated with a nomadic or semi-nomadic way of life. In the absence of a unifying force the tribe tends to disintegrate into smaller units. The size and the organizational patterns of the tribal units are determined to a considerable extent by economic and security factors. But fundamentally the tribal regime is based on the assumption that all the members of the tribe are descended from a common ancestor, whose name they usually bear. The subdivision of the tribe into families and father's houses is merely a division into smaller units descended from a common ancestor, who in his turn is a descendant of the ancestor of the entire tribe. According, every group — whether it be a nation, a league of tribes, a tribe, a family, or a father's house — is separated by an interval of generations from the direct descendants of the ancestor common to that group, the closeness of kingship among tribes or peoples being proportionate to the generations separating them from their common ancestor. According to the tribal concept neither social-political regime nor territorial principle determine the formation of national units, but solely the genealogical factor.

This tribal concept is clearly expressed in the Bible in all the records of the generations and the genealogical lists, from the Creation and the table of the nations (Gen. 10) to the family and individual genealogies in the Book of Chronicles (I Chron. 2–9). All people are descended from a common ancestor, Adam, whose offspring subdivided into nations, tribes, and families throughout the world. Among them figure the Israelites, all of whom are descendants of a common ancestor, Jacob-Israel, whose sons are the fathers of the twelve Israelite tribes. Besides their detailed genealogies according to families, it results clearly from the genealogical lists that the Bible applies the tribal concept also to the nations related by origin to Israel, who are, according to the Book of Genesis, the posterity of Terah, Abraham and Isaac. These nations and tribes, which are enumerated in the lists of the sons of Nahor (Gen. 22:21–24), of the East (Gen. 25:1–4), of Ishmael (Gen. 25:12–16), and of Esau (Gen. 36) are all — whether main units or the latter's sub-units — the descendants of ancestors who bear the names of tribes or tribal groups.

The biblical concept of an ancestral house turning into a nation following a natural growth process during which its posterity subdivided into tribes and clans, is identical with the traditions of the Arab tribes. Among them there also took shape detailed genealogies which ascribe the filiation of all the Arab tribes to a common ancestor whose offspring are the fathers of tribal associations, tribes and clans.[7] Needless to say, this oversimplification has no basis in fact. No large tribal association has ever come into being through natural increase of the descendants of a single father, this being feasible only with regard to comparatively small units. While in the complex process of the formation of tribes and tribal associations it sometimes undoubtedly happened that a large unit split up into several parts, tribal leagues usually resulted from the merger of a number of independent tribes. Even the tribes themselves, especially those consisting of many families, were the outcome not of the natural increase of a common ancestor's descendants, but of the union of various families.

Nonetheless, the assumption that the tribe is an extended family has a certain basis in reality. Concerning their structure, the tribe and its subunit are neither class nor territorial groups, as in some types of regime, but family units. The unifying factor in tribal society is the principle of blood relationship which left its imprint on the life of the tribe, even as among the ancient Semitic nomads it was the fundamental basis of a compact society with its own institutions. It is this principle that defines the code of rights and the duties of individuals and the various social units.[8] Hence the great importance that attaches in nomadic tribal society to the institution of the blood-avenger, an institution that provides protection for, and is the basis of the security of the individual in a tribal society which has no central authority nor communal power to restrain the individual. Only a person belonging to a group where blood-avengers are prepared to defend him feels secure in life and property.

This situation accounts for the considerable cohesion prevailing in tribal society. On the face of it, the individual is free to leave his tribe or family, but if he is rejected by his people his social position and personal safety are completely undermined. Hence, communal living and communal wandering are characteristic features of the basic group in tribal society.

Such a group, then, constitutes the fundamental unit in tribal society, larger ones having apparently resulted from the merger and amalgamation of these smaller groups either through pacts between those of equal status or through the annexation of a small group by a larger one. It is improbable that this basic unit represents a tribe in the biblical sense of the word. The Bible itself mentions families which were absorbed by various tribes, that is, individual groups, which later subdivided and joined different other tribes or transferred from one tribe to another.[9] The small family unit, the "house" in its restricted meaning, could not have been the basic unit, and this for two reasons. First, it was too small to sustain a separate existence. Secondly, in the course of a few generations a father's house could under favorable conditions increase and become a family consisting in the main of actual blood relations. It appears, then, that this unit, larger than a house but smaller than a tribe, was the basic association of blood-avengers. Consisting of the "people" or "kindred" of the man, it was sometimes a clan, and sometimes, when the family had grown and increased, more limited. It is coextensive with the archaic biblical term ḥay (I Sam. 18:18) which is none other than the word ‎حي of the ancient Arab nomads.[10] This is a unit in which blood vengeance is not practiced toward its own members: someone who kills a member of his own family is not put to death but cast out from among his people and denied asylum (cf. Gen. 4:8–14).[11] But should a member of the family be killed by an outsider, all his relations are his blood—avengers.

The family, then, is the basic tribal unit. Its members live together, migrate together, and most of them are descended from the father of the family whose name they bear. In contrast to the restricted family unit — the father's house in which the father enjoys complete and absolute authority over all his offspring — the head of the family has no such authority over its other branches, which in theory enjoy social equality, but as he is naturally at the same time also the head of a father's house, he there exercises complete authority. The size of a family does not depend exclusively on natural increase, since it includes to a smaller or larger extent additions from without as also the offspring of servants and slaves, whose position is at first inferior to that of the actual members of the family, but who are in the course of time absorbed by it either by marrying into the family or by claiming genealogical descent from one of its fathers.

The same processes that were responsible for the consolidation and growth of the family through external additions also led to the formation of tribes by families joining together. Among neighboring tribes that wandered in adjacent areas practical ties were created resulting in the establishment of tribal associations. Some of these ties within the tribes and between tribal associations were of an enduring nature. But separation and secession also occurred. A family would separate from a declining tribe to seek protection with another that was stronger and more prosperous, or a family that had increased in size would break away to become an independent tribe. Among groups of nomads the formation of new tribes and families is as a rule connected with the real or imaginary decline of their predecessors. In all these shifts and changes the genealogical principle that all the members of the tribe and even of the tribal association are descended from a common ancestor constitutes the basis of the tribal regime. This principle is, as previously stated, largely unrealistic. Nevertheless, although not the offspring of a common ancestor, tribes or tribal associations generally share the same ethnic origin, and the genealogical concept is merely a schematization of kinship and origin ties existing among tribes and families.

Even as the father's house is not subject to the absolute rule of the family, the family is not subject to the rule of the tribe, either, since nomadic life makes it comparatively easy for the former to free itself from the authority of the latter. However, under tribal conditions there is as a rule no reason to adopt such a course, since almost no restrictions are imposed on the family within the tribal structure, especially in times of peace; the activities involving the tribe as a whole being mainly wars, raids, migrations, and the search for fresh pastures. In times of peace the tribal head has no power of coercion, he is a leader rather than a ruler, for in a tribe based on the principle of blood kinship, in which all its members apparently enjoy equal status, there is no established and absolute authority, no permanent rule.

This brief survey of tribal society is based largely on the customs of societies in which a tribal regime still obtains or on those of ancient tribal societies on which information is available. As regards Israel, despite the fact that only late traditions and some general information on its pre-Conquest social structure and form of government, were preserved the biblical tradition is clear about the actual existence of a tribal regime in Israel before the Settlement. It may therefore be assumed that the Israelite tribes lived as did the nomadic and semi-nomadic tribes in the border areas of Canaan. Only on this basis is it possible to explain the impact that the tribal traditions had on the formation of the social institutions and religious outlook of Israel even after these traditions had lost their inner content.

D. The Tribe as a Social and Political Unit during the Conquest and the Settlement

One of the principal results of the Conquest and of the Settlement — a result which found expression only much later — was the complete disintegration of the tribal regime. True, the tribes maintained their traditional relationship to a common ancestor, the consciousness that they formed one nation even strengthened and deepened among them, and the tribes and families continued to preserve the tribal tradition. But with the Settlement the inner content and social significance of the tribal institutions underwent a complete transformation, though in name and outward form they persisted for a long time.

In the process of settling, the Israelites came into close contact with the earlier inhabitants of the country, who had, living as they did in towns and villages, an urban and agricultural civilization. This contact exerted considerable influence on the Israelites' institutions and regime, but even without it this process would have been inevitable for nomads and semi-nomads now transformed into a nation living on its own land. In the course of settling in the country the tribes and families lost the characteristic feature of their society in which the ties, duties, and rights of individuals and of secondary groups were based on family relationship. Nonetheless, outwardly, the tribal structure was preserved, and fathers' houses and families that had wandered together generally settled together.

Neither did genealogy lose its former importance during the period of the Settlement, for it alone conferred on the individual Israelite the status of a settler and of a privileged citizen among his people. During this period this principle was to a considerable extent fictitious. But the very existence of the fiction tended to give a measure of national cohesion to the tribal groups then absorbing foreign elements from among the population of the country. A considerable number of urban settlements of the country's earlier inhabitants were incorporated as families and fathers' houses within the tribal structure. Nor was the genealogical concept of the settling tribes undermined by the continuous wandering of individuals and small groups in search of an inheritance, which resulted in fathers' houses and families leaving their original tribal framework, in their settling within the borders of another tribe, and in their genealogical inclusion within that tribe. Thus despite the disintegration of the tribal regime, the process of the consolidation of the tribes did not end with the Settlement, but continued until the families and fathers' houses had settled down in their permanent abode. Even after the Settlement and until the beginning of the monarchy, the regime in Israel was fundamentally tribal and familial, adapted to the changed conditions of a settled country. The organic social unit — the city with its dependent villages — was regarded as a father's house or a family. Gideon's city, Ophrah, is for example, called in Jud. 6:24 "Ophrah of the Abiezrites," that is, of the family of Abiezer, one of the chief families in the tribe of Manasseh.

The elders of the family, that is, the heads of the fathers' houses, were the leaders of the city and its environs,[12] which may explain the term "heads of their fathers' houses" to denote the princes, the authorized leaders of the tribes (Num. 7:2; 36:1; Josh. 22:14; I Kings 8:1). In several passages "princes" occurs in parallelism with "elders" (Jud. 8:14 — "And he wrote down for him the princes of Succoth, and the elders thereof"), or signifies the elders of the families (Jud. 5:15 — "the princes of Issachar"; Jud. 10:18 — "the princes of Gilead"), a usage that testifies to governance, by the elders of the family, during the period of the Judges.

The city elders were responsible for law and order in the city, and for the community's discharging its obligations toward the individual, the orphan and the widow, the sojourner and the stranger. In times of war the heads of the fathers' houses summoned the warriors; they met with the elders of other places in the tribal council which convened at the sacred site in the tribal territory on days of public assembly and of festival. They were authorized to deal primarily with legal and religious matters within the sphere of family law — with bloodshed and murder, landed and other property, marriage and levirate marriage.[13] In all these matters the city elders exercised the authority formerly enjoyed by the patriarchal head of the family. They sent for the wilful murderer from the city of refuge so as to hand him over to the blood-avengers (Deut. 19:12), granted asylum, in the city of refuge to the unintentional murderer, and made atonement for the person found slain within or near the city limits (Deut. 21:1–9). They confirmed the laws of inheritance and redemption of land (Ruth 4:1ff.), decided which member of the family was debarred from inheriting in his father's house (Jud. 11:1–2, 7), played a leading role in the ceremony connected with a levirate marriage (Deut. 25:5 ff.), whose purpose is to perpetuate the memory of the man who died childless and thereby to preserve the continuity of the family, and decided the fate of the stubborn and rebellious son who was liable to the death penalty (Deut. 21:18–21).

Family and tribal law was most clearly expressed in the laws of inheritance,[14] especially as applied to the daughters of Zelophehad who inherited their father in the absence of male heirs: they were bidden to marry members of their own tribe, "Thus no inheritance shall pass over from one tribe to another but the Israelite tribes shall remain bound each to its portion" (Num. 36:9). This principle most probably lies at the root also of the laws of the Jubilee and of the redemption of land (Lev. 25:8–34), which ensure the return of landed property to the family and which charge a member of the family to redeem from a stranger, insofar as he is able to do so, the property of his kinsman. It is characteristic of tribal society that the Bible contains no adoption laws. For in theory, if not in practice, belonging to a family — and hence inheriting the family property — is determined solely by descent, and the individual has no right to change social arrangements based on blood kinship.

As this social organism adapted itself to a settled urban life, the various professional craftsmen organized themselves into separate groups. There was also a growing social gap between the members of the families that had entered upon their inheritance and those who had devoted themselves to the service of God and who supported themselves from the offerings of the others. Not only the priests and those who, being well versed in wisdom and in song, ministered in the sanctuary (and who were accounted Levites), but also the craftsmen, among them men with special skills (cf. I Chron. 2:55; 4:21, 23), traced their lineage back to a common ancestor. Any outsider who joined these theoretically closed groups automatically established his descent from the father of the tribe or of the family. One of the most conspicuous examples of this is the genealogy of Samuel's family: according to I Sam. 1 he was an Ephraimite dedicated to the service of God, but is included in the genealogical lists in I Chron. 6:18–23 among the Levites, the sons of Kohath.

Several passages dating from the Settlement and the beginning of the monarchy refer to divine service within the family circle. A family sacrifice was customary in Israel (I Sam. 20:29), and so highly esteemed that it was considered an adequate excuse for David's absence from the king's table. Passover was basically a family festival, the paschal lamb being slaughtered according to families (Ex. 12:21). Divine service within the home was an important factor as can be seen from the presence of a priest in a father's house and in a family (Jud. 18:19). In the course of time this family aspect became blurred and the individual served his God as a member of the Israelite community.

Although adapting itself to urban conditions, the family unit was still bound to the institutions characteristic of the tribal regime. At festivals and appointed times pilgrimages were made to the sacred tribal sites, constituting in fact the main bond among the various families in days of peace. In times of war and of enemy raids the men of the families rallied in defense of the tribe's territory, a duty that generally devolved upon the warriors[15] who were men of standing and of property among their people.

This transitional period saw the emergence of a unique type of leader and ruler — the charismatic leader who arose in times of trouble to save his own or several neighboring tribes. The Bible refers to him as a "savior" (Jud. 3:9, 15) and also as a "head and chief" (Jud. 11:11), but the biblical narrator usually designates him "Judge". As a rule he is not a judge in the legal sense, nor a leader by virtue of his standing in the tribe,[16] but someone who is impelled by the divine spirit which directs him and invests him with authority to unite families and tribes for a specific purpose. Once he has successfully repelled the enemy, he acquires judicial authority and the status of a leader among the tribes and families. Nonetheless he is not an absolute ruler nor is his position generally an hereditary one.

The institution of a "Judge" is indicative of a disintegrating tribal regime. Under an agricultural regime the head of the tribe no longer enjoyed the authority which had been his during migrations and the recurrent raids and wars that took place under nomadic conditions. At this juncture neither the monarchy nor any other form of government based on a permanent army had as yet been established in Israel. There was even strong opposition to a monarchy — an opposition rooted in the tribal tradition. It was during the transitional period from the regime of tribal heads, whose position had become devoid of all substance, to a monarchical regime, that the charismatic judge arose. Due to prevailing conditions the judge became a king. The personality of Saul, the first king in Israel, and the circumstances of his accession bear a marked resemblance to those of a charismatic judge.

With the progressive consolidation of the monarchy the foundations of tribal privileges were increasingly undermined. The tribes were obliged to relinquish individual freedoms and to accept obligations hitherto unknown: taxes, *corvée*, military service, and so on. Thus ended the decisive stage in which the tribe, from being a free unit based on genealogical ties that were founded on the concept of kinship, was transformed into a quasi-state subject to a king who was outside and above the tribal framework. With the passage of time the inner tribal divisions in Israel were blurred, several tribal names being assigned to districts (cf. I Kings 4:15–18). Although the tradition of belonging to a certain family and tribe was preserved at least among aristocratic families, the tribe as an actual social unit receded and succumbed before the growing consolidation of the institutions of a monarchical regime in Israel.

E. The Tribal League and its Institutions

Although the patterns of life and the family regime in the period of the Settlement tended to intensify division among the tribes, there is a clear and explicit tradition of their unity at that time. When the tribes coalesced into a nation or when a sense of national unity arose among them is a question to which no definite answer can be given. According to the biblical account the tribes were from the outset united and acknowledged a single leader. At the time of the Settlement there was indeed no central government in Israel, but this does not contradict the assumption that close ties existed among the tribes that had entered Canaan. Whereas the division into two kingdoms, which was due to local interests, took place only after the disintegration of the tribal institutions and following a lengthy period of centralized rule under David and Solomon, the ties uniting the twelve tribes, based on the consciousness of their common origin, were not affected during the entire period of the Settlement, which was one of independence for each tribe. This basic fact can only be explained on the assumption that in pre-monarchical times the congregation of Israel, that is, the league of the twelve tribes, enjoyed a certain measure of consolidation and authority. Nor was this a mere abstract concept of relationship, for common institutions which preserved the bond uniting the tribes were maintained. In the absence of coercion and of a centralized government, these institutions were necessarily associated with central cultic sites which, hallowed in ancient times, were common to all the tribes, but were by themselves unable to foster a consciousness of the unity and distinctiveness of the Israelite tribes as reflected in the biblical account.

The tradition of the tribal league is, then, bound up with the actual emergence and consolidation of Israel as a nation in the pre-Conquest period. Hence the assumption — almost identical with the biblical conception — that the tribes had a common ancient center for the worship of God where they concluded a solemn covenant. A common faith, comprising belief in the God of Israel, and the institution of common cultic practices ensured the continuance of the covenant which could be indefinite as to its details, thus permitting the tribes a considerable measure of freedom regarding arrangements and action. Although the tribal settlement was effected in stages, for, as seems probable, the tribes did not enter Canaan together, no lengthy intervals separated the different waves of settlers,[17] nor did this circumstance impair the tribes' sense of unity.

A salient feature of the Israelite tribal league is the number of twelve tribes belonging to it, a number which, far from being fortuitous, constitutes one of its essential elements.[18] A tribe might cease its independent existence (for example, the tribe of Levi) or be subdivided into two (like Ephraim and Manasseh), but the overall number of the tribes did not change. The Bible applies the principle of twelve tribes also to associations of other tribes related to the Israelites by common descent, such as the Ishmaelites (Gen. 25:13–16), the sons of Nahor (Gen. 22:20–24), and perhaps also of Joktan (Gen. 10:26–30) and of Esau (Gen. 36:10 ff). In these lists, as in those of the twelve Israelite tribes, the division of the tribes and peoples tends to be according to the sons of the different mothers, some wives, others concubines. To a certain extent, these differentiations, like the pattern of the twelve tribes, have their roots in historical factors.[19] This principle recalls the ancient *amphictyonies*, confederations of tribes and peoples (ἔθνε̆), which existed in Greece, in Asia Minor, and in Italy among the Etruscans. Of these the earliest and most important, as also the best known as regards its structure and institutions, is the Delphic *amphictyony*, evidence of whose existence date from the 8th century B.C.E. and onwards, but which was undoubtedly much earlier. The distinctive features of the *amphictyonies*, are, first, the explicit principle of twelve (or twice twelve) units associated in the *amphictyony*, and, secondly, the significance attached to a central temple uniting the members of the *amphictyony*. From the very outset apparently an association of peoples lived near the site of the temple, the word ἀμφικτυονία being composed of ἀμφί "round" and κτίζω "to dwell, settle (in a region), found" (a city, temple), and thus signifying "those who dwell round about" (the temple). The basis of the Greek *amphictyony*, at least in historical times, was the maintenance of a particular temple and the defense of those making the pilgrimage to it in order to participate in ceremonies and festivities conducted there at fixed times. It was to these ends that the laws and institutions of the *amphictyony* were directed.[20] It is doubtful whether there are in the available information on Semitic tribal confederations any references to all this. Yet despite differences in social and cultural background and in institutions between the *amphictyonies* of the classical world and the confederation of the twelve tribes mentioned in the Bible, it is precisely such evidence from a remote culture which shows that a league of twelve tribes, with its fixed and defined number, is no mere theoretical arrangement but is sustained by a specific social reality. This presupposes that the tribal league was associated with a common cultic site, the responsibility for the maintenance of which was assigned for a certain period during the year first to one tribe and then to each of the others in turn. It may therefore be assumed, despite the absence of evidence to this effect, that the Semitic confederations of twelve tribes also had a central cultic site where the tribes gathered for cult purposes, and that the tradition of the twelve tribes was connected with their participation in this cult.

When it consisted of nomadic tribes, the ancient Israelite tribal league, the congregation of Israel, was not associated with a particular sacred site, but with portable cultic objects, especially the Ark of the Covenant which contained the tables of the testimony and which in times of migration and of war was carried before them. According to biblical tradition, Kadesh-barnea, on the borders of the Negev, was for a long time the permanent center of the tribes in their migrations. With this area, too, the Sinai tradition is linked. While Kadesh-barnea was an ancient center of the Israelite tribal league, it does not apparently represent the earliest phase in the history of the league, the tradition of which is not connected with the name of Jacob but with that of Israel, as in the biblical expressions "tribes of Israel," and "children of Israel." Thus Israel's name is linked with the formation of the tribal league, which originated neither at Kadesh-barnea, nor at the revelation at Mount Sinai, nor in the Israelite wanderings in the wilderness, but at another, apparently earlier, stage in the history of the tribes described in the Book of Genesis in the migration of Jacob and his sons from the region of the Euphrates to Canaan (Gen. 32:25–31).

The location of the site of the ark of God and of the center of the tribal league in the early days of the Settlement is bound up with the divergent views on the various stages of the Settlement.[21] There is only sparse evidence as to the tribal league's central cultic site. But insofar as there was a fixed center, it was at Shiloh. There, according to the Book of Joshua, all the children of Israel assembled, there they set up the tent of meeting and placed the Ark of the Covenant, there Joshua decided the division of the country according to tribes (Josh. 18:1–10). There, too, was the seat of the chief priestly house in Israel which traced its descent from Aaron the high priest, there was celebrated every year a feast to which people from all Israel came to sacrifice unto the Lord (Jud. 21:19; I Sam. 1:3).

That Shiloh, in the territory of Ephraim, became the home of the Ark of the Covenant and of the tent of meeting was due to the rise of the House of Joseph (or, more precisely, the tribe of Ephraim) to a position of hegemony in the tribal league. This status, enjoyed by Joseph, is referred to in the biblical account regarding the birthright given to Ephraim after the decline of Reuben (cf. I Chron. 5:1 — "Forasmuch as he defiled his father's couch, his birthright was given unto the sons of Joseph the son of Israel"). In contrast to the other tribal cultic centers in Canaan, Shiloh is not mentioned in the patriarchal narratives as a holy site, but was nevertheless chosen as the center of the league, primarily on account of the supremacy of the tribe in whose territory it was situated. With its destruction it ceased to be a cultic center.

On the other hand, the biblical sources furnish no evidence of the existence in the period of the Judges of a tribal league, the congregation of Israel, with its own specific regime under the leadership of the tribal heads. True, the Book of Numbers depicts such a regime during the wandering in the wilderness, when the twelve princes of the tribes were at the head of the congregation of Israel, participated in the cult in the Tabernacle, and assisted Moses in governing the people. The question that arises is to what extent this description reflects the social situation in the nomadic period or in that following the Conquest. No contemporary historical data exist as regards the former period. But if it is accepted that the Israelites were associated in a league of twelve tribes before the Conquest, and that the tribes settled in Canaan conscious of their common descent and unity, they must have had some definite form of association and the tribal princes must have enjoyed a considerable measure of authority. This assumption holds good whether, as the Bible states, all the Israelite tribes entered Canaan together under the leadership of Joshua, or whether they did so in several waves that followed one another at brief intervals.

A regime of the congregation of Israel at the beginning of the Settlement is attested by the account in Josh. 9 of the covenant between the Gibeonites and the settling Israelites. While the account is stylized and tendentious,[22] it embodies historical evidence of the submission of the Gibeonites, and of the congregation of Israel as a united and consolidated body headed by the princes. Confirmation of this is found in the Book of Samuel (II Sam. 21:2 ff.) in the Gibeonites' request to David for the blood of the house of Saul because the latter had slain some of them, thereby violating the oath taken by the Israelites at the time of the Conquest. But during the period of the Judges, there is evidence neither of a regime of the congregation nor of a consolidated tribal league led by princes. On the contrary, each tribe or limited group of tribes fought their own battles while the others held aloof. Only in times of great peril did several tribes undertake joint action under a charismatic leader, a judge who was above the tribal league, and not a recognized tribal leader. The historical narrative of the period of the Judges contain no reference to the tribal princes, so characteristic of the nomadic way of life, but whose continued existence was doubtful once the city-family[23] had become the focal point of the social regime. The tent of meeting at Shiloh, which contained the Ark of the Covenant, was the assembly center of the tribes of Israel; but it was primarily a religious center. There the Israelites went on pilgrimage to sacrifice and to worship unto the Lord. There also, the traditions about the Patriarchs and the exploits of the Israelite tribes were shaped into songs and parables of the kind preserved in the blessing of Jacob (Gen. 69) and in that of Moses (Deut. 33), to be recited at festivals and appointed times. Nevertheless the priesthood at Shiloh had no authoritative power, nor could they summon the tribes' assembly for any special action. Characteristically, the only instance in the Book of Judges in which all the tribes participated, namely the war against the tribe of Benjamin resulting from the outrage upon the concubine at Gibeah (Jud. 19–21), was not connected with the center at Shiloh but with Mizpah (Jud. 20:1), on the border of Ephraim and Benjamin, near Gibeah of Benjamin. The historical authenticity of the incident is open to doubt, since the fictional element in it is particularly prominent,[24] and it cannot be regarded as evidence of the existence of a regime of the congregation in the days of the Judges. Nevertheless, there was a certain measure of national unity in this period. Saul's action of summoning the tribes of Israel to come to the rescue of the inhabitants of Jabesh-gilead by sending throughout the land twelve hunks of raw meat from a yoke of slaughtered oxen (I Sam. 11:7), and the similar manner in which the tribes of Israel were summoned in the episode of the concubine at Gibeah (Jud. 19:29), indicate a nucleus of unity among the tribes. But this sense of unity originated neither in the conditions prevailing in the days of the Judges nor in an attachment to a specific sacred site, but in the tradition of the congregation dating from the early days of the Conquest, a tradition rooted in the social realities that preceded the separation of the tribes and their settlement in cities and villages.

F. The Basic Principles of the Tribal Genealogical Lists

It is not known when written genealogical lists were first introduced in Israel, but as previously stated the genealogical tradition is very old.[25] Not only the tracing of descent from a common ancestor but the system that sets down the relationships of nations, tribes, and families as a continuous genealogical structure almost certainly preceded the Settlement, and was transmitted as an oral tradition. But this does not mean that the number and names of the tribes, and the order of the families belonging to a tribe are identical with those which were transmitted later in the biblical tradition. The narrative that treat of the ancestors of the nation and of the tribes, their genealogies, and their connections through marriage may, with some reservations, be regarded as an abstract of the relationships existing at a certain stage between the Israelite and the neighboring tribes, as also among the tribes themselves.[26] In these narratives, for which there are analogies in the ancient Greek traditions, the father of the nation or of the tribe — the eponym (ἥρως ἐπώνυμος) — may be regarded as a personification of the homonymous ethnic or geographical group. With the consolidation of the monarchical regime in Israel at the conclusion of the process of settlement, the tribal framework disintegrated and attachment to the tribal tradition of genealogy weakened. Belonging to a certain tribe or even to a family was now no longer as important as formerly. Nevertheless, there was still much vigor in the modes of life retained by the people, as well as in the hallowed traditions of the past, some of which were even committed to writing. It is not known what were the nature and scope of the genealogical lists in Israel, nor to what extent and where they were preserved.[27] Most probably they were largely lists of families and of fathers' houses, rather than of individuals, several of which were drawn up for official purposes, such as a national census, military service, and so on. This is suggested by some of the usages of the verb *hityiahes* which occurs in the genealogies in the Book of Chronicles[28] in an almost identical sense as that of *hitpaqed* (= "to be numbered").

The genealogical lists in the Bible comprise two principal types: a) those which mainly reflect historical, ethnographical, and even mythological traditions,[29] and which, occurring chiefly in the Book of Genesis, are introduced by the expressions "the generations of," or "the book of the generations of" (Gen. 5:1; 6:9; 10:1; etc.); b) those comprising lists of tribes and fathers' houses, as in the census lists in the Book of Numbers and in the genealogical chapters in the Book of Chronicles. There are, moreover, genealogies which set out the order of the successive generations in a family. No distinction is made between various kinds of relationship, and the historical-ethnographical and tribal lists are, as stated above, given solely with the view of establishing that a nation or tribe grew from a father's house. To distinguish precisely between the different types of genealogies is not always possible, it being extremely difficult to differentiate between schematic tribal lists and realistic genealogical ones of certain families incorporated to them. The redactors of the comprehensive lists — principally those in the Book of Chronicles — did not have a clear and coordinated set of genealogies available but only fragments of lists and traditions which they combined by bridging and joining together different lists that had taken shape at various times and which differed in importance. This procedure, while preserving the original character of the different lists, was made possible by the redactors' formal viewpoint that these comprehensive lists were the genealogies of individuals, some of whom were also fathers of tribes and of families.

The considerable degree of schematization in the tribal genealogies — in some of which this being a matter of system — has led to the realization that these genealogical schemata embody ethnographic memories of, and information on, the manner in which the tribes and families settled, as well as the connections that existed among them. Consequently, attempts have been made to establish the principles on the basis of which these ancient genealogical schemata were formulated and compiled.[30] Thus it has been suggested that the merger of any two groups, is at times depicted as a marriage, symbolizing the union of two families or tribes, in some instances of common ancestry and equal status, in others of unequal standing, this being apparently the meaning of "taking a concubine." The merging of a tribe settling in a new area with the earlier inhabitants of the locality is portrayed as the marriage of the father of the tribe (eponym) with one of the local women. "Daughters" generally refer to settlements dependent on the principal city, "sons" to secondary tribes or families. Elder sons represent families or tribes that are old or strong. The inclusion of outside individuals in the tribal genealogy usually implies the annexation of weak families by a stronger tribe but sometimes indicates attempts by the weaker ones to establish a relationship between themselves and those stronger or more important, and so on.

Although no single set of rules can satisfactorily explain the family relationships, such as father, mother, son, etc., in the various genealogies, these rules do seem to apply at least to a considerable section of the genealogical lists and furnish information on the ethnic connections of the Israelite tribes and their settlement. Thus, for example, the formula "father of so and so" in the genealogies in the Book of Chronicles points in the main to a connection between a family and a locality, such as "Shobal the father of Kiriath-jearim" (I Chron. 2:50), "Salma the father of Bethlehem" (I Chron. 2:51), and similarly "Mesha his first-born, who was the father of Ziph" (I Chron. 2:42) or "And in Gibeon there dwelt the father of Gibeon" (I Chron. 8:29).

Nevertheless, no far-reaching conclusions can be drawn from an interpretation of the genealogies on the basis of these rules. For part of the narratives and of the various traditions of family relationships, even some that are contained in the genealogical lists, undoubtedly have their origin in popular tales, being a schematic description made up of historical facts, legendary material, and popular anecdotes. Moreover, the tendentiousness evident in various lists, in that they set out to prove the direct descent of families and individuals from the Israelite tribes, diminish their value as an ethnographic and historical source. Since the lists sought to incorporate all the Israelite tribes and their settlements in one homogeneous genealogical schema that would allocate to each family, father's house, or settlement a place, according to its size and status, in the genealogical pattern of the tribe and also incorporate, the political relations and those regarding the settlements in the structure of ancient ties of kinship, it was on occasion necessary to insert imaginary ancestors in the genealogies, that is, names that represent neither tribes nor families nor historical persons. At times ancestors were even invented by repeating certain names or introducing personal ones in the schematic genealogies.

A frequent feature of the schematic genealogies is the appearance of a name, on one occasion as a father, on another as a son, on one occasion as a brother, on another as an uncle, in various genealogical schemata or even in a composite one. The same name occurs likewise in various ethnic or tribal groups in different genealogies.[31] Naturally, two of these could have the same name. But generally the recurrence in several lists of a certain name — if it is clearly that of a tribe or family (that is, if it is the son of the ancestor, the son or grandson of the father of the tribe, or the name of a place or district) and not that of an individual — supports the assumption that it refers to the same tribe or family, even though the relationship changes from list to list. The reasons for this may vary but the change was sometimes due to an error on the part of the compilers of the comprehensive genealogical schemata. Many of them, however, reflect modifications in the historical conditions and in the balance of power among the tribes, families, and fathers' houses at various periods. From the very nature of the genealogical schemata it is evident that lists which were drawn up at a certain time do not agree with those compiled at another stage. It is precisely the differences in the status of the families and fathers' houses in the various complete or partial lists that make it possible to elucidate the process of the consolidation of the tribal groups and the settlement of families and fathers' houses in Canaan. Differences in the relationship of a family or tribe to its ancestor in different lists tend to indicate its superior standing and the dependence of others on it at a certain period, as also the decline of one group and the rise of others at another. The recurrence of a name in various ethnic or tribal groups points to the migration of families or fathers' houses from one area to another, the merging of different ethnic elements, or the absorption of local populations by their conquerors, and so on.

G. The Historical Significance of the Lists of the Twelve Tribes

The schema of the twelve Israelite tribes, who are the sons of Jacob, occurs in several versions[32] in which the tribes are enumerated in different orders. These schemata of Jacob's sons are of consequence for a consideration of the historical significance of the tribal genealogies. The historical importance of the number of twelve tribes, which appears regularly in the various lists, and its place in the tradition of the tribal league, have previously been discussed. In the tribal and other lists as well as in the passages that enumerate the tribes in their order (whether they are narratives of the birth of Jacob's sons, a list of the heads of the congregation or of the spies, a description of the division of the tribal territories, etc.) two main groups can be distinguished: in one Levi is included among the tribes and Joseph is counted as a single tribe, in the other Levi is no longer counted as a tribe and the list is complemented by reckoning Ephraim and Manasseh, the sons of Joseph, as two tribes. This clearly reflects the discontinuance of Levi as a lay tribe,[33] and the rise of Joseph to a dominant position in relation to the other tribes. These facts emerge clearly from the biblical narratives and accounts.

In the tribal lists to which the genealogical principle applies (Gen. 46:8-27; 49:3-28; Ex. 1:1-4; etc.) a distinction is made between the sons of the Matriarchs, Leah and Rachel, and those of the handmaids. The relationship of the various tribes to their mothers is given only in the account of the birth of Jacob's sons (Gen. 29-35), this being indicated in the different lists by the order in which the tribes are enumerated.

In the tribal league there is no fundamental difference in status among the sons of the two Matriarchs or between them and the sons of the hand-maids. Nonetheless, the sons of the Matriarchs are the more important and honored tribes, the lesser importance of the handmaids' sons in the tribal league being shown not only by their being referred to as the sons of concubines but also by the varying order in which they appear in the different lists, the position of the tribes descended from the Matriarchs being generally constant.

First in the enumeration of the tribes and senior in the order of their birth are four of Leah's six sons: Reuben, Simeon, Levi, and Judah. Hence at an early period in the history of the tribal league the sons of Leah were the strongest and most important of the tribes. In the course of time the first three lost their status, Levi ceased to be a lay tribe, nor did it inherit a territory. Reuben and Simeon became tribes of secondary importance, Simeon being finally absorbed by the tribe of Judah. That Reuben and Simeon continued as semi-nomads even after the Settlement and lived in the border regions of the country are significant factors in determining at what stage in the history of the tribal league these tribes were its leaders. Furthermore, the fact that Leah's six sons constitute a group in the tribal genealogies — the rest comprising the two sons each of Rachel, of Leah's handmaid, and of Rachel's handmaid — indicates the principal position occupied, at the outset of the tribal league, by the sons of Leah headed by Reuben. The rise of Rachel's two last born sons, Joseph and Benjamin, to a position of pre-eminence, as expressed in the tribal lists which include Ephraim and Manasseh, Joseph's sons, among the tribes, occurred after the Settlement. It is to this development that the chronicler refers in I Chron. 5:1 when stating: "And the sons of Reuben the first-born of Israel — for he was the first-born; but, forasmuch as he defiled his father's couch, his birthright was given unto the sons of Joseph the son of Israel, yet not so that he was to be reckoned in the genealogy as first-born."

In several other lists the tribes are enumerated in the order of their settlement (Num. 34:17–29; Deut. 33:6–25; Josh. 13–19). But since with one exception — the blessing of Moses (Deut. 33) — these are lists of the tribes' inheritances, it is not surprising that they are based on a geographical principle. There are also other lists, such as those dealing with the Israelites' encampment in the wilderness (Num. 2:1–31; 7:12–83) and with the tribal census (Num. 1:20–46; 26:5–56), which are drawn up in geographical order, even though they naturally have no direct connection with the territorial arrangement in Canaan. From all these lists no information can be gained regarding either the history of the tribal league during its early stages or the process of the settlement before the tribes established themselves in their permanent homes. The order in which, according to Deut. 27:11 ff., the tribes stood on Mount Gerizim and Mount Ebal represents a special case: apparently the more important tribes, consisting of the sons of Rachel and some of those of Leah, were to pronounce the blessing, and the others, the less important ones, the curse.[34]

Even from the tribal lists based on a genealogical principle no far-reaching conclusions can be drawn about the process of the Settlement. Many scholars contend that the tribal league came into being only after the tribes had settled in Canaan. Hence they conclude from the tribal list that the tribes of Leah settled first and were united in a tribal league, that they were subsequently joined by the tribes of Rachel who, they maintain, entered Canaan at a later stage. In view of the league's development and institutions, it is difficult, as previously stated, to accept the assumption that the tribal league crystallized only after the Settlement, or to explain, on the basis of this assumption, the juxtaposition of Issachar and Zebulun to the other tribes of Leah. In the list of the tribes of Leah there is no territorial continuity or any other geographical principle, nor does it accord with the historical position obtaining after the Conquest. It is more probable that the tribal list based on the genealogical principle corresponds to the pre-Conquest status of the tribes. Hence the fact that the tribes of Leah were the earliest members of the tribal league does not contradict the theory that the sons of Joseph entered Canaan before those of Leah.[35]

H. Some Aspects of the Tribal History

The genealogies of families and fathers' houses, in particular those in I Chron. 2–9 and in Num. 1; 26, contain information on several aspects of the settlement of the tribes, on the relationships among the tribes and the families, and on their contacts with foreign peoples. In various chapters in this volume which describe the history of the Conquest and the Settlement, the main issues are discussed and summarized on the basis of data contained also in other sources. Here it will suffice to deal with several basic features that emerge from the tribal genealogies.

An outstanding example of the migration of families in search of a tribal inheritance is that of the Danites who moved northward from their home in the center of the country (Jud. 18). Here is precise information on the transfer of a whole tribe, although numbering only one family, from its place of domicile. Indeed, until the end of the process of settlement, — i.e. close to the monarchical period — not all the families had settled down permanently. Various fathers' houses and apparently whole families moved from their homes to other localities and were finally included in the genealogies of tribes other than those in which they were first enumerated. The frequent occurrence of this is attested by the already mentioned fact that several family names recur in two or even in three tribes.

Of four family names in the tribe of Reuben (Hanoch, Pallu, Hezron, and Carmi — Gen. 46:9; Num. 26:5–6; I Chron. 5:3), two, Hezron and Carmi, are also family names in Judah. In the genealogical schema in I Chron. 2, Hezron son of Perez (Gen. 46:12; Num. 26:21) appears even as the father of most of the families in the hill-country of Judah; while Carmi is descended from Zerah (Josh. 7:1;[36] I Chron. 2:7; 4:1), the son of Judah and Tamar. That these are not different families is proved by the fact that they are considered two of the chief families of these two tribes and also from other evidence. For example, in the description of the boundary between Judah and Benjamin there occurs the place-name "The stone of Bohan the son of Reuben" (Josh. 15:6). This place lies east of the land of Judah, not far from Jericho and the Valley of Achor mentioned in the story of Achan the son of Carmi of the tribe of Judah (Josh. 7). The name points to an association, apparently during the early stages of the Settlement, between Reuben or a Reubenite family and the eastern slopes of the hill-country of Judah. However, I Chron. 2:21 refers to Hezron of the tribe of Judah who married the daughter of Machir the father of Gilead, and to Jair, one of their descendants. Hence families of Judah migrated to the land of Gilead at a later stage of the Settlement, for in the early stages and even subsequently Machir lived in Cis-jordania (cf. Jud. 5:14). It is surprising to find a connection between Judah and Machir on the one hand and the semi-nomadic sons of Jair,[37] inhabitants of the villages, on the other. There were, more probably, genealogical connections between the sons of Jair and those of Hezron in Transjordan, that is, with the sons of Reuben who did not, even at a later period, adopt a settled form of life. Thus I Chron. 5:9–10 tells of Reubenite families who dwelt "eastward" as far as the Euphrates "because their cattle were multiplied in the land of Gilead." Only after the genealogical traditions had assumed definite form were the sons of Jair, living in northern Transjordan, connected genealogically with Machir the son of Manasseh, and hence the tradition of their origin from Hezron and from Machir the father of Gilead. The genealogical connection of Hezron with Judah in one genealogy supports, however, the assumption of ties, based on origin, between the family of Hezron in Reuben and the families of Hezron in Judah. These sparse data do not as yet provide a basis for elucidating in detail the subdivision of the families of Hezron and Carmi or the question of their original connection. They do however furnish evidence of some such process.

This circumstance of identical names of families, testifying to their having originally been one family, is also found among other tribes. Becher is the son of Ephraim, and the Becherite family one of the chief families of Ephraim (Num. 26:35), but Becher is also the son of Benjamin (Gen. 46:21) and the progenitor of a large Benjaminite family (I Chron. 7:6, 8–9). Beriah is one of the families of Ephraim (I Chron. 7:21–24) and of Benjamin (I Chron. 8:13) as well as one of the chief families of Asher (Gen. 46:17; Num. 26:44; I Chron. 7:30). Shema is one of the families of Judah (I Chron. 2:43–44) and also of Benjamin (I Chron. 8:13). Zerah is one of the chief families of Judah (Gen. 46:12; I Chron. 2:4) but also one of Simeon's sons (Num. 26:13; I Chron. 4:24). These families belonged to tribes which lived near one another, the identical family names pointing to the migration, within narrow limits, of families or fathers' houses from the territory of one tribe to that of another, or even to the affinity of families settled in the border areas of neighboring tribes. It is not always possible to determine the connections between families bearing identical names and living in different tribes. But here is clear evidence of the subdivision of families in their search for a territory, and of the formation of family genealogies based on the territorial principle.

The family of Beriah, mentioned above, which belonged partly to Ephraim and partly to Benjamin, besides being one of the chief families of Asher, subdivided at an early stage into three families, two of which were descended from Beriah's sons, Heber and Malchiel (Gen. 46:17; Num. 26:45). The families and father's houses, descended from the Asherite Beriah, included Birzaith the son of Malchiel (I Chron. 7:31) and Japhlet and Shemer the sons of Heber (I Chron. 7:32 ff). The Asherite family of Birzaith may be connected with the place-name Birzaith in Ephraim's territory, known from sources of the Second Temple period (Josephus, *Antiquities*, xii, § 422). The name Japhlet is also found in the hill-country of Ephraim and is mentioned in Josh. 16:3 as marking the boundary between Ephraim and Benjamin, while Shemer is likewise the name of a Benjaminite family (I Chron. 8:12). Here is evidence of connections between the Asherite family of Beriah and the hill-country of Ephraim and the Ephraimite family of Beriah. Either the family of Beriah was originally descended from the tribe of Asher which first lived in the hill-country of Ephraim and later migrated northward while several fathers' houses of this family remained in their original locality, or these were fathers' houses of the Ephraimite family who migrated northward and joined the tribe of Asher.

Some families of the tribe of Issachar, who were also connected with the hill-country of Ephraim, finally settled in the Valley of Jezreel. One of the Judges, Tola son of Puah, a man of Issachar, dwelt in Shamir in the hill-country of Ephraim and there he judged Israel and there he was buried (Jud. 10:1-2). The family of Puah, to which he belonged, was one of the most important in Issachar (Gen. 46:13; Num. 26:23). At that time, at least part of it, if not the entire family lived in the hill-country of Ephraim. The names of two other families of Issachar — Jashub and Shimron (Gen. 46:13; Num. 26:24) — are place-names in the hill-country of Ephraim, in the territory of Manasseh.[38]

The connections between the tribes in Cis — and Transjordan form a separate subject. Mention has previously been made of the connections of Reuben with Judah and of the Hezron families of Judah with Machir the father of Gilead. The connections of Benjaminite families with the inhabitants of Gilead are known from the relations between the people of Jabesh-gilead and Gibeah of Benjamin (Jud. 21) as well as the House of Saul (I Sam. II; 31:11-13).[39] That there were connections between Benjaminites and Transjordan may also be deduced from the fact that Bela is the name of a Benjaminite (Gen. 46:21; I Chron. 8:1) but also of a large Reubenite family (I Chron. 5:8), and that Ezbon is the name both

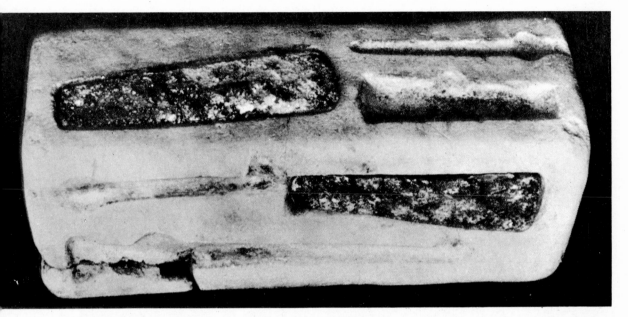

A Middle Bronze Age II pottery mold for casting implements with two axes or chisels in place, from Shechem.

IDA, Jerusalem.

Late Bronze Age copper ingots from Cyprus.
Dr. S. Alexion, Heraclion Museum, Crete.

Late Bronze Age Canaanite gold bowl from Ugarit.
Prof. Claude F. A. Schaeffer, Paris.

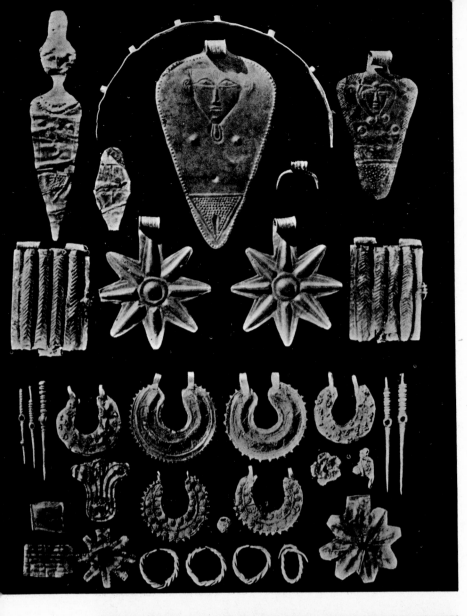

Late Bronze Age
gold work: double-head
from Megiddo;
jewelry from
Tell el-'Ajjul.

Oriental Institute,
University of Chicago;
Institute of Archaeology,
University of London.

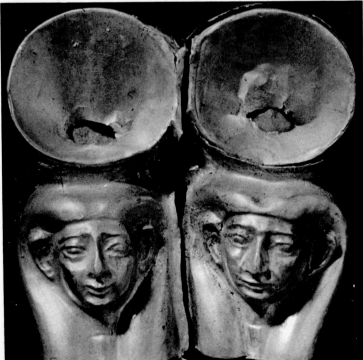

Middle Bronze II Age weapons found in a tomb at Megiddo.
Oriental Institute, University of Chicago.

Late Bronze Age Hittite
battle-ax from Beth-shean.
IDA, Jerusalem.

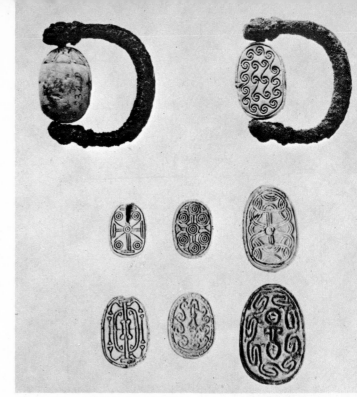

Right: Middle Bronze II Age group of scarabs from
Tell el-'Ajjul;
Left: two Egyptian scarabs of the New Kingdom period
found at Lachish and Beth-shemesh.

Institute of Archaeology, University of London;
The Wellcome Trust, London.

Late Bronze Age Mitannian style
cylinder seals from Hazor.

Prof. Y. Yadin, Jerusalem.

Late Bronze Age faience vase with
cartouche of an Egyptian Queen
found in a temple of Tell Deir 'Ālla.
Prof. H. J. Franken, Leiden.

Egyptian Middle Kingdom
excration figurine from Sakkarah.
National Museum, Brussels.

Ivory plaque bearing the cartouche of Ramses III, from Megiddo.
Oriental Institute, University of Chicago.

14th century B.C.E.
cuneiform tablet from
Megiddo;
fragment from
the Gilgamesh epic.
IDA, Jerusalem.

14th century B.C.E. clay cuneiform
letter from Abdu-Hepa,
King of Jerusalem, to Pharaoh
Akh-en-Aton, found at
Tell el-Amarna.
Staatliche Museen, Berlin.

15th century B.C.E. clay model of
liver with cuneiform inscriptions
used in divination, from Hazor.
Prof. Y. Yadin, Jerusalem.

12th century B.C.E. Ugaritic
alphabetic script, on a clay tablet
found at Taanach.
BASOR, U.S.A.

Clay tablet with an unknown alphabetic script found at Tell Deir ʻÀlla; end of the 13th,
beginning of the 12th century B.C.E.
Prof. H. J. Franken, Leiden.

Proto-Canaanite
inscription on stele
fragment found
at Shechem.
IDA, Jerusalem.

16th century B.C.E.
Proto-Canaanite
inscription on dagger
from Lachish.
The Wellcome Trust.
London,

Proto-Canaanite
ostracon from
Tel-Nagila
Mrs. Ruth Amiran,
Jerusalem.

Proto-Canaanite inscription
on bowl from Lachish.
The Wellcome Trust, London.

Alphabetic inscription in Sinaitic script,
on a statue from Ṣerabit el-Khadem.

View inside Middle Bronze I Age tomb at Jericho.
Prof. Kathleen M. Kenyon, London.

Jericho. View of the interior of Middle Bronze II Age tomb containing remains of wooden furniture, pottery vessels and straw basket.
Prof. Kathleen M. Kenyon, London.

Middle Bronze II Age tomb from Tell el-'Ajjul with burials of a man and a horse.
Institute of Archaeology, University of London.

Late Bronze Age stone-built tomb in the Mycenaean style from Ugarit.
Prof. Claude F. A. Schaeffer, Paris.

Philistine pottery from Megiddo.
Oriental Institute, University of Chicago.

Philistine anthropoid clay coffin
from Beth-shean.
University Museum, Philadelphia.

Philistine spouted jug found in a tomb at Tell E?
Mr. G. Edelstein, IDA, Jerusa.

Bronze cult object and
weapon found in stratum XI
at Hazor; 11th century B.C.E.
Prof. Y. Yadin, Jerusalem.

Clay cultic stands found in stratum VI at Megiddo;
11th century B.C.E.
Oriental Institute, University of Chicago.

Two inscribed spearheads found near Bethlehem; 12th–11th centuries B.C.E.
BASOR, U.S.A.

of a family of Gad (Gen. 46:16) and of a father's house descended from Bela the son of Benjamin (I Chron. 7:7).

These connections between tribes of Cis — and Transjordan do not signify a tribal connection with Gad, Reuben, or Machir, but rather with the whole land of Gilead. In the genealogies of Manasseh, Gilead is usually mentioned as the son of Machir. However, the Song of Deborah has Gilead apparently instead of Gad (Jud. 5:17), for according to some biblical texts the land of Gilead was given as an inheritance to Reuben, Gad, and the half-tribe of Manasseh (Num. 32:1; Josh. 22:9; etc.). That tribes in Cisjordan were connected with Gilead is apparent from the genealogies of the families of the tribe of Manasseh itself, part of which settled in Cis-jordania and part in Gilead.

Although the genealogical lists of the families of Manasseh,[40] and especially the fragmentary list in the Book of Chronicles, are complicated and contradictory, all of them mention Machir as the father of Gilead. But whereas one list gives the remaining families of Manasseh — Abiezer, Helek, Asriel, Shechem, Hepher, and Shemida — as the sons of Manasseh himself and thus as the brothers of Machir (Josh. 17:1–3), another states that they were the sons of Gilead the son of Machir the son of Manasseh (Num. 26:29–33). Should it however be contended that this latter list is corrupt and that in its original version all the families of Manasseh in Cisjordan were the sons of Manasseh, there is the independent tradition regarding the daughters of Zelophehad who was the son of Hepher the son of Gilead the son of Machir the son of Manasseh (Num. 27:1; Josh. 17:3), and was at all events of the children of Gilead the son of Machir the son of Manasseh (Num. 36).

Several names of Zelophehad's daughters and that of Hepher his father were place and regional names in Cis-jordania. Hepher, as also Tirzah, the name of one of Zelophehad's daughters, were the names of Canaanite royal cities which the Israelites possessed (Josh. 12:17, 24), while the names of two other daughters, Hoglah and Noah, were those of regions mentioned in the Samaria ostraca.[41]

Thus families which derived their descent from Machir dwelt in Cis-jordania. Machir himself, that is, families of Joseph descended from Machir, were still living there at the time of the war of Deborah, for in the Song of Deborah Machir is mentioned with Ephraim and Manasseh among the tribes that took part in the battle (Jud. 5:14), while Gilead in Transjordan is included, together with Reuben, among those who held aloof. Thus at the time Machir dwelt in Cis-jordania, Gilead was regarded as an independent group.

These data are proof that at first all the families of Manasseh, together with the rest of Joseph's sons, settled in Cis-jordania. At that time Machir was probably accounted a leading family of Manasseh and the latter's only son (cf. Gen. 50:23) from whom the other families of Manasseh were descended. It was only some time later that the families of Machir settled in Gilead, in consequence of which Machir was finally identified with Gilead and made Gilead's father. The genealogical connections of the other families of Manasseh are an echo of their connections with Machir from the time he lived in Cisjordan. For since Gilead was regarded as Machir's only son, these families claimed descent from him. The process whereby the sons of Manasseh settled in Gilead indicates the manner in which the families and fathers' houses of Judah and Benjamin as also the other tribes of Cisjordan settled in the land of Gilead. The settlement of the families of Machir was, however, the cardinal factor.

In the tribal genealogies the associations between families and fathers' houses on the one hand and places of settlement on the other testify, as previously stated, to the settlement of various families within the tribe's territory and their later dispersion. Such data are found especially in the genealogies of Judah in I Chron. 2–4.[42] These relate about the settlement of the families of Shelah in the west of Judah, the settlement of the families of Jerahmeel in the southern hill-country of Judah, and in the northern Negev, of Caleb in the central hill-country of Judah, of Hezron in the neighborhood of Bethlehem, and so on. These lists also indicate the expansion of the families of Judah in the region of Kiriath-jearim and in the vicinity of Zorah and Eshtaol, that is, in the area of Benjamin's inheritance and in the territory inhabited by the Danites before their migration northward.

I. Tribal Connections with Foreign Ethnic Elements in the Light of the Genealogical Lists

The genealogical connections between families and fathers' houses on the one hand and ancient settlements, on the other, generally testify to the merging of the Israelites with the local population. The extent of that process cannot, however, be determined even where the names of Canaanite royal cities, such as Hebron, Gibeon, and Hepher, occur in the tribal genealogies, for at times they merely indicate the settlement of Israelites in these places. Nor is there a satisfactory criterion for judging when the genealogies that attribute an ancient place-name to an Israelite tribe or family constitute evidence of a fusion with the earlier inhabitants and when these are merely fathers' houses named after their new places of settlement.

On the other hand, the assimilation of the local population to the settling Israelite tribes is evidenced by the marriage of fathers of families with local women whose names are mentioned in the patriarchal narratives in the Book of Genesis, and in the tribal genealogies, this being particularly apparent in the case of the tribe of Judah. Gen. 38 contains an account of Judah's marriage to a daughter of a Canaanite named Shua. Their sons — Er, Onan, Shelah — were the fathers of mixed Jewish-Canaanite families. Whereas the families of Er and Onan disappeared at an early stage, the descendants of Shelah, mentioned in the genealogies of the tribe of Judah, lived on the western slopes of the hill-country of Judah in the vicinity of Mareshah (cf. I Chron. 4:41 ff.). The other families of Judah who were descended from Perez and Zerah, the sons of Judah and Tamar (Gen. 38), were accounted the chief families of Judah, and settled in the hill-country of Judah. The extent of their intermingling with the local population is attested by the marriage of the fathers of these families with women whose names are recorded, as for example Ephrath (I Chron. 2:19) or Atarah (v. 26); and even with concubines, such as Ephah (v. 46) or Maacah (v. 48). Similar, though more meager, information is contained in the fragmentary genealogies of other tribes. Thus Maacah, mentioned in I Chron. 2:48 as Caleb's concubine, was also the wife of the father of Gibeon who traced his filiation back to Benjamin (I Chron. 8:29). She represents what was apparently a large Canaanite family, part of which assimilated with the sons of Judah and part with those of Benjamin. The sons of Manasseh in Transjordan were, according to I Chron. 7:14, descended from Manasseh's Aramean concubine, thus indicating the assimilation of Aramean elements who were neighbors of the inhabitants of Gilead,[43] and so on.

In the pre-Conquest period the local population in Canaan undoubtedly included Hurrian elements.[44] That some of these merged with Israelite families is an assumption for which support may be found in the identical names borne by several families among the inhabitants of northern Judah[45] and recurring in the list of the sons of Seir the Horite (= "Hurrian") in Gen. 36. Thus Shobal is the name of one of the sons of Seir the Horite (Gen. 36:23) and also of a family descended from Judah, whose place of settlement was in the neighborhood of Kiriath-jearim (I Chron. 2:50; 4:1). Manahath is the name of one of the sons of the Horite Shobal (Gen. 36:23) as well as of a family of Judah descended from Shobal (I Chron. 2:52), while Bilhan, which occurs in the genealogy of the Benjaminites

(I Chron. 7:10), is also the name of a descendant of Seir the Horite (Gen. 36:27). Other names of the latter's sons appear among the offspring of Jerahmeel who lived in southern Judah and in the Negev, but these were apparently tribal elements from Mount Seir that had merged with the families of the border region of Judah.

Other tribes, too, had ethnic elements in common with the nomadic peoples on the frontiers of Canaan. Mibsam and Mishma are the names not only of two of the twelve Ishmaelite tribes (Gen. 25:13–14) but also of two of Simeon's families (I Chron. 4:25–26). The name Jair, by which the nomadic families of the eastern border district of Gilead were known, may point to ties with non-Israelite nomadic tribes living in that area.

To this subject of genealogical connections with non-Israelite tribes and peoples belongs the ethnic origin of the large family groups of Caleb, Kenaz, and Jerahmeel in the tribe of Judah. The list of the families of Judah in Num. 26:20–21 comprises the family of the Shelanites and that of the Perezites which is subdivided into the families of the Zerahites, the Hezronites, and the Hamulites — "these are [all] the families of Judah according to those that were numbered of them." This schema of the families of Judah recurs at the beginning of the tribal genealogies in I Chron. 2:3–4. Later however only a few descendants of Zerah and Shelah, none of Hamul, but a large number of those of Hezron son of Perez are mentioned. The sons of Hezron, who inhabited the whole of the hill-country of Judah and the Negev area, included a considerable number of families that were in fact secondary groups of the tribe. Prominent among these were Caleb and Jerahmeel,[46] who lived in the hill-country of Judah from Beth-zur southward, in the Negev, and in the wilderness of Judah. The families of Kenaz were related to the sons of Caleb (I Chron. 4:13), for according to the traditions of the Conquest, Caleb, the central figure among those sent to spy out the land of Canaan, conquered from the sons of Anak, Hebron, which was assigned to him as his inheritance, while his brother Othniel son of Kenaz took Debir to the south of Hebron (Josh. 15:13–19; Jud. 1:12–15).

In addition to the fact that these prominent families of the tribe of Judah are not included in the list of Judah's families in Num. 26, there are other data which suggest that also after the Conquest they constituted special ethnic and territorial groups in Judah. The Negev of the Jerahmeelites and the Negev of Caleb are mentioned beside the Negev of Judah (I Sam. 27:10; 30:14). Nabal of Carmel was called a Calebite (I Sam. 25:3). Caleb himself is called a Kenizzite (Num. 32:12; Josh. 14:14) and, as previously stated, he was related to Othniel the son of Kenaz, thus indicating Caleb's family connections with the Kenizzites who are also reckoned among the Canaanite peoples (Gen. 15:19) and partly included in Edom (Gen. 36:11, 15; etc.). In the families of Caleb and Jerahmeel the foreign elements — Edomite and Hurrian — occuring in the genealogies of the tribe of Judah are much more pronounced than in the other families of Judah. Hence there are grounds for assuming that they represent ethnic elements related to the Israelite tribes by common descent, but not included from the outset among the twelve tribes, being from early times genealogically related to the inhabitants of Mount Seir. However since they lived in the area situated between Judah and Edom, their fate was linked to that of the tribe of Judah from the first stages of the Settlement, as is apparent from the accounts of the Conquest regarding Caleb and Othniel. During the period of the settlement these families preserved a measure of ethnic and territorial cohesion, and were accordingly at that juncture not completely absorbed by the tribe of Judah. And yet the picture that emerges from the genealogies in the Book of Chronicles depicts them as families of Judah in every respect and as descended from Hezron the son of Perez the son of Judah. On the basis of the geographical and historical data in them, the tribal genealogies of the families of Judah in I Chron. 2–4 date from the beginning of the monarchy.[47] It was therefore at that time that the process of the total merging of the families of Caleb, Kenaz, and Jerahmeel with the tribe of Judah was completed.

The subjects discussed here reflect only the principal tendencies and processes undergone by the Israelite tribes after the Settlement. The migrations of fathers' houses in search of territories to settle in were responsible for the transfer of tribal attachment from one tribe to another. Daily contact with the earlier inhabitants of the country whom the Israelites were unable to dispossess led to the inclusion of local ethnic elements in the Israelite tribal structure. Tribal and family groups, originally not reckoned as Israelite tribes, attached themselves to Israelite tribes living on the borders of the country. Contemporaneously with these processes, as the Israelites settled in Canaan and the former nomadic tribes became urban and rural tillers of the soil, the economic and social foundations of the tribal structure were undermined, and the tribal concept of life was increasingly relegated from everyday life. Nonetheless, throughout the entire biblical period there existed in Israel the social and religious outlook that was based on traditions which the settling Israelite tribes brought with them to Canaan.

THE RELIGIOUS CULTURE OF THE JEWISH PEOPLE IN ITS BEGINNINGS: THE FAITH AND THE CULT

by J. Wiener

A. THE MULTIPLICITY OF VIEWS ON THE ORIGIN OF THE JEWISH FAITH

BIBLICAL RESEARCH offers many answers to the various problems raised by Jewish monotheism and the place of Moses in the history of the Jewish faith. We cannot describe all these answers in detail, but we shall briefly present the main schools of thought, emphasizing their points of difference.

1. The first subject of dispute is the view held by part of the scholars that Jewish monotheism should be regarded as a continuation of a foreign monotheistic stream, Babylonian or Egyptian, while others ascribe the creation of monotheism to the Jewish people itself. Proponents of the Babylonian monotheism theory regard the religion of Israel as one of the consequences of the henotheistic tendencies of the Babylonian priests, who strove to unite all the gods in the figure of one god, and to describe all the deities as different manifestations of the one god, Marduk, king of the gods, creator of heaven and earth. Advocates of the Egyptian theory see Moses as a continuer of Akh-en-Aton's sun worship. In favor of proponents of the independent creation theory, who today represent the preponderant majority among the scholars, is the point raised by Wellhausen: "One cannot believe that any Egyptian deity whatsoever could have inspired the Hebrews in Egypt to undertake a struggle against the Egyptians, or that any abstraction whatsoever of esoteric thought could have been converted into the national deity of Israel."[1]

2. The second controversy opposes the scholars who attribute the invention of monotheism to Moses to those who maintain that the religion established by Moses in Israel was not monotheistic to begin with.

3. Opinions are divided as to the actual extent of the religion of JHWH in Israel; there are scholars who consider this to have been the legitimate religion of the people, and others who argue for the existence of esoteric sects of believers in JHWH who succeeded — after a protracted struggle with the idolatrous majority — to impose that religion in Israel.

THE RELIGIOUS CULTURE OF THE JEWISH PEOPLE IN ITS BEGINNINGS

4. There are those who think that these sects belonged to foreign groups, e.g. Kenites, and others who see in the stories of Jethro in the Pentateuch evidence of the conversion of the ancient Israelite religion to that of Jethro, the priest of JHWH. The question of the origin of the name JHWH and its original form has exercised the scholars considerably. In the view of some he was an ancient tribal god or one of the deities of the ancient Hebrew pantheon; others consider him to be the original invention of Moses.[2]

5. The question of the origin of the name has significance only if we assume that the religion of JHWH, as Moses proclaimed it, was not entirely an innovation, but the continuation of an earlier religious situation. On this point opinion is also divided. On the one hand, many scholars tend to see in the message of Moses—whatever its content—the laying of the foundations of a new religion; on the other hand, there is a tendency to regard Moses as the worker of a fateful change in the life of the Israelites through absorption from the fund of existing religious concepts.

None of these points of difference are expressions of accidental textual variations; they are the result of different basic assumptions about the laws of the formation of human ideas, and different conceptions with respect to the life of the cultures of man. We can thus define groups which hold similar views as schools of thought divided in accordance with their fundamental approach to the problems of the history of culture. Let us examine some of these and summarize the opinions of their outstanding representatives.

B. Moses and the Jewish Religion in the Eyes of the Evolutionary School

The evolutionary school — Wellhausen's school — regards monotheism as the fruit of slow development, the result of the protracted struggle of the prophets of Israel. In the beginning of its history, the religion of the Jewish people was monolatrous (though neither to it were the people faithful), a primitive religion which expressed itself in the worship of the national god. Julius Wellhausen was the founder of the school which regards the history of the faith, in the period of the First Temple, as an evolutionary development from the primitive religion — that worships its national god, but recognizes the existence of other gods in the world — to the higher religion which recognizes but a single God, the creator of heaven and earth, and the master of the whole world. According to this view, Moses was the founder of a national monolatrous religion, basing the national unity of the tribes of Israel on their religious unity. Wellhausen summarizes the essentials of this religion as follows : JHWH (the Lord) is the God of Israel, and Israel is JHWH's people. This faith, due to Moses' enterprise, fashioned the history of the Jewish people; it was responsible for the very creation of the people and constituted the base of its existence.

Laying down the Jahvistic religion as the foundation of the entire history of the Jewish people does not exhaust all of Moses' accomplishments: it is also he who takes the people out of the land of Egypt, it is he who establishes law and order in social life; he is teacher and judge. As the leader he possesses judicial authority, and this he exercises in accordance with the instructions of God — transmitted to him at En-mishpat which is in Kadesh — and thus he becomes the Father of the Law in Israel. That Law, according to Wellhausen, is not a normative book, but a collection of rulings, based on divine or priestly decisions. Ancient Israel did not have a Book of the Law, but the word of a living God, which was made known to the priests who sought it.[3]

God, on whose special relation with the people Moses based the religion of his nation, is not a new and unknown deity, but the god of one of the tribes — the tribe of Moses, or the House of Joseph.[4] And not only was the character of the Lord not the original discovery of Moses, but even the idea of divinity itself, which was known in the ancient Israelite religion, was nothing new. Therefore, one should not ask: What is the source of the Israelite idea of divinity? But since this superfluous question has been asked, Wellhausen calls attention to fact that, of all the possible answers, the one that links the religion of Moses with the wisdom of the priests of Egypt is the worst, for the simple reason that the abstract deities of the sages of Egypt did not have the ideational weight required to fortify, and inspire the Israelites in their historical enterprise.

Apart from the principle, "The Lord is the God of Israel; Israel is the people of the Lord," one cannot find any element in the ancient Jewish faith that can be ascribed to Moses. It is generally supposed, of course, that at least the Ten Commandments are the work of Moses; but Wellhausen considers even this view doubtful, for four reasons: 1) the difference between Exodus 20 and 34; 2) the prohibition against images does not belong to that period, and the proof can be found in the serpent of brass, in which Wellhausen sees the Lord's image[5]; 3) the Commandments bear a universal, ethical character; 4) the Commandments presuppose the existence of actual monotheism.[6]

What certainly was Moses' handiwork was the Ark, the symbol of the covenant between God and Israel. In a sense, the Ark was the principal (and only) sanctuary of the people of Israel at the time of Moses. Wellhausen is not sure that there were tablets in the Ark, and if there were, we do not know what, if anything, was written on them.

The essence of Moses' accomplishment was not the writing of the Law, but the creation of the Jewish nation, the shaping of its particular national character through his activity as leader, judge, and welder of the national covenant; and that was his life's work.

But Moses did not bring to his brothers the faith that God, the Lord of heaven and earth, had chosen them to serve Him and to know Him; the contrary is true: Moses allowed the people to view the nature of God, as their fathers had.

The man Moses created the nation, with its character and its ideas; the nation was not created by the Prophets — they themselves were created by it (although the Prophets, to be sure, had a large share in shaping the special character of the Jewish nation). However, Moses did not invent monotheism. That new religion was created at a later period, as a result of two factors:

(1). The ideational development of the nature of JHWH who in His capacity of national god became a god of justice and morality, so that in the course of time He came to be regarded as the supreme power in heaven and on earth and, finally, as the sole force.[7]

(2). The destruction of the Temple, which raised the question: if Babylonia had defeated Israel did this not mean that the gods of Babylonia had defeated the Lord? The best way out of this impasse lay in the argument that there are no other gods at all, that God does not need His people and His Temple, but that He directs world history as He chooses. In addition, there was the view that the destruction of the Temple was a punishment for worshiping idols — and the total atonement for that sin formed the basis of monotheism.

The Wellhausen school and those who carry on its literary and historical method, in whose approach one recognizes elements of evolutionism and rationalism, became within a short time the dominant school in the study of the history of Israel's religion. Many of its followers criticized Wellhausen's views and sought innovations of their own; but on the basic points most scholars accept the portrait of Moses as Wellhausen drew it, that is: the content of Moses' message is the establishment of national monolatry in Israel by means of a covenant between JHWH (who originated in ancient Israel) and the nation. From the same evolutionist school branched out various approaches, such as that which regards the whole story of the Exodus as false, and the people of Israel as the fruit of slow growth on the soil of Canaan.

C. OTHER IMPORTANT SCHOOLS

The critics of Wellhausen's evolutionist view are divided into a number of groups. There are those who reject the very assumption that it is permissible to learn about the development of the faith from the biblical text, which in their opinion is mainly a creation of the Second Temple period — whose views it expresses; hence the complaint about the erection of an entire structure of Jewish history on the basis of philological criticism. This Masoretic-historical school (so-called because of its appreciation of the role of the Oral Tradition-[Masora]), also known as the Scandinavian school,[8] rejects all attempts to reconstruct the events of Moses' time. Asserts one of its spiritual fathers: the events of Mount Sinai became the foundation of the nation's life, and for that reason each generation attributed to Moses everything important and essential in its life, and projected against the background of the desert period its laws and the source of its social and spiritual arrangements. Hence, "we have no means of answering the question what Moses was, from a historical point of view." The same is true of the exodus from Egypt and the wanderings in the desert, which "have been elaborated from the point of view of fully finished Israel."[9]

Other scholars hold a similar view, even though they use different points of departure.

Another group of Wellhausen's critics or, to put it differently, another approach for criticizing his system, is based on the objective fact that eighty years have passed since he wrote his *Prolegomena*, a period which has abounded in archeological discoveries and has advanced the scientific attitude in all fields. The archeological discoveries have nullified one of Wellhausen's main assumptions about the Priestly Code. Because of the multiplicity of details on ceremonies and the rules of purification, he regarded it as a later priestly creation; but it has since been found that, essentially, it is not different from all the other literature on the rules of worship in the Ancient East.

The progress of the view concerning the history of cultures and of human thought has changed the concepts of the 19th century as to the nature of evolution, and has curbed our tendency to exaggerate in seeking analogies between the histories of different cultures. This does not mean that we can point to a biblical-scientific stream that has exploited all the advantages that Wellhausen missed. But these eighty years have left their mark on the development of biblical science.

However, to whom does this apply? To scholars and thinkers who are

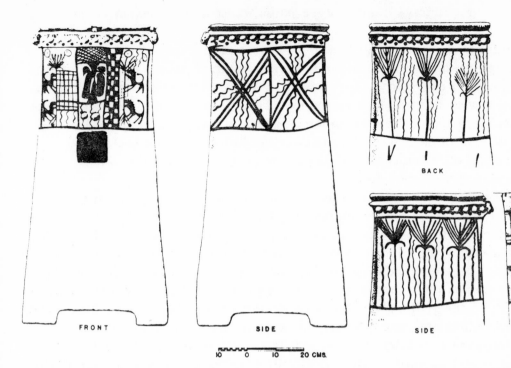

Fig. 28.

Incense burner from Megiddo, Late Bronze.

G. Loud, *Megiddo* II, Chicago, 1948, pl. 251.

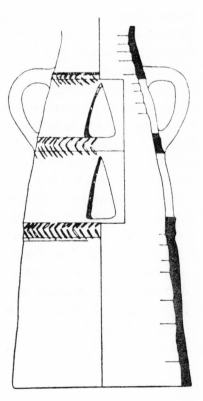

Fig. 29.

Incense burner from Hazor, Late Bronze.

Hazor III–IV, pl. CCLXVIII.

faithful to the point of departure of historical-philological research, which uses all possible tools in order to reveal historical truth. But the removal of the point of departure from historical research to an altogether different area is also fruitful. It is easier says Paul Volz[10] to study the people of Israel as people, than to understand everything that happens from the view-point of the call of God to man.[11] And he, Volz, chooses the hard way: the study of the enterprise of Moses, that mighty personality, whose genius is not of the common run.

Moses effected a tremendous revolution: he abolished idol-worship in Israel and established monotheism; of the Ten Commandments he made a covenant between God and the people; at the head of the Decalogue there stands the expression of the monotheistic faith and the demand of faith. The commandment of the observance of the Sabbath — and the very idea of the Sabbath — are the original invention of Moses which in itself is enough to place him among the geniuses who have raised the value of mankind, and have given it its greatest achievements. The abolition of polytheism as religious idea and the establishment of the monotheistic idea among an entire nation would also have been a sufficient achievement for any thinker or leader of genius. But Moses, in addition, put an end to magic, and even uprooted from the hearts of the people the desire to make idols. Moses' achievement is greater yet: he even instilled in the people the feeling that responsibility rests on each individual (and there is no need for intercessors between the individual and his God), thus destroying the hegemony of the priests.

The Law of Moses is not the end of a long road in the development of human thought, the expression of an ideological stream, but, on the contrary, a new creation which stands in opposition to the past. It is an effort that succeeded, in contrast to attempts at introducing monotheism that had preceded it, and which had only temporary significance. In addition to the doctrine of unity, the Decalogue and the Sabbath, Moses built the Ark of the Covenant.

Volz calls the Law of Moses — Protestantism of the ancient times. And in fact, Luther abolishes hagiolatry and Moses — polytheism; Luther bans pictures, abolishes the priesthood, makes the individual responsible to his Creator. Nevertheless, Protestantism was created in the 16th century, preceded by what went before it, and it expressed tendencies hundreds of years old, and strivings of thousands of years — whereas Moses worked virgin soil, both as thinker and as fighter.

We shall not linger over the approach to the history of human culture that is reflected in the results of Volz' study; of his book Martin Buber has said[12] that it is "valuable and stimulating, but too general, and... does not deal adequately with the basic problems of the biblical text." Volz' view is not his alone, but the expression of a school of Bible scholars.

D. Moses as the Father of the Israelite Style of Creation

Another approach is taken by Yehezkiel Kaufmann in his comprehensive work, *Tol*e*dot ha-'Emuna ha-Yisra'elit — History of the Israelite Religion*. With an observation no less penetrating than that of Wellhausen, and richer than it by eighty years of research and development of human thought, Kaufmann draws an entirely different picture of the history of monotheism in Israel. Instead of the superficial discernment of such concepts as "a primitive people working its land" which served Wellhausen as a point of departure in his evolutionary structure, Kaufmann postulates a theory of national groups who create various spiritual assets. In place of evolutionism, he assumes the sudden appearance of an idea. In effect, although he does not say so explicitly, Kaufmann accepts the view of modern research as to the general ways of development: discontinuous development, invisible processes, and sudden revelation of the new. Kaufmann believes that the Israelites before Moses practiced idol-worship in its higher stages, so that the very monotheistic idea is a new developmental stage in human religion.

These assumptions free research of its naive attempts at explaining every detail in the invention of monotheism in the manner of simple rationalism. The result obtained from combining these assumptions into a splendid analysis of the biblical text, into the ability to grasp the nature of things, and the like, is a new edifice to the history of the Israelite faith, which begins with the monotheistic message of Moses, and which proceeds — by virtue of the independent, national, style of creation, and of the ideas connected with the very nature of monotheism — towards the peaks of human creation in prophecy.

True, the written Law of Moses plays in this system the same role it did in Wellhausen's theory: it is the beginning of the road of Second Temple Judaism (at the same time Kaufmann rejects all of Wellhausen's literary conclusions, but that cannot be gone into here); but the monotheistic idea, the doctrine of Moses proclaimed at Mount Sinai, is what predominates in the life of the Israelites since the time of the Exodus. Moses invented monotheism and the tribes accepted it. By means of a short and decisive war against idolatry, which the Israelites waged in Egypt, Moses prepared the people to receive the great message.

This message changes the concepts of the nation: the way of thought that is reflected in the entire Bible is absolutely monotheistic, according no recognition to Gentile idolatry, free of concepts of mythology and magic. The Israelite sees the whole world as subject to the dominion of God, though denied knowledge of Him and the grace of His revelation, and therefore doomed to idolatry. There is in the Bible no understanding of idolatry, and no war against it — neither the ancient and usual Israelite idolatry, nor the Gentile variety. There is only war against fetishism, the worship of wood and stone, with no recognition of the symbolic significance of the images, and no understanding of polytheistic mythology. Even the idols — worshippers among the Israelites do not know their true nature. At the revelation of Sinai Moses completes the task of establishing monotheism in Israel.

The monotheistic idea flashed through his mind — the mind of a creative genius — and gained dominion over the people; since then it has been educing all the forces latent in the essence of monotheism. That essence is the establishment of the will of God in everything, the abolition of His dependence on the forces of ancient being, which in every polytheistic religion operate without recourse to God, or even against His will. The monotheistic God is not enslaved to fate, to the changes of time, or to any of the independent and momentous factors which operate in polytheistic religion. For this reason magic does not exist in Israel; Israelite worship is not conceived as participation in the life of the god (feeding him, washing him), which leads to the diminution of his image.

Yet another original creation emerges with the birth of monotheism: emissary prophecy, which constitutes a new stage, as compared with the ancient Hebrew seer, common to many peoples, and whose message was only mantic.[13]

The religion of Moses is an original creation in the faith of Israel, but it inherited from the highest polytheistic religions — including the Hebrew — institutions of worship, priesthood, sacrifice, mantic prophecy, concepts and laws, and even mythological remnants empty of content (every mythological allusion in the Bible is interpreted in this system as a remnant from the time before the new message). But it contains no inheritance from the religion of the Patriarchs, who were idol-worshippers—only the later scribes turned them into believers in the oneness of God — because they could not conceive of them otherwise. Even in Egypt the Israelites did not worship JHWH, the proof being that even though the Lord reveals Himself to Moses as the God of his fathers, Moses does not know His name.

E. The Religion of Moses, Its Roots and Its Content

We cannot understand the nature of Moses' message without a knowledge of the religious and cultural background against which he acted. The general assumption that the Israelites were familiar with the higher culture of polytheism, like the assumption that they were a primitive people, prevents us from understanding the peculiar nature of the phenomenon. The latter becomes clear only when we view the Israelite way of life in the period of the Patriarchs as something unique, both from the social and the religious aspects.

In the life of the Hebrews, which we know from the external documents, and which is reflected in the stories of the Patriarchs, unique social concepts are evident. The members of the Hebrew group enter into treaty-relations with the rulers of various countries, and in return for various services (mainly, assistance in war) they obtain land of their own for pasturage and tillage. They are accustomed to live on the land of others, to do the work of their allies, while at the same preserving a degree of autonomy in the internal life of the community. The treaty ties give the Hebrew community the protection of its allies, and the right to live on their land.

The religious life of the Hebrews, which is also that reflected in the life of the Patriarchs, has been investigated and explained by Alt.[14] He has shown that the religion of the Patriarchs was based on the belief that the chief of every group chooses whatever name he likes for the god of his fathers, and establishes a special tie with him, a covenant-attachment which we may regard as an idea created against the background of the life of human society. The divine ally, like the earthly ally of the Hebrews, grants his worshippers his protection, sees to their security and their success, and, in return, he demands the fulfilment of all his commands and absolute loyalty.

These religious concepts were not monotheistic — since the very principle of freedom in the choice of the deity assumes the existence of many gods — but neither were they polytheistic in the accepted sense, for the Hebrew tribe has no pantheon, it has no saga narrating the fate of the gods, it has no opportunity of creating legends about the relations between different gods. This religious view is a unique phenomenon also because a new idea, unknown to the great polytheistic religions, was created in it: a special affinity between the god and man (or a group of men), and a demand to carry out all of the god's commands.

This attachment between the god and his people is the special factor that is revealed in the religion of Moses; many Israelite religious conceptions substantiate this assumption. The religious ideas concerning the land belonging to the Lord and the children of Israel being "strangers and settlers with Me" and his servants, the concept of walking in the ways of the Lord, which is not a theological abstraction about imitating the traits of God — as tradition interprets it — but a reminder of historic reality, which knew that the Hebrew was obliged to go in the ways of his ally and hearken to his voice; the very idea of the prophetic mission, whose purpose it was to make known the will of God to His people — all these point to the fact that the religion of Israel is the creation of a special socio-religious way of life, not merely the belief in a national god, neither the creation of a new conception against the background of the higher polytheistic culture.[15]

In the stories about the fathers of the nation, the God of the Patriarchs is referred to by various names. It may be assumed that the Israelite tribes in Egypt had a single, crystallized religion; they believed in the gods of their fathers, and called them by different names or titles. But they had one religious idea, common religious concepts. And they possessed in common the deep yearning to be free of Egypt's yoke.

To the Hebrew tribes living in Egypt, comes Moses. What is his historic task, what message does he bring? His natural task is to educe the ideational forces latent in the world of thought and faith of the Hebrews in Goshen. The idea of the ancient covenant, the faith in the saving power of the divine ally — it was these that could arouse the Hebrews and lead them on the way toward the materialization of the Patriarchs' vision; the conquest of the land of Canaan.

The belief in the pledge of God, made in the distant past to the fathers of the people, to give the land to their children, is surely not the invention of Moses himself; Kaufmann's analysis of the question of the boundaries of the Promised Land has shown that the promise of the land to the Patriarchs was one of the spiritual assets of the tribes in Egypt. This faith was bound up with the ancient Hebrew traditions. In order to convert it into an active factor, Moses had to revive those very traditions, rather than bring the tidings of a new religion.

But it is clear that the belief in man's ability to choose a god for himself, as he pleases, operated for the last time when the covenant was made at Sinai. The covenant with God is binding forever, and it cannot be changed. Moses united all the deities and identified all of them as the God of his fathers — the God of Abraham, Isaac and Jacob — and thus he created the unity of JHWH, the God of Israel, and the unity of the Israelite people.

Moses introduces the name of the deity (actually it appears that the name was new only to part of the tribes), but he does not innovate the religious idea itself; he builds the edifice of the religion of Israel on the ideational assumptions that existed before him. But he changes the religion; the basis of the covenant is the recognition that JHWH is the God of Israelite history, that henceforth the history of the people depends on loyalty to the God of the people and on the observance of His covenant. The people were given a visible symbol of their eternal bond with God: the Ark of the Covenant and the early version of the Ten Commandments, which undoubtedly included only the special terms of the covenant, but not the general rules of morality.

How shall we define this religion? It is not monotheism—this conjecture if refuted by the Scriptures themselves—but neither do we exhaust its contents if we define it as the worship of only one god. It is religion of the Covenant, different from the religious concepts of the idol-worshippers. A religion of discipline and mission, of divine will and divine grace, it is a new conception of God, not because of a special theological theory, but because of an independent fundamental approach. It is an entity unto itself. However, in classifying it according to the standard types of religion, we must define it as monolatry, since it does not deny the existence of other gods in the world. The transition to monotheism is effected by virtue of later processes; indeed, the very possibility of their occurence stems from the special nature of the religion of Moses.

F. The Scriptural Evidence

In various places the Bible mentions the period of wandering in the desert and the revelation at Sinai. The most interesting reference is found in Jeremiah, 7:23, which briefly gives the content of the covenant entered into at Mount Sinai: "Hearken unto My voice, and I will be your God, and ye shall be My people; and walk ye in all way that I command you, and it may be well with you." The Israelite tradition knew that the terms of the Covenant did not include commandments pertaining to worship (this is not the result of Jeremiah's ethical tendencies but an understandable fact to which we shall return), and was also aware of the original nature of the covenant idea. On the other hand, the later tradition, formulated in the prayer in Nehemiah 9:5 ff., regards the revelation at Sinai as the act of the giving of laws by Moses, and does not mention the idea of the covenant at all. The times of Nehemiah do not know the formula: JHWH is the God of Israel, Israel is the people of JHWH; but, the Lord, the God who chose Abraham because He found his heart faithful to Him.

These two pieces of evidence are not important in themselves; they simply hint at the fact that the Judaism of the Second Temple period prefers the idea of the giving of the Law to that of the covenant, and the concept "to be a God to someone" is not pleasing to the ears of those (in Nehemiah's day) who make a covenant.

The main evidence for the events we are discussing is to be found, of course, in the books of the Pentateuch. We have been given four versions of the story, four views of what transpired. But before we attempt to consider the viewpoint of each source, we must determine their original composition, for collections of laws that are not connected with Moses — nor for that pretend to be connected with him — have been interwoven in the fabric of the stories. These are not laws which someone attempted to impose and validate by attributing them to Moses, but ancient legal literature that was ascribed to Moses at the time when all the legislation began to be ascribed to him, to the point that one of the collections of laws is called "The Book of the Covenant" (Sefer ha-bᵉrit).

But the determination of the original composition of each source still does not enable us to understand its point of view; between the intention of the biblical text and our understanding of it there stands the block of the conventional interpretation, the assumption that the Law contains the same things that Nehemiah found in his day. Nor is the traditional interpretation subscribed to by traditionalists alone; even the most critical scholars, who have no compunction about casting doubt on the truth of the biblical text, balk at the very idea that the biblical text constitutes faithful evidence, and that only the later interpretation does not reflect the historical truth.

We have already seen an example of this approach, when we encountered the argument that all the evidence about the connection between the new religion and that of the Hebrew Patriarchs is invalid because it is simply a copy of the later conception of the monotheistic people, who wished to see in their forefathers early monotheists. For this reason the people in the later period believed that Moses was not an innovator, but only a continuer of the Patriarchs' religion — of their belief in the one God.

But on this point there are scholars who sin against the biblical evidence, a sin derived from our dependence on the accepted exegesis, when attempting to understand what is written in the Bible. We are prepared to reject the testimony of the biblical text about the events, but we shrink from rejecting an interpretation that has been accepted for two thousand years or longer. We must not forget that the same conventional interpretation, which we are unwilling to deviate from, was born out of the same faith whose emergence we are investigating.

The sources of the Pentateuch before Deuteronomy, do not say that the Patriarchs believed in one God or that they were true saints. Even the Priestly Code can only say that Abraham made a covenant with *El Shadday*, who, in return for certain promises, demanded that he serve and be faithful to him. The argument that Abraham knew that the one who appeared before him was the creator of the universe belongs to the interpretation and not to the Priestly Code. The sources of the Pentateuch say explicitly that Moses was sent by the God of the Patriarchs to take His people out of Egypt and to bind them by a new covenant, so that they would become the people of God.

There are those who hold that the sources of the Pentateuch believe in the monotheistic character of Moses' message, that is, that God chose the people of Israel in order to demand of them the fulfillment of special commandments, in return for a special relationship. For that reason He informed the people of His divinity and bound them by a covenant to Him, in order to oblige them to fulfill all His commandments. But only in one place — Exodus 19:5–7 — does the Pentateuch tell us that before the making of the covenant the Israelites knew of the divinity and unity of their god. And those verses, which belong to the J source, seem to have been added according to the deuteronomist school; in any case a certain confusion is evident, as a result of which, instead of being the people of God, the Israelites become "a kingdom of priests and a holy nation." This confusion stems from the contradiction between the idea of the covenant and that of the cosmic authority of God, which strikes the biblical author.

It is of interest that the P source also does not recognize the idea of election, and except for one place, it makes no mention, either, of the idea that the Lord God is the creator of heaven and earth.

It might be added that the two early pentateuchal sources know such expressions as: "I will mete out punishments to all the gods of Egypt" (Ex. 12:12), and "Who is like You, O Lord, among the celestials?" (Ex. 15:11); but these are not enough to prove the purely monolatrous character of the religious revolution effected by Moses. It is only when we approach the latest source that this character becomes apparent. Here the real confusion begins: in it the idea of election seems to be essential in explaining the contradiction between monotheism and national covenant. Even more tangible is the fact that in all three early sources there is no hint of positive monotheistic proclamations.

However, the ordinary Israelite belief that there is something in the covenant idea that deviates from its ideational structure found expression in the prayer in Nehemiah 9, which concludes a summary of the history

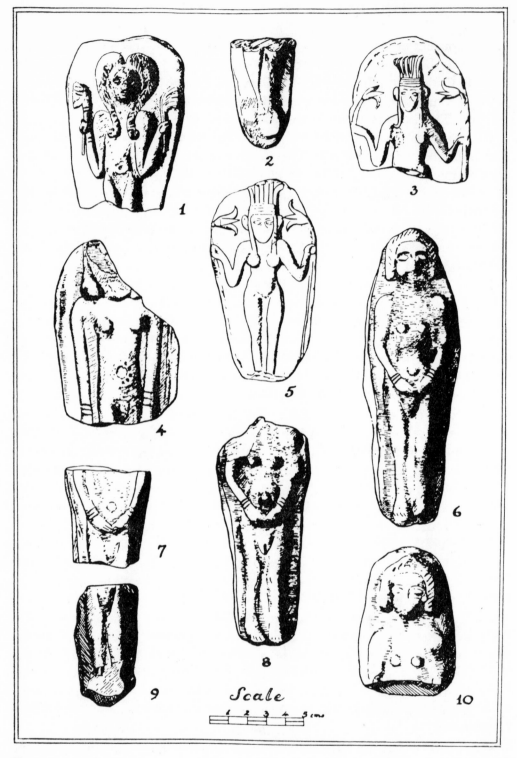

Fig. 30.
Tell Beit Mirsim. Clay tablets bearing the images of fertility goddesses.
Prof. W. F. Albright.

of the nation in the spirit of the Second Temple period; and thenceforth —
in Jewish tradition — the revelation at Sinai became the occasion upon
which the Law as well as the law of the Sabbath were given. All the
distinctiveness of the Israelite covenant relationship disappeared, and made
way for the idea of Abraham's, the righteous man's, love of God.

At Mount Sinai a covenant was concluded between God and Israel. How
was the covenant concluded and what was its content? Exodus 24:2–9
(E source) relates that Moses went up to meet the Lord by himself. When
he returned he told the people all the words of the Lord ("and all the
ordinances" is an addition), and upon the people's acceptation of them,
Moses arranged a covenant-making ceremony in accordance with ancient
custom. Before doing so, he wrote all the words of the Lord in the Book
of the Covenant.

It is reasonable to conclude that this book was preserved, or was copied
onto the tablets, in any case, mention of its contents should be sought in
the biblical material. We are not called upon to prove that the reference
is not to a collection of laws called the Book of the Covenant. The question
is only this: are the words of the Lord, which constitute the basis of the
covenant, identical with the Ten Commandments in Exodus 20, or part
of them, or are they perhaps identical with the cultic commandments in
Exodus 34? The decision must go against the latter hypothesis

There are at least two reasons for this: 1) The command, "You shall
not make molten gods for yourselves" (Ex. 34:17). If there really had been
such a basic provision, it would have prevented the making of idols and
molten images in the times of the Judges; at the very least, the author of the
Book of Judges would have denounced the temple at Dan. But it is only in
the pragmatic compilation, which follows the episode of Gideon, that the
compilers of the Book of Judges get around to denouncing the making
of the *ephod*; in Gideon's time the Israelites knew nothing about that grave
prohibition.   2) Jeremiah 7:22 not only rules out the possibility that anything was said at Sinai concerning burnt-offerings or sacrifices, but it even
sums up the positive content of the covenant, as the creation of "The Lord
is the God of Israel, Israel is the people of God" relationship i.e. hearkening
to the voice of the Lord, absolute obedience to a god who promises to do
well by His people. Such an idea is to be found only in the version: "I the
Lord am your God..." We must therefore seek the wording of the covenant
in Exodus 20. It is probable that this version included the following commandments:

"I am the Lord...," which is actually the core of the Covenant; "You
shall have no other..." — which is a reinforcement of the demand for

absolute faithfulness ("You shall not make" and its whole continuation is a later commentary on the commandment "You shall have no other," its aim being to identify "other gods" with "idol");

"You shall not take the name...", which in the opinion of many scholars is a prohibition against the administration of an oath with the intention to harm;

"Remember..." until "to keep it holy." This is not the place to go into the true significance of this commandment (or of the idea of sabbath in general).

The remaining commandments do not belong to the original content of the Sinaitic covenant, not because they are "ethical-universal," but because they have no connection with the first four which build the basis of a faith of generations.

The religion of JHWH, which Moses established in Israel, did not introduce a new cult, or reveal a different way of serving God. The various cultic ordinances ascribed to Moses are later creations. It is therefore difficult to discover the manner in which the ancient Israelites worshipped God.

G. An Outline of the Ancient Israelite Cult

In seeking to comprehend the Israelite cult in the period between Moses and Eli the priest, we must rely mainly on the description, to a large degree objective and historical, we find in the Book of Judges, and the beginning of the Book of Samuel. The laws of worship in the Pentateuch, even in the ancient layers of the JE source, are no firm support for a description of the cultic practice in the days of the Judges — apart from the fact that they are inadequate for a complete picture.

Holy Places. We can nevertheless distinguish cultic institutions which were an innovation, as against the previous period in the history of the people in its land. The main institution whose origin is surely from the time of Moses is the Ark of the Covenant. This Ark was placed at Shiloh, and a sort of cultic center was established there, but this was not the only holy place. What distinguishes it from all the other holy places is its ancient origin, the location of the Ark of the Lord there, and the fact that a family of priests served there which could trace its lineage to the time of the Exodus from Egypt. The tabernacle at Shiloh was a place of pilgrimage, but we have no evidence that there were fixed times for this pilgrimage.

The worship of God included the bringing of sacrifice, the offering of gifts, and the burning of incense. There is no evidence of other types of sacrifices. The tabernacle also served as a place for the discharge of vows and as a house of prayer — and apparently also as the place for consulting the judgment of the Urim and Thummim. In addition, there is an allusion in Judges, 21:19, to a periodical holiday connected with Shiloh.

Judges 20:26–27 relates that in the days of the Judges the Ark was at Beth-el, which place also served as a cultic center in a certain sense, and a place for communicating with God. Critical research does not regard this account as reliable.

In various places in the country we find the worship of God performed in front of a molten image, in the manner of the tribal temple of the Danites. In front of the image there officiates a priestly family of the tribe of Levi.

We also find a local temple at Ophrah in the time of Gideon, which also serves as a sort of cultic center.

Another temple, of the time of Abimelech, has been located in Shechem, but not all scholars consider this an Israelite temple, because it was called "the house of Baal-berith," according to the biblical text this was a temple of idol-worship.[16] If we assume that this was an Israelite temple, we regard it as an urban temple which served as a center for assemblies of the people, and also contained a treasury, which may hint at priestly taxes.

Private Worship. The worship of God in the times of the Judges is not restricted to the temples; it is free, and any person can erect an altar (Jud. 6:17 ff.), offer sacrifices, and even make a molten image (Jud. 17), and appoint a private priest (Jud. 17:5), or hire a priest from the tribe of Levi (Jud. 17:10). The form of the altars was certainly not fixed, but on the basis of the available writings we can conjecture that they were built of stone, with an *Ashera* tree plated by them. The customary sacrifices were the *'ola* and *minḥa* (meat and *mazzot*).

It may also be assumed that human sacrifice was practiced, but undoubtedly only in special cases. The text in Exodus, 22:28, apparently refers to that ancient period; everywhere else in the Pentateuch the significance of the demand, "You shall give Me the first-born among your sons" was changed, by an addition, into the commandment to redeem Man's first-born.

Cultic Commandments and Holidays. Up to this point we have surveyed the worship of God, as it is reflected in the early historical writings. But we have not found in these sources any allusion to a fixed book of laws, such as exists even in the most primitive religions, nor any evidence of the existence of cultic commandments. This is surprising, because the Passover festival and the sacrifice of the first-born connected with it certainly existed even before the Exodus. And the code of the JE source may also prove the existence of the law of the first fruits and the law of the Passover in the ancient period, not because it commands their observance, but because it warns against forbidden cultic practices: Exodus 34:25–26 does not command the observance of the Passover or the bringing of the first fruits, but forbids the sacrifice of leavened bread, the leaving of the sacrifice until morning, and the seething of a kid in its mother's milk at the time of the bringing of first fruits.

On the other hand, we find Elkanah going every year up to Shiloh to offer his sacrifice (I Sam. 1) — but there is no indication that this is the Passover sacrifice. Even more doubtful is the observance of the commandment of the three pilgrimages. Nor is there evidence of the bringing of the first fruits to the Temple.

The Sabbath and the Sabbatical Year, which are among the main commandments in the Priestly Code, are also found in the JE source (Ex. 23:10–12). Even though this is one of the few places where the commandment of the Sabbath is juxtaposed to the commandment of the sabbatical year- undoubtedly a sign of the antiquity of the law — there is no assurance that either one of these commandments was actually observed in that period.

The Cultic Commandments as an Ancient Idea. Even though we have no evidence of the observance of the cultic commandments in JE, either in the ancient period or afterwards, it may be assumed that the commandments existed and were observed by the priests as a religio-cultic demand. The very fact that D abolishes the commandment to let the land lie fallow (Deut. 15:1 ff.), and that the later period invents various reasons for the commandment of the Sabbath (a sign of covenant, the Exodus from Egypt, a remembrance of the creation of the world), shows that the later period required an explanation, which would have been superfluous in the ancient period, for the things were then self-evident.

The admonitions (*"Beḥuqotai-"* Lev. 26), in the Holiness Code, which does not appear to be particularly late, associate the subject of rest of the land with the threat of exile: the non-observance of the sabbatical year will be punished with exile, and its length will depend on the number of sabbatical years the land did not rest when the people dwelt in it (Lev. 26:33–35). But already in D there is no mention of rest for the land — which means that the commandment was very ancient.

The highlights in the general picture resulting from the study of the biblical sources are the following: in the ancient Israelite cult there is no fixed form for the worship of God, and no written constitution is known. Gifts to the priests are given at the time of the sacrifice, but are not defined; there is no evidence of the existence of the laws of the Sabbath and the sabbatical year.

CHAPTER XI

LAW

by S. E. Loewenstamm

L IKE EVERY LAW in the world early Israelite law also reflects the social structure and its correspondent way of life, in abstract and clear formulation; it is therefore an important historical source of information about the People of Israel in ancient times. This generally is valid concerning the law accepted by the people since the Exodus and handed down by the Bible as fixed legal rules, but is not the case of the tradition from the Patriarchs' times. These traditions were not transmitted formulated as legal principles but we learn of them from isolated allusions contained in the stories of the Patriarchs.

A. THE PERIOD OF THE PATRIARCHS

The clearest amongst these references touch on the life of the family which the head of the family rules. This regime is clearly demonstrated in the episode of Judah and Tamar. When Judah heard that his son's widow had played the harlot, he sentenced her to death: "Bring her out and let her be burned" (Gen. 39:24). This shows that the head of the family had the right to have members of his family killed. The position of the head of the family is also recognized by the laws of levirate marriage in this story, for on the strength of it Judah was accused of not having given the widow of his dead son to his younger son in marriage (Gen. 38:11, 26). Hence, it was the head of family who was responsible for arranging the levirate marriage and not the brother of the deceased husband. The nature of family life at the time of the Patriarchs is also demonstrated in the stories of Sarah and Hagar, Rachel and Bilhah, Leah and Zilpah. They testify to an ancient custom which obliged a barren woman (or a woman who had ceased bearing children) to give her handmaid to her husband "to be built up through her." Such a custom was bound to cause upheavals in the life of the family, like the crisis that forms the background to the story of Hagar. We read that after conceiving, Hagar taunted her barren mistress, and Abraham let Sarah "deal harshly" with her handmaid (Gen. 16:4–6). One cannot ignore the similarity of this incident to the problem of the *naditum* (the priestess forbidden to bear sons), discussed in the Code of Hammurabi § 146. This law states: If the *naditum* has given her handmaid to her husband, and the latter claims the same status as her mistress after having borne sons, the wife is entitled to reduce her rival to the position of a simple maidservant again, the latter keeping only one advantage over the other servants, namely, her mistress is not allowed to sell her. We also learn from the story of Hagar that a wife might one day demand the expulsion of her bondwoman's son, especially if she has meanwhile borne a son of her own (Gen. 21:10). This family problem is also mentioned in a Mesopotamian document from the period of the Patriarchs — the marriage contract from Nuzi — under which the wife is obliged to give her husband a handmaid in case she herself does not bear him any sons. Furthermore, the wife is expressly forbidden to send away the maidservant's son.[1] A number of details in the stories of the Patriarchs, such as the story of Rachel stealing the *teraphim* of Laban her father (Gen. 31:19–35), became clear in the light of the legal documents from Nuzi. In one of these contracts a man adopts his daughter's husband and specifies that if he himself were to have a son, the inheritance of the adopter would be divided equally between his own and the adopted son, however, he excludes his household gods from this rule. His natural son will inherit those.[2] This contract clearly shows the great esteem in which the household gods were held in the days of the Patriarchs and explains Rachel's action.[3]

B. The Nature of the Law in the Ancient East.

After these observations about law at the time of the Patriarchs, and before we turn to the pentateuchal law, we ought to make a brief survey of the nature of law in the Ancient East as a whole. In the entire Ancient East the head of the people acted as supreme judge, this function pertaining to his task of looking after the welfare of his people. The common morality of all the peoples of the Ancient East demanded from the judge in general, and from the supreme judge in particular, that he discharge this duty honestly and justly, that he protect the weak from oppression and see that justice is done for the orphan and the widow.[4] These elementary require-ments demonstrate the nature of that law, which is not subjected to any written rules. We have here a picture that differs from the pattern of the famous lawsuit dating from the beginning of written law in Rome. In that case the person who demands redress for the destruction of vines (*actio de vitibus succisis*) loses his claim because the law only recognises a claim for the destruction of trees (*actio de arboribus succisis*). The plaintiff in the case of the destruction of vines had to phrase his claim as if he sued for the destruction of trees — if he wanted to have his case accepted.[5] Such an approach was foreign to the spirit of the peoples in the Ancient East, whose judges were free to hand down in every lawsuit decisions according to plain justice.

Obviously this does not imply the absence of rules in the law of the Ancient East. From the decisions taken there naturally crystallized an oral legal tradition. Moreover, recent discoveries have proved that Mesopotamian kings put this tradition into writing hundreds of years before Hammurabi, King of Babylon,[6] with the intention (explained in the Code of Hammurabi)[7] that every citizen might know beforehand what to expect if he found himself in any of the cases mentioned. But being written, did not basically change the character of the law. There was no attempt at drawing up an exhaustive system of state laws. One looks in vain in all those laws for a paragraph which defines ownership of any kind. Even terms which all laws use, such as theft, do not rate a legal definition. There is manifestly no room for abstract terms, such as power of attorney and the like. In the light of this situation it is quite obvious that even after writing down the law an extensive area was covered by the oral law. In general legislation did not influence the accepted form of the course of judgement. This accounts for the phenomenon which so amazes the jurist of our time: no Mesopotamian judge ever gives reason for his decision by reference to paragraphs in the law.[8]

C. The Nature of Israelite Justice before the Monarchy

It would appear that this was also the position in Israel. The leader was also the supreme judge, not only during the monarchy,[9] but since the days of Moses and during the entire period of the Judges, whose very title points to their judiciary function. Moreover, in Israel written law was nothing but a kind of completion to the oral law, handed down to us only in the late form it assumed in the Talmud. A perfect example of the incompleteness of the Written Law is the version of the law of corporal punishment in Deuteronomy: "When there is a dispute between men and they go to law, and a decision is rendered declaring the one in the right and the other in the wrong — if the guilty one is to be flogged, the magistrate shall have him lie down and be given lashes in his presence, by count, as his guilt warrants. He may be given up to forty lashes, but no more, lest being flogged further, to excess, your brother be degraded before your eyes" (Deut. 25:1–3). The content of the law is clear enough, but its applicability is problematic, since — in contrast to Assyrian laws[10] — we have not found in the whole of the Pentateuch a single clear case in which the guilty man is sentenced to be scourged;[11] but at the most an isolated allusion to the condemnation of a man who brings a false charge against his wife, claiming that he has not found her a virgin. Of such a man it is said: "The elders of that city shall then take the man and flog him" (Deut. 22:18). A criterion according to which the Pentateuch puts laws into writing is not existent, or at least, is not known to us. In the above case it might just possibly be argued that the entire nation was well aware what offences deserved flogging, and it was only necessary to stress the warning not to exceed the number of lashes. This argument does not, however, apply to all laws. There is, for instance, in the Book of the Covenant the law dealing with the sofar harmless ox who has gored another ox (Ex. 21:35), codified already in the law of Eshnunna (§ 53) which precedes the Code of Hammurabi. This implies that we have here a very old law, and there was no special need to repeat it.

So far we have discussed the common aspect of the biblical laws and those belonging to the Ancient East in general, but that does not mean that one can compare biblical law in all its aspects with the rest of the laws of the Ancient East. Biblical law does not merely differ from them in this or that detail, but in its very character, being a fundamentally religious law (similar to Islamic law)[12] and therefore different from Eastern secular law in quite a number of ways: 1) The Pentateuch emphasizes time and again that the source of its laws is God's word to Moses, whether it says so explicity as for instance: "And the Lord said to Moses: Tell the Israelite people" ... or whether it invests the idea of divine revelation with a dramatic force as in the impressive description of the Revelation at Mount Sinai. The rest of the laws in the Ancient East do not allude to a superhuman source, and even in the Code of Hammurabi the allusion to a god looks merely like a figure of speech which does not decrease the king's credit as a legislator. Hammurabi boasts: "A righteous King, upon whom Shamash [the god of the sun and of law] has bestowed justice, am I,"[13] but he tones down this formula at great length, stressing that it is indeed he who is the lawgiver. At the end of the introduction it is again mentioned that it is the king who at the order of the god Marduk has introduced law and justice into the land;[14] 2) The Pentateuch attaches the idea of the covenant to the divine source of the law: mankind undertook to observe the word of God.[15] The concept of a covenant, which the Pentateuch mentions for the first time when speaking of the covenant that God made with man after the Flood, reaches its climax with the covenant God concluded with Israel at Mount Sinai. Later on it recurs in the description of the covenant concluded on Mount Ebal and Mount Gerizim

(Deut. 27), at Joshua's covenant (Josh. 24:25), and lastly in the purely historical description of the covenant concluded by God, Josiah and the entire nation (II Kings 23:3). All these traditions point to the ancient custom of a nation receiving its laws in the course of a solemn religious ceremony. However, with the other nations of the Ancient East the king's legislation does not require the people's sanction; 3) It is in the above that the distinctive literary character of pentateuchal law has its roots. The giving of the laws in the Pentateuch is part of the description of the acts of the Lord, who led His people out of the land of Egypt bringing them to the land of Canaan, and gave them laws and statutes on the way. From the literary viewpoint the laws fit therefore into a historical account of a clearly theological nature, while the laws of other nations in the Ancient East are contained in collections of laws which form independent codes. In the Pentateuch civil and criminal laws are all mixed with moral precepts and even with cultic statutes as for example the rules of sacrifices, festivals, defilement and purity, etc. The other law collections of the Ancient East confine themselves to the sphere of civil and criminal law, resembling also in this respect modern codification. If they do contain ethic statements, their place is only in the introduction or conclusion, but they are never included within the actual formulation of the laws. The result is that with these nations civil and criminal laws, ethics and cult constituted three separate domains;[16] 4) Only part of the pentateuchal legislation is formulated in dry, legal terminology, most of it being written in a rhetorical style which reasons, persuades and instructs. It seems as though one can hear the sermonizing of the Levites who wrote them: "They shall teach Your norms to Jacob, and Your instructions to Israel" (Deut. 33:10). The ancient Eastern laws are all of them written in a dry, technical language, without any undertone. Quite clearly then, any attempt at outlining the secular law of the Pentateuch meets with serious difficulties. The rules of the law are put down without any definite order, moral and religious elements mingle to such an extent that anyone attempting to separate the secular law from the moral and religious elements comes up against the gravest doubts. Furthermore, no protocols of trials or contracts have come down to us, which might serve as a source of information showing how the rules were applied, or separate them from principles of a purely ethical character.

D. The Historical Problem

The difficulties mentioned increase even more when one attempts a historical analysis of biblical laws. The question immediately comes to mind whether in ancient Israel one and the same law was applied by all the tribes. This question arises in particular concerning the laws of levirate marriage, redemption and inheritance which, according to the Book of Ruth, were practised in Bethlehem, but which do not appear at all clear from the pentateuchal laws.[17] This contradiction led to the assumption that in ancient times the pentateuchal laws of redemption and inheritance were customary only in northern Israel. One might furthermore ask whether contradictions within pentateuchal law cannot be explained in the same way or if they might be solved by assuming that they do not belong to one and the same period. The difficulty involves the problem of dating the pentateuchal laws. This matter, which forms the subject of continuous differences of opinion among scholars, turns any attempt at describing Israelite law in the period before the monarchy into purely subjective hypothesis.

The suggestions made by scholars for dating the laws can be divided into three types:

(1) There is the attempt to attribute a definite time of conclusion to every collection of laws. The conclusions reached by these studies did not meet with unanimous agreement,[18] though there is a general tendency to raise the date of the Book of the Covenant (Ex. 20–23:19) as against the other collections, i.e., the Law of Holiness (Lev. 17–26), the law of Deuteronomy (Deut. 13–26) and the laws scattered in Numbers. Further, dating the time a collection of laws was concluded by means of a hypothesis leaves open the question whether all the laws it contains, or a part, need to be considered several centuries older than the date of conclusion.

(2) There is the attempt at differentiating the several layers by means of analysing the various formulations. It is obvious that the pentateuchal laws are not formulated according to a single pattern, but are cast in different stylistic moulds. We have already mentioned that part of the pentateuchal laws are in the nature of purely legal instructions, while with others the legal nucleus is clothed in a homiletical and moralizing style. But this is not all. Even the technical, legal formulation shows far-reaching differences. The casuistic law in the Book of the Covenant generally refers to its subject by a verb, beginning with the word "if" (*ki*) and continues with "if" (*im*), e.g. "if you buy a Hebrew servant... if he came in single" ... (Ex. 21:2–3). Yet close by we have the solemn parcipial formulation e.g. "Whosoever lies with a beast shall surely be put to death" (Ex. 22:18) which recalls the imprecation: Cursed

be he who lies with any beast" (Deut. 27:21), or even the formulation in the imperative: "You shall not tolerate a sorceress" (Ex. 23:17). Things become even more complicated when we come to investigate the rest of the collections. In the Priestly Law there frequently recurs the casuistic formulation: the man that does such and such a thing (cf. for example Lev. 20); the participial formulation from the Book of the Covenant: "He who reviles his father or his mother shall be put to death" (Ex. 21:17) is repeated here: "If any man insults his father or his mother, he shall be put to death" (Lev. 20:9). The apodictic rule which does not generally take easily to legal details is liable to assume a form quite close to the formulation of the casuistic law, e.g. "Every seventh year you shall practice remission of debts," and further on: "This shall be the nature of the remission" (Deut. 15:1–2). After the introduction the text explains the release procedure in detail. The evaluation of these and similar differences in formulation is the subject of a scholarly dispute. As against the point of view that every shade of formulation represents evidence for a specific source,[19] there is the view which sees no basis for analysis in the different styles, and assumes that precisely differences of style suit the fluid rhetorical language of the Bible.[20] The daring suggestion was even made that a casuistic formulation is evidence for an early Canaanite law, while an apodictic formulation is proof of its being a legal innovation of the Israelites.[21] Against this supposition it was argued that the amorphous structure of society and the primitive economy reflected in the casuistic laws of the Pentateuch do not agree with our knowledge of the life of Canaanite society which had a clear social stratification and a developed economy.[22] Also the Hittite international contracts contain both passages of a casuistic formulation along with apodictic passages;[23] and even the laws of the Ancient East bear traces of apodictic formulation[24] (Assyrian laws, tablet A §§ 40, 57–59, tablet B § 6, the Code of Hammurabi §§ 36, 38–40). The doubts are further increased by the ancient law of Eshnunna, which is conspicuous for the absence of a uniform formulation. As against the passages which begin with *šumma*, i.e. "for," paragraphs 1–4, 7–16, 18A, 19, 51, 52 are formulated in widely different styles. It was specially pointed out that the style of paragraphs 15, 16, 51, 52 is purely apodictic, while paragraphs 12, 13 and 18 begin with *awīlum ša*, i.e. "the man that," like the New Babylonian laws and similar to the formulation patterns in Leviticus.[25] The point of view which deprives the difference in formulation of any critical value is inacceptable. The claim that a rhetorical style excludes monotony ignores the obvious fact that part of the pentateuchal laws is formulated in a technical, legalistic style, lacking any trace of rhetoric, and that the actual fundamental difference between a dry, simple, legal formulation and a rhetorical formulation points to different manners of editing. The same applies, for example, to the difference between the casuistic formulation of the rules in the Book of the Covenant and the casuistic formulation of the rules in the Priestly Law. Furthermore, one cannot ignore the fact that even rhetorical formulations are occasionally peculiar to one collection of laws, such as the warning "Show him no pity or compassion," which recurs five times in Deuteronomy (Deut. 7:16; 13:9; 19:13; 19:21; 25:12). It must therefore be admitted that differences in formulation constitute evidence of a complicated editing history. At the same time we have to realize that our ignorance of this history prevents us from using it as a criterion for the chronology of the texts.

(3) The third way of dating the pentateuchal laws is the examination of their background and contents. As we have said, their narrative background is the story of the Exodus, and an analysis of the contents strengthens the assumption that in their main outlines the pentateuchal laws crystallized at an early period. In the Pentateuch allusions to the period of the Monarchy are extremely meager and are limited to warning the king not to abuse his position (Deut. 17:20) and to the regulation of a supreme court of law (Deut. 8:13).[26] The elders and priests apparently served as judges. The Pentateuch contains no laws concerning the professional soldier (which play a considerable role in the Code of Hammurabi), that is to say, a class which did not develop in Israel before King David's time. The Pentateuch considers participation in a battle the concern of the entire nation, based on the principle of volunteering, with the proviso of discharging the faint-hearted (Deut. 20:8). The strong hand of the king is not felt in a single pentateuchal law, nor is there in it room for a law like that in the Code of Hammurabi which holds financially responsible for an act of robbery the city within whose boundaries the delict was committed (§ 23). The very language of the law reveals the weakness of the regime, for when the Pentateuch comes to restrict the right of the creditor to seize a pledged article

it appeals to the heart of the creditor: "If you take your neighbor's garment in pledge, you must return it to him before the sun sets; it is his only clothing, the sole covering for his skin. In what else shall he sleep? Therefore, if he cries out to Me, I will pay heed, for I am compassionate" (Ex. 22:25–26). The restriction of the creditor's rights is formulated here as an appeal to the creditor's conscience accompanied by a threat of heavenly punishment. Hammurabi's law on this subject — though far-reaching — contents itself with a dry and practical passage: "If a man pledges a bull, a third *minah* he shall pay" (§ 241). This means that it imposes a fine on the creditor who transgresses that commandment, and while the Pentateuch requests compassion, the Babylonian law speaks of prohibition and punishment. In Israel there is no sign of government interference. In contrast to Mesopotamian laws[27] the Pentateuch supplies no tariffs for services and merchandise. Likewise it lacks the emphasis so frequently encountered in the Code of Hammurabi — that contracts must be confirmed in writing.[28] Only a single document is mentioned in the entire Pentateuch, it is the act of divorce which the husband is ordered to hand to his wife at the time of the separation (Deut. 24:1). This rule differs from the formulation of the rest of the pentateuchal laws, and it is thought to be a regulation dating from the time of the Monarchy. Economic life, founded on a familial-tribal basis was certainly primitive. In contrast to the Mesopotamian law, the Pentateuch contains no laws of land tenancy; this implies that it does not recognize the figure of the large landowner who lives in the city and leases out his land, but only the peasant who farms his land himself, or at most with the help of his slaves.[29] There are no commercial laws. The laws concerning the sale of land and money lending are in the nature of an exception which proves the rule that the man who sells or leases out his land, or the man who borrows money, is not considered as transacting ordinary business, but as a citizen who has a hard time, is forced to take steps from economic necessity, and therefore comes under the protection of the law. There are, furthermore, no laws in the Pentateuch which point to a high standard of material culture, as for example the Mesopotamian laws concerning physicians or architects. Briefly, the society reflected in the pentateuchal laws is based on a loose tribal-familial regime that lacks the force of a powerful state. The general picture fits the period of the Judges. The view is therefore justified that the pentateuchal laws precede the period of the Monarchy, without ruling out the possibility that one or another law was brought up to date at a later time.

E. CIVIL LAW

In discussing the civil law we start with the laws that clearly deal with the social structure and we shall add to them those laws which indirectly shed light on the life in society.

1. *Marriage Laws.* We have already mentioned that the way of life in ancient Israel was based on a tribal-familial regime. Before we deal with these characteristic arrangements, let us look at the marriage laws. Biblical law does not limit the number of women that a man is allowed to wed, in contrast to the tendency of the Mesopotamian law to make the permission to marry an additional woman dependent on the first woman being barren.[30] In the Bible a man's right to marry a woman is limited by a series of prohibitions all of which derive from the rule that "None of you shall come near anyone of his own flesh to uncover nakedness" (Lev. 18:6–18; 20:11–12; 14, 17, 19–21). Only few of these prohibitions are enforced by death penalty, namely intercourse with a father's wife, a son's wife and with both a mother and a daughter (Lev. 20:11, 12, 14). This led to the assumption that the rest of the prohibitions were laid down later. This hypothesis is also supported by the story of Tamar who tells Amnon, her brother on her father's side, that the king would not reject his request to marry her (II Sam. 13:13). To these restrictions is added the one in Deuteronomy that a man is not allowed to marry the wife he divorced and who had been married to another man after their separation (Deut. 24:1–4), as well as the special prohibition for priests to marry a widow, divorcée, harlot or defiled woman (Lev. 21:7, 14). As against these prohibitions there is the ordinance of the levirate marriage. If two brothers live together, and one of them dies childless, it is the duty of the surviving brother to marry the widow (Deut. 25:5–10). The express intention of this law is for the deceased husband's brother to produce a child for the dead man, ruling that the first born to the dead husband's brother and the widow is legally considered to be the son of the deceased. The law demonstrates the intense concern that the name of the dead man be not extinguished among his people, a concern which is also displayed by the genealogical lists that perpetuate the names of men who died childless (Gen. 38:7–10; Num. 26:19; I Chr. 2:30).[31] However the law of the levirate marriage is considerably milder in the Pentateuch, in

comparison with the ancient law reflected in the story of Judah and Tamar, for the Pentateuch explicitly permits the brother to refrain from a levirate marriage by undergoing the ceremony of *haliẓah*.

In contrast to the Mishna (Qid. I, 1) the Pentateuch sets no fixed rules as to the manner in which a woman is acquired, i.e. becomes a man's wife, and the little information we do possess on the subject originates from the exceptions through which we learn something of the rule. We read in the Book of the Covenant: "If a man seduces a virgin for whom the bride price has not been paid, and lies with her, he must make her his wife by payment of a bride price. If her father refuses to give her to him, he must still weigh out silver in accordance with the bride price for virgins" (Ex. 22:15–16). The ruling in Deuternomy 22:29 fixes the dowry in such a case at fifty pieces of silver. These laws and the story of David's marriage to Michal, Saul's daughter, (I Sam. 18:25–27; II Sam. 3:14) inform us that a man bought himself a virgin by concluding a betrothal contract with her father. This contract obliged him to pay a certain sum called a dowry. From then onwards the virgin was considered engaged, but remained in her father's house until her wedding. This law appears to be based on an ancient Canaanite law, as shown in the Ugaritic inscriptions where the verb *mhr* (dowry) has the same meaning as in the Bible.[32] We do not know how the betrothed virgin became a wife, i.e. whether it required a ceremony, a kind of marriage blessing, or if it was enough for the girl to enter her husband's house for the purpose of becoming his wife. The Bible contains no clear evidence of a dowry the woman received from her father. It is, however, difficult to assume that in contrast to the custom of the Ancient East[33] and that stated in the Talmud[34], a daughter of Israel left in ancient times her father's house empty handed. Even if there is no outright evidence of a dowry, there is an allusion to it in the story of Caleb who gave his daughter, the wife of Othniel, as a "blessing," i.e. a gift, "springs of water" (Jud. 1:14, 15). The Bible has furthermore preserved the legal term for the daughter's dowry, namely the word *shilluḥim* (I Kings 9:16) which is nothing but the Ugaritic *tlḥ* occuring in the Ugaritic inscriptions as a parallel of the *mlg*[35] corresponding to the talmudic *mᶜlog*. In the case the father of a virgin had died, his place was very likely taken by her eldest brother. The important part played by Jacob's sons in the affair of Dinah is not the only allusion to it, but also the instructive fact that the eldest brother in the genealogical lists in Chronicles is frequently called "the chief" (e.g. I Chr. 5:7, 15; 9:17; 12:3); it also happened that a father appointed as chief one of the sons who was not his first-born (I Chr. 26:10).[36] In addition to the marriage of a virgin, we must also mention the marriage of a woman who is not a virgin, i.e., a widow, divorcée, harlot or defiled woman, marriages which are permitted to all Israelites except priests. The laws governing such marriages are not known, but it is to be assumed — from the story of David and Abigail (I. Sam. 25:40–42) — that such a woman married of her own accord. This is also proved by the precept that the vow of a widow or divorcée "shall be binding upon her" (Num. 30:10), which means she is independent. The marriage of a handmaid, mentioned in the Book of the Covenant, belongs to a special category, it obliges the man who purchases a maidservant with the intention of making her his or his son's wife, but has not carried out his purpose, to do everything to have her redeemed, and in no case sell her to foreign people (Ex. 21:7–10). The difference in status between the wife and such a handmaid cannot be determined precisely, but the law's concern for her raiment, conjugal rights, and food imply that her status approached that of her mistress. A similar precept applies to woman captives "of goodly form" (Deut. 21:11–14). He who has taken such a beautiful woman is forbidden to sell her after he has tired of her, he has to send her away, i.e. to divorce her, or to free her. The common denominator of all the marriage forms we have mentioned is that the woman enters her husband's house. Only in exceptional cases does the man become attached to the woman's family. There is a reference to such a marriage in the Book of Chronicles, in the genealogical list of Sheshan who married his daughter to his Egyptian servant, Jarha. In such a case the sons count as members of the mother's family, and not the family of their father (I Chr. 2:34–41); and this is also where the laws concerning the daughter who inherits come in (cf. below).

The Pentateuch does not deal with the laws ruling the monetary aspects of marriage, such as the question of a husband's liability for his wife's debts, or the other way round. Similarly, there is nothing about the rights of a widow who is not entitled to an inheritance (cf. below). Not for nothing did scholars find it difficult to explain the story in the Book of Ruth where Naomi, the widow of Elimelech, sold her husband's field to the redeemer on condition that he marry the wife of her husband's dead son.[37] We have already mentioned the hypothesis that this reflects a law peculiar to the land of Judah, which in the Pentateuch was given up in favor of the laws of northern Israel.

It is the husband's privilege to divorce his wife if he discovers some unseemly thing in her, as mentioned in Deut. 24:1–4, it being stressed that he must give her a bill of divorcement. Even if the antiquity of the law concerning the bill of divorcement is questionable (cf. above), there is no doubt that the husband was entitled to divorce his wife. The term "some unseemly thing" is not clear; it is certain, however, that it refers to a serious reason. No law in the Pentateuch entitles the woman to demand under certain conditions a divorce from her husband. There may be reference to it, though, in the law concerning the handmaid who goes free if her husband took another wife and for that reason diminished her food, raiment and conjugal rights (Ex. 21:10, 11). This assumption also emerges in the light of the obvious tendency of the Pentateuch to limit the authority of the head of the family with respect to the precept of the levirate marriage, and, even more clearly, the law of the rebellious son. The text implies a restriction of the father's right to kill his son. Instead, both parents are entitled to bring him before the elders of the town and to demand the death penalty for him (Deut. 21:20–21).

2. *The Inheritance Laws.* More characteristic than the marriage laws for the background of Israelite society in ancient days are the laws based on blood kinship. To begin with we must point out a basic difference between the Israelite laws (including the laws of the Talmud) and those of Mesopotamia, Rome and Greece. Israelite law does not recognize adoption, that is, a person's right to bestow on a stranger the legal status of a son. The individual's privilege to change the laws of society which are founded on the history of the tribe and the family, is foreign to the spirit of biblical law. The Pentateuch knows no family relationship apart from blood kinship. And blood relationship means from the father's side only, relatives on the mother's side are not called family. This principle, called the principle of the agnatic family in Roman terminology, is common to most ancient laws,[38] and is founded — according to the commonly held view — on the structure of the patriarchal family. According to this principle, to the family belong only those people who are subject to the head of the family, or who were subject to him in his life time, and no others.[39] The law in Numbers presents us, however, with an additional reason, the concern lest an inheritance pass from one family to another, or even from tribe to tribe. It is this concern which governs the laws of inheritance whose entire purpose is the perpetuation of the territorial arrangements and family matters which were established at the time of the conquest of Canaan. The principle of the law determines that: "If a man dies without leaving a son, you shall transfer his property to his daughter. If he has no daughter, you shall assign his property to his brothers. If he has no brothers, you shall assign his property to his father's brothers. If his father had no brothers, you shall assign his property to his nearest relative in his own clan, and he shall inherit it" (Num. 27:8–11). A supplement to this law says

that a daughter who inherits shall marry into a family of her father's tribe (Num. 36:6), and the execution of the law (Num. 36:11) shows preference for the sons of the father's brothers i.e. for those men to whom the inheritance would have come in the end, were it not for the daughter inheriting. These laws merely supplement the laws ruling the division of the land according to tribes and families (Num. 26:53 ff.), which grant the individual his inheritance as a member of the tribe and the family, for the sole purpose that "the Israelite tribes shall remain bound each to its portion" (Num. 36-9). The substance of the inheritance legislation becomes clear only when we realize that its aim is to maintain a solid familial-tribal framework. The principle that only the father's kin is recognized as family prevents any transfer of the inheritance to another family. There is no mention of legal problems that do not refer to this central problem, such as the question who inherits the possessions of a woman who is not a daughter entitled to inherit, since an ordinary woman has no part of the tribe's inheritance; or the question of the responsibility of the heirs for the dead man's debts. A comparison of biblic law with mishnaic law (B. Bathra 8:1–2) is highly instructive. As we said, according to the Pentateuch the inheritance of a childless man passes to his brothers. But according to the Mishna the father has priority over the brothers. This difference is characteristic. The biblical law is only concerned with immovables which are passed on from generation to generation; it starts out from the assumption that a son has no possessions in his father's life time. While according to the point of view on which the Mishna is based, a son has possessions of his own, and is even portrayed as buying immovable property for himself. Therefore it is perfectly understood that the father has priority over the brothers, since he is closer to the son than the brothers. In most instances, however, the mishnaic laws merely explain the pentateuchal laws according to their original meaning, in conformity with the rule that if a person precedes in inheritance, his heirs have precedence and he passes the inheritance to his sons when he dies. For example: If a man had two sons, one of whom died in his father's life time and left only two daughters, then the living son takes his part and the daughters of the dead man divide their father's part between themselves. The basic laws of inheritance are supplemented by the law of the first-born. This law, which Deuteronomy mentions as a well known rule and not as an innovation, allots to the first-born a double portion of his father's inheritance, i.e., twice as much as each of his brothers.[40] (Deut. 21:17).

3. *Property Laws*. We stressed that the laws of inheritance are essentially concerned with the division of the land inheritance. But implicitly the

same laws also apply to the inheritance of movable property, which means that the laws of inheritance do not differentiate between immovable and movable property. But this distinction does exist if a man sells his possession during his lifetime. The Pentateuch imposes no restrictions on the sale of movable property, since their transfer does not affect the order of society. On the other hand, the law disapproves of the transfer of immovable property, which tends to undermine the tribal and familial regime fixed at the time of the Conquest. The principle that the land shall not be sold irrevocably (Lev. 25:23) was reinforced in the Jubilee and redemption laws which complement each other. The law of the Jubilee sees to it that sold land returns to its owners in the Jubilee year (which appears to coincide with every seventh sabbatical year). This turns every sale of land into a kind of lease for a number of years. It follows that the price of land is determined in accordance with the number of years for which it was sold (Lev. 25:27). The result of this law is that with every Jubilee the social situation returns to its former state. Many scholars consider this legislation to be merely utopian. However, this criticism ignores three facts: i) In the view of Scripture the individual's right to ownership of the land results from his belonging to a familial-tribal regime which conquered the land, and one cannot therefore evaluate the concept of such ownership according to the criterion of an individualistic-capitalistic point of view. ii) The Pentateuch established exceptions to this rule in favor of religious endowments (Lev. 27:16–21), and in favor of the buyer of a dwelling-house within a walled city, as long as it does not belong to Levites (Lev. 25:29–34). The sale of such a house is permanent if it is not redeemed within one year since its sale. Such casuistic distinctions make no sense in utopian legislation. They are quite logical, however, in a legislation to be carried out in practice, which is concerned with the welfare of the religious endowments, and reckons with the disintegration of the familial-tribal regime in the cities which have absorbed people of different origins, have become the center of an economic life not based on agriculture, and developed beginnings of individualistic and capitalistic concepts. iii) It ignores the law of the Jubilee in the story of Zelophehad's daughters (Num. 36:4), whose actual background is beyond question. It is true that even after all these considerations the law of the Jubilee remains difficult for a modern jurist. A secular law objecting to the individual's free ownership of land would have limited the validity of the law of transfer to a certain number of years since the year of sale, but would hardly have introduced such a peculiar rule as that of all lands returning to their owners at one and the same time irrespective of their date of sale. This principle can only be understood in the light of the religious character of the Jubilee law, which is expressed in the commandment of sanctifying the Jubilee year (Lev. 25:10).[41] This precept is well suited to connect the law of the Jubilee to the law of leaving the field fallow during the sabbatical year (*ibid.* 1–7; 20–24), i.e. the law which commands the peasant to rest from his work during the entire seventh year. This too is clearly a religious law, dating apparently from the time of the conquest of Canaan, since it can hardly be assumed that such a restriction was renewed amongst a farming community that had been working its fields for many generations.

The Jubilee law is not the only one that limits the sale of land. Before the Jubilee the seller is free to redeem his land from the buyer at any time, if he can afford it (Lev. 25:26, 27). The relative of the seller has the same right (*ibid.*:25); it results that an impoverished man offers his land first to a relative (cf. Jer. 32:9).

4. *Social Laws.* Concern for the fate of the impoverished Israelite, as shown by the laws of the Jubilee and the redemption, has also put its stamp on the credit laws. Like the man who sells his field, so also the man who borrows is considered a poor man who needs the money for his livelihood and not a person who looks for money to develop his enterprises. Only against this background can it be understood that the law never defines the rights of the creditor positively, but clearly restricts the rights of the man who lends money to his Israelite brother — the obvious purpose of these restrictions was to turn the contract of loan into an act of philanthropy. The Pentateuch does not therefore content itself with restricting the creditor's right of seizing the property of the man who does not repay his debt (Ex. 22:26; Deut. 24:10–13[42]) — this has its parallels in Hammurabi's Code and in modern laws — but it even prohibits taking interest (Ex. 22:24; Lev. 25:35–37; Deut. 23:20).[43] In addition it decrees the remission of all debts in the sabbatical year (Deut. 15:1–11),[44] along with strict injunctions for the rich not to withhold his hand from his poor brother with the approach of the sabbatical year, meaning by it that he should be prepared to make a loan which is practically a gift. However, the very formulation of these laws raises the doubt as to their actual implementation, or whether they were regarded as moral precepts. The law does not stipulate that a contract about charging interest is legally void, it merely tries persuasion: "If you lend money to My people, to the poor who is in your power, do not act toward him as a creditor: exact no interest from him." (Ex. 22:24). This warning follows upon the prohibition: "You shall not afflict any widow, or fatherless child" (Ex. 22:21), which

is accompanied by the threat of heavenly punishment. Also the words "... do not act toward him as a creditor" is an allusion that an ordinary creditor receives interest. Thus we also found that to David came: "Everyone that was in debt" (I Sam. 22:2). In the final analysis it transpires that the credit laws express a general social request: "Open your hand to the poor and needy kinsman in your land" (Deut. 15:11). It does not grant the poor a legal right, but merely approaches the rich with a religio-ethical appeal. These laws did not diminish the creditor's right of enslaving the man who did not repay his debt (Prov. 22:7); furthermore, he was entitled in such a case to make the debtor's son his slave (II Kings 4:1).[45] The following prohibitions belong to that same category: "You shall not subvert the rights of your needy in their disputes" (Ex. 23:6). The practical implication of this prohibition becomes clear further on in this passage: "Do not take bribes" (Ex. 23:8). Such warning concerning miscarriage of justice as the result of accepting a bribe occur repeatedly in Deuteronomy (Deut. 16:19; 27:25), implying that the Bible was speaking of a widespread evil. However, we have not found the law decreeing that the court punish the bribe taker, it merely alludes to heavenly punishment, contained in the somewhat surprising statement that God "shows no favor and takes no bribe" (Deut. 10:17). The legal aspect is more evident in laws that deal with the poor as a class and assure them of some sustenance, such as the laws of gleanings, the overlooked sheaf and the poor man's tithe[46] (Lev. 19:10; 23:22; Deut. 21). But even the extent to which these laws were carried out depended on the goodwill of the rich landowner (cf. Ruth 2). The same applies to the request to let the poor have the crop of the sabbatical year (Ex. 23:11), but which is whittled down to near annulment in Lev. 25:6. To these laws Deuteronomy adds the allocation of the second tithe to the poor of the land every third year (Deut. 14:28, 29). The antiquity of this law is doubtful, however.

Along with the poor, biblical law frequently mentions the sojourner, the resident alien and the hired laborer, and in Deuteronomy also the Levite. Each one of these groups requires separate treatment.

The antiquity of the Levites' social and legal distinctiveness is demonstrated not only by their being set apart from the rest of the settlers in the land (Num. 26:62) but also by the various pentateuchal traditions concerning their consecration to the service of God during the wandering in the wilderness (Ex. 32:29; Num. 3:40–51; Deut. 10:8; 33:8–10). These traditions are supported also by the story of the graven image of Micah (Jud. 17:7–13) which is based on the assumption that a cultic priestly office can be given only to a Levite. It is therefore quite certain that already at the time of the Conquest the Levites constituted a special social unit, in which the office of divine service passed from father to son. Therefore, it is quite plausible that already in ancient times they benefited from specific laws which ensured their livelihood. But this general conjecture is not sufficient to support the antiquity of all the laws concerning the Levites which have come down to us, and their historical explanation meets with serious difficulties. As against the regulation which denies the Levites a tribal inheritance, there is the regulation which allocates to them towns surrounded by pasture land for their cattle (Num. 35:1–8). Its implementation is described in Josh. 21 which enumerates the cities that every single tribe granted the Levites. This regulation is surprising for several reasons. To begin with, it contradicts the principle that the Levite has no portion and no inheritance in Israel. Furthermore, in Deut. 12:18 we read: "The Levite in your settlements," which implies that the Levites dwelt among the rest of the Israelites and not in special cities; we also saw in the story of Micah's graven image that a Levite lived in Bethlehem (Jud. 17:7) which is not enumerated among the cities of the Levites. Moreover, the schematic way in which the Levites's pasture land is described in the body of the regulations gives an impression of artificiality. In the light of all these difficulties many scholars have come to the conclusion that the law concerning the cities of the Levites must be viewed as a late construction, lacking all basis in reality. This assumption does not, however, agree with the historical analysis of the list of the cities of the Levites, which dates them for the period of the monarchy,[47] nor with the early law of the Jubilee (cf. above) which assigns to the dwellings of the Levites in the walled cities the same status as to the village dwellings which are perpetually redeemable, and strictly forbids the sale of their plots of land. These contradictory verses encourage the assumption that the Levites' lack of an inheritance as early as the period of the Judges led to the amphictyonic decision to allocate them dwellings and pasture land in certain towns, and that this development came to an end at the time of the United Kingdom. The houses and pastures were not sufficient for their needs, and the pentateuchal regulations therefore provided for the Levites plenty of additional sources of income (Lev. 27:22–30; Num. 18:21–24; Deut. 18:1–5). Thus we come back to the question: what caused the comparison of the Levites to the poor in Deuteronomy? It seems that the answer must be looked for in the instability of the political regime, which made the execution of the regulations in favor of the Levites dependent to a considerable extent on the good will of the well-to-do, to whose generosity Deuteronomy appeals. Maybe these appeals mainly refer to those Levites who did not obtain a cultic appointment?[48] It is therefore not necessary to accept the view of those scholars[49] who consider the passages dealing with the Levites in Deuteronomy as an echo of Josiah's reforms which reduced the priests of the high-places to the rank of incomeless Levites, and that it was only then that a special class of priests crystallized, who differed from the Levites as to their tasks and sources of income (Num. 18:25–32). There is no evidence that differences of status among the Levites developed only at the end of the First Temple period, nor must one ignore the figure of the poor Levite described in the account of Micah's graven image.

The sojourner is included among the needy about whom the Pentateuch is concerned. The Pentateuch prohibits oppressing him (Deut. 24:14), commands not to wrong him (Ex. 20:10; 23:9), not to pervert his justice (Deut. 23:17; 27:19) and to help him like the needy of Israel (*ibid.* 14:29; 16:11, 14); it even commands to love him (Lev. 19:34; Deut. 10:18, 19). The Pentateuch frequently repeats the principle of one and the same justice being applied to the sojourner and the citizen (Ex. 12:49, Lev. 24:22, Num. 15:15–16). This principle also applies to the religious duties (Lev. 16:19; 17:12, 13, 15, 20:2; 22:18; Num. 9:14; 19:10). But from here one cannot simply deduct that the sojourner was equal to the citizen in every respect. The repeated warnings prove that the precept of loving the sojourner required inculcation. Moreover, the Pentateuch's sympathy was vouchsafed the sojourner only as long as he resembled the Israelite poor. It was considered a curse if the sojourner rise up, if "he shall be the head, and you the tail" (Deut. 28:44). We need to pay attention to the reservation in the religious assimilation of the sojourner to the Israelite citizen. The law in Numbers 9:14 obliges and entitles the sojourner to participate in the Passover feast without any reservations, while the law in Exodus 12:48–49 does have its reservations, and makes the participation of the sojourner in the Passover sacrifice dependent on his first being circumcised. The law in Leviticus 17:15 obliges the sojourner to observe the precepts of not eating "what has died or has been torn by beasts," yet according to the law in Deuteronomy 14:21 the sojourner is expressly permitted to eat that which dies of itself. The difference in status between the citizen and the resident alien (*tōshāv*) stands out most strongly in the laws ruling serfdom (in Lev. 25:45–49) which permit the enslavement of a resident alien as a life-long slave and command the redemption of the Israelite who was sold to a sojourner.

From all these laws there emerges a class of non-Israelite people who live permanently among the Israelites, but have neither part nor lot in the nation and who require protection and fair treatment. Their precise identification is fraught with difficulties.[50] It is clear that the sojourner is not identical with the stranger. The Pentateuch expressly permits taking interest from him (Deut. 23:21) and collecting a debt from him after the sabbatical year (Deut. 15:3). But we have no clear distinguishing mark between the stranger and the sojourner. The gravity of this question is demonstrated by the rule which prohibits the Ammonite and the Moabite entering the Lord's congregation forever (Deut. 23:4–7).[51] This implies that their descendants are considered strangers; however, from the Book of Ruth, in general, and from the kinship of King David and Ruth the Moabite woman in particular, we see that such a conception was not customary in Israel in all generations. Further on, in that same difficult legal statement we read that it is forbidden to abhor an Edomite or an Egyptian and that their children of the third generation may enter the congregation of the Lord. This comes to show that the law counts them as sojourners, but it distinguished between the first two generations and the third. We do not find anything like this in the laws of the sojourner. It is doubtful whether it can be assumed that the third generation were considered full citizens.

The concept of the hired laborers in the Pentateuch is close to that of the sojourner. The hired laborer is mentioned next to the resident alien as not partaking of the Passover sacrifice (Ex. 12:45). A study of the laws governing the consumption of the Passover sacrifice (Ex. 43:49) clearly shows that he was considered uncircumcised. Similarly, the hired labourer was considered a sojourner (Lev. 22:10, 25:6, 40). Only Deuteronomy mentions: "a needy and destitute laborer, whether a fellow country-man or a stranger" (Deut. 24:14); the situation is quite clear, the sojourner lacking an inheritance worked as a hired laborer for an Israelite who owns an inheritance. At the time of the Settlement the Israelite had his own inheritance, it was only later that a class of Israelite hired servants without an inheritance came into being. The status of the hired servant, who was a free man, was superior to that of the bondman as we see from the injunction: "... do not subject him to the treatment of a slave. He shall remain under you as a hired or bound laborer ..." (Lev. 25:39–40). Even so, his dependent position required warning his employer not to oppress him (Deut. 24:4), and not to hold back the wages of a hired servant until the following day (Lev. 19:13). The hired servant was not a day labourer, the length of his service was measured in years, as can be seen from such expressions as: "Within a year, according to the years of a hired servant" (Isa. 21:16), i.e. in exactly a year's time. The length of his service also shows the proximity of the terms resident alien and hired servant.

5. *Laws of Slavery*. The limited power of implementation of the laws which protected the needy, the citizen and the sojourner are demonstrated by the possibility of their becoming the slaves of their creditors. But there is an important difference here. The sojourner was liable to be perpetually enslaved as was the case with all non-Israelites, and there is even a suggestion that it was permissible to rule them with rigor (Lev. 25:45–46). In principle, an Israelite does not serve his master for more than a definite number of years. The law in the Book of Covenant limits the period of servitude of the Hebrew slave, i.e., Israelite,[52] to six years (Ex. 21:3), similar to the Code of Hammurabi which limits a citizen's period of servitude to three years (§17). However, in contrast to the Code of Hammurabi the Book of the Covenant recognizes the possibility that at the end of his period of servitude the slave may announce that he loves his master and would like to remain so for ever (Ex. 21:5–6; cf. Deut. 15:16, 17). Furthermore, this same law considers female slaves as concubines, who do not leave in the seventh year, unlike the law in Deuteronomy according to which the handmaid is simply a female slave who is also freed in the seventh year (Deut. 15:12). The law in Deuteronomy still adds the injunction not to let the hired servant and the maid-servant go out empty handed (*ibid.* 13–15). These regulations are completed by the law in the Book of the Covenant which commands the master to free before the legal date of release the slave whose eye he has put out, or whose tooth he has knocked out (Ex. 21:26, 67). The law in Leviticus, on the other hand, postpones the release of the Hebrew slave until the year of the Jubilee (Lev. 25:40–41), i.e., the same year in which the restoration of his property assures him a livelihood, and adds the warning not to rule him with rigor (Lev. 39–46). It is impossible to explain the open discrepancy between the law in the Book of the Covenant and the law in Leviticus by the hypothesis that if the Jubilee occurred earlier than the six years he had to serve, it set him free (according to Rashi). This interpretation does not explain the law of redemption of the Hebrew slave who was sold to a stranger and whose redeemer is obliged to pay the price of the slave according to the number of years yet to flow between the redemption and the year of the Jubilee (Lev. 25:50–53). This led scholars to assume that the law of the redemption of slaves in the Jubilee year was amended only after the failure of the law of their release in the seventh year had become obvious, and that this law was simply an attempt at creating some kind of alternative to an ancient law that could not be implemented.[53] This assumption does

not, however, suit the ancient character of the law of the Jubilee. It is therefore preferable to assume that in ancient times the law of the Jubilee was observed only by the northern tribes, and that is why we find it mentioned in the story of the daugthers of Zelophehad which is linked to the history of the tribe of Manasseh, and it may be that the law in the Book of the Covenant was observed at first only in the land of Judah. We have already found support in the Book of Ruth for the assumption that in ancient times the pentateuchal laws of inheritance were also observed only in the north.

The severity of the law concerning the slave was softened by his religious attachment to the Israelite people. We read in the statute regulating the Passover sacrifice: "But any slave a man has bought may eat of it once he has been circumcised" (Ex. 12:44), which means that a Hebrew slave anyway partook of the sacrifice. In the same way the slave was also protected by the ordinance of the Sabbath rest (Ex. 20:10; 23:12; Deut. 5:14). However, no conclusions of the slave's social status can be drawn from a law which extends the same protection to the ox and the ass. A fundamental reservation against the very institution cf slavery may be felt, perhaps, in the prohibition in Deuteronomy: "You shall not turn over to his master a slave who seeks refuge with you from his master. He shall live with you in any place he may choose among the settlements in your midst, wherever he pleases; you must not ill-treat him "(23:16–17). From the apodosis of the law it appears that the prohibition refers to the extradition of the slave who fled to the land of Israel. It seems that this law is directed against international agreements concerning the extradition of slaves who fled to another country. So far only such agreements from the pre-Israelite period have been found.[54] But we may be permitted to deduct that they were observed also in biblical times. It is not to be assumed that this law applied also to a slave who fled from his Israelite master. However, the way of thinking expressed in this law fully explains why the Pentateuch does not contain parallels to the paragraphs in the Code of Hammurabi which imposes a heavy punishment on the person assisting a slave to flee from his master (§§ 15,16) and promises a reward to him who returns the fugitive to his master (§ 17).

6. *Various Civil Laws.* This brings us to the end of the survey of civil legislation with direct bearing on the social structure. But the rest of the laws also help us towards an understanding of the sociological background of ancient Israel — for instance the laws of damages — which shed much light on the life of the farmer and the shepherd. The law imposes payment of compensation upon the man into whose uncovered pit an ox or ass has

fallen (Ex. 21:33–34), upon the man who let his cattle graze in a field which he does not own (Ex. 22:4), or if he lit in his field a fire which burnt his neighbor's corn[55] (Ex. 22:5). To the same rustic environment is directed the law of the owner of the ox who gored the ox of his neighbor (Ex. 21:35). To these laws must be added the laws concerning a person who injured his fellowman, to be discussed further on, along with the penal laws. As with the laws regulating payment of damages, so also with the laws regulating restoration of lost property the agricultural background stands out. The Book of the Covenant only mentions the loss of cattle: "When you encounter your enemy's ox or ass wandering, you must take it back to him" (Ex. 23:4). Deuteronomy enlarges the basis to: "...anything that your fellow loses and you find," but it too begins with the ox, sheep and ass (22:1–3). Contractual laws are extremely limited. The laws ruling acquisition and sale are confined to an exhortation not to cheat over weight and measure (Lev. 19:35, 36; Deut. 25:13–15). We find more details — apart from the laws of credit which were discussed above in the laws regulating safekeeping. These laws differentiate between the safekeeping of money or objects, and that of animals. When ruling: if articles in his safekeeping are stolen from him, he is not held responsible (Ex. 22:6, 7), the text refers to an unpaid keeper, as Rabbi Samuel ben Meir explains: "They are movable goods and were handed over to be kept in his house alongside the rest of his property. Therefore, if they were stolen from his house he is not liable, since he kept them as he kept his own belongings." The laws dealing with the safekeeping of animals distinguish between the person who is paid to keep someone's cattle, and the person who borrows an animal (free of payment) to work with it. There appears to be a reference also to the person who hires someone's beast, that is to say, works someone's beast against payment. He who keeps someone's beast for payment is held responsible for the theft. If, however, the animal died, was torn to pieces or seized by an animal of prey, this is considered force majeure and the keeper is not liable for payment (Ex. 22:9–12). The most heavy responsibility naturally rests upon the man who borrowed an animal, since the agreement works only in favor of the borrower, and he has to make restitution even if the beast died or was torn, in case the owner was not present (Ex. 22:13). The last item in the law is not clear. The traditional explanation seems reasonable, namely that it intends to compare his responsibility to that of the person who is hired to keep someone's animal and who has to pay restitution in case of theft, but does not have to in case the animal died or broke a bone.[56]

F. Criminal Law

The religious character of the pentateuchal law stands out very clearly in the penal laws, as we see from the discussion of the following fundamental questions: who bears the responsibility of a criminal act, and who imposes the punishment.

As to the first question, it must be pointed out right from the beginning that this responsibility does not fall only upon human beings, but also upon any other creatures, a concept which is definitely foreign to the secular jurisprudence of the Ancient East. The incidence of laws inflicting punishment upon animals is referred to already in the covenant with Noah: "But for your own life-blood I will require a reckoning: I will require it of every beast;" (Gen. 9:5). From this religious principle derives the rule in the Book of the Covenant that the ox which has gored a man to death, shall be stoned and its meat not be eaten (Ex. 21:28–32). But since the death penalty falls also upon any animal with whom a man or a woman has lain (Lev. 20:15–16), in the light of the explicit ruling concerning the goring ox it seems that the prohibition of eating the meat of the animal applies also in this case.

In general, the responsibility for a person's crime is borne solely by the perpetrator of the crime, and it is specifically said in Deuteronomy: "Parents shall not be put to death for children, nor children be put to death for parents" (24:16). The principle does not, however, agree with the religious concept that God visits the iniquity of the fathers upon the children unto the third and fourth generation (Ex. 20:5, Num. 14:18; and cf. Lev. 26:39). This shows that in ancient Israel they did not observe the rule of individual responsibility in the case of a transgression which according to the view of that generation brought down God's wrath upon the entire people. We read that God sets His face not only against the father who gives his son to Molech, but also against his whole family (Lev. 20:2–5). There are instances of a criminal being punished by human agency along with his whole family in order to avert God's wrath from his people. There is the classic example of Achan who took from the banned booty (Josh. 7). According to the text, God punished the entire nation because of this transgression and caused a great many of them to die, He even informed the nation that there could be no atonement unless the accursed thing in its midst were annihilated. This annihilation was not confined to Achan; along with him were wiped out his sons and daughters, his oxen, asses, his sheep and his tent, and all his possessions (Josh. 7:24–25). Moreover, as late as the period of the monarchy we find that a man who cursed God or a king was put to death together with his sons (II Kings 9:26). Murder was one of the transgressions which was liable to bring calamity upon the entire people as we see from the story of the famine that ravaged the land in retribution for Saul's spilling the innocent blood of the Gibeonites. The famine did not cease until David atoned for this sin by handing Saul's sons over to the Gibeonites who made them expiate for the blood of their brethren (II Sam. 21:1–10 and cf. II Sam. 3:29).

At the same time we ought to realize that not one of the pentateuchal laws mentions the principle of the family's collective responsibility for the crime of one of its members in front of a law-court. This leads to the assumption that since the beginning the law strove to place the responsibility upon the individual.[57]

More easily understood than the above discussed question of responsibility, is the distinction between divine punishment and that meted out by the court of elders. One of the rare instances of punishment by God in the Pentateuch is the law which refers to people who have commerce with ghosts and familiar spirits: "I will set My face against that person and cut him off from among his people" (Lev. 20:6). Occasionally divine punishment comes in place of punishment meted out by fallible human beings. The relationship between these two kinds of punishment is expressed in the law of him who offers his son to Molech: "Any man ... who gives any of his offspring to Molech, shall be put to death; the people of the land shall pelt him with stones ... And if the people of the land should shut their eyes ... I Myself will set My face against that man and his kin, and will cut off from among their people both him and all who follow him" (Lev. 20:2, 4, 5). To the sphere of divine judgement belong also all the laws which do not say in so many words that it is God who metes out punishment, but which use the impersonal passive, such as: "That soul shall be cut from his people" (Gen. 17:14), "From among his people" (Ex. 31:14), "From Israel" (Ex. 12:15), "From the congregation of Israel" (Ex. 12:19), "From the midst of the assembly" (Num. 19:20), or "And that man shall be cut off from among his people" (Lev. 17:4), "From his people" (Lev. 17:9) or briefly "Shall be cut off" (Lev. 17:14). The argument that all these expressions refer to divine punishment only is supported by a number of considerations, such as the laws concerning the Day of Atonement where the expression he "shall be cut off from his kin" (Lev. 23:29) acts as a synonym for the wording: "I will cause that person to perish from among his people" (Lev. 23:30). About the man who eats three days old sacrificial meat, we read that he bears his iniquity: "And that person shall be cut off from his kin" (Lev. 19:7–8). Yet the same law exists in a parallel formulation which stipulates that if the sacrifice be eaten on the third day "It shall not be acceptable . . . and the person who eats of it shall bear his guilt" (Lev. 7:18). The plain meaning of this law is that the bringer of sacrifice is not accepted by God, who will punish him. The expression "cutting off the soul" and "bearing the guilt" interchange in a similar manner in other laws too (Lev. 7:21; Num. 9:13). In the laws dealing with incest the expression "cutting off" is accompanied by such formulations as: "They shall die childless" (Lev. 20:20), "They shall be childless" (Lev. 20:21). Quite obviously all these regulations fall within the sphere of religion and not the authority of the courts of justice. There emerges no support for the view held by some scholars that the precise phrasing "And that person shall be cut off from his people" alludes to secular punishment, such as casting the criminal out of society by means of banishment, outlawing[58] and the like. Similarly, we have to reject the view that the sentence of "cutting off" mentioned in all or some passages was passed by a court.[59] This view is based on the somewhat unclear law concerning the person who profanes the Sabbath (Ex. 31:14) where the wording "shall be put to death" occurs next to "that person shall be cut off from among his kin." This law must also be explained in accordance with the already mentioned law concerning the person who offers his son to Molech, namely, that the profaner of the Sabbath is sentenced to death by a court, and if the court ignores his transgression then he is doomed to suffer divine punishment.

This explanation that punishment by destruction is actually a divine retribution also fits the nature of the transgression for which it is incurred; in the majority of cases one of the cultic commandments (Gen. 17:14; Ex. 12:15, 19; 30:33; Lev. 17:4, 9; 22:3; Num. 9:13; 19:13, 20). To these we are to add the laws punishing incest (Lev. 18:29; 20:17–18); their religious evaluation is explained by the warning that is attached to them: "So let not the land spew you out for defiling it" (Lev. 18:28). Here belong also the laws that read: "He shall bear his guilt" which is synonymous with the expression "cutting off", and which in the majority of cases refers to cultic transgressions also (Ex. 28:43; Lev. 22:9; Num. 5:31; 18:22). To these laws must be added the one concerning the person who blasphemes God (Lev. 24:15) — with the proviso that in case the transgressor uttered the name of God he is to be handed over to a court and sentenced to death — (Lev. 24:16), — as well as the law of the witness who did not testify even though he heard the voice of adjuration (Lev. 5:1) i.e. God will punish him if he does not do his duty (cf. Num. 5:21). The tremendous power of the oath is made clear in the law of the adulteress (Num. 5), that is, the woman whom her husband suspects of adultery without having sufficient evidence. In such a case the husband is entitled to take her to the priest who will put the woman before the Lord (i.e., before the altar or some other holy vessels which symbolize the presence of God), and will cause her to answer "Amen" to an adjuration and make her drink water of bitterness, while at the same time bringing a meal-offering of jealousy — "if she has defiled herself by breaking faith with her husband, the spell-inducing water shall enter into her to bring on bitterness, so that her belly shall distend and her thigh shall sag; and the woman shall be a curse among her people" (Num. 5:27). The law concludes with the words: "And that woman shall suffer for her guilt" (Num. 5:31). This makes the synonymy of the terms "to bear one's iniquity" and destruction very clear in the Pentateuch.

The transgressions which deserve divine punishment are atoned for by sin-offering and guilt-offering (Lev. 4, 5). In general these offerings only bring remission of a sin committed by error (Lev. 4:3, 4,18). However, several transgressions depart from the rule and the priest can absolve of them under certain circumstances, even if they were perpetrated deliberately. What these transgressions have in common is that they harm another person, and to a modern mind they appertain to the sphere of secular law; as for instance the transgression of the person who did not bear witness in spite of having heard the voice of adjuration (Lev. 5:1). Such a witness can atone for his sin if he confesses to a priest and offers a sacrifice. One may assume that first of all the priest forced the man to testify. Similarly, atonement through the priest is accepted even in the case of a few deliberate transgressions — if they are not punishable by excision — as for example the law concerning the seduced bondmaid. If a man has slept with a bondmaid who was meant for someone else before her liberation: "With the ram of guilt offering the priest shall make expiation for him before the Lord for the sin he has committed; and the sin he has committed will be forgiven him" (Lev. 19:22). More than that, the priests were authorized to administer justice in a whole group of transgressions belonging to the domain of civil law. Among these belong not only the law concerning the person who misused sacred property and the perjure (Lev. 5:21, 24), but even the law concerning the man who embezzled a desposit or appropriated a lost article (Lev. 5:21, 22), as well as the law dealing with the man who robs the poor or oppresses them, that is the person who disobeyed the social prohibition of abusing the weak (Lev. 6:21–22). The proximity of these laws to the secular sphere of jurisdiction is expressed by the fact that here the transgressor is not absolved by merely bringing a sacrifice and confessing, he also has to compensate the injured party and add a fifth of the amount of the damage (Lev. 6:6). Thus, apart from purely religious transgressions, religious law applies also in a few offences which are at the same time the concern of secular law, such as perjury, or even transgressions of a completely secular nature like embezzlement.

As against this, the secular law of the elders deals also with some religious offences. Among these belong — apart from those dealing with the man who offers his son to Molech, the man who desecrates the Sabbath and he that blasphemes the name of the Lord — the prophet who prophesies in the name of strange gods and the false prophet (Deut. 18:20–22). According to the Bible to this category seems to belong also the law: "You shall not let live a sorceress" (Ex. 22:17). This law is not peculiar to Israelite legislation, it also appears in Mesopotamian legislation (the Code of Hammurabi § 2; Assyrian legislation, tablet A § 47). It is aimed at protecting people from the ill luck which black magic (called *Kišpu*) can bring upon them. This aspect is not, however, clear in the Bible, since Deuteronomy mentions the sorcerer along with those who practice other kinds of magic that do not harm another person, such as the man who consults a necromancer and soothsayer, or communicates with the dead (Deut. 18:10–11). Those who indulge in such practices are explicitly called an abomination unto the Lord, that is to say, transgressors of religious laws. The laws concerning prohibited sexual practices punishable with death belong clearly also to the religious domain. Among these belong the laws concerning the adulterer and the adulteress (Lev. 20:10), the man who cohabits with his father's wife (*ibid.* 20:11), the father who cohabits with his daughter-in-law (*ibid.* 20:12), the male homosexual and the man who commits bestiality (*ibid.* 20:13, 16). We have mentioned already that all these practices are considered abominations defiling the land, which will vomit out its inhabitants (Lev. 18:25–28).

This is also where belongs the law concerning "He who strikes his father, or his mother, shall be put to death" (Ex. 21:15), a stern formulation which has its parallel in: "And he who insults his father or his mother shall be put to death" (Ex. 21:17; Lev. 20:9), and which is the first interdictory decree to derive from the moral principle: "Honor your father and mother" (Ex. 20:12; Deut. 5:16). It is negatively formulated in the imprecation: "Cursed be he who insults his father or his mother" (Deut. 27:16).

The religious aspect is also evident in the law concerning murder. Even though murder is primarily an injury caused to the murdered man's family, the religious concept of a murder defiling the land comes into it: ". . . and the land can have no expiation for blood that is shed on it, except by the blood of him who shed it" (Num. 35:33). Two conclusions were drawn from this concept: a) the prohibition of taking blood money instead of the life of a murderer (Num. 35:31–34), in contrast to the Assyrian law which presents the avenger of the blood with the choice of having the murderer killed or accepting ransom (tablet B § 2); b) the law of the "beheaded heifer" which restricts the idea that the land can be ransomed only by the blood of the murderer if he has been identified. If he is not known it is permitted, even obligatory, to ransom the land by means of a special expiatory ceremony. Deuteronomy commands such a ceremony to be held in case a corpse is found in a field far from a town. The people must measure which city is nearest, and the elders and the priests of it are charged with performing the ceremony (Deut. 21:1–9). It is not the intention of the law to let off from the ceremony of "beheading the heifer" the inhabitants of the town inside which, or in front of whose gates a corpse was found, but to emphasize that this ceremony is necessary in any case, even if it is impossible to know, without measuring, which town is obliged to perform it.

All this shows that the wish of the public to avenge the blood of the murdered does not coincide with the interest of society to preserve law and order, but derives from religious concepts. In spite of the people's concern for exacting the blood of the murderer in expiation for the spilt blood, pentateuchal law does not deviate here from the principle that punishment is the concern of the kinsman, not of society. Biblical law deviates from this principle only in cases which involve other than private damage, such as the case of Achan, or the prophet who prophesies in the name of strange gods, and the like. The Pentateuch reveals the institution of blood redemption in its most primitive form, namely by the obligation of the blood avenger to kill the murderer without the agreement of the transgressor's family and without any kind of trial, unlike Assyrian law (tablet B § 2) which entitles the blood avenger to demand the murderer's extradition from his family. This implies that in the event of a refusal there is the possibility of a legal claim, and the murderer is killed only with his family's consent or by the decree of a court of justice. Pentateuchal laws mitigate the rigor of this principle by distinguishing between the deliberate murderer, who is the only one who deserves the death penalty, while the inadvertent murderer is exempt of the death penalty (Ex. 21: 12–14; Num. 35:16–25; Deut. 19:1–5),[60] and they leave it to the court to decide whether it was wilful or accidental murder. At the same time the pentateuchal laws have retained a trace of the early state where the permission given the blood avenger to kill the inadverted murderer was only rescinded after the latter reached the city of refuge and only while he was actually inside it; if he left the city, the blood avenger was entitled to kill him. There is no unanimity on the question when the law of the inadvertent murderer was mitigated in Israel. Many scholars postpone the law of the cities of the refuge to the period of the United Kingdom,[61] others claim on the basis of considerations due to historical topographical research — that the list of the cities of refuge (Josh. 21:13, 21, 27, 32, 36) must be attributed to this very period. But by way of hypothesis we may go further and attribute this institution to the first beginnings of the development of Hebrew law, though its functioning was improved during the United Kingdom.[62] This hypothesis is supported not only by the primitive and casuistic formulation of the concept of inadvertency, but also by comparing the laws in the Book of the Covenant with those in Deuteronomy. The Book of the Covenant contents itself with the vague formulation: "I will assign you a place to which he can flee" (Ex. 21:13), the reference appearing to point to only one city.[63] Deuteronomy voices the apprehension: "Otherwise, when the distance is great, the blood-avenger, pursuing the manslayer in hot anger, may overtake him and kill him; yet he did not incur the death penalty, since he had never been the other's enemy. That is why I command you: set aside three cities" (Deut. 19:6–7). This opens the door to the assumption that the purpose of this injuction is the reinforcement of the innovation: "Set aside three cities" and not just one as before. The legislation dealing with murder is repeated three times in the Bible (Num. 35:9–34; Deut. 19:1–10; Josh. 20: 1–6). By combining these prescriptions we succeed in reconstructing the legal institution as a whole. The person who killed a man and claimed inadvertency had to flee to a city of refuge, but as long as he had not reached it the blood avenger was entitled to pursue and kill him (Deut. 19: 6). On arriving at the city of refuge the murderer had to request its protection from the elders at the gate, and it is clear that the decision of the elders rested solely upon the word of the man seeking refuge (Josh. 20:4). However, the avenger of the blood could come and claim that the murderer had lied and that his crime had been intentional. In that case the murderer was handed over to the elders of his own city and judged. If he was considered guilty they had to "hand him over to the blood-avenger to be put to death" (Deut. 19:12). But if he was considered innocent: "The assembly shall protect the manslayer from the blood-avenger, and the assembly shall restore him to the city of refuge where he fled, and there he shall remain until the death of the high priest . . ." (Num. 35:25). However, the law explicity adds a strict warning: "But if the manslayer ever goes outside the limits of the city of refuge where he fled, and the blood-avenger comes upon him outside the limits of his city of refuge, and the blood-avenger kills the manslayer, there is no bloodguilt on his account" (*ibid.* 35:26–27). This implies that the law restricted the right of the blood avenger in the case of inadvertent murder, but did not abolish it altogether.[64]

The act of murder, which appears to be the cause of a distinction being made between premeditated and unintentional sin, first introduces in Israel speculation upon a different general problem — the causal connection between the transgressor's action and its consequences. The reason of it is obvious: it is not a rare occurrence that the victim dies sometime after the attack, whereby the question arises whether the assaulter is responsible for his death. The law in the Book of the Covenant answers this fundamental question as follows: "When men quarrel and one strikes the other with stone or fist, and he does not die but has to take to his bed — if he then gets up and walks outdoors upon his staff, the assailant shall go unpunished, except that he must pay for his idleness and his cure" (Ex. 21:18–19). This implies that if the victim dies before recovering sufficiently to walk about with the help of a stick, the assaulter is considered a murderer. But if he dies later, it suffices to pay compensation for loss of income and reimbursement of medical expenses. On the other hand biblical law did not formulate at all under what circumstances it is permissible to kill, and it contains no ruling such as the talmudic principle: "If someone comes to kill you anticipate in killing him." But there is a reference to this problem in the law concerning the thief who is discovered breaking in, that is to say breaking through the wall of house. If the thief broke in during the night "There is no bloodguilt in his case" (Ex. 22:1), i.e. it is permissible to kill him but "If the sun has risen on him, there is bloodguilt in that case" (Ex. 22:2).[65]

As against the detailed laws dealing with the murder of a freeman, the law concerning the murder of a slave is brief and obscure. In contrast to the rest of the laws of the Ancient East the Pentateuch does not formulate the law concerning the murder of someone's slave (but cf. below the law of the goring ox). Instead it clarifies the law ruling the case of the master who kills his slave as follows: "When a man strikes his slave, male or female, with a rod, and he dies there and then, he must be avenged. But if he survives a day or two, he is not to be avenged, since he is the other's property" (Ex. 21:20–21). This law clearly compromises between the consideration that even a slave is a human being and his murder requires punishment, and the opposite, namely that he is merely his master's chattel. However, the vague formulation of the law arouses the question whether it also applies to the perpetual slave, or whether such a slave was considered his master's property in all respects. Neither is the formulation "He shall surely be punished" sufficiently clear. It should be noted that the Samaritan text reads here: "He shall surely die." If we accept the interpretation which lies at the basis of this textual change, we must admit that the law refers solely to the Hebrew slave, since the Canaanite slave had no avenger.

Two specific laws are added to the general legislation dealing with murder, these are the law concerning the ox whose owner has been warned, and the law concerning the pregnant woman who dies of a miscarriage following a blow received. The distinctiveness of these two laws is inherent to the tradition of the Ancient East. The Code of Eshnunna (§ 54), and also of the Code of Hammurabi (§ 251), devote special paragraphs to the punishment of the owner of a goring ox which has killed a man after the local elders had warned him; in such a case both laws impose a heavy fine on the owner of the ox. In the Book of the Covenant this law is extremely strict and condemns the owner of the ox to death, but immediately mitigates: "If ransom is laid upon him, he must pay whatever is laid upon him to redeem his life" (Ex. 21:30). To this law the Book of the Covenant adds a law similar to the Code of Hammurabi — concerning the owner of a goring ox which has killed someone else's slave — and obliges the owner to pay thirty shekels (Ex. 21:32). This is the only law in the Pentateuch which deals with bodily harm caused to another man's slave.[66]

The legislation concerning blows administered to a pregnant woman also has its roots in the laws of the Ancient East. The Code of Hammurabi judges the man who beats a pregnant woman and sentences him to pay a fine if she aborted (§ 209), but exacts his own daughter's death if the woman dies (and cf. also in the Assyrian laws, tablet A, §§ 21, 50–52 and in Hittite law § 17). In the Book of the Covenant the law concerning the pregnant woman appears to have got mixed up with the law about the man who maims another man's limb during a dispute. In spite of the confusion one can differentiate between the two laws. The law concerning the pregnant woman who loses her child following a blow received, reads: "The one responsible shall be fined according as the woman's husband may exact from him" (Ex. 21:22). But it the woman dies as a result of a miscarriage the principle of a life for a life applies, i.e. the man who struck the blow dies. In the Book of the Covenant the law concerning the man who maims another man's limb is casuistically formulated: "Eye for eye, tooth for tooth, hand for hand, foot for foot, burn for burn, wound for wound" (Ex. 21:24–25). In Leviticus the fundamental and general formulation is repeated: "If anyone maims his fellow, as he has done so shall it be done to him: fracture for fracture, eye for eye, tooth for tooth. The injury he inflicted on another shall be inflicted on him" (Lev. 24:19–20). The wording of the rule leaves no doubt that it literally means an eye for an eye and not payment of compensation. This is also confirmed by the Code of Hammurabi, in which the formulation of the principle of an eye for an eye is casuistic too (§§ 196, 197, 200), but which restricts its incidence to the case where the injured is an *awīlum*, i.e. a member of the upper class. It adds that injuring the limb of a man belonging to another class merely entails payment of a fine, a distinction which leaves no doubt whatsoever that in the first case the reference is literally to an eye for an eye.[67] At the same time it is clear that the Pentateuch does not prohibit the payment of a compensation. Hence, the pentateuchal law does not differ from the ancient Roman law of the Twelve Tables which establishes *si non pacit, talio esto*, i.e., bodily punishment was carried out only if the parties could not reach a compromise concerning the ransom.

Included among the laws dealing with the maiming of limbs is the law of the woman who injures a man's genitals (Deut. 25:11, 12). The special character of this law is better understood when we compare it with its parallel in the Assyrian law: "If in a quarrel a woman injure a man's testicle, one of her fingers is to be cut off. If also the second testicle is damaged and inflamed even if a physician bandaged it, or she damaged the second testicle in a quarrel, her two [. . . . .]" (Tablet A, § 8).[68] The Assyrian law thus takes care to make the woman's punishment fit the extent of the physical damage, contenting itself with cutting off a finger in the case of injury to one testicle. As against this, the biblical law is stricter, decreeing the loss of the whole hand, even if the man has suffered no damage whatsoever, and enforces this severity by forbidding to show mercy to the woman even if her act was prompted by a wish to save her husband. All these show that the biblical law saw in the woman's action first and foremost a sexual transgression, an abominable deed deserving severe punishment, regardless of its consequences.

This brings us to the laws of sexual transgressions which take up considerable room in the pentateuchal legislation. We have already mentioned the prohibitions of intercourse within the family, among men, as well as with an animal. These laws are complemented by the law dealing with adultery which sentences to death the adulterer and the adulteress (Lev.

20:10; Deut. 22:22). The claimant is, of course, the woman's husband and there is a slight allusion that at times he might be satisfied with a large compensation (Prov. 6:35). The law concerning the man who commits adultery with a married woman resembles that of the man who commits adultery with a betrothed virgin (Deut. 22:23–27). Also this law imposed principially the death penalty on man and woman alike, but it spared the life of the woman if the man abused of her in a field where there was nobody to save her.[69] On the other hand, the laws concerning intercourse with an unbetrothed virgin are somewhat obscure. We have already mentioned that a man who seduced an unbetrothed virgin was obliged to marry her. This implies that there is no question of punishment here, since it is possible to repair the misdemeanor. This law is, however, restricted by two qualifications: 1) "When the daughter of a priest degrades herself through harlotry, it is her father whom she degrades; she shall be put to the fire" (Lev. 21:9). This severity is understandable in the light of the law's special concern for the absolute purity of the priestly families, which is also expressed in prohibiting the priest to marry a divorced or profaned woman, or a harlot. This shows that the talmudic explanation which restricts the applicability of this law to the betrothed or even married daughter of a priest (B.T. Sanh. 49b–51b),[72] is not in accordance with the plain meaning of the text; 2) More problematic is the law concerning the woman whose husband charges "I found that she was not a virgin" (Deut. 22:14). The woman will be stoned, if her parents cannot produce evidence of her virginity (Deut. 22:21). The Rabbis explained that this also refers only to a woman who had lain with a man while she was betrothed (B.T.Keth. 44, 45). But neither here is the traditional explanation supported by the pentateuchal text. It seems that the law considered the virgin's act deserving of punishment, but waived it in the hope that the girl would marry the man who seduced her, and in that way the misdemeanor would be put to rights. If, however, the girl kept quiet and agreed to marry another man, who believed her to be a virgin, she had to suffer the full severity of the law. The fact that a woman was sentenced to death in such a case explains also the punishment inflicted upon the husband who has brought a false charge against his wife. Such a man is to be chastised by the city elders (Deut. 22:18) and has to pay a hundred shekels to his wife's father (cf. Deut. 22:19), i.e., twice the sum of the bride price.

Among the laws which safeguard human life belongs also that concerning kidnapping. The law in Deuteronomy decreed that the Israelite kidnapper shall be put to death since he kidnapped a man "enslaving him [i.e. sells him for gain] or selling him" (Deut. 24:7). The law in the Book of the Covenant, which apparently also refers to an Israelite, imposes the death penalty on the kidnapper, irrespective of whether the victim has been sold or is still in his possession (Ex. 21:16; and cf. Ex. 22:3)[71]. The severity of the punishment is understandable. A person was kidnapped for the purpose of being sold to another people, since it was practically impossible for the kidnapper to keep his victim in his own house for any length of time, or to sell that person to a fellow Israelite (cf. the story of Joseph, and the Hittite laws which explicitly mention the sale of a kidnapped person to another country, §§ 19, 20).

There are only a few penal laws safeguarding property. Most of these concern theft of property. The general law dealing with theft is implied in the law of the keeper which reads: "When a man gives money or goods to another for safekeeping, and they are stolen from the man's house — if the thief is caught, he shall pay double" (Ex. 22:6). This means that an ordinary thief is charged to pay twice the value of the stolen object. The law also applies to a cattle thief, if the stolen animal was found with him (Ex. 22:3), and another decrees: "When a man steals an ox or a sheep, and slaughters it or sells it, he shall pay five oxen for an ox, and four sheep for a sheep" (Ex. 21:37). That same punishment of double fine is also imposed on the person who damages or misappropriates an object that was given into his safekeeping (Ex. 22:8)., and cf. below.

G. Legal Procedure

1. *Laws of evidence.* In the norms of legal procedure first place is accorded to the principles ruling evidence given by witnesses. No distinction is made between the witnesses who saw or heard the occurrence by chance and the witness who was specially invited to give evidence in an important matter, as we saw in the Book of Ruth, where Boaz invited ten city elders to be present when he asked the redeemer, who was a closer relative than himself, whether he intended to claim the field (Ruth 4:2). We cannot, however, deduce from Boaz's action that in a civil case more than one witness was needed, though in a criminal case at least two witnesses[72] were required to convict the accused (Deut. 19:15). This principle is emphasized particularly in capital offences (Deut. 17:6). If a man is executed — "Let the hands of the witnesses be the first against him to put him to death" (Deut. 17:7). This means that the person instrumental in the verdict is ordered to carry it out and will tend to consider seriously the evidence he is giving. The legal responsibility the witness bears for the evidence he gives is

determined according to the principle of "measure for measure," namely, to a false witness shall be done as he had schemed to do unto his fellow man (Deut. 19:19). The same rule appears to apply to civil as well as to criminal law, as explained in the Code of Hammurabi (§ § 3, 4). A reference to this principle is also found in a 13th cent. B.C.E. Egyptian protocol. In this case, in which the parties quarrelled over the ownership of slaves, one of the witnesses said: "We shall speak the truth. If we do not speak the truth, let our slaves be taken from us,"[73] which leads one to assume that the law dealing with false evidence was current in the whole Ancient East.

Only rarely is there a reference to exhibits brought as evidence before the court. A shepherd who claims that an animal was torn to pieces has to bring it as evidence (Ex. 22:12), i.e. he shall bring it to its owner, or in the case of a trial — to the court. This is particularly the case with the garment of the woman wantonly accused by her husband: her parents have to spread it out in front of the city elders (Deut. 22:17).

2. *The Ordeal.* If there is no possibility of getting at the truth by means of witnesses or exhibits, the law occasionally transfers to God the responsibility of making the decision. This is the case when an oath is administered, since the person taking it invites divine punishment if he has falsely sworn. As an example of an ordeal in the Bible, we have the law of the adulteress mentioned above, where the legal procedure consists of an oath and a trial. But we must also mention here the laws in Ex. 22:6-10. If an unpaid keeper claims that an object which was deposited with him was stolen from him, then: "The owner of the house shall depose before God that he has not laid hand on his neighbor's property" (Ex. 22:7). According to the Mesopotamian[74] parallels it is clear that here the original meaning of the word "God" is not the judge, but an object which symbolizes the presence of God in the place. The verse keeping silent, however, on the procedure of the trial before God, the scholars were led to put forward numerous hypotheses.[75] The most likely assumption is that the master of the house was put under oath. There are two reasons for this assumption: a) In the case of a paid keeper who claims that an object deposited with him was lost under circumstances for which he was not responsible then "an oath before the Lord shall decide between the two of them that the one has not laid hands on the property of the other" (Ex. 22:10). It seems reasonable to explain the two similar laws by one another, that is to say, that in both instances the keeper was taken before God and put under an oath; b) We found in the laws of Eshnunna that the keeper whose house collapsed and thus lost the depositor's goods, is ordered to approach the gate of the

god Tishpak's temple and to swear that the deposited object was lost along with his own belongings and that he did not lay hand on it (§ 36). The law: "In all charges of misappropriation — pertaining to an ox, an ass, a sheep, a garment, or any other loss, whereof one party alleges, "This is it" — the case of both parties shall come before the Lord: he whom God declares guilty shall pay double to the other" (Ex. 22:8) is obscure. It is clear that here the claimant points to a certain object and argues that the defendant has misappropriated it. The latter is than charged with double payment, according to the law of theft. It is also clear that the losing claimant must pay the defendant double if God proves the accused is innocent. Similarly, it transpires that such a trial is applicable only in a case where no witnesses are available. However, the procedure in the ordeal is obscure, and we do not know by what process God convicts the guilty.[76]

CHAPTER XII

THE SEER-PRIEST*

by H. M. Orlinsky

A. Divination as a Craft in the Ancient East

DURING THE FIRST thousand years of its diversified and exciting career, covering the period of the Patriarchs, of the Eisodus and the Exodus, of the Judges, and of the United Kingdom, ancient Israel shared — more than it did during the several centuries of relative sovereignty that followed — many social, economic, religious, legal, and cultural features with the various peoples with whom it came into contact. It was really not until Israel had experienced a national life of its own for a few hundred years, from about 1100 to after 900 B.C.E., that its own genius came to express itself in these several phases of national activity.

An excellent case in point — indeed, it would be difficult to find a better one — is the common Egypto-Asiatic phenomenon of divination, and how, in Israel alone, it came, not to develop into, but to be opposed and largely replaced by, prophecy.

All peoples in the ancient Near East practiced divination. How else could they stand up before the whim of the gods who controlled their destiny? The forces of nature, on which their very existence depended, and which they but ill understood, had to be brought under some kind of control; at least the attempt had to be made — and when unsuccessful had to be made again and again — to limit and perhaps even bend the otherwise unlimited will of the divine beings. The past had to be studied for the benefit of the present, and the future had to be foreknown and if possible even predetermined. J. A. Wilson's clear statement[1] on Egypt holds true for the Near East generally: "Magic had always been an element of Egyptian life. Amulets are known from the earliest periods, and the Pyramid Texts are full of promotive or protective charms. This later period [ca. 1325–1100 B.C.E.], however, showed an increased reliance upon various magical techniques and powers. Insecurity brought a longing for greater protection through some kind of external potency. Men turned to magic scrolls and images of prophylactic power; they went through elaborate rituals when they recited charms. They tried to counteract the new fatalistic cast of life by summoning the gods for magical support. Man was no longer strong enough in himself."[1]

Divination took on many forms. It was a complex business. The beliefs and practices associated with the profession were so varied and intricate that one who wished to put them to successful use had to devote himself to studying them and working at them; there were, further, trade secrets and vested interests to be protected. And thus there arose throughout the ancient world guilds of diviners, after the pattern of guilds generally, with set rules governing masters and apprentices in divination as surely as if they were stonemasons or smiths. The novitiate in divination, like the worker in textiles or metals, had to spend many years of hard and closely supervised work in learning his trade. He had to memorize incantations of all sorts. He had to learn to interpret the flight of birds, the formation of livers (hepatoscopy) and entrails (extispicy), the lay assumed by sticks of wood, arrows, or stones cast out of a container, the casting of lots, the formation and direction of smoke (incense) emanating from a container (libanomancy) or of oil in a special cup or other vessel of water (lecanomancy), the significance of dreams and of signs in general, the relative position and other aspects of the heavenly bodies (astrology); and the like.[2]

B. The Biblical Terms for Seer-Priest and Prophet

Ancient Israel, too, recognized the diviner in its midst. The Bible has preserved a number of references to the "visionary" (*hoze*) "seer" (*ro'e*), "man of God" (*ish [ha-] Elohim*), and "prophet" (*navi*). All four expressions, as technical terms, were employed for the diviner in the earlier period, before Hosea, Amos, Isaiah, and Micah of the 8th century appeared on the scene; but only the last-mentioned, the term *navi*, came to be used as a technical term for the exponents of classical prophecy. (See Excursus I, below, on the terminology for the biblical "seer-priest.")

Let it be stated at once what significant elements the seer-priest — for which the shorter term "seer" will usually be employed here[3] — and the canonical prophet shared, and in what essentials they differed. Both the seer and the prophet experienced the phenomenon of ecstasy; they differed only in that the former practiced several recognized techniques to induce it that the latter did not. Unlike the prophet, the seer employed music, dance, and group participation to work himself up into a state of ecstasy, even frenzy.[4] Thus Asaph, Heman, and Jeduthun are said to be "visionaries" and also members of the musical guild under King David[5] (cf., for example, I Chron. 25:1 ff., where we are told of "the sons of Asaph, Heman, and Jeduthun, who were to prophesy with lyres, harps, and cymbals;" I Sam. 10:5 ff. mentions "a band of prophets" whom Saul would meet as they were "coming down from the sanctuary led by harp, tambourine, flute, and lyre as they were prophesying"). The prophets of the Lord who gave advice to the kings of Israel and Judah — advice which the prophet Micaiah son of Imlah flatly contradicted — acted very little differently from the prophets of Baal (I Kings 22:9 ff.; 18:26 ff.); Elisha asked for a music-maker (m'naggen) so that "the hand of the Lord" might descend upon him (II Kings 3:15), that is, that he might achieve ecstasy, and thereby God's message. In general, both the seer-priest and the prophet received directives from God in much the same way, through dreams, objects, and sounds.

Again — and this must not be overlooked — members of both categories spoke in the name of the same single God and practiced that same monotheism. That the Hebrew seer worked at what was a common craft in antiquity, whereas the prophet was a uniquely Hebraic product, should not obscure this important fact. Both groups in Israel declared themselves proponents of God's word; both asserted, and were much concerned to make the general population believe, that they received authority from God. When seer-priests differed with one another, or when the classical prophets denounced and scorned the seer-priests, or when the classical prophets differed among themselves (so that some prophets were denounced as "false prophets" to whom God had not really spoken), the basic causes of these differences derived from the group interests which the seer-priest or prophet in question championed; the fact that the expressions and formulas employed in the sundry denunciations were couched in theological-covenant terms (how else could they then have been?) — so that the one who was criticized was accused of one kind or another of idolatry and covenant-breaking — should not blind the historian to the basic social-political-economic factors involved.

Finally, it is quite likely that already in the period of the Judges, as elsewhere in the Near East at the time, scribal activity was associated with the seer-priesthood and the shrines. Some half-dozen seers are specifically credited with having written royal chronicles: Samuel, Nathan, Iddo, Gad, Ahijah, and Shemaiah recorded something of the reigns of David (presumably something also of his predecessor, Saul), Solomon, Rehoboam, his son Abijah, and Jeroboam (I Chron. 29:29; II Chron. 9:29; 12:15; 13:22). However, as the seer-priesthood became increasingly a function of the royal court after the monarchical institution in Israel was firmly established, so did the scribe become independent of the seer-priesthood and a distinct functionary in the royal service; but at the numerous sanctuaries (*bamot*) in the land, the local seer-priest continued scribal activity for his clients round about.

C. The Difference Between the Seer-Priest and the Prophet

It is the points of difference, however, that stand out between the seer and the prophet. In the first place, the seer was usually a member of a guild or group, and he learned the craft from a master; the seer, furthermore, was associated with a sanctuary. Thus Samuel was trained under Eli the priest at Shiloh; the "band of prophets" to which Saul attached himself was associated with a sanctuary (*bama:* I Sam. 10:5); and Elisha was trained by Elijah (I Kings 19:21 — "and he became his *mᵉsharet*." And see below, on the guilds). The prophet, on the other hand, was individualistic;[6] there is no record of a prophet having learned prophecy in association with or under another prophet, or of having acquired his calling by enrolling in a guild of prophets.[7] Indeed, there is reason to believe that membership in guilds of seer-priests, as in guilds generally, was sometimes hereditary; thus Micah (Micaiah) ordained one of his own sons to serve as seer-priest in his "house of God" (Jud. 17:5), and Jehu the "visionary" was the son of Hanani the "seer" (II Chron. 16:7–10; 19:2; I Kings 16:1, 7).[8] This was so, because the craft of the father, providing as it did a ready source of income and prestige, frequently attracted the son, whereas the prophet, making a living from another source, was drawn into his calling directly and (though only seemingly) against his will.

In his craft, moreover, involving individual Israelites and God, the seer was the person to whom the people came for advice, to help them in problems that a mere, untrained mortal, without special access to God, could not solve. For these services the seer was paid. One cannot imagine an Amos or Jeremiah or Deutero-Isaiah being approached thus and making a living in this manner. (See Excursus II, below, on the seer and divination.)

Again, fundamentally the Israelite seer predicted the future and attempted to control it. He performed miracles. The prophet however unreservedly opposed divination and miracle-making in every form.[9] He did not know the future; he did not predict it or try to control it.[10] He knew that Israel's transgression of its covenant with God called for punishment; but also that this punishment, in all or in part, could be prevented or mitigated not by magic or incantation — any more than by formal, insincere sacrifice and prayer — but by a heartfelt return to God.[11] Another and historically more correct and intelligible way of putting it would be: the prophet, claiming to speak directly and exclusively for Israel's God, warned those in power, both within and outside the government proper, that unless they acted politically and socially in accordance with his proposals they would suffer defeat and even destruction.

In this difference between them, the seer was basically a man of action, the prophet a man of words. The former, a craftsman, did things: he offered sacrifices, he interpreted dreams, he predicted events, he performed miracles, and sometimes he was in charge of a shrine and of apprentices. The prophet on the other hand opposed everything that smacked of the seer as a craftsman. To have his way with his fellow Israelites, the prophet had to resort to another method. That method was argument, reasoning, exhortation — in short, words. And what the prophet did with words, and with the older concepts of monotheism, covenant, justice, and the like — the writings of the prophets from first to last bear the most eloquent testimony to their universal and lasting influence in the realm of religion, literature, law, and ethics. But this theme cannot be pursued here.[12]

D. The Seer-Priest in Ancient Israel

It has scarcely been recognized that the diviner and the priest were one and the same in early Israel, as elsewhere in the Near East. Thus already Jastrow[13] recognized Samuel as "a priest and a diviner," and noted in that connection the role of the *bārû*, the Babylonian divining priest. An excellent example of this is provided by the account (widely accepted as old and authentic) preserved in Jud. 17–18. There we are told that a certain Micah (Micaiah) of the hill country of Ephraim owned " a house of God," that is a local sanctuary, along with the appropriate equipment: a sculptured image, a molten image, an ephod, and household gods (*t'rafim*); and he ordained one of his sons to serve as priest (Jud. 17:4–5). Subsequently, an itinerant levite (that is, one who was associated with the craft of divination-priesthood),[14] who had left his home in Bethlehem of Judah to go seeking more attractive employment (verse 8), happened across Micah's shrine. When Micah learned that the traveler was a levite looking for work, he at once offered him the post of priest in his shrine (verse 10);[15] for unlike the son who had been ordained *ad hoc* for the post, the levite was a professional diviner-priest.[16] The offer provided ten pieces of silver, the necessary garments, and food and lodging; and the levite accepted it. Micah then ordained the levite as his diviner-priest (verses 10–13).

Some time later, a group of Danites, in search of a homestead for their clan, also found itself at the house of Micah, and they recognized the levite by the sound of his voice (Jud. 18:3); apparently he had at one time worked also in their territory, being a poor itinerant diviner-priest. When they asked him what he was doing in Micah's house, he told them the circumstances under which Micah had hired him to be his priest (verse 4), whereupon they asked him to divine for them whether their mission would be successful or not. "And the priest said to them: 'Go in peace; the Lord looks on you with favor'" (verses 5–6).[17] For the priest was a diviner and the diviner was a priest.

Let us go back to Samuel for a moment. It is true that Eli, the mentor of Samuel, is referred to only as a "priest", whereas Samuel is specifically designated "seer," "man of God," and "prophet"; but this should not obscure the basic fact that their functions were essentially identical, that Samuel the apprentice was simply following in the footsteps of Eli his master, and that, like him, he is also said to have "judged" (shafat) Israel. Observe also that just as Eli's two sons, Hophni and Phinehas, were "priests" under their father at Shiloh (I Sam. 1:3; 2:11–17), just so was Samuel "girded with a linen ephod" (I Sam. 2:18); and he officiated at sacrifices (I Sam. 9:9 ff.; 16:5). As a matter of fact, however, a closer look at I Sam. 2:13, 35 indicates at once that the term "priest" (kohen), too, was applied to Samuel; for verse 13 describes the duties of the priest's assistant (na'ar ha-kohen), referring back to Samuel the assistant (na'ar) of Eli the priest in verse 11, and a priest is what Samuel would become when he grew up and succeeded Eli. This is precisely what verse 35 explicitly says in the name of God: "I will raise up for Myself a faithful priest," in place of Eli's two sons, to succeed Eli. The main difference between Eli and Samuel was that the latter was a much more powerful seer-priest than the former, and helped to raise the shrine at Shiloh to a level of authority it had not previously enjoyed in Israel. M. A. Cohen has put it well: "Samuel's importance derived not from his role as shofet or military leader or from his role as prophet, but from his actual position as the Shilonite seer-priest."[18]

That it has become necessary for the modern scholar to prove that Samuel, like Eli and others, was a priest as well as a seer is due to the fact that the old institution of seer-priesthood ceased to be correctly comprehended after the priestly group acquired power in post-exilic Judah and supplied the literary framework in which the older materials (J, E, D, and the older parts of P) were brought together in their preserved form. Naturally, the hierocratically minded editors furnished the kind of data that gave their group antiquity, continuity, and authority; also, the "priest" element in the seer-priest of old became extremely blurred; and finally, the relationship between a "levite" and a "priest" was distorted beyond recognition, and the two were turned into members of an allegedly original tribe by the name of Levi. Hence one of the more important and urgent tasks in biblical research today — no less than in the pre-archeology days of the 19th century — is the attempt to reconstruct historically the growth of the P document and the role of the priest in ancient Israel, from the period of the Judges to the rise of the theocratic-hierocratic state of Judah in the 6th century B.C.E.[19]

That the seer and the priest in ancient Israel were really one should occasion no surprise; it would be surprising if they were not. For in the ancient Near East they were one, as the Semitist has long recognized. There, too, the priesthood was an organized guild of craftsmen, and there, too, the temples and shrines played central roles in the economy, politics, and culture of the country. The various categories and strata of the priesthood had their specific functions to perform. But, of course, the Mesopotamian and Egyptian social structures were more complex than was early Israel's polity, and far more is known of their priestly structure and functions than of the biblical.[20]

E. THE SEER-PRIEST AS A MEMBER OF A GUILD. MASTER AND APPRENTICE

It is now widely recognized that the expression *benei ha-nevi'im* (lit, "the sons of the prophets") means "members of the prophet's guild, order."[21] This term, just like "visionary"[22] and "seer", is never applied to any of the literary, canonical prophets, for they did not constitute guilds or orders. And so, whenever a group of prophets is spoken of in the Bible, it is the seer-priests of the pre-classical prophetic period who are meant. Eli the "priest" in all probability,[23] just as Samuel after him, was the master of such a group associated with the shrine at Shiloh. One of Samuel's signs and predictions in connection with the anointing of Saul as king was that "a band of prophets" (*ḥevel nevi'im*) would be descending from the shrine (*bama*) at Gibeah in prophetic ecstasy (*mitnabbe'im*) to the accompaniment of instrumental music (I Sam. 10:5, 10) — an event that gave rise to the popular saying, "Is Saul also among the prophets?" (verses 11–12).[24] It would not be easy to imagine a Saul "prophesying" in the manner of an Amos or Micah or Deutero-Isaiah!

It may well be[25] that Saul recognized Samuel's ghost, brought up by the woman of En-dor through necromancy, by the garment he was wearing (I Sam. 28:14; cf. 15:27; perhaps this is intended by the garment of Ahijah in I Kings 11:29 ff.). Zech. 13:4 is a clear reference to the "hairy mantle" that at least some prophets wore. Elijah was recognized by King Ahaziah by the description given of him as one who wore "a garment of haircloth, with a girdle of leather about his loins" (II Kings 1:8).[26] And it was through this mantle that Elijah transferred his authority to Elisha (II Kings 2:8, 13 ff.).

The seer, at least the wealthier or more important one, had an apprentice attendant about him (na'ar; m'sharet), who sometimes succeeded him. Samuel was the attendant-apprentice of Eli,[27] and I Sam. 2:13 ff. describes some of the duties of the seer-priest's attendant (na'ar ha-kohen). The references to such attendants are more numerous in connection with the careers of Elijah, Elisha, and others.[28] On the other hand, there is no record of a classical prophet, qua prophet, having such an attendant.

F. The Seer-Priest as an Integral Part of Israelite Society

The seer-priest constituted an integral part of ancient Israelite society, usually playing a direct and important role in it; after all, his authority stemmed from the belief that he had direct access to God and some influence with Him. The preserved text of the Book of Samuel is authority that the leadership of parts of Israel was in the hands of Eli, and then of Samuel. The unidentified "messenger (mal'ak) of the Lord" in Jud. 6:11 ff. chose Gideon as the military chieftain (shofet) of Israel, following the Lord's condemnation through "a prophet" (ish navi) of their idolatrous practices (verses 7–11). Another nameless "messenger of God" (Jud. 13) predicted to the barren wife of Manoah the Danite that she would bear a son who would lead Israel in successful battle against its subjugators; Samson was that leader. The levite who became Micah's priest foretold the success of the military venture of the Danites against the inhabitants of Laish (Jud. 18:5). Samuel chose Saul as his successor in leadership (I Sam. 9), and — if I Sam. 16 is to be followed — David after him.[29]

The seer-priest's monopoly in the field of religion gave him, especially if he was the head of a shrine and a guild, considerable political, economic, and social authority. Like everyone else with a vested interest, the seer vigorously opposed any encroachment upon his domain, and was always

on the alert to extend it. Hence, apart from religious considerations, the
seer whose authority was bound up with the Lord (Yahweh) fought
tooth and nail against the devotees of Baal or Asherah or Baal-zebub
or the like; indeed, the seers of the Lord fought no less violently among
themselves when they presented clashing statements of the Lord's in-
tentions, that is, when their interests clashed. Samuel could say — in
the name of God — that the Lord brought about Eli's fall because of the
wickedness of his two sons; but when his own leadership was repudiated
by the people, Samuel — again in the name of God — was quick to
blame not the wickedness of his own two sons but the people themselves, for
they were repudiating God!

It is unfortunate that we no longer possess the data for reconstructing
in detail the structure of ancient Israelite society and the precise roles
played by the various groups in the period of the Judges and the early
monarchy: the landowners, petty farmers, merchants, slaves, seer-priests
and their shrines, craftsmen, money-lenders, and the like. Nevertheless,
enough material is available for a reasonable attempt at comprehending
the process of social forces at work even here.

About the middle of the 11th century B.C.E. the sundry tribes of
Israel, for the first time since their conquest of Canaan, found themselves
in real trouble, for the military might of the Philistines threatened to crush
them one and all. The hitherto politically and militarily independent
tribes,[30] each with its own city-states and governed by a group of "elders"
(*z^eqenim*), now found themselves compelled to set up a chieftain over
them all, to lead them in organized battle against the common enemy,
the Philistines. Unwilling, however, to relinquish more of their autonomy
than was absolutely necessary, they sought the means by which to keep
under reasonable control the authority of the new leader. This means
was ready at hand in the form of the seer-priesthood at Shiloh.

All the tribes acknowledged the authority of the Lord (Yahweh).
The seer-priest of the shrine at Shiloh, centrally located in Israel, was
considered a — if not the — major spokesman of the Lord. And at this
point the interests both of the tribal leaders and of the seer-priesthood
at Shiloh (that is, Samuel) coincided. This has been very well stated by
M. A. Cohen: "The divining-priesthood is the only supra-tribal institution
of the pre-monarchical period that is mentioned by the Bible and therefore
the only one capable of furnishing an ideology of tribal unity . . . The
priesthood [however] possessed no military power; it therefore had to
depend for support upon the leadership of the individual tribes. It had
every reason to expect, and surely received, enthusiastic support. All

the tribes, whatever their provenance, had attached themselves to the traditions of Yahwism. The leadership of each tribe subscribed to the ideology of Yahwism. The loyalty of their subjects also derived from Yahwism. Yahweh, in turn, guaranteed tribal autonomy and hence the positions of each tribe's leaders; at the same time He transcended tribal limits and provided for a spiritual brotherhood of all Israel . . . It would have been too much to expect the old guard leaders to abdicate all their power. They were compelled to invest the monarchy with sufficient strength to carry out its primary mission, that of defeating the [Philistine] enemy. At the same time, however, they . . . would insist on retaining for themselves as much power as circumstances permitted. This they could accomplish only by controlling the monarchy. They had at hand one institution, dependent and loyal, which was ideal for the purpose. This was the Yahwistic priesthood at Shiloh . . . The old guard leadership hoped that by subordinating the monarchy to the priesthood, it might be kept weak, and that if it should seek to increase its strength at their expense, the priests might hear Yahweh's voice dismissing the king from office. This is exactly what happened in the case of Saul . . ."[31]

The seer-priests located at shrines and the roving bands (of the kind associated with Elijah and Elisha) depended for a living mainly on the relatively stable agricultural elements, the landed gentry, and the petty farmer; and when the monarchy came along, they were anti-monarchical in principle, though in practice they would have to compromise with this new institution.

The seer-priest began to lose ground as first the United and then the Divided Kingdom established itself. This was true far more in Judah, where the Davidic dynasty became firmly established, than in Israel to the north, where the different circumstances prevented any dynasty from maintaining itself for more than a generation or two. Thus "Gad the prophet" was David's "visionary" (II Sam. 24:11), just as Nathan served the king as prophet, and as Asaph, Heman, and Jeduthun were his "visionaries."[32]

It appears that the reign, and even the very person, of Solomon dealt the power of the seer-priests a very heavy blow. The Bible makes it clear (I Kings 3:5–15 // II Chron. 1:7 ff.; I Kings 8–9) that this monarch himself constituted priest and diviner[33] (as well as merchant, government head, etc.), as witness his central role in offering sacrifices to God and in receiving dream-messages from Him.[34]

In the Northern Kingdom, however, where the landed gentry were too strong for a dynastic regime to establish itself and yet not strong enough to prevent the rise of monarchs, the seer-priests were content to settle for the clear-cut recognition of Yahwistic exclusivism and the monopoly control of the oracles and sacrifices by Yahwistic spokesmen. Hence Elijah was uncompromising and sought the support of those elements in society that were threatened by the urban-commercial-Baal orientation of the House of Omri. The Naboth incident (I Kings 21) was thus not primarily an ethical-moral issue, but one in which urban-commercial-Baal interests threatened the free peasant class and presumably other groups in the economic and social structure. And what Elijah sought and fought for, his disciple Elisha succeeded in achieving through the Jehu revolution.[35]

G. The Uniqueness of the Prophet in Israel

We are now, finally, in a position to relate some extra-biblical data to the biblical. Methodologically, it is possible to reconstruct the history of ancient Israel only in the light of the history of the peoples and cultures with which they had contact; and so the extra-biblical data that are constantly coming to light are most urgently needed and welcome. But an improperly understood biblical phenomenon must lead to utter confusion, both in the biblical and extra-biblical data, when applied to the larger body of data.

Scholars had long sought the pre-Israelite origins of prophecy (as of monotheism, the covenant, the concept of history, and the like) in some other culture in the ancient Near East, with but indifferent results — until the cuneiform texts (ca. 18th century B.C.E.) from the notable excavations at Mari began to appear. Similarities between the latter and biblical prophecy were at once noted.[36]

One text from Mari[37] tells of the reply that a king (presumably Zimri-lim) received from the priestly representative of the god Adad, in response to the king's request for information and advice. Whereas some scholars found in this text something of the origins and character of biblical prophecy, it is clear, as the biblical parallels collected by A. Lods indicate,[38] that it is only the period and career of the priest-diviner that is involved. The interests of the priesthood and temple of Adad are at stake, and the king is "influenced" to continue the alliance as before.[39] This interpretation is seen even more clearly in the light of a second Mari text describing how the priesthood of the temple of the god Dagan in Terqa attempted to increase its prestige and income through a dream-message to King Zimri-lim.[40]

Hardly more pertinent for the role of the classical prophet, but fully parallel to that of the seer-priest and his period, is the 11th century B.C.E. Egyptian tale of Wen-Amon:[41] "Now while he (Zakar-Baal, King of Byblos) was making offering to his gods, the god seized one of his youths and made him possessed.[42] And he said to him: 'Bring up (*the*) god! Bring the messenger who is carrying him out! Amon is the one who sent him out! He is the one who made him come!'" This episode clearly bears no relationship to an Hosea or a Micah or a Jeremiah!

To sum up. Divination nowhere developed into prophecy, no more than polytheism developed into monotheism, or, to give a more recent analogue, no more than the guild system developed into trade unions. Divination was a common ancient Near Eastern phenomenon; prophecy is a uniquely Israelite phenomenon. The difference between divination and prophecy, clearly perceived, enables us to see how it is divination, and not prophecy, that finds its parallels in the Mari and other social structures and documents in the Fertile Crescent of old.[43]

CHAPTER XIII

THE MANNER OF THE KING

by E. A. Speiser

A. The Terms Shōfēṭ and Mishpāt and their Meaning

T HE QUESTION AT ISSUE in this chapter is the basic concept of
state in ancient Israel and, more particularly, the introduction of
kingship as a replacement for the system previously in force. The answer
to this question involves problems in the fields of linguistics, society, and
cultural and political history. But the effort is justified, even in broad
terms, for the results have an intimate bearing on the whole biblical way of
life.

The biblical phrase that summarizes the question is *mishpāṭ ha-melek* (I
Sam. 8:11).[1] These two words together take in the underlying semantic
issue in its entirety. The first is genetically related to *shōfēṭ*, the technical
term for the chief official under the outgoing system of government; the
second describes the head of state in the new scheme of things. The compound *mishpāṭ ha-melek* thus underlines the transition from *shōfēṭ* to *melek*:
the *shōfēṭ* was to give way to the king. But what did the former function
actually imply? Strange as it may seem, this point is as yet far from settled.

The root *shpṭ* is the basis for some of the most intimate terms in the
vocabulary of biblical society. Yet no vocable of like importance has been
subjected to as monolithic a treatment at the hands of innumerable generations of translators, ancient and modern. Beginning with the Greek render-
ings, the pertinent verb has been given all too frequently the rigid meaning
of "to judge." Accordingly, *shōfēṭ* became specialized as "judge." And since
this technical value does not link up of itself with political leadership,
modern scholarship has sought to establish the necessary bridge by explaining the *shōfᵊṭīm* as "charismatic judges." But this has merely served to
compound an obscurity. The *shōfēṭ* as such was no more and no less
charismatic than the *melek*. A Samson, for instance, until personal tragedy
had humanized him, reflected little divine grace, let alone judicial conduct.
If the position of the *shōfēṭ* was thought to be charismatic, it was not
because of anything that was inherent in the meaning of the term. But
if the *shōfēṭ* was something other than "judge," the translation of *shᵊfaṭīm*

as "acts of judgment" must likewise be reconsidered, however felicitous it might appear to be on the surface.

When it comes to *mishpāṭ*, it was evident from the start that "judgment" could not begin to suit all the occurrences. The familiar English translations, among others, recognize this fact by resorting to "justice, ordinance, rule, due, manner," and the like. Obviously, all these diverse meanings could not readily be traced back to an underlying connotation "to judge." Some other primary meaning of the root would thus seem to be indicated.

Etymological correspondences within a given linguistic family must always be evaluated with all due caution; they should never be permitted to override the evidence of actual usage. Yet such comparisons, if correctly adduced, can at least throw light on basic semantic values. In the case of *shpṭ*, we have now the independent testimony of the Mari texts. The new evidence is significant on several counts. For one, the pertinent Mari occurrences are unambiguous in their bearing. For another, they are not so much Akkadian as "Amorite," and hence that much closer to Canaanite. And for still another, the Mari texts date from the Old Babylonian period; they thus reflect earlier linguistic conditions than are to be encountered in the Bible. On all these counts, therefore, the Mari evidence in regard to *shpṭ* promises to be highly important.

We find, then, in Mari a functionary called *šāpiṭum;* this term is an exact linguistic analogue of Heb. *shōfēṭ*. The authority of the *šāpiṭum* is described as *šāpiṭūtum*, his activity is indicated by the verb *šapāṭum* (Heb. *shāfoṭ*), and the corresponding action noun is *šipṭum* (which would be *shefeṭ* in Heb.; cf. *shefaṭīm*).[2] Now the one thing that is clear at a glance is that *šāpiṭum* is not "judge." For, as one literary text informs us, the god Shamash is *šāpiṭ ilī u awēlūtim* "the *šāpiṭ* of gods and men" as well as *dayyān šakin napištim* "the judge of living creatures."[3] In other words, the *šāpiṭum* and the *dayyānum* perform separate functions; and since *dayyānum* is definitely "judge," *šāpiṭum* must be something else. Elsewhere we learn that the *šāpiṭum* was one who could issue and carry out the *šipṭum*, which in turn was a disciplinary warning or act.[4] Normally such activities lay within the province of governors. But they could be delegated to special officials who then bore the appropriate title of *šāpiṭum*.

The corresponding biblical terms are all of later date, but their basic meaning remains substantially the same. Thus *shefaṭīm* refers unmistakably to "acts of discipline," hence "punishment" or the like.[5] Accordingly, the *shōfēṭ* was originally someone with authority to decide what administrative action was needed and, when necessary, to issue warnings and mete out punishment. He was arbiter or punitive officer, as the case might be, one whose duties were administrative rather than legal, although they naturally involved both judgment and devotion to justice. And if the analogy of Mari society is valid, the *shōfēṭ* was subject to higher authority as much as the *šāpiṭum*. In the biblical instances, however, that authority was divine rather than human. In this respect the *shōfēṭ* was not unlike the Mesopotamian *iššakku* or "governor."

As regards *mishpāṭ* — which has not turned up at Mari — we should now expect it, theoretically, to mean something like "standard, regulation," and hence conduct, custom, manner, or characteristic behavior in general. In point of actual fact, the biblical uses of this term reflect every one of these nuances. The underlying connection may well have been "norm," based on a noun meaning "discipline," or the like, if not on a verb with the sense of "to regulate, administer." It may be noted in passing that the only Akkadian term which approaches the range of *mishpāṭ* is *parṣu*, which reflects the complex Sumerian concept of *m e*, approximately "norm, nature." Indeed, a recently published text from Alalakh speaks of a gift presented *kīma paraṣ* (URU) *Ḫalab* (KI) "according to the custom of the land of Aleppo."[6] In a Hebrew text this would have to be turned into *kᵉ-mishpāṭ ḥalab*.

In summary, the semantic range of *shpṭ* is by no means oriented toward the legal concept "to judge." The strictly judicial aspect is here tangential or incidental at best.

B. THE NATURE OF KINGSHIP IN ANCIENT ISRAEL

Turning now to the matter of kingship, we find in the key passage about it in I Sam. 8 not only the noun form *mishpāṭ*, but also the simple verb *shpṭ*, which occurs twice in the significant combination *melek lᵉ-shofṭenu* (verses 5, 6). The obvious meaning in this phrase is not "a king to judge us," which clearly would be out of place, but "a king to govern us (like all the nations)," precisely what the foregoing discussion would lead us to expect. The next question before us is the exact force of *mishpāṭ ha-melek* in the sequel. Does *mishpāṭ* refer in this phrase to the "rule, discipline" that the prospective king would impose? Or alternatively, is the sense "nature, habit, manner," that is to say, conduct habitual with kings? Since the term itself can have more than one meaning, we have to look to the context for the answer. But the context, too, happens to be ambiguous. Samuel is dealing with the *mishpāṭ ha-melek* in order to warn the people against the king whom they had just requested; whether he is thus referring to the king's "rule," or to his "conduct," the picture remains just as grim. A possible hint of the intended meaning may be contained, however, in the related passage in Deut. 17:14–20.[7] There the subject matter is a list of various things that a king must be careful to avoid; it is a sort of negative *Fürstenspiegel*. Samuel on the other hand chooses to stress the things that the wrong kind of king is sure to do. In either instance the emphasis would thus seem to be conduct. On this basis, therefore, the traditional "manner of the king" may be said to strike the proper note.

In any case, however, there need be no doubt about the biblical concept of kingship in general.[8] In deciding to be ruled by a king "like all the nations," Israel had a choice of two prevailing systems which had long been established in the neighboring lands. One was peculiar to Egypt; it featured a deified ruler, and hence an absolute form of government which made the king's authority supreme both in theory and practice. To Israel such a way of life could have meant only the most abject kind of surrender, spiritually as well as socially. Small wonder, then, that the Bible dwells constantly on the theme of Egyptian bondage in a manner that physical oppression alone would not have been sufficient to justify. Rather it was the horror of an utterly alien social system that made the memory of the Egyptian experience so acute and repelling. Thus "the manner of the king," as it is stigmatized in I Sam. 8:11–18, could just as aptly have been labeled in that context "the Egyptian manner." And it may safely be assumed that this is how the pronouncement was meant and understood.

The other system with which pre-monarchic Israel could not help being acquainted was at home throughout the Fertile Crescent. Its principal, and apparently original, exponent was Mesopotamia. Under that concept of state, the king was distinctly a mortal ruler whose authority was subject to two ever-present checks: one by the assembly of his elders, the other by the gods to whom the king was ultimately responsible for his acts. The law was impersonally conceived and it applied to the ruler and the ruled with equal force in guiding the king and safeguarding his subjects at one and the same time. To be sure, sporadic attempts were made in parts of Mesopotamia to invest the king with divine authority. But these were limited and short-lived in their effect. They failed to involve such strong personalities as Sargon of Akkad and Hammurabi, and they never spread to Assyria. The prevailing culture rejected all such pretensions as incompatible with the very spirit of the native civilization. And many other cultures found the basically democratic system of Mesopotamia attractive enough to copy its features and its numerous by-products.

Israel was on many basic counts a representative member of Fertile

Crescent society. It would be very strange, therefore, if it failed to conform also on the all important issue of the fundamental concept of state. Nevertheless, one school of modern scholarship has been at pains to uphold the view that the idea of divine kingship was central to biblical thought. This interpretation however starts out with the demonstrably faulty premise that the Ancient Near East as a whole shared the same ideology. Actually Egypt alone was thus involved, in sharp contrast with the rest of the region. The resulting ideological curtain proved to be a more formidable barrier than any conceivable physical obstacle.

There is, moreover, ample direct evidence to show conclusively that kingship in Israel was regarded as man-made in origin and limited in scope and authority. It was "the people" who "made Saul king" in Gilgal (I Sam. 11:15). Following Saul's death, "the men of Judah . . . anointed David king over the house of Judah" (II Sam. 2:4). This was later repeated when "the elders of Israel . . . anointed David king over Israel" (II Sam. 5:3), except for one highly significant added touch: they first obtained assurance against autocracy in the form of a solemn "covenant." Later on, "all Israel" was prepared to approve Rehoboam as king following the death of Solomon (I Kings 12:1). But when the people discovered that Rehoboam would oppose badly needed reforms, they promptly summoned Jeroboam before "the congregation" and "made him king over all Israel" (verse 20).[9] In this passage the assembly plays the same decisive role that it enjoyed traditionally in Mesopotamia.

The authenticity of the instances just cited has never been disputed by the leading critical schools. The same cannot be said of Samuel's ominous warning about "the manner of the king," which gave the present chapter its title and starting point. For one reason or another, that passage has been assigned by the critics to a later period. It is wholly immaterial for our purpose whether this evaluation is right or wrong. What matters is that the spirit of the statement is fully in harmony with the other evidence concerning the nature of the Israelite kingship. The actual king-makers were the leaders of the people; and such authority on the part of the people is literally "democracy."

C. The Introduction of Kingship in Israel

While there may thus still be some doubt as to the nature of Israelite kingship, no such uncertainty need exist concerning the reasons for the change from the previous system. The evidence on this point is both explicit and implicit, biblical and extra-biblical, but never really ambiguous.

It remains only to view this evidence in its proper historical and cultural perspective.

The Philistines had arrived in the land from distant parts at the beginning of the 12th century B.C.E. They evidently required several generations to establish themselves securely in the coastal plain. In any case, by the end of the 11th century they were sufficiently entrenched and consolidated to make a bid for the control of neighboring areas farther inland. That expansion however was bound to run up against the counter-drive of the Israelites, who had been undergoing a similar process of settlement and consolidation for a slightly longer period than the Philistines. A head-on collision between these two dynamic forces was thus only a matter of time.

An important factor, however, in the impending struggle was the difference in the backgrounds of the respective opponents. The Israelites had started out as a number of separate tribes intent on taking up settled occupation of the land. They had a common body of religious beliefs and practices, but otherwise their interests and their prospects varied from place to place. Economic and political procedures had to be improvised and adjusted. And although a national consciousness had been solidifying for some time, the machinery to implement it was yet to be devised and developed.

The Philistines on the other hand had started out as a compact and well-organized social group. Otherwise they could not have embarked on a long journey across the sea, with the goal of conquest and settlement on their arrival. Such evidence about the Philistines as we do have points to a homogeneous social and political organization and an urban economy. All this was in sharp contrast with the unregimented ways of the Israelite tribes.

There was also one further factor which for a long time bade fair to outweigh all the others. This was the overriding technological factor at one of the decisive junctures in the advance of mankind. It falls under the heading of the Coming of Iron. The Iron Age had been ushered in only a bare few centuries earlier. It had a truly epochal impact on a very broad front. Industry and economy throughout the Mediterranean world were drastically affected; politics and warfare were revolutionized; large portions of the world's population were on the move. The so-called Sea-Peoples put an end to the Hittite empire, overran Syria, and posed a mortal threat to Egypt. The incursion of Philistines into a land that was henceforward often to be called after them was but one of the innumerable reverberations of the advent of the Iron Age. Understandably, the newcomers were better schooled in the new vital iron technique than the older inhabitants.

Indeed, a regretful tribute to Philistine superiority in this field has found its way into the Bible (I Sam. 13:19–20).[10] They had mastered the new art and were provident enough to treat it as their secret weapon while keeping that knowledge from potential enemies.

The inevitable clash between the Philistines and the Israelites thus loomed for the latter as a battle against seemingly impossible odds. They lacked the weapons and training, the social coherence and organization, to face this challenge to their very existence as a nation. The emergency called for heroic measures, for sacrifices and changes commensurate with the existing danger. And the common answer was embodied in the popular demand for a king, so that Israel might be put on a par with "all the nations."

What, then, did the introduction of kingship in this case actually imply? It could not mean the establishment of absolute rule, for the Israelite idea of kingship, as indicated above, involved a man-made ruler of an essentially democratic state. Nor was it simply a matter of changing from a theocratic to a secular regime. The old *shōfēṭ* was not appreciably more charismatic than the new *melek*. Nor is there much difference between these two terms, semantically speaking. If one has to give a workable translation of *shōfēṭ*, it would have to be something like "arbiter, person in authority," or just simply "leader." On the other hand, *melek* is etymologically no more than "counselor," as is abundantly clear from the uses of the corresponding verb, especially in Akkadian and Aramaic. It thus follows that the actual difference between these two terms was not so much one of kind as of degree. The same should also hold true of their respective functions.

In their former inchoate state the individual tribes were headed by chieftains set up by the more influential clans. Such heads bore the title *nāsī*,[11] which probably signified someone who had been "elevated" by the assembly of the leaders. When several tribes had to act in concert — in the face of a common danger, or for purposes of a joint religious undertaking — they would need an over-all "arbiter" or "leader," in short, a *shōfēṭ*. This was necessarily a loose and casual set-up, with little if any governmental machinery. The arrangement would often not outlast the given emergency or joint enterprise. There was manifestly nothing permanent, let alone dynastic, in the concept of a *shōfēṭ*.

What "all the nations" had under their royal system was a head of state who was at the helm for life and would be succeeded by a logical representative of the same line. This applied not only to totalitarian Egypt but also to the anti-authoritarian systems of Mesopotamia, Syria, and Anatolia. And even where royal succession was not hereditary in theory, it was so normally in practice. The system was conducive to stability and efficiency. It meant proper administrative organization on a permanent basis, taxes,[12] and personal services to the state, including military obligations. Inevitably, bureaucracy would encroach on personal liberties, and regimentation would tend to curb individualism. But these were the facts of political and economic life in an increasingly international world. They could spell the difference between survival and extinction.

NOTES AND BIBLIOGRAPHY

NOTES

CHAPTER I
THE HISTORICAL DEVELOPMENT

1 Cf. J. Wilson, *ANET*, p. 233. Sharuhen is known from Thut-mose III's Annals, as well as from Egyptian rosters of Canaanite cities, as a fortress located at the south-western tip of the country; in Josh. 19:6 it is mentioned as a town on the border of Simeon's tribal territory. The discoveries at this large tell (Petrie, *Beth Pelet* I, London, 1930) made Albright suggest its identification with Tell el-Far'ah.

2 Cf. W. Helck, *Die Beziehungen Ägyptens zu Vorderasien im 3. und 2. Jahrtausend vor Christ*, Wiesbaden, 1962, pp. 109 ff.

3 The Land of Canaan (*mât Kinaḫḫi*) is first mentioned in the inscription of Idrimi, King of Alalakh, probably from the beginning of the 15th century B.C.E. The reference is to Syria's coast (S. Smith, *The Statue of Idrimi*, Ankara, 1949). For the land of Canaan in the Tell el-Amarna Letters, in Egyptian documents and in the Bible cf. B. Maisler (Mazar) *Untersuchungen*, p. 54 ff.; A. F. Rainey, *IEJ*, 13 (1963), pp. 43 ff.; and for the meaning of the name cf. B. Maisler (Mazar), *BASOR*, 102 (1946), 7 ff.; and see W. F. Albright, *The Bible and the Ancient Near East*, New York, 1962, p. 356 note 50. In the Egyptian documents, beginning with the time of Thut-mose III there also occurs quite frequently the name Djahi which is apparently co-extensive with Canaan; and cf. Helck, *op. cit.*, p. 274.

4 Cf. Wilson, *ANET*, p. 234 ff. On Zephath and its identification with Khirbet Sitt Leila, see Y. Aharoni, *IEJ*, 9 (1959), pp. 110 ff.

5 Papyrus Harris 500;. cf. Wilson, *ibid.*, pp. 22–23.

6 See J. Simons, *Handbook for the Study of Egyptian Topographical Lists Relating to Western Asia*, Leiden, 1937, pp. 27 ff., and cf. the detailed discussions of Thut-mose's lists—M. Noth, *ZDPV*, 61 (1938), pp. 26 ff.; S. Yeivin, *JEA*, 34 (1950), 51 ff.; Y. Aharoni, *The Land of the Bible*, 1967, pp. 143 ff.; M. Astour, *JNES*, 22 (1963), 220 ff. The nature of Thut-mose's list of Canaanite towns is a controversial subject. Some scholars believe that it reflects the order of Thut-mose's military expedition (Noth) or the list of Canaan's administrative divisions (Yeivin), while others deny it any intentional sequence, although it contains rosters of towns arranged in definite geographical units, such as the list of towns along the *Via maris* or the list of towns in Bashan (Mazar, Aharoni). The Leningrad Papyrus is one of the documents presenting a special interest for the geography of Canaan at the time of Thut-mose III, cf. A. H. Gardiner, *JEA*, 1 (1914), 20 ff.

7 See R. O'Callaghan, *Jahrbuch für Kleinasiatische Forschungen*, I (1950) 309 ff.; Helck, *op. cit.*, pp. 522 ff.

8 Cf. B. Mazar, *JBL*, 80 (1961), pp. 16 ff.

9 Concerning Gaza cf. A. Alt, *Kleine Schriften*, I, pp. 202 ff. Gaza was a very important Egyptian stronghold in Canaan, but it is hard to agree with the hypothesis of some scholars that it represented the capital of the Egyptian province in Asia. For Jaffa cf. J. Kaplan, *The Archeology and the History of Jaffo–Tel Aviv*, (Hebrew), Tel-Aviv, 1959, pp. 50 ff.

10 From one of the Taanach Letters (No. 5, and cf. below note 16) it can be concluded that in the second half of the 15th century the Canaanites of the Plain of Jezreel area used to hand in their taxes at the Egyptian fortress of Megiddo, while a Canaanite ruler resided in Taanach (cf. B. Mazar, in *The Beth-Shean Valley* [Hebrew], Jerusalem,

[1962], 14). Later on, during the Amarna period, Biridiya, a local ruler who is known from his letters to Amen-hotep IV, resided in Megiddo.

11   One of the Tell el-Amarna Letters mentioned the men of Gath-carmel as forming the garrison of Beth-shean, and it seems reasonable to assume that the reference is to the garrison of the Egyptian fortress about which we know from the excavations at Tell Beth-shean. It would appear that the remains in stratum IX, including the sanctuary put up by the Egyptian authorities, are to be attributed to the Amarna period; and cf. below note 13 and the discussion of the problem of the chronology, W. F. Albright, *AASOR*, 17 (1938), 76 ff.

12   The sanctuary was discovered outside the walls of the Late Bronze city of Lachish. The excavations revealed three phases in the existence of the sanctuary, the erection of which began apparently in the days of Thut-mose III, and its destruction is to be dated to the end of the 13th century; cf. O. Tufnell, C. H. Inge and L. Harding, *The Fosse Temple* (= *Lachish, III*), London, 1940. For the sanctuary in Megiddo see G. Loud, *Megiddo* II, Chicago, 1948, pp. 102 ff. For the sanctuary in Shechem see L. E. Toombs and G. E. Wright, *BASOR*, 169 (1963), 5 ff. The two last-mentioned structures of the fortified sanctuary type (tower-sanctuary, cf. B. Mazar "Migdāl," *Encyclopaedia Biblica* IV [Hebrew], cols. 633–635), which apparently began to be built at the end of the Middle Bronze Period and were finally destroyed in the Early Iron Age. The sanctuary in Shechem is apparently the House of Baal-berith (Jud. 9:4); cf. G. E. Wright, *Shechem*, New York, 1965. The plan of the sanctuary discovered in Hazor (Y. Yadin *et alii*, *Hazor*, 3–4, pls. CI ff.) which originates from the Middle Bronze II Period and was destroyed by the Israelites, must be viewed as a Late Bronze prototype of Solomon's Temple in Jerusalem.

13   For the sanctuaries in Beth-shean see A. Rowe, *The Topography and History of Beth-Shan* I, Philadelphia, 1930; A. Rowe and G. M. Fitzgerald, *The Four Canaanite*

Temples of Beth-Shan I–II, Philadelphia, 1930–1940. For the Egyptian sanctuaries in Canaan erected under the Nineteenth Dynasty, cf. A. Alt, *Kleine Schriften*, I, pp. 216 ff.

14   Cf. Wilson, *ANET*, pp. 245 ff.; E. Edel, *ZDPV*, 69 (1953), 98 ff.; B. Mazar, *Jerusalem*, 4 (Hebrew), (1953), 13 ff.; Y. Aharoni, *JNES*, 19 (1960), 177 ff.; A. Malamat, *Scripta Hierosolymitana*, 8 (1961), 218 ff.

15   Concerning the Mycenaean imports see among others: H. J. Kantor, *The Aegean and the Orient in the Second Mill. B.C.*, Bloomington, 1947; F. H. Stubbings, *Mycenean Pottery from the Levant*, Cambridge, 1951; R. Amiran, *Eretz Israel*, (Hebrew), 6 (1961) 25 ff.; for the commercial relations between Egypt and Canaan see Helck, *op. cit.*, pp. 391 ff. Tell Abu Huwām provides an instructive example of a harbor town which had close connections with Cyprus and the countries of the Aegean Sea; see R. W. Hamilton, *Quarterly of the Department of Antiquities in Palestine*, 4 (1955), 1 ff.; cf. B. Maisler (Mazar), *BASOR*, 124 (1951), 21 ff.

16   The Taanach Tablets were published by F. Hrozný *apud* E. Sellin, *Tell Ta'annek*, Vienna, 1904; *Idem, Eine Nachlese auf dem Tell Ta'annek*, Vienna, 1906; and the translations of B. Maisler (Mazar) in *Klausner Volume* (Hebrew), Jerusalem, 1937, pp. 44 ff.; W. F. Albright, *BASOR*, 94 (1944), 12 ff.; cf. A. Malamat, *Scripta Hierosolymitana*, 8 (1961), 218 ff.

17   Three hundred and fifty-eight letters have been published so far, the great majority in the edition of J. A. Knudtzon, *Die Tell El Amarna Tafeln*, Leipzig, 1907–1915, and others by F. Thureau-Dangin, *RA*, 19 (1922), 91 ff. Some of the documents were translated anew by Albright, *ANET*, pp. 483 ff., and cf. J. de Köning, *Studien over de El-Amarnabrieven etc.*, Delft, 1940; E. F. Campbell, *The Chronology of the Amarna Letters*, Baltimore, 1963; W. F. Albright, *CAH* II (2nd. ed), Chapter XX, 1966.

18   See K. A. Kitchen, *Suppiluliuma and the Amarna Pharaohs*, Liverpool, 1962.

19   For the Amurru kingdom see H.

Klengel, *Mitteilungen des Instituts für Orient-forschung* 10 (1964), 57; Helck, *op. cit.*, pp. 293 ff.

20   See *ANET*, p. 486.

21   See W. F. Albright, *ANET*, p. 487; Thureau-Dangin, *RA*, 19 (1922) 106; Albright lowers the date to the days of Akh-en-Aton.

22   On Hor-em-heb see Helck, *op. cit.*, pp. 199 ff.

23   See Wilson, *ANET*, p. 253.

24   See B. Grdseloff, *Une stele Scythopolitaine du roi Sethos I*, Cairo, 1949; Albright, *BASOR*, 125 (1952), 24 ff., as well as B. Mazar and S. Yeivin in *The Beth-Shean Valley* (Hebrew), 16 ff., 26–27.

25   See B. Grdseloff, *Revue de l'histoire juive en Egypte*, 1 (1947), 74 ff.

26   For the documents of Seti I, see N. Noth, *ZDPV*, 60 (1937), 213 ff.; and Y. Aharoni, *The Settlement of the Israelite Tribes in Upper Galilee*, (Hebrew), Jerusalem, 1957, pp. 55 ff.

27   For details see A. Alt. *Kleine Schriften*, I, pp. 216 ff.; III, pp. 107 ff; Helck, *op. cit.*, pp. 480 f. Some Egyptian fortresses in Canaan were named for Pharaoh Mer-ne-Ptah. It was suggested that one of these, the well of Me(r)-ne-Ptah in the mountains, be identified with the spring of the Waters of Nephtoah (Josh. 15:9). Papyrus Harris I from the time of Ramses III is of special interest because it mentions among the estates of the temple of Ammon in Thebes a number of cities in Canaan; see Wilson, *ANET*, pp. 260 ff.

28   For the battle of Kadesh see C. Kuentz, *La bataille de Kadech*, Cairo, 1928; J. Sturm, *Der Hettiterkrieg Ramses II*, Vienna, 1939; Helck, *op. cit.*, pp. 208 ff.

29   See B. Mazar, *Encyclopaedia Biblica*, (Hebrew), I, col. 694.

30   See Wilson, *ANET*, pp. 199 ff.; A. Goetze, *ANET*, pp. 201 ff.

31   See B. Maisler, (Mazar), *Yediot*, (Hebrew), 12 (1946), 91 ff.

32   For Papyrus Anastasi I see Wilson, *ANET*, pp. 475 ff.; Y. Aharoni, *The Settlement*, etc. (Hebrew), pp. 120 ff.; Helck, *op. cit.*, pp. 328 ff. About Asher cf. the Egyptian documents — A. H. Gardiner, *Ancient Egyptian Onomastica*, I, Oxford, 1947, pp. 191 ff.; Y. Aharoni, *The Settlement, etc.*, (Hebrew), pp. 53–65 ff.

33   See Wilson, *ANET*, pp. 376 ff.

34   For the last stage in the history of the Hittite empire cf. now H. Otten, *MDOG*, 94 (1963), 1 ff.; G. Güterbock, *JNES*, 26 (1965), pp. 73 ff.; W. F. Albright, *Jahwe and the Gods of Canaan*, London, 1968, pp. 139 ff.

35   For details see S. Yeivin, in Volume II, Chapter III; of the same series; F. M. Cross Jr., *BASOR*, 134, (1954), 15 ff.; *Eretz Israel*, 8 (1967), pp. 8*ff.

CHAPTER II

THE EGYPTIAN DECLINE IN CANAAN
AND THE SEA-PEOPLES

1   A. H. Gardiner, *Egyptian Hieratic Texts*, I, I: *Papyrus Anastasi* I . . ., Leipzig, 1911; *ANET*, pp. 475 ff. The document apparently reflects the situation in Canaan in the later years of Ramses II. For a brief summary of the sources dealing with Canaan from the time of Ramses II, cf. A. Malamat, "Syrien-Palästina in der zweiten hälfte des 2. Jahrtausends," *Fischer Weltgeschichte*, III, Frankfurt a/M, 1966, pp. 196 ff., 349.

2   See *ANET*, p. 258; and R. A. Caminos, *Late Egyptian Miscellanies*, London, 1954, pp. 108 ff. Of particular interest there is the name "The Wells of Me(r)-ne-Ptah which is in the mountains" (*ibid.*, lines 4–5). This has been equated with the biblical "The fountain of the waters of Nephtoah" mentioned as a locality on the border between Benjamin and Judah, near Jerusalem (Josh., 15:9; 18:15). Indeed, the Hebrew text contains a tautology, and *ma'yan mē neftōaḥ* should thus be interpreted as "The fountain of Me(r)-ne-Ptah." For a contrary opinion, see D. Leibel, *Yediot*, 28 (1964), 255–256 (Hebrew).

3   Note especially Mer-ne-Ptah's title "Binder of Gezer," Breasted, *ARE*, III, § 606. The excavations at Gezer have yielded objects bearing his name: (a) an ivory sundial of Egyptian type; (b) a statue-pedestal (and not dating from the Twenty-Ninth Dynasty, as pointed out to me by Dr. R. Giveon). Cf. R. A. S. Macalister, *Gezer*, II, London, 1912, pp. 313, 331. For (a), see now K. A. Kitchen, *Ramesside Inscriptions*, IV, 1, Oxford, 1968, p. 24.

4   See J. Černý, *apud Lachish*, IV, London, 1958, p. 133. In another view, the date refers to the reign of Ramses III.

5   W. F. Albright, *BASOR*, 74 (1939), 20 ff.; *idem*, *Yahwe and the Gods of Canaan*, London, 1968, p. 139. The archeological context, including the bowl sherds, is not clear-cut and it cannot be unreservedly claimed, as done by Albright, that it belongs to the actual destruction layer of Late Bronze Period Lachish. Cf. now the remarks of R. de Vaux in *Near Eastern Archaeology in the Twentieth Century* (ed. A. Sanders), New York, 1970, p. 77. In any case, Egyptian rule at both Gezer and Lachish at this time could illuminate an episode of the Israelite Conquest. According to Josh. 10:33, Horam, King of Gezer, rushed to the aid of Lachish even though he had not joined the southern Canaanite coalition opposing Israel. His move may have been inspired by Egypt, who would have ordered military cooperation between the two centers under its domination. Cf. A. Malamat, "External Sources on the Conquest of Canaan," *Studies in the Book of Joshua*, 1960, p. 195, (Hebrew).

6   Recent years have seen the growth of an abundant bibliography on the Sea-Peoples; for summaries with bibliographical references, see W. Helck, *Die Beziehungen Ägyptens zu Vorderasien im 3. und 2. Jahrtausend v. Chr.*, Wiesbaden, 1962, pp. 240 ff.; and R. D. Barnett, "The Sea-Peoples," *CAH* II (rev. ed.), ch. XXVIII (1969). The chief proponent in recent years for the Anatolian hypothesis has been G. A. Wainwright who presented his views in a series of studies, the latest summary being "Some Sea-Peoples", *JEA*, 47 (1961), 71 ff. For the Aegean-Pelasgian origin, cf. W. F. Albright, "Syria, the Philistines and Phoenicia," *CAH* II (rev. ed.), ch. XXXIII (1966), pp. 24 ff. For an appraisal of the various assumptions from the viewpoint of classical sources, cf. F. Lochner-Hüttenbach, *Die Pelasger*, Vienna, 1960.

7   Concerning these identifications, see note 6. For the Lukka (see also below, C), as well as the equation of the Aḫḫiyā(wa) — who are mentioned in Hittite sources as dwelling on the western coast of Asia Minor, with their centers beyond the sea — with the Greek Achaeans, see further A. Malamat, "Western Asia Minor in the Time of the Sea-Peoples," *Yediot*, 30 (Hebrew), (1966), 195 ff.; for the rejection of

the latter equation see G. Steiner, "Die Aḫḫiyāwa Frage heute," *Saeculum*, 15 (1964), 365 ff. An appealing but unconvincing reference to an invasion of Egypt by the Aqawasha in the days of Mer-ne-Ptah has been sought in the *Odyssey* (XIV, 246), where Odysseus's nine boats landed in Egypt on their return journey. The name of the Teresh-Tyrsēnoi may occur in the biblical Table of Nations (Gen. 10:2) as Tiras, a "son" of Japheth.

8   Cf. Breasted, *ARE*, III, § 580, and Wainwright, "Menephtah's Aid to the Hittites," *JEA*, 46 (1960), 24 ff., who also adduces Hittite sources alluding to a famine felt particularly in western Anatolia. A Hittite mission to Egypt in Mer-ne-Ptah's 4th year, possibly to be inferred from a text at Amada, may have been concerned with such grain-shipments; see A. A. Youssef, "Merenptah's Fourth Year Text at Amada," *Annales du Service des Antiquites de l'Égypte*, 58 (1964), 273 ff., where quite a different interpretation is given.

9   In one Hittite document mention is made of Mer-ne-Ptah (*Keilschrifturkunden aus Boghazköi*, III, no. 38, vs. 7), while in another (*ibid.*, XXVI, no. 33), one of the last documents to be deposited in the royal archives, Egypt is mentioned (column 3, line 7) in a military context, but because of the poor state of the tablet, it is not clear whether it is as a friend or a foe. Cf. A. Malamat, *JNES*, 13 (1954), 238.

10   Mer-ne-Ptah's name occurs on a sword found there; cf. C.F.A. Schaeffer, *Ugaritica*, III, Paris, 1956, pp. 169 ff. Further, letters from the tablet oven (in the destruction layer at Ugarit; see below C, and note 33) indicate that merchant vessels still plied to Egypt, and that an Egyptian agent at Ugarit was supplied with oil (*PRU*, V, 59: 11; 95:4).

11   For a treatment of this rather obscure period, where even the sequence and length of the kings' reigns are controversial, see A. Malamat, "Cushan Rishathaim and the Decline of the Near East around 1200 B.C.," *JNES*, 13 (1954), 231 ff., and the literature quoted there (pp. 233 ff.); for more recent discussions of this period, see E. Drioton and J. Vandier, *L'Égypte* (4th ed.), Paris,

1962, pp. 655 f.; R. D. Faulkner, *CAH*, II (rev. ed.), ch. XXIII (1966), pp. 21 ff. L. H. Lesko, "A little More Evidence for the End of the Nineteenth Dynasty," *JARCE*, 5 (1966), 29 ff.

12   For the Tell el-Far'ah jar, cf. E. Macdonald, J. L. Starkey and L. Harding, *Beth-Pelet*, II, London, 1932, pp. 28–29; for the Tell Deir 'Alla find, see J. Yoyotte "Un souvenir de 'Pharaon' Taousert en Jordanie," *VT*, 12 (1962), 464 ff. Interestingly enough, in the same level were unearthed inscribed clay tablets, some signs on which resemble closely the Minoan Linear A script, while in a subsequent stratum "Philistine" pottery was found; see W. F. Albright, *CAH* (rev. ed.) ch. XXXV, p. 27, and the literature below in the chapter "The Period of the Judges," note 48.

13   For the quotation from Papyrus Anastasi IV, see Caminos, *op. cit.*, p. 138; on the emissary, see Breasted, *ARE* III, § 651.

14   For Papyri Anastasi V and VI, see *ANET*, p. 259 and Caminos, *op. cit.*, pp. 254 ff., 293 ff. For the problem of the site of Tjeku — possibly to be identified with the Succoth of the Exodus tradition (and Pe[r]-atum with biblical Pithom), cf. W. Helck, "Ṯkw und die Ramsesstadt," *VT*, 15 (1965), 35 ff.

15   Papyrus Harris I, 75:2–5; cf. Breasted, *ARE*, IV § 348; J. A. Wilson, *ANET*, p. 260 and note 6. Some take the word *ꜣi.ꜣir.św* not as the name Irsu but as an Egyptian verbal form meaning "[a Syrian] who made himself". This name, however, is attested in other Egyptian sources; for references see A. Malamat, *JNES*, 13 (1954), 234, note 26; J. Černý-A. H. Gardiner, *Hieratic Ostraca*, Oxford, 1957, pl. 19, no. 1:5; pl. 31, no. 2:5. Interestingly, it also appears at Ugarit as a personal name; cf. C. H. Gordon, *UT*, p. 366 (no. 368).

16   See A. H. Gardiner, *JEA*, 44 (1958), 12 ff.; Helck, *Beziehungen*, pp. 247 ff.; J. Černý, "A Note on the Chancellor Bay," *ZÄS*, 93 (1966), 35 ff.

17   For the following discussion, see in detail A. Malamat, *JNES*, 13 (1954), 231 ff.; other approaches concerning Cushan-Rishathaim are reviewed there and are found to be unsatisfactory. Cf. also below in the chapter "The Period of the Judges," par. E.

18 Thus, e.g., the biblical account in Gen. 14 of four Eastern rulers joining in a campaign against five petty kings of the Dead Sea area. The historical kernel of such a story could make sense only in the context of a campaign passing through Canaan but directed ultimately against Egypt.

19 Albright, too, is inclined to date Cushan-Rishathaim around the end of the Nineteenth Dynasty; see his *Archaeology and the religion of Israel*, Baltimore, 1942, p. 110. For another appraisal of the significance to Israelite history of Egypt's decline at this time, see, e.g., M. B. Rowton, "The Problem of the Exodus," *PEQ*, 85 (1953), 46 ff., who asserts that the majority of Israelite tribes then left Egypt for Canaan and conquered it. This view, however, has been countered by H. H. Rowley, "A Recent Theory on the Exodus," *Orientalia Suecana*, 4 (1955), 77 ff.

20 Cf. O. R. Gurney, *CAH*, II (rev. ed.), ch. XV (a), pp. 20 f.; O. Carruba, "Die Chronologie der heth. Texte und die heth. Geschichte der Grossreichszeit," *ZDMG*, Suppl. 1, Wiesbaden, 1969, pp. 266 ff., who dates also the inscriptions of Arnuwanda III to an earlier period. Cf. now also P. M. J. Houwink Ten Cate, *The Records of the Early Hittite Empire*, Istanbul, 1970, pp. 2, 80. But for a contrary view, see A. Kammenhuber, *Or*, 38 (1969), 548 ff.; 39 (1970) 278 ff.; idem, *Münchener Studien zur Sprachenwissenschaft*, 28 (1970), 51 ff.

21 See now H. Güterbock, "The Hittite Conquest of Cyprus Reconsidered," *JNES*, 26 (1967), 73 ff.; and also A. Goetze, *CAH*, II (rev. ed.), ch. XXIV, pp. 51 f.

22 On Alalakh see L. Woolley, *A Forgotten Kingdom*, London, 1953, pp. 162 f. On Ugarit, J. Nougayrol, *PRU*, IV, pp. 113 ff.; Schaeffer, *Ugaritica*, III, pp. 14 ff. On Amurru, O. Szemerényi "Vertrag des Hethiterkönigs Tudhalija IV mit Ištarmuwa von Amurru," *Oriens Antiquus*, (1945), 113–130; H. Klengel, *Geschichte Syriens im 2. Jahrtausend v. u. Z.* II, Berlin, 1969, pp. 320 ff.

23 E. Weidner, *Die Inschriften Tukulti-*Ninurtas I (=*AFO* Beihefte, 12) Graz, 1959, pp. 26 ff. (Nos. 16 & 17). Helck (*Beziehungen*, p. 239, note 83) considers the abovementioned campaign to Amurru to have brought about the end of its independence, while Woolley (cf. above, note 22) attributes the destruction of the Alalakh temple (level I, phase 2) to an assumed local uprising, in the wake of the Assyrian successes. Albright (*Yahwe*, pp. 139 f., 235 f.) doubtfully finds a reflection of Tukulti-Ninurta's campaign in a letter from the Hittite king found at Ugarit (PRU, V n.60), mentioning the Assyrians (according to his unfounded reading) as enemies.

24 See E. Laroche, "Šuppiluliuma II," *RA*, 47 (1953), 70 ff.; H. Otten, "Neue Quellen zum Ausklang des hethitischen Reiches," *MDOG* 94 (1963), 1 ff. From a new document published by Otten (ibid., pp. 16–17), mentioning "Shuppiluliuma the son of Tudhaliya the grandson of Hattusilis," the sequence of the last Hittite kings seems settled. We can no longer uphold the reconstruction given in *JNES*, 13 (1954), 238 f. For the last Hittite kings, see also A. Goetze, *CAH*, II (rev. ed.), ch. XXIV, section IV. For the naval battle with Cyprus, see also note 21.

25 On the destruction of the Hittite empire and the subsequent ethnic and political changes, cf., e.g., H. Schmökel, *Keilschriftforschung und alte Geschichte Vorderasiens*, Leiden, 1957, p. 139; A. Goetze, *Kleinasien*, (2nd ed.), Munich, 1957, pp. 184 f.; G. L. Huxley, *Achaeans and Hittites*, Oxford, 1960. and most recently E. O. Forrer, "Der Untergang des Hatti-Reiches," *Ugaritica* VI, Paris, 1969, pp. 207 ff. The ethnic upheavals in the interior of Anatolia, which followed the Sea-Peoples' invasion, are also echoed in the inscriptions of Tiglath-pileser I who relates that fifty years earlier (i.e. in the mid-12th century) there appeared in the Upper Tigris region Mushku tribes which seem to have been affiliated with the Phrygians; cf. Goetze and Forrer above. For the peoples and countries on the western and southern seaboards of Asia Minor, cf. A. Malamat, *Yediot*, 30 (Hebrew), (1966), 195 ff. and map below, p. 00.

26 This depends, *inter alia*, on the lowest possible dating of the Mycenaean (Late Helladic III B) ware found in destruction layers at the Late Bronze Period sites. For the difficult dating of the archeological material, see V. R. Desborough, *The Last Mycenaeans . . .* , Oxford, 1964, pp. 207 ff., 237 ff.

27 L. Woolley, *op. cit.*, p. 164; *idem, The Excavation of Alalakh*, Oxford, 1955, p. 374, ascribes the town's final destruction to the Sea-Peoples in Ramses III's 5th year, which he puts in 1194 B.C.E. (And cf. there the abortive attempt to renew the settlement half a century later, as indicated, *inter alia*, by the discovery of a scarab of Ramses VI.) It has been suggested, however, that this destruction occurred a generation earlier, in accord with a higher *terminus ad quem* for the LH IIIB ware; cf. P. E. Pecorella, "Sulla data della distruzione di Alalakh," *La Colombaria (Atti - Memorie Accad. Toscana di Scienze e Lettere)*, 24 (1960–61), 145 ff.

28 See R. W. Hamilton, *QDAP*, 4 (1935), 1 ff. and cf. B. Maisler (Mazar), *BASOR*, 124 (1951), 21 ff.

29 This view is preferable to that attributing the initial conquest to the Israelites, as has been suggested for Jaffa by J. Kaplan, *The Archaeology and History of Tel Aviv-Jaffo* (Hebrew), Tel Aviv, 1959, pp. 56 ff., (but after the 1970 season he now attributes both destruction layers to the Sea-Peoples). and for Ashdod by M. Dothan, *IEJ*, 14 (1964), 84, and in *Ashdod*, I ('*Atiqot* VII), Jerusalem, 1967, p. 81; for Tel Mor, see *idem, 3rd World Congress of Jewish Studies*, (Hebrew) Jerusalem, 1965, 295 ff. Interestingly, enough in the 1968–69 seasons at Ashdod, the first "Philistine" level above the destruction of the Late Bronze Period city (stratum 13; 1st half of the 12th century) has yielded a local imitation of LH III C1 ware found particularly in Cyprus, as well as several seals bearing signs resembling the Cypro-Minoan script. Cf. *IEJ*, 19 (1969), 244 f. Cf. *ibid.* p. 243 for two waves of Sea-Peoples also at Gezer, as reported by W. G. Dever in the log of the 1969 excavations there.

30 See E. Meyer, *Geschichte*, II, 2 (2nd ed.), Stuttgart, 1931, pp. 79 f. B. Mazar rejects this conclusion (cf. "The Philistines and the Rise of Israel and Tyre," *Proceedings of the Israel Academy of Sciences*, I, 7 [1964], 5 and note 11). The Sea-Peoples' conquest of Ashkelon may be reflected in the classical legends surrounding the hero Mopsus; cf. G. A. Wainwright, *JEA*, 47 (1961), 80; and R. D. Barnett, *Journal of Hellenic Studies*, 73 (1953), 142 ff.

31 Josephus, in *Ant.* VIII, iii, 1 (probably basing on an early Hellenistic source), relates the foundation of Tyre to 240 years before the building of Solomon's Temple, i.e., ca. 1200 B.C.E. This tradition, however, is of doubtful value. For Sidonian coins mentioning Sidon as the "Mother of Tyre," cf. G. F. Hill, *Catalogue of the Greek Coins of Phoenicia*, London, 1910, pp. 155 f.

32 See *PRU*, V, no. 59; and J. Sasson, *JAOS*, 86 (1966), 137.

33 The contents of the tablet kiln have been published by Ch. Virolleaud, in *PRU* V, pp. 81 ff.; 180 ff. The Akkadian documents have been dealt with in several preliminary surveys; see J. Nougayrol, *CRAI*, 13.5 (1960), 163 ff.; H. Otten, *MDOG*, 94 (1963), 8 f.; M. C. Astour, "New Evidence on the Last Days of Ugarit," *AJA*, 69 (1965), 253 ff.; and now the long-awaited final publication by Nougayrol, in *Ugaritica*, V, Paris, 1968, pp. 79 ff.; and cf. Schaeffer's commentary on pp. 607 ff. On the Alashya letters cf. now the textual remark of R. P. Berger, *Ugarit Forschungen*, 1 (1969), 217 ff.; and on the impact of the material on the problem of the Sea-Peoples in general, my lecture at the Israel Exploration Society's excursion in the Mediterranean, fall 1969 (to be published).

34 For this alignment of forces, see *Yediot*, 30 (1966), 199 f. Albright, on the other hand, has perceived here an alliance between Mer-ne-Ptah and the Assyrians directed against the Hittite camp, the former having diverted the hostility of the Sea-Peoples toward Hatti; see *Yahwe*, pp. 141 f. For still another view, see note 36.

35 This earlier date for the city's fall could further be indicated by the fact that no Hittite king after Tudhaliya IV is explicitly mentioned at Ugarit. It would also be in

accord with Albright's recent dating — based on a rather speculative synchronism with Tukulti-Ninurta I's campaign (cf. above, note 23) — i.e. about 1230 B.C.E. Helck, *Beziehungen*, p. 234, even dates the destruction of the Hittite empire to the time of Mer-ne-Ptah, which hardly seems likely since Shuppiluliuma II most probably outlived Mer-ne-Ptah. On Ugarit's final period see also M. Liverani, *Storia di Ugarit*, Rome, 1962, pp. 131 ff.

36   But not so late as contended in Schaeffer's lengthy historical discussion of the new Ugaritic material (in *Ugaritica*, V, pp. 607 ff.), where he claims that 'Ammurapi turned coat when confronted by increasing pressure, and joined the Sea-Peoples. Equally doubtful is his assertion that a most intriguing letter ("lettre de Général"—*ibid.*, no. 20), written to the King of Ugarit by one of his commanders in Ammurru, is to be linked with Ramses III's campaign against Amurru in his 8th (sic?) year (cf. below). This letter, however, would fit in much more aptly with the circumstances of the Battle of Kadesh (Ramses II), a hundred years previously; see H. Cazelles' forthcoming study in *Mélanges offerts à M. Dunand*, and already Liverani, *op. cit.*, pp. 77 f.

37   Cf. W. F. Edgerton – J. A. Wilson, *Historical Records of Ramses III*, Chicago, 1936, pl. 45, p. 53; *ANET*, p. 262.

38   For traces of the Sea-Peoples at Enkomi, see Schaeffer, *Enkomi-Alasia*, Paris, 1952, pp. 37 ff., 156 ff., 371 ff. For Enkomi ivories depicting warriors resembling typical Sea-Peoples — most likely Tjeker (see below) — see Wainwright "A Teucrian at Salamis in Cyprus," *Journal of Hellenic Studies*, 83 (1963), 146 ff., and also T. Dothan, *The Philistines and Their Material Culture* (Hebrew) Jerusalem, 1967, p. 219, fig. 67 (a similar depiction on a seal). Cf. now also K. Galling, *Ugaritica* VI, Paris, 1969, pp. 247 ff. For the double extensive destructions of Enkomi, see P. Dikaios, "Excavations and Historical Background: Enkomi in Cyprus," *Journal of Historical Studies*, 1 (1967), 41 ff.; see also the excavator's, P. Dikaios, recent summary.

39   For the identification of these peoples,

see note 6 above. On the Denen and their identification with the Danaoi of the Greek sources, see the detailed discussion by M. C. Astour, *Hellenosemitica*, Leiden, 1965, pp. 1 ff. On a presumed identification with the Israelite tribe of Dan, cf. Y. Yadin, *Australian Journal of Biblical Archaeology*, 1 (1968), 9 ff.

40   For this inscription see Edgerton-Wilson *op. cit.*, pp. 19 ff. (pls. 27–28). On the historical reliability of the Amurru campaign, cf. Malamat, *JNES*, 13 (1954), 240 f. Recently, R. Stadelmann has negated altogether the historicity of any of Ramses III's campaigns into Asia — whether of the 5th, 8th or any other year, rejecting any notion of his control over Canaan; cf. *Saeculum*, 19 (1969), pp. 156 ff. This seems to be going too far, however.

41   Cf. Papyrus Harris I, 76; 7 ff.; *ANET*, p. 262, which also gives a summary of Ramses's victories over the Sea-Peoples.

42   Cf. the previous note and F. Bilabel, *Geschichte Vorderasiens*, Heidelberg, 1927, p. 128. For a recent discussion of the location of Seir (to the west of the Arabah), see J. R. Bartlett, *Journal of Theological Studies*, N.S. 20 (1969), 1 ff.

43   Papyrus Harris I, 78: 5 ff.; Breasted, *ARE*, IV, p. 204, § 408. Cf. the first report of these discoveries, made in 1969 by B. Rothenberg, in *Illustrated London News*, Nov. 15, 1969, pp. 28 f. and Nov. 29, 1969, pp. 31 f., and *PEQ*, 101 (1969), 57 ff. The Egyptian material will be published by R. Giveon and A. Schulman.

44   The reliefs were republished in *Medinet Habu*, I-II, pls. 87–88, 90; on the city of Amurru, *ibid.*, pl. 94; and cf. Helck, *Beziehungen*, p. 248.

45   J. J. Simons, *Handbook for the Study of Egyptian Topographical Lists relating to Western Asia*, Leiden, 1937, pp. 77 ff., pp. 164 ff., and most recently M. C. Astour, *JAOS*, 88, (1968), 733 ff.

46   Cf. Breasted, *ARE*, IV, § 225; *ANET*, p. 261 (D).

47   Edgerton-Wilson, *op. cit.*, p. 43, and also note 21a there.

48   Scarabs of Ramses III were discovered at sites such as Tell el-Fara'h (south),

Tell Jemmeh, Lachish, Beth-shemesh, Megiddo and Beth-shean; cf. A. Rowe, *A Catalogue of Egyptian Scarabs in the Palestine Archaeological Museum*, Cairo, 1936.

49 On the Gezer jar, see Macalister, *Gezer*, II, p. 236, fig. 388, where the name is mistakenly read as Ramses II. For the correct reading, cf. B. Porter and R. L. B. Moss, *Topographical Bibliography of Ancient Egyptian Hieroglyphic Texts*, VII, Oxford, 1951, p. 374. On the Megiddo material, see G. Loud, *The Megiddo Ivories*, Chicago, 1939, pl. 62: 377; *ANET*, p. 263.

50 The excavators ascribed this stratum to Seti I; cf. A. Rowe, *The Four Canaanite Temples of Beth-Shan*, I, Philadelphia, 1930. For the correct dating, however, cf. B. Maisler (Mazar), "The Chronology of the Beth-shean Temples," *Yediot*, 16, (Hebrew), (1951), 14 ff., and cf. now F. W. James, *The Iron Age of Beth-shean*, Philadelphia, 1966; for the hieroglyphic inscriptions there, see W. A. Ward., *ibid.*, pp. 161 ff. Two temples existed there until the Israelite Monarchy and are apparently the "House of Dagon" and the "House of Ashtaroth" (I Chr. 10:10 and I Sam. 31:10 respectively).

51 Cf. A. Alt, "Ägyptische Tempel in Palästina," *Kleine Schriften* I, pp. 216 ff.; R. Stadelmann, *Syrisch-Palästinensische Gottheiten in Ägypten*, Leiden, 1967.

52 This ivory, together with others of the same cache, may be earlier than the time of Ramses III. See above, note 49, end. The minstrel of the god Ptah was called Kerker (Kelkel) and she seems to have been of a type of Canaanite temple singer which, in the time of David and Solomon, was integrated into the Israelite cult (cf. I, Kings 5:11); cf. W. F. Albright, *Archeology and the religion of Israel*, p. 127. Ptah's title may allude to his having "succeeded" the local dynasty as "the Great Prince (*wr*) of Ashkelon," after its conquest by the Egyptians; but see Helck, *Beziehungen*, p. 480.

53 Papyrus Harris I, 9:1; *ANET*, pp. 260 f. It is interesting to note that a list of gifts Ramses III sent to one of his officials includes two silver vessels from Ashkelon; cf. Helck, "Materialien zur Wirtschafts-geschichte des neuen Reiches," V, *Abhand. Akad. Wissensch. u. Liter. Geistes u. Sozialwiss. Klasse*, Mainz, (1964), 752.

54 *ANET*, p. 271; and cf. A. Malamat, quoted in B. Mazar, *Studies in the Book of Joshua* (Hebrew), p. 173.

55 For the Twentieth Dynasty after Ramses III and the Twenty-First Dynasty, cf. J. Černý, *CAH*, II (rev. ed.), ch. XXXV, and cf. also E. F. Wente, "On the Chronology of the Twenty-First Dynasty," *JNES*, 26 (1967), 155 ff.; E. Hornung, *Untersuchungen zur Chronologie u. Geschichte des neuen Reiches*, Wiesbaden, 1964, pp. 95 ff.

56 See A. Malamat, *JNES*, 22 (1963), 10 ff.; *idem, The Biblical Archeology Reader*, II, New York, 1964, pp. 89 ff.

57 See *Megiddo*, II, Chicago, 1948, 135 ff. This base must have originated from stratum VII A, which was still under Egyptian influence.

58 See W. M. F. Petrie, *Researches in Sinai*, London, 1906, p. 108; A. H. Gardiner, T. E. Peet and J. Černý, *The Inscriptions of Sinai*, II, London, 1955, nos. 290-3.

59 Cf. Porter and Moss, *op. cit.*, pp. 370 ff. For the cartouche of the Gezer ring, see Macalister, *Gezer*, III, pl. 195:74. The name here was mistakenly read as that of Ramses X; it should be noted that the name on the ring (Nefer-Ka-Re) can also be that of Nephercheres, son of Psusennes I of the Twenty-First Dynasty.

60 For Heri-Hor's rule contemporary with Ramses XI, cf. Černý, *CAH*, II (rev. ed.), chap. XXXV, pp. 32 ff.; Heri-Hor's 5th year would synchronize with the 24th year of Ramses, i.e. 1089 B.C.E. according to Černý's reckoning.

61 For Assyria at the time of Tiglath-pileser I, see S. Smith, *Early History of Assyria*, London, 1929, pp. 283 ff., E. Forrer, *Reallexikon der Assyriologie*, I, pp. 268 ff.; D. J. Wiseman, *CAH* II (rev. ed.) ch. XXXI (1965), pp. 17 ff.

62 In addition to the bibliography in note 61, see A. Malamat, *The Arameans in Aram Naharaim and the Rise of their States* (Hebrew), Jerusalem, 1952, p. 1 ff., *idem* "The Arameans," in *The People of the Old Testament*, (ed. D. J. Wiseman), Oxford (in press). See also on the campaign to the west,

E. Weidner, "Die Feldzüge und Bauten Tiglatpilesers I," *AFO*, 19, (1957–8), 343 ff.

63 See E. Michel, *Welt des Orients*, 2 (1954–59), 38 f.; A. Malamat, "Campaigns to the Mediterranean . . . " *Studies in Honor of B. Landsberger* (= *Assyriological Studies*, 16), Chicago, 1965, pp. 371 f.

64 For the above, see in greater detail A. Malamat, in *Western Galilee and the Coast of Galilee* (Hebrew), (1965), pp. 89 ff., the section of "Assyria and Egypt on the Phoenician Coast in the time of Tiglath-pileser I." For the shipment of animals, see Weidner, *op. cit.*, Text II, 11, 27–28, and *idem*, *AFO*, 6 (1930–31), 88 ff. The inscription on the ornament found at Tanis was published by E. Dhorme, *apud* P. Montet, *Psousennes — La necropole de Tanis*, II, Paris, 1951, pp. 139 ff.; and cf. R. Borger, *Einleitung in die assyrischen Königsinschriften*, I, Leiden, 1961, pp. 20 f. The fact that the daughter of a high Assyrian official is mentioned in the inscription may point to a diplomatic marriage to a pharaoh.

65 This English version, of the Hebrew original published in 1967, was revised and brought up to date at the beginning of 1970.

CHAPTER III

SOCIETY AND ECONOMIC CONDITIONS

1 Cf. A. Alt, "Die Landnahme der Israeliten in Palästina," *Kleine Schriften*, I, pp. 89–125.
2 Knudtzon, *EA*, nos. 148 : 6–13, 28–34; 149 : 49–53.
3 *Ibid.*, no. 287 : 26–8.
4 J. Nougayrol, *PRU*, III, 1955, p. 134, no. 15. 137 : 12; and see *ibid.*, p. 234.
5 S. Smith, *The Statue of Idrimi*, London, 1949, p. 25; W. F. Albright, "A Prince of Taanach in the Fifteenth Century B.C.," *BASOR*, 94 (1944), 23, 24.
6 Knudtzon, *EA*, nos. 102 : 22; 138 : 49.
7 J. A. Wilson, *JNES*, 4 (1945), 245; and cf. Jud. 9 : 2; Ezek. 27 : 9.
8 H. L. Ginsberg, *The Legend of King Keret*, New Haven, 1946, p. 24, col. 4, lines 6–7.
9 Knudtzon, *EA*, nos. 59, 100.
10 Nougayrol, *PRU*, III, p. 225; Gordon, *UH*, nos. 110, 111.
11 Wiseman, *Alalakh*, no. 108 : 6.
12 Nougayrol, *PRU*, III, p. 54, no. 15 : 90.
13 Cf. Virolleaud, *Syria*, 18 (1937), 164; cf. Gordon, *UH*, nos. 108, 109; I. Mendelsohn, *BASOR*, 85 (1942), 15 ff.
14 Albright, "A Prince of Taanach," *loc. cit.*, 22.
15 F. Thureau-Dangin, *RA*, 19 (1922), 97.
16 Cf. Wiseman, *Alalakh*, nos. 128–235; Gordon, *UH*, nos. 119, 329.
17 Wiseman, *Alalakh*, p. 9.
18 Nougayrol, *PRU*, III, pp. 226 f.
19 *Ibid.*, p. 159, no. 16 : 256; etc.
20 Cf. *ibid.*, pp. 230 f.; and so, too, *ḥofshī* in I Sam. 17 : 25.
21 Nougayrol, *PRU*, III, p.112, no. 15:114; p. 140, no. 16: 132; p. 107, no. 16:238; etc.
22 Cf. Wiseman, *Alalakh*, p. 11.
23 *Ibid.*, no. 15.
24 Nougayrol, *PRU*, III, p. 140, no. 16 : 132; Gordon, *UH*, no. 300; Ch. Virolleaud, "Un état de solde provenant d'Ugarit," in *Mémorial J. M. Lagrange*, Paris, 1940, pp. 39–41.
25 Albright, "A Prince of Taanach," *loc. cit.*, 24; B. Maisler (Mazar), "Luḥot Ta'anak," *Sefer Klausner* (Hebrew), Jerusalem 1937, pp. 53–4.

26 Gordon, *UH*, no. 113 : 60; *ARE*, III, no. 302; A. H. Gardiner, *Egyptian Hieratic Texts*, Part I: The Papyrus Anastasi I, Leipzig, 1911, p. 19, no. XV. For the interpretation of *nᵉʻarim* in II Sam. 2 : 14 ff. as "warriors," see Y. Sukenik (Yadin), "Let the Young Men, I Pray Thee, Arise and Play before Us," *JPOS*, 21 (1948), 110–16.
27 *ARE*, II, nos. 436, 585, 590.
28 *Ibid.*, no. 790; cf. B. Maisler (Mazar), "The Military Campaign of Amenhotep II in the Land of Canaan" (Hebrew), *Yerushalayim*, 4 (1953), 20.
29 Wiseman, *Alalakh*, nos. 129–78. Cf. I. Mendelsohn, "The Canaanite Term for 'Free Proletarian,'" *BASOR*, 83 (1941), 36–9; *idem*, "New Light on the Ḥupšu," *ibid.*, 139 (1955), 9–11. The Alalakh tablets use the term *ṣabē namē* "rural population, peasantry," which includes the *ḥupšu* class of tenant-farmers. The documents from the royal palace in Ugarit employ the term *namūtu* with the same connotation; cf. Nougayrol, *PRU*, III, p. 116, no. 16 : 148, verso 10.
30 See W. F. Albright, *JPOS*, 14 (1934), 131 note 162.
31 Knudtzon, *EA*, no. 125 : 27–30; see also nos. 85:11–5; 139:39 ff.
32 *Ibid.*, no. 118:36–9.
33 *Ibid.*, no. 112:10-2; see also no. 117:90.
34 *Ibid.*, no. 77 : 36–7.
35 Cf. R. De Langhe, *Les textes de Ras Shamra-Ugarit et leurs rapports avec le millieu biblique de l'Ancien Testament*, II, Gembloux, 1945, pp. 378–99.
36 See I. Mendelsohn, "Guilds in Ancient Palestine," *BASOR*, (1940), 17–21.
37 *Idem, Slavery in the Ancient Near East*, New York, 1949, pp. 106–17.
38 Wiseman, *Alalakh*, nos. 230–4; I. Mendelsohn, "On Slavery in Alalakh," *IEJ*, 5 (1955), 65–72.
39 Cf. *ARE*, II, nos. 436, 447, 462, 480, 482, 518.
40 Cf. Ch. Kuentz, *Deux stèles d'Amenophis II*, Le Caire, 1925; and see Maisler

(Mazar), "The Military Campaign of Amenhotep II", *loc. cit.*

41 Knudtzon, *EA*, no. 288 : 20; see also nos. 301, 309.

42 *Ibid.*, nos. 74:15–7; 85:10–5; and see no. 120:22 where the round number of male and female persons sold during a long period of time is given as 9,000.

43 Cf. *ARE*, II, nos. 434–6, 471, 482, 509, 790, etc.

44 Cf. Knudtzon, *EA*, nos. 126, 151, 254, 288, 301, 309, 313, 327, etc.

45 *ARE*, II, no. 462.

46 Cf. B. Maisler (Mazar), "Canaan and the Canaanites," *BASOR*, 102 (1946), 7–12.

47 Cf. N. Glueck, "Copper and Iron Mines in Ancient Edom," in *Trade, Industry and Crafts in Ancient Palestine* (Hebrew), ed. by S. Yeivin (Library of Palestinology, IX–X), Jerusalem, 1937, pp. 51–60.

48 Wiseman, *Alalakh*, nos. 227, 397, 425–31; Gordon, *UH*, nos. 114:8; 308:6, 8.

49 *ARE, II*, no. 435, etc.; Knudtzon, *EA*, no. 99 : 12–5.

50 Cf. A. G. Barrois, *Manuel d'archéologie biblique*, I, Paris, 1939, pp. 363–402.

51 *ARE*, II, nos. 471, 482, 490, 491.

52 Wiseman, *Alalakh*, no. 227.

53 Cf. I. Ben-Dor, "Trade Relations between Palestine and Egypt in the Canaanite Period," in *Trade, Industry and Crafts in Ancient Palestine*, pp. 31–50.

54 *ARE*, II, nos. 447, 462, 472, 473, 491, 509, 510.

55 Knudtzon, *EA*, no. 120 : 26.

56 Cf. W. F. Albright, "The Role of the Canaanites in the History of Civilization," in *Studies in the History of Culture* (Presented to Waldo G. Leland), ed. by P. W. Long, Menasha, Wis., 1942, p. 26; H. J. Kantor, "The Aegean and the Orient in the Second Millennium B.C.," *American Journal of Archaeology*, 51 (1947), 1–103.

57 Cf. Maisler (Mazar), "Canaan and the Canaanites," *loc. cit.*, 10.

58 Wiseman, *Alalakh*, nos. 18–31, 52–4.

59 Nougayrol, *PRU*, III, pp. 31 f.

60 Knudtzon, *EA*, nos. 113:14; 114:17–8; 126:4 ff.; Albright, "A Prince of Taanach," *loc. cit.*, 17.

61 Knudtzon, *EA*, nos. 67:10–1; 105 : 83–4; 117:12–7; 127:17–9; and see *ibid.*, p. 1216.

62 G. Dossin, *RA*, 31 (1934), 126 ff.; and see the translation by W. F. Albright, *ANET*, p. 487.

CHAPTER IV

CULTURAL AND RELIGIOUS LIFE

1 See C. H. Gordon, *Ugaritic Manual*, Rome, 1955. (Now revised as *Ugaritic Textbook*, Rome, 1967.)

2 Cf. J. Nougayrol, *PRU*, III, 1955. (See now also *PRU* IV, 1956; and *Ugaritica* V, Paris, 1968, by Nougayrol *et alii*.)

3 For the bibliography, see M. S. Ruipérez, "Les études sur le linéaire B depuis le déchiffrement de Ventris," *Minos*, 3 (1955), 157–67. (Note also M. Ventris and J. Ghadwick, Documents in Mycenaean Greek, Cambridge, 1956.)

4 Gordon, *op. cit.*, p. 244, no. 296a.

5 See the monograph on this text by J. Gray, *The Krt Text in the Literature of Ras Shamra*, Leiden, 1955. (The latest complete translation of Ugaritic literature is C. H. Gordon, *Ugarit and Minoan Crete*, New York, 1966; paperback ed., 1967.)

6 See C. H. Gordon, "Biblical Customs and the Nuzi Tablets," *BAr*, 3 (1940), 1–12. Additional material may be found in *idem, Introduction to the Old Testament Times*, Ventnor (N. J.), 1953, pp. 100-19. The latter has been revised under the title *The Ancient Near East*, New York, 1965.

7 For the repertoire of Egyptian stories, see G. Lefebvre, *Romans et contes égyptiens de l'époque pharaonique*, Paris, 1949.

8 See the bibliography in C. H. Gordon, "Homer and the Bible: the Origin and Character of East Mediterranean Literature," *HUCA*, 26 (1955), 43–108; and in L. A. Stella, *Il Poema di Ulisse*, Florence, 1955.

9 Since this article was written it has become clear that the Minoan language of Crete was Northwest Semitic, closely related to Hebrew, Phoenician and Ugaritic. The Philistines worshipped a Semitic god, Dagon. Their personal and place names are largely Semitic. They never needed interpreters to communicate with the Hebrews. It appears that they came from the Aegean to Palestine speaking Canaanite dialects akin to Hebrew. See C. H. Gordon, *Evidence for the Minoan Language*, Ventnor, N. J., 1966; and *Forgotten Scripts*, New York, 1968, pp. 147–161.

10 See *Antiquity*, 29 (1955), 148–9, and pl. VII.

11 Cf. D. Barthélemy and J. T. Milik, *Qumran Cave* I, Oxford, 1955, pp. 121 f.

12 It is absent from the older codes of Babylonia down through Hammurabi's; but it occurs in the Nuzi tablets, the Middle Assyrian laws, the Hittite code, and in Hebrew Law, all in areas and periods of Indo-European influence.

13 C. H. Gordon, "Sabbatical Cycle or Seasonal Pattern," *Orientalia* (n.s.), 22 (1953), 79–81.

14 *Idem, UM*, p. 269, no. 766.

15 For the evidence, see *idem*, "The Patriarchal Age," *Journal of Bible and Religion*, 21 (1953), 238–43.

16 El of Ugarit is of importance in this connection. See, on this topic, M. H. Pope, *El in the Ugaritic Texts*, Leiden, 1955. See also the original and stimulating studies on the Ugaritic pantheon by J. Aistleitner, "Götterzeugung in Ugarit und Dilmun," *Acta Orientalia Hungarica*, 3 (1953), 285–312; *idem*, "Ein Opfertext aus Ugarit," *ibid.*, 4 (1954), 259–70; *idem*, "Ein Opfertext aus Ugarit mit Exkurs über kosmologische Beziehungen der ugaritischen Mythologie," *ibid.*, 5 (1955), 1–23.

17 See the stone relief from the reign of Tukulti-Ninurta I (ca. 1243–1207) reproduced by W. von Soden, *Herrscher im Alten Orient*, Berlin-Göttingen-Heidelberg, 1954, p. 73.

CHAPTER V

THE EXODUS FROM EGYPT AND THE CONQUEST
OF PALESTINE

1 As it would appear from the Ugaritic and the Arabic; see W. F. Albright, BASOR, 62 (1936) 30.

2 See below, in the chapter "The Religious Culture of the People of Israel in its Beginnings: Faith and Worship." On Moses' character and work, see, *inter alia*, H. Gressmann, *Moses und seine Zeit*, Göttingen, 1913; J. Martin, *Moise, homme de Dieu*, Paris, 1952; H. Cazelles and A. Gellin, *Moses in Schrift und Überlieferung*, Düsseldorf, 1963, pp. 11 f.; R. Smend, *Das Mosesbild* etc. Tübingen, 1959; Y. Kaufmann, *A History of the Israelite Faith*, (Hebrew), IV, 33 ff.; 334 ff. On the tradition of the exodus from Egypt, see S. Loewenstamm, *Masoret Yᵉṣiʾat Miṣrayim Bᵉhishtalshᵉluta* (Hebrew), Jerusalem, 1965, and the detailed bibliography given there.

3 On the battalion as a 600 men military unit, see A. Malamat, *Encyclopaedia Biblica* (Hebrew), II cols. 432 ff. Cf. now *idem*, *Biblica*, 51 (1970), 9 f. Various suggestions have been advanced to explain the number 600,000, such as that of W. M. F. Petrie, *Egypt and Israel*, London, 1911, pp. 42 ff. that *elef* simply means "father's house" (also see G. E. Mendenhall, JBL, 77 [1958], 52 ff.), or that of W. F. Albright, *JPOS*, 5 (1925), 20 ff., that the figure reflects the position at King David's time.

4 See A. Gardiner, *JEA*, 19 (1933), 127.

5 See *idem, ibid.*, 6 (1920), 109.

6 *ANET*, p. 259.

7 See G. Posener, *Syria* 14 (1937), 185; *idem, apud* J. Bottéro, *Le problème de Habiru* Paris, 1954, pp. 166 ff.; Alt, *Kleine Schriften*, III, pp. 80 ff.

8 On Per Ramses and the problems connected with it, see in particular A. H. Gardiner, *Ancient Egyptian Onomastica*, II, Oxford, 1947, pp. 171 ff.; B. Couroyer, *RB*, 60 (1953), 111 ff.; Alt, *Kleine Schriften*, III, pp. 176 ff.; D. B. Redford *VT*, 13 (1963) 401 ff.

9 On the problem of the exodus from Egypt and the determination of its date see,

inter alia, W. F. Albright, *From the Stone Age to Christianity*, Baltimore, 1940, pp. 190 ff., H. H. Rowley, *From Joseph to Joshua*, London, 1950, pp. 24 ff., T. J. Meek, *Hebrew Origins*, New York, 1950, pp. 28 ff.; R. de Vaux, *RB*, 58 (1951) 278 ff.; H. H. Rowley, *Orientalia Suecana*, 4 (1955), 77 ff.; S. Lowenstamm, "The Exodus from Egypt" *Encyclopaedia Biblica* (Hebrew), III, cols. 754 ff.; H. Lubsczyc, *Der Auszug aus Ägypten*, Leipzig, 1963.

10 See W. F. Albright, *BASOR*, 99 (1945), 9 ff. On the Four Hundred Year Stele, see the chapter "The Chronology of the Ancient East in the Second Millennium" section 11a in the volume *The Patriarchs*. Among the various published articles on this stele, that by P. Montet, *Kemi*, 4 (1933) 191 ff., deserves particular mention.

11 Recently Albright suggested (*BASOR*, 163 [1962] 50 f.) that the concept "generation" in Genesis 15:16 — "And they shall return here in the fourth generation" — should be interpreted as parallel to the four hundred years mentioned in verse 13, meaning a complete cycle in the life of man; see also H. M. Y. Gevaryahu, *Beit Miqra*, 7, 3 (1962) 87 ff.

12 See J. Sturm, *Der Hethiterkrieg Ramses II*, Vienna, 1939, as well as the detailed survey of W. Helck, *Die Beziehungen Ägyptens zu Vorderasien* etc., Wiesbaden, 1962, pp. 204 ff.

13 See B. Mazar, *Encyclopaedia Biblica* (Hebrew), I cols. 694 f.

14 See M. Diman (Haran), *Yediot*, 13 (1947) 17 ff.

15 See K. A. Kitchen, *JEA*, 50 (1964), 47 ff.; B. Grdseloff, *Revue de l'histoire juive en Egypte*, 1 (1947), 69 ff. The Egyptian sources from the time of Ramses II testify to heavy wars in the lands of the Shasu, including Mount Seir, and to the destruction of settlements in these areas. From the inscription of Ramses II, which was discovered in the temple at Luxor and was published by Kitchen, we learn that the Egyptians conquered a series of fortified

cities, including Batora in the land of Moab (apparently the later Rabbath-batora) and probably Dibon, both of them on the main highway. A separate problem arises in connection with the stele from Khirbet Balu'a in Transjordan, which is apparently from the 13th century B.C.E. The inscription on the stele has not been deciphered yet and according to one of the doubtful conjectures it is Egyptian; see W. A. Ward and M. F. Martin, *Annual of the Department of Antiquities of Jordan*, 8–9 (1964) 5 ff.

16 For details see: N. Glueck "Exploration in Eastern Palestine," *AASOR*, 14–15 (1933–35), 18–19 (1937–39), 25–28 (1945–49), *passim*.

17 See S. Loewenstamm, "Reed Sea", *Encyclopaedia Biblica* (Hebrew) III, cols. 695 ff., where a detailed bibliography is given. As for the suggested identification with Jebel Hilāl, see C. S. Jarvis, *PEQ*, 1938, 25 ff.; J. Gray, *VT*, 4 (1954), 148 ff. Further arguments for locating the site of Mount Sinai in the southern part of the Sinai Peninsula are presented by Y. Aharoni, *The Land of the Bible*, (Hebrew) Jerusalem, 1963, pp. 170 ff. (= *The Land of the Bible, A Historical Geography*, Westminster Press (Philadelphia), 1967.) see also B. Mazar, *Historical Atlas of the People of Israel, Biblical Times*, Tel Aviv, 1957, map 2.

18 See Gardiner, *op. cit.*, II, p. 201.

19 See Gardiner, *JEA*, 6 (1920), 99 ff.

20 See O. Eissfeldt, *Baal Zaphon . . .* Halle a/S, 1932; W. F. Albright, in *Festschrift Bertholet*, Tübingen, 1950, pp. 1 ff.

21 See B. Mazar, "Book of Numbers" *Encyclopaedia Biblica* (Hebrew), II, cols. 144 f.; cf. H. Cazelles, *RB*, 62 (1955), 321 ff.

22 Concerning all the problems connected with the families of Jethro, Reuel the Midianite and Hobab the Kenite, see J. Liver, "Midian" *Encyclopaedia Biblica* (Hebrew) IV, cols. 686 ff (and the bibliography included); S. Abramsky, *Eretz Israel* (Hebrew) III (1954) 188 ff.; B. Mazar, *Eretz Israel* VII (1964), 1 ff.; W. F. Albright, *CBQ*, 25 (1963), 1 ff.; Cazelles, *Moses*, pp. 18 ff.

23 On the Cushite woman, no doubt the daughter of a family which originated in Cush-Cushan (cf. Habakkuk 3:7) — a group of nomadic tribes who assimilated with Midian — see *Eretz Israel*, III, 20.

24 On Kadesh-barnea, see M. Dotan, in *Elath* (Hebrew), Jerusalem, 1963, pp. 100 ff.; on the halt at Kadesh, see E. Meyer, *Die Israeliten und Ihre Nachbarstämme*, Halle a/s, 1906, p. 72; Rowley, *From Joseph to Joshua*, pp. 106, ff.

25 It transpires that the tradition according to which the Israelites smote the king of Arad at Hormah (Num. 21:3) was influenced by the story of the conquest of the South of Arad by the sons of Judah and Simeon (Jud. 1:17). On Hormah, which apparently was the capital of the kingdom of Arad, see Mazar, *Eretz Israel*, VII, 2.

26 See Mazar, "Book of Numbers", *Encyclopaedia Biblica* (Hebrew), II.

27 The theory that the sons of Joseph preceded the rest of the tribes in the exodus from Egypt (and not from Kadesh) has been put forward by various scholars; see *inter alia*, W. F. Albright, *BASOR*, 58 (1935) 16 ff.; 74 (1939), 21 f.; T. J. Meek, *Hebrew Origins*, pp. 28 ff.; S. Mowinckel, *BZAW*, 77 (1958), 129 ff.

28 On Jaazer, see M. Noth, *ZDPV*, 75 (1959), 52 ff.

29 This emerges in the light of the excavations at Tell Deir'Ālla, apparently the site of Succoth, and at Tell Sa'idiyeh the site of Zaphon. Both of these Canaanite cities were destroyed in the 12th century B.C.E., apparently at the beginning of the century. On the excavations at Tell Deir 'Ālla see H. J. Franken, *VT*, 11 (1961), 361 ff.; 14 (1964), 377 ff.; 15 (1965), 150 ff., where the enigmatic inscriptions discovered in the temple area are also discussed.

30 See the detailed discussion in A. Bergman (Biram), *JPOS*, 16 (1936), 244 ff.; N. Glueck, *AASOR*, 18–19, 25–28, *passim*; R. de Vaux, *Vivre et Penser*, 1 (1941), 16 ff.

31 Of the literature on the conquest of Canaan, see in particular; H. H. Rowley, *From Joseph to Joshua*; Alt, *Kleine Schriften*, I, pp. 89 ff.: 176 ff.; G. E. Mendenhall; *BAr*, 25 (1962), 66 ff.; B. Maisler, (Mazar), *Toledot Eretz Isra'el* (Hebrew), Jerusalem, 1938, 280 ff.; S. Yeivin, "The Conquest" *Encyclopaedia Biblica* (Hebrew), IV, cols.

79 ff.; Y. Kaufmann's commentaries on the Books of Joshua and Judges; and E. Jenni, "Zwei Jahrzehnte Forschung an den Büchern Josua bis Könige," *Theologische Rundschau* (NF), 27 (1961), 07 ff.

32 *ANET*, p. 378, and see below.

33 See W. F. Albright, *BASOR*, 125 (1952), 24 ff.; S. Yeivin in *Biq'at Beth-shean* (Hebrew) (anthology), Jerusalem, 1962, 21 ff.

34 *ANET*, pp. 476 ff.; also see Y. Aharoni, *The Settlement of the Israelite Tribes in Upper Galilee*, Jerusalem, 1957, pp. 120 ff.

35 See W. F. Albright, *JAOS*, 74 (1954) 222 ff.; A. Gardiner, *Ancient Egyptian Onomastica*, I, pp. 191 ff.

36 See the report of Y. Yadin *et alii*, *Hazor* (Hebrew), I, Jerusalem, 1958; II, 1959; and also F. Maass, *BZAW*, 77 (1958) 158 ff.

37 See Aharoni, *op. cit.*, pp. 17 ff.

38 See B. Maisler (Mazar), *HUCA*, 24 (1952/53), 80 ff.

39 See the latest surveys in *BASOR*, beginning with issue 55 (1934) and more recently in issue 164 (1962).

40 See J. Marquet-Krause, *Les fouilles de 'Ay*, (*Et-Tell*), 1933–35, Paris, 1949; and the recently published work of J. A. Callaway, *BASOR*, 178 (1965), 13 ff.

41 See K. M. Kenyon, *PEQ*, 83 (1951), 101; 92 (1960), 88 ff.; also N. Avigad, "Jericho" *Encyclopaedia Biblica* (Hebrew), III, cols. 839 ff. It is quite possible that the buildings, attributed to the Late Bronze Periods I and II, on the hillock west of the spring (the "Middle Building" by J. Garstang, *Annals of Archeology and Anthropology*, 21 [1934] pl. XIII–XIV) and the remains north of this building are remnants of the city's stronghold dating from the 14th and the first half of the 13th century B.C.E.

42 See in particular Alt, *Kleine Schriften*, I, pp. 176 ff.; Noth, *Josua* (2nd edition) Tübingen, 1953, *passim*.

43 The latter hypothesis is that of Y. Yadin. Also see note 41, above.

44 See, *inter alia*, W. F. Albright, *BASOR*, 58 (1935), 15; Rowley, *op. cit.*, pp. 19 f.; M. Noth, *PJB*, 31 (1935), 7 ff.; J. M. Grintz, *Biblica*, 42 (1961), 201 ff.

45 See J. B. Pritchard, *Gibeon, Where the Sun Stood Still*, Princeton, 1962; *idem*, *The Bronze Age Cemetery at Gibeon*, Philadelphia, 1963.

46 See in particular, Albright, *AASOR*, 17 (1932); 21–22 (1941–43), *passim*; *BASOR*, 74 (1939) 20 ff.

47 See O. Tufnel and others, *Lachish*, II, London, 1940; *Lachish* III, 1953, pp. 51 f.; *Lachish*, IV, 1958, *passim*. Among the finds within the area of the citadel which can be attributed to the times of Ramses III are sherds (including those of Late Mycenaean III C type), a scarab of Ramses III, and a bowl with a hieratic inscription from the fourth regnal year apparently of Ramses III and not that of Mer-ne-Ptah (Albright). In addition to two anthropoid coffins of mercenaries from among the Sea-Peoples, these graves contained utensils typical of the beginning of the Bronze Period.

48 These sources allude not only to wars with the Midianites (Joshua 13:21: "The chiefs of Midian . . . the princes of Sihon, that dwelt in the land"), but also to the plague that broke out in the camp, which the author ties to the fact that the children of Israel had attached themselves to Baal-peor.

49 It is instructive that Joshua rebuilt Timnath-serah north of Beth-horon (Khirbet Tibneh near 'Abud), and that on the border of his inheritance in this place in the hill-country of Ephraim they showed his grave (Josh. 19:49–50; 24:30; Jud. 2:9). This tradition is tied up with the data in the genealogical lists of Asher, one of whose sons was Beriah and who had a daughter Sheerah, and of the Ephraimite family Beriah, whose daughter Sheerah, built Beth-horon and Uzzen-sherah (I Chron. 7:23–28; and see also the later source I Chron. 8:13 on the relationship of the children of Aijalon to the Benjaminite families of Shema and Beriah). It emerges that the widespread family of Beriah, which belonged to Ephraim and had absorbed Asherite families, spread out from the Birzaith area north of Beth-el (I Chron. 7:31) to Beth-horon and Aijalon and bordered on Timnath-serah. Not for nothing did the author of I Chronicles 7:23 ff. link the genealogical list of Joshua, son of Nun with Beriah, son of Ephraim.

[50] Gilgal, east of Jericho, was the main camp of Joshua son of Nun, on the west of Jordan, and during the period of the Settlement and the Kingdom it was regarded as a place of assembly and worship for the families of Benjamin and Ephraim, i.e. the House of Joseph. And see the recently published K. D. Schunck, *Benjamin*, Berlin, 1963, pp. 39 ff.

[51] Concerning this problem, see Alt, *Kleine Schriften*, I, pp. 176 ff. and Schunck *op. cit.*, pp. 28 ff.; and on the Gibeonites, see M. M. Haran in *Yᵉhuda vᵉ Yᵉrushalayim* (Hebrew), 1957, 77 ff.

[52] Some scholars maintain that the words of Joshua to the children of Joseph — "If thou be a great people, get thee up to the forest, and cut down for thyself there in the land of the Perizzites and of the Rephaim; since the hill-country of Ephraim is too narrow for thee" (Josh. 17:15) — refer to the settlement of the children of Joseph in Gilead; see C. F. Burney, *Israel's Settlement in Canaan*, London, 1919, pp. 20 ff.; M. Noth, in his commentary on the Book of Joshua considers that in the dialogue between Joshua and the children of Joseph two sources have been joined, one of them referring to the mountains of Ephraim and the other to Gilead.

[53] Surveys recently conducted in central Sharon have shown that settlements of semi-nomads were established there at the beginning of the Iron Age. In that connection, mention should be made of the list of Canaanite kings in Joshua 12:7–24, which presumably summarizes the names of the royal cities that were conquered (see Aharoni, *The Land of Israel in Biblical Times* [Hebrew], pp. 195 ff.). Actually, it specifies the names of the cities which the author found in stories of the Conquest and the wars in Canaan, including some not known to us from the Books of Joshua and Judges, such as Aphek of Sharon (according to the Septuagint version) and Hepher (cf. I Kings 4:10).

[54] See Aharoni, *The Settlement* etc., pp. 69 ff.

[55] See W. F. Albright, *BASOR*, 125 (1952), 24 ff.

[56] See S. Yeivin, "Judah", *Encyclopaedia Biblica* (Hebrew), III cols. 489 ff.

[57] On Bezek, see P. Welten, *ZDPV*, 81 (1965), 138 ff.

[58] On the problems concerning Jerusalem, see B. Maisler (Mazar), *AJSL*, 49 (1932), 248 ff., and J. Liver, "Jebus, Jebusites" *Encyclopaedia Biblica* (Hebrew), III cols. 447 f.

[59] See B. Mazar, *Encyclopaedia Biblica* (Hebrew), I cols. 694 ff., and on the problem in general, Rowley, *op. cit.*, p. 4 ff., and G. E. Wright, *JNES* 5 (1946), 105 ff., who is sceptical about the historical value of the description in Judges 1.

[60] See B. Mazar, *Eretz Israel*, VII (1964), 1ff.

[61] See Y. Kaufmann, *The Book of Judges* (Hebrew), Jerusalem, 1962, pp. 3 ff., pp. 61 ff.; J. Liver, "Caleb" *Encyclopaedia Biblica* (Hebrew), IV, pp. 106 ff.

[62] See the theory of A. Malamat, *JNES*, 13 (1954), 231 ff.

[63] See S. Yeivin, "Judah" *Encyclopaedia Biblica* (Hebrew).

[64] See note 58, above.

[65] See the summation of Aharoni, *The Land of the Bible*, p. 209.

[66] See Alt, *Kleine Schriften*, I, pp. 261 ff., and B. Mazar, *ibid.*, 4, and the chapter, "The Philistines and their Wars with Israel" in the volume.

[67] The theory that the battle of Deborah preceded that of the waters of Merom has been proposed by B. Mazar, *Yediot*, 11 (1945), 35; *HUCA*, 24 (1952–53), 80 ff.; and following him, by Aharoni, *ibid.*, 188 ff. Various theories have been put forward by: A. Malamat, in the chapter, "The Period of the Judges," in this volume; M. Engberg and W. F. Albright, *BASOR*, 78 (1940), 4 ff.; Alt, *op. cit.*, I pp. 256 ff.; S. Yeivin, in *Mélanges A. Robert*, Paris, 1957, p. 103.

CHAPTER VI

THE SETTLEMENT OF CANAAN

1 M. Zohari, *Encyclopaedia Biblica* I (Hebrew), Jerusalem, 1950, cols. 650 ff.; Map of the Flora, *ibid.*, cols. 651–652; *ibid.*, III, cols. 722 ff.

2 B. Grdseloff, *Une Stele Scythopolitaine du roi Sethos I*, le Caire, 1949; W. F. Albright, *BASOR*, 125 (1952), 24–32.

3 Albright (*ZAW*, 44 [1926], 231) suggested its identification with Kaukab el-Hawa which is the highest place in this area.

4 A. H. Gardiner, *Egyptian Hieratic Texts*, Series I, Part I: The Papyrus Anastasi I and the Papyrus Koller, together with the Parallel Texts, Leipzig, 1911.

5 Cf. in particular "Amalekites dwell in the Negeb region; Hittites, Jebusites, and Amorites inhabit the hill country; and Canaanites dwell by the Sea and along the Jordan" (Num. 13:29); the Hittites and the Jebusites are specific ethnic elements, but the Amorites represent here a collective name for the autochtonous population of the mountains, as distinct from the Canaanite inhabitants of the plains. Cf. also Josh. 10:5; 11:3, *passim*.

6 Jerusalem and its allies (Josh. 10:5 ff.); Shechem (Gen. 48:22), the Gibeonite cities (II Sam. 21:2). Usually they are more precisely called Hivites (or Hurrians, according to the Septuagint, Josh. 9:7), but here the reference is general meaning the autochtonous inhabitants of the mountains — the Amorites.

7 E. Meyer, *Die Israeliten und ihre Nachbarstämme*, Halle a/S, 1906, p. 512. M. Noth, *Das Buch Josua*, (2nd ed.) Tübingen, 1953, p. 106, is of the opinion that two parallel sources were amalgamated here; the earlier one, which speaks of the forest covered hill-country of Ephraim was placed after the later tradition, which refers to the settlements in Transjordan.

8 This brand of agriculture is occasional and seasonal work, e.g. Gen. 26:12, which does not require a stay of more than a couple of months in the same locality.

9 E. Meyer, *op. cit.*, pp. 303 ff. It is worthwhile noting that Abraham served his visitors milk and not wine (Gen. 18:8), and so did Jael, the wife of Heber the Kenite, who still lived in a tent (Jud. 4:18–19; 5:24–25).

10 W. F. Albright, *The Archaeology of Palestine*, Harmondsworth, 1960, p. 110; H. H. Rowley, *From Joseph to Joshua*, London, p. 22.

11 A. Barrois, *Manuel d'archéologie biblique*, I, Paris, 1939, pp. 239–243; W. F. Albright, *From the Stone Age to Christianity*, Baltimore, 1940, p. 212; A. Alt, *Kleine Schriften*, I, pp. 140 ff., M. Noth, *Geschichte Israels*, (3rd. ed.), Göttingen, 1956, pp. 67 ff.

12 A. Alt, "Erwägungen über die Landnahme der Israeliten in Palästina" *PJB*, 35 (1939) 24 ff.; *idem*, *Kleine Schriften*, p. 140; M. Noth, *op. cit.*, pp. 67 ff.

13 A comparison of Ammon and Moab's borders with Palestine's Map of the Flora (see note 1 above) shows that these nations lived mainly outside the afforested areas, which might be one of the reasons for their rapid settlement and consolidation.

14 In the Masoretic text "Manasseh" is written with a suspended *nun*, which leaves no doubt of the original reading "Moses," as it was preserved in the Septuagint manuscripts, in the Vulgate and also by the Talmud scholars (Baba Bathra 109:2), cf. C. F. Burney, *The Book of Judges*, 1920, pp. 434 ff.

15 His designation of a young man does not refer to his age, but to his function or status (cf. W. F. Albright, *JBL*, 51 [1932], 82 ff.), but neither does it hint to his being on old man.

16 Hence the widely held view that the Danite migration was connected with the Philistine expansion, cf. H. H. Rowley's bibliography, *op. cit.*, p. 84 note 2. Some scholars even read "Philistines" for "Amorites" in Jud. 1:34, cf. F. Schmidtke, *Die Einwanderung Israels in Kanaan*, Breslau, 1933, p. 181. According to Noth (*op. cit.*, p. 67, note 1) "Amorites" is used here in a wider sense, and the reference is to the Philistines.

17 For a summary of the different views and the bibliography cf. H. H. Rowley, *op. cit.*, pp. 81 ff. The view that this still refers to southern Dan is less probable. It is not likely that the Danites became a seafaring tribe immediately after settling there, since it is doubtful whether they even reached the seaboard. In this instance one cannot rely on the city list which apparently belongs to the period of the monarchy, cf. Y. Aharoni, *The Land of the Bible* London, 1967, pp. 265 ff.

18 Noth, *op. cit.*, p. 68 ff.

19 Y. Kutscher, *Tarbiz* 11 (1940) 17 ff.

20 "And Malchiel, who was the father of Birzaith" (I Chron. 7:31); as usual, the designation "father of" denotes the domicile of the family.

21 The name of the family of Serah might be connected with Timnath-serah in the hill-country of Ephraim, Joshua's city (Josh. 19:50; 24:30), though in Jud. 2:9 the place is called Timnath-heres.

22 S. Yeivin, *Encyclopaedia Biblica* I, col. 779.

23 As mentioned, Beriah also occurs among the families of Asher.

24 Y. Aharoni, "The Northern Boundary of Judah" *PEQ*, 90 (1958), 27 ff. At the south the border of Canaan is the primary source which is utilized for the description of Judah. The actual Judean border point was Mount Halak (Josh. 11:17; 12:7) c. 40 km. south-east of Beer-sheba, cf. Aharoni, *op. cit.*, pp. 70, 215 ff.

25 Y. Aharoni, *IEJ*, 8 (1958), 26 ff.

26 It is worth noting that in the end the same action was attributed to all Israel under Joshua's leadership (Josh. 10:36–37).

27 In later days this conquest was also attributed to all Israel under Joshua's leadership (Josh. 10:38–39).

28 The name Wadi el-Qinī, south-east of Arad has been preserved to the present day, and also Kain (Zanoah-ha-Kain according to the Septuagint, Josh. 15:56–7) north of Arad is perhaps called after them.

29 Shishak's list mentions the "Haggarim of Arad Rabbath and of Arad of the house of Jeruham." J. Simons, *Handbook for the Study of Egyptian Topographical Lists relating the Western Asia*, Leiden, 1937, p. 185, notes

107–112; M. Noth. *ZDPV*, 61 (1938) 277 ff. B. Maisler (Mazar) in *Epstein Volume*, (Hebrew), Jerusalem, 1950, pp. 316 ff.

30 Jud. 1:17; the list of Simeon's cities is preserved in Josh. 19:1 ff.; I Chron. 4:28 ff,

31 S. Klein, *Eretz Yehuda* (Hebrew), Tel-Aviv, 1939, p. 140; B. Maisler (Mazar), "Kiriath-arba – is Hebron," in *Dinaburg Volume*, (Hebrew), Jerusalem 1949, p. 322 note 13.

32 B. Maisler (Mazar), *ibid.*, p. 323, note 14.

33 Ginsberg–Maisler, *JPOS* 14 (1934), 262 ff.

34 S. Abramski, "The Kenites," *Eretz Israel*, 3 (1954), 116 ff.

35 "These are the sons of Rechah;" must doubtlessly be read Rekab as in the Septuagint (I Chron. 4:12). Cf. also S. Talmon, *IEJ*, 10 (1960), 174–180.

36 Cf. *Biblia Hebraica*, (5th ed.) Stuttgart, 1949, p. 365.

37 E. Meyer, *op. cit.*, pp. 433 ff.

38 For the identification of Tamar with 'Ain Ḥuṣb, cf. Y. Aharoni, *IEJ*, 13, (1963), 30 ff.

39 For this road, which the Bible calls "The way of (the wilderness of) Edom", see Y. Aharoni, *IEJ*, 8 (1958), 35.

40 On the strength of this fact S. Klein suggests to identify the place with Beth-ashbea, cf. *Studies of the Genealogical Chapters in Chronicles*, (Hebrew) Jerusalem, 1930, 29–31.

41 In the Septuagint the original reading of this name is doubtless Kiriath-sopher, for Josh. 15:15–16; Jud. 1:11–12.

42 O. R. Sellers, *The Citadel of Beth-Zur*, Philadelphia, 1933; *idem*, *BA* 21 (1958), 71 ff.; O. R. Sellers *et al.*, *AASOR* 38, 1968.

43 However, it has been argued recently that the reference is rather to Beth-horon, cf. Z. Kallai and H. Tadmor, *EI* 9 (1969), 138 ff.

44 Neither is Keilah, 5 km south of Adullam, mentioned in the accounts of the Conquest, though it was known as a Canaanite town from the Tell Amarna Letters. It is interesting that we have no information either of the conquest of Jarmouth on the road from Adullam to

Timnah, in spite of its being mentioned among Jerusalem's allies, in the beginning.

45   This is apparently how it must be read instead of Lecah.

46   H. H. Rowley, *From Joseph to Joshua* 4; 101 ff.; and *ibid.* the bibliography. There is also the view that in the beginning the "Judean Mountains" was the name of a region, like Mount Gilead, and perhaps the hill-country of Ephraim (cf. H. H. Rowley, *ibid.* note 5). However, even if this view were correct, it does not follow that Judah was originally an autochthonous Canaanite tribe, but that the name of the region stuck to the settling tribe as in the case of the Gileadites in Gilead.

Recent excavations at Hebron are in very preliminary stages, cf. Ph. Hammond, *BA*, 28, (1965), p. 28 f.

47   This might also account for the tradition that Benjamin was born in Canaan. The Mari documents speak of a strong tribal league by the name of Benjamin existing in the 18th century in the Euphrates region next to a tribal league called Banu Sim'al, i.e. Children of the North. One cannot infer connections of origin on the strength of the clearly geographical meaning of this name, in spite of the warlike characteristics shared by the tribes of Benjamin in Mari and in Canaan, cf. bibliography: H. H. Rowley, *op. cit.*, p. 115 note 4.

48   A man of Ephraim was called an Ephratite.

49   According to one view there was here a place called Ephraim, an assumption based in particular on II Sam. 13:23; and cf. W. F. Albright *JPOS*, 3 (1923), 36 ff.; *idem.*, *AASOR*, 4 (1924), 127 ff.; A. Alt, *PJB*, 24 (1928), 35 ff.; M. Noth, *Geschichte Israels* (8th ed.) p. 60. But this lacks sufficient basis.

50   The only military informations which deal with this area refer to the southern tribes (Gen. 34; Jud. 1:4 ff.) but they are not connected with the settlement of the House of Joseph.

51   A. Alt, *BWAT*, 13 (1913), 1 ff., *idem*, *PJB*, 21 (1925), 100 ff., F. M. Abel, *Géographie de la Palestine*, II, Paris, 1938, pp. 79 ff. These conclusions still hold good in spite of various recent attempts to reject

them, cf. Z. Kallai, *The Tribes of Israel*, Jerusalem, 1967, pp. 43 ff.; G. E. Wright, *EI*, 8 (1967) 61* ff.

52   Aphek, at the southern limit of the Sharon, is mentioned as the place where the Philistine army encamped (I Sam. 4:1; 29:1); in Dor, at the northern limit of the Sharon, lived the Tjeker, one of the Sea-Peoples according to Wen-Amon, cf. *ANET*, p. 26.

53   Cf. K. Ohata, M. Kodiavi, *et al.*, *Tel Zeror* 1–11, Tokyo, 1966–7.

54   Manasseh's northern border line is missing altogether, but since Issachar is not included in the border descriptions, Naphtali's southern border north of the plain must be identical with the northern border of Manasseh.

55   Noth's assumption (*Das Buch Josua*, [2nd ed.], pp. 102 ff.) that the appearance of Machir in the description of Manasseh's western inheritance in Josh. 17:1 proves that also the original description of the tribal lots recognized Machir here, is unnecessary. With the migration of a good part of Machir to Transjordan he became "the father of Gilead," and the remaining clans became "the rest of Manasseh."

56   Just like the reference to Simeon's towns in the midst of the tribal inheritance of the children of Judah (Josh. 19:1, 9).

57   W. F. Albright, *BASOR*, 29 (1928), 9 ff.; 35 (1929), 5; 55 (1934), 23 ff.; 56 (1934), 2 ff.; 57 (1935), 27 ff.; 58 (1935), 13; 74 (1939), 17 ff.

58   H. Kjaer "The Excavation of Shiloh 1929," *JPOS*, 10 (1930), 87 ff.; *idem. Det Hellige Land*, Copenhagen, 1931. The material has now been published by Mrs. M. L. Buhl, *Shiloh*, Copenhagen, 1969; however her chronological conclusions are unreasonable. The date of the collar-rim jars is definitely not later than mid-twelfth century, as concluded by Kjaer, and her suggested comparison with Iron Age II jars from Hazor is erroneous.

59   Horite — according to the Septuagint, Josh. 9:7. Of the four Gibeonite cities, Gibeon itself was identified with el-Jib, Chephirah with Khirbet el-Kafira, and Baalah (Kiriath-jearim) with Deir el-'Azar (Abū Ghosh). The place of Beeroth has not

so-far been definitely identified, its identification with el-Bīra near Beth-el is not convincing.

60 W. F. Albright, *BASOR*, 52 (1933), 6 ff.; L. A. Sinclair, *AASOR*, 34–35 (1960), 16 ff.; W. F. Badé, C. C. MacCown, J. C. Vampler, *Excavations at Tell en-Nasbeh*, I–II, Berkely and New Haven, 1947. At this place were also found remains from the Early Bronze Period, but it was rebuilt at the beginning of the Iron Age, after an interval of more than a thousand years.

61 This does not refer to Gath of the Philistines, but to Gath-Gittaim west of Gezer, which was identified by B. Maisler (Mazar) with Ras Abu-Ḥamid: see B. Mazar, "Gath and Gittaim," *IEJ*, 4 (1954), 227 ff.

62 I. W. Lapp, *BASOR* 185 (1967), 2 ff.; *BA* 30 (1967), 1 ff. This makes it very probable that Megiddo's much debated Stratum VI was already Israelite. The destruction of Statum VII A is contemporary with the destruction of Taanach, and all the public buildings ceased to exist, like the temple, the palace and even the fortifications. It becomes clear that the discussed biblical sources predate c. 1125 B.C.E.

63 A. Saarisalo, *The Boundary between Issachar and Naphtali*, Helsinki, 1927, pp. 23 ff.; pp. 130 ff.

64 Which is the biblical Adami-nekeb, cf. A. Saarisalo, *op. cit.*, 31 ff.; Y. Aharoni, *The Settlement of the Israelite Tribes in Upper Galilee*, (Hebrew), Jerusalem, 1957, pp. 77 ff.

65 H. H. Rowley, *op. cit.*; and cf. J. Simons, *Handbook*, p. 198, in disagreement with Albright (W. F. Albright, *JAOS*, 74, [1954], 222 ff.). Even if Albright were right that there are several places of this name, it does not rule out the identification of Asher in the Egyptian sources, especially in the light of the reference to "the head [of the tribe] of Asher" in Papyrus Anastasi I.

66 To the correct reading Abdon (Josh. 21:30; I Chron. 6:74) and not Ebron (Josh. 19:28) testifies the identification of Khirbet 'Abda.

67 A. Alt, "Neues aus dem Archiv Amenophis IV," *PJB*, 20 (1924), 34 ff.

68 Some scholars consider the name "the hill-country of Naphtali" evidence that originally this was the name of a region which later became the name of a tribe, similar to Gilead and perhaps to the hill-country of Ephraim and the Mountains of Judah, but this lacks sufficient basis.

69 There are no data for establishing the exact border line between Naphtali and Asher. However, from the border point of Kabul (Josh. 19:27), in western Lower Galilee, it appears that Asher's inheritance was restricted to the western slopes of Galilee.

70 Y. Aharoni, *The Settlement*, etc., pp. 8 ff.

71 This type of pottery was discovered in Hazor in a layer following the Canaanite one, dating from between the 13th and the 10th cent. (Solomon). There are so far no data to permit a more precise dating but it seems that the Israelite settlements in Galilee were founded somewhat earlier than the settlement of Hazor, which took place only after the destruction of the Canaanite city. This rules out the view that originally Naphtali lived in the south together with Dan, K. Steuernagel, *Die Einwanderung der israelitischen Stämme in Kanaan*, Berlin, 1901, pp. 12 ff.; C. F. Burney, *Israel's Settlement in Canaan*, London, 1919, pp. 51 ff.

72 Y. Aharoni, *The Settlement*, etc., pp. 70 ff.

73 Num. 32:38 alludes perhaps to the similar process of the occupation of Heshbon and its cities by Reuben (cf. below).

74 One must reject the view that the reference here is to Dan's southern inheritance, since in its attempt to settle there, in the region of Zorah and Eshtaol, the tribe was a long way from the coast, and the borders of Dan's inheritance (Josh. 19:41 ff.) do not reflect this early reality. For the composition of the list of Dan's cities cf. F. M. Cross–G. E. Wright, *JBL*, 75 (1956), 210 ff.; B. Mazar, *IEJ*, 10 (1960), 70 ff.

75 In the Bible *'Eiver ha-Yarden* may mean also the western side of the Jordan, particularly in the period of the Settlement (cf. Num. 32:19; Deut. 3:20, 25; 11:30; Josh. 9: 1, etc.), but usually it refers to Transjordan.

76 Cf. in particular Glueck's comprehen-

sive survey: N. Glueck, "Explorations in Eastern Palestine" I–IV, *AASOR*, 14(1934); 15 (1935); 18/19 (1939); 25/28 (1951).

[77] Josh. 22:11; The region about the Jordan ("The regions of the Jordan") are the regions of the various tribal lots in the eastern Arabah, opposite the Land of Canaan, i.e., outside the Land of Canaan; as against this, the text in verse 10, which speaks of "the region about the Jordan, that is in the land of Canaan" is corrupt.

[78] The half tribe of Manasseh is an addition also here, like in most of the early chapters, as clearly seen from this verse.

[79] This event might be connected with an earlier attempt to set up a common amphictyonic center in this area, maybe in the town of Adam, according to the allusions in Ps. 78:57–60; and cf. also Ps. 68:19, cf. S. D. Goitein, *Yediot*, 13 (1947), 86–88.

[80] This is the accepted view, in contrast to A. Bergman, *JPOS*, 16 (1936), 233 ff.

[81] Tell edh-Dhahab el-Gharbiyeh. The two tells which we called Tulul edh-Dhahab and which rise up opposite each other on both sides of the Jabbok, were identified by different scholars as Mahanaim on the one hand and with Penuel on the other, from the assumption that the two tells belong to the same city. But in spite of their proximity, the Jabbok does divide them and therefore it appears that they supported two neighboring cities, the western one (north of the Jabbok)—Mahanaim, and the eastern one (south of the Jabbok) — Penuel. This assumption has now been fully confirmed by the discovery of both cities, next to each other, in Shishak's roster, cf. B. Mazar, *VTS*, 4 (1957), 60 ff.

[82] W. F. Albright, *BASOR*, 89 (1943), 7 ff.

[83] Cf. particularly in the Song of Deborah: "Gilead abode beyond the Jordan" (Jud. 5:17), also Jephthah the Gileadite who was connected with Mizpeh of Gilead (this Mizpeh is apparently Gad's Ramath-mizpeh, Josh. 13:26) and in the north (Jud. 12:7 according to the Septuagint Mss. — *Biblia Hebraica*, [5th ed.], p. 388), ευ Σεφε which is mentioned among the cities of Gad and its families. Solomon's twelfth district consisted of the land of Gilead according to the Masoretic text, and of the land of Gad according to the Septuagint (I Kings 4:19), and cf. Jud. 11:29, I Sam. 13:7.

[84] A. Bergman, *JAOS*, 54 (1934), 169 ff.

[85] The system of counting ancient tribes which had attached themselves as the sons of concubines is clearly illustrated in the genealogical table of the Aramean sons of Nahor (Gen. 22:24), Cf. E. Meyer, *Die Israeliten und ihre Nachbarstämme*, p. 241; B. Maisler (Mazar), "The Genealogy of the sons of Nahor and the Historical Framework of the Book of Job," *Zion*, 11 (1946), 8 ff.

[86] Noth and Alt try to see a continuation of the system of the boundaries of the tribes of western Palestine in the description of the tribal lots of Reuben–Gad, and since the towns mentioned here are the main cities situated among the mountains, they believe this to be the boundary line of their ancient area of settlement, and that the area extended only over the western slopes of the Transjordan hill-country, M. Noth, *ZDPV*, 58 (1953), 230 ff.; A. Alt, *PJB*, 35 (1939), 19 ff.; *idem*, *Kleine Schriften*, I, p. 20. However, this assumption lacks any basis, for there is actually no border system of the Transjordanian tribes (cf. below), instead there is a description of the regions which they occupied, and cf. N. Glueck, *AASOR* 18/19 (1939), 249 ff. Instead of the verbs usually employed in the description of the borders, there are general indications — from such and such a town — and these are the chief or outlying cities in various districts, e.g. "And from Heshbon unto Ramath-mizpeh and Betonim; and from Mahanaim unto the border of Debir" (Josh. 13:26). Actually Noth and Alt's far-reaching theory is based solely on this attempt of turning the enumeration of the mentioned districts into a regular border list.

[87] Perhaps the name Mount Gilead, like the appellation hill-country of Ephraim, originally involved a more restricted area, but extended with the expansion of the Israelite settlement in the northern parts of Transjordan, until, in the end, it designated sometimes the whole area of the

Israelite settlement in Transjordan, see R. de Vaux, *Vivre et penser* I, Paris, 1941, 16 ff.; M. Noth, *PJB*, 37 (1941), 51 ff.

88 E. Z. Malamat, "Benjamin and Gilead" *Tarbiz*, 5 (Hebrew), (1934), 121–125.

89 According to one view this is a reference to the family of Hezron the son of Reuben (I Chron. 5:3), cf. E. Meyer, *op. cit.*, p. 519. However, in the light of many instances of family relationships between western tribes and inhabitants of Gilead there is no reason to doubt the biblical tradition.

90 Though according to a number of passages the *Havoth-jair* were in Bashan (Deut. 3:14; Josh. 13:30), but since they were fortified cities and not farms, it is possible that the children of Jair expanded northwards at a later period. The localization of Havoth-jair in Gilead is proved from various passages (Jud. 10:4; I Kings 4:13; I Chron. 2:22–23). In Num. 32:41 one has to read *Hāvath-ham* instead of *Havotheihem* (A. Bergman, *JAOS*, 54 [1934], 176) the reference being to Ham in northern Gilead, which is already mentioned in Gen.

14:5. The burial place of Jair the Judge was Camon (Jud. 10:5) perhaps Kam, north-west of Ham.

91 B. Maisler (Mazar), *Tarbiz*, 15 (Hebrew), (1944), 63–64.

92 The reference is to the description of the borders, for most of the rosters of towns were established later and belong to the period of the monarchy.

93 En-dor is probably a dittography of Dor and it is missing in Judges 1.

94 Rehob was perhaps in Western Galilee, cf. Y. Aharoni, "The Settlement etc.," pp. 51–52.

95 Maisler (Mazar), *Untersuchungen*, 59 ff.; Noth, *Das Buch Josua*, (2nd. ed.) pp. 73 ff.

96 The first to evaluate these circumstances and their importance in the Settlement and the creation of the Israelite Monarchy was Alt, cf. Alt, *Landnahme der Israeliten in Palästina*, Leipzig, 1925; *idem*, *Kleine Schriften* I, pp. 89 ff.; 126 ff.; *idem*, "Erwägungen über die Landnahme der Israeliten in Palästina, *PJB*, 35 (1939), 8 ff.

CHAPTER VII

THE PERIOD OF THE JUDGES

[1] These question are discussed at great length in the numerous commentaries on the Book of Judges; see the general bibliography for this chapter, below, pp. 000; and cf. O. Eissfeldt, *The Old Testament, An Introduction*, Oxford, 1965, pp. 257 ff.; E. Sellin–G. Fohrer, *Einleitung in das Alte Testament* (11th edition), Heidelberg, 1969, pp. 223 ff. Cf. also E. Jenni, "Zwei Jahrzehnte Forschung an den Büchern Josua bis Könige," *Theologische Rundschau*, (NF), 27 (1961), 1 ff.; 97 ff.

[2] On this framework cf. the specific discussion by W. Beyerlin, "Gattung und Herkunft des Rahmens im Richterbuch," *Festschrift A. Weiser*, Göttingen, 1963, pp. 1 ff. The author diminishes the importance of the deuteronomic editing of the framework; and cf. in particular W. Richter, *Die Bearbeitungen des "Retterbuches" in der deuteronomischen Epoche*, Bonn, 1964. This author distinguishes between several strata in the deuteronomic recension, which in his view was preceded already by a comprehensive work dealing with the deliverer-judges and not by separate tribal accounts. On the contrasting pre-deuteronomic and deuteronomic views of this period, cf. also M. Weinfeld, "The Period of the Conquest and of the Judges as Seen by the Earlier and the Later Sources," *VT*, 17 (1967), 93 ff.

[3] On the double aspect of the nation's deliverance in the Book of Judges, which ascribes it on the one hand to divine providence, and on the other to human valor — concepts which exist side-by-side in biblical historiography — cf. I. L. Seeligman, "Menschliches Heldentum und göttliche Hilfe," *Theologische Zeitschrift*, 19 (1963), 385 ff.

[4] M. Weber, *Aufsätze zur Religionssoziologie*, III, Tübingen, 1923, pp. 47 f.; pp. 93 f.; *idem, Wirtschaft und Gesellschaft* (Grundriss der Sozialökonomik), (2nd edition), Tübingen, 1925, pp. 140 ff., pp. 753 ff. and cf. pp. 662 ff.; W. F. Albright, *From the Stone Age to Christianity* (2nd edition), New York, 1957, pp. 283 f. In recent years the previously neglected social aspect of the concept of "charisma" has been stressed (an aspect which is certainly of consequence for Israelite history); see, e.g., W. H. Friedland, "For a Sociological Concept of Charisma," *Social Forces*, 43 (1964), 18 ff.; E. Shils, "Charisma, Order and Status," *American Sociological Review*, 30 (1965), 199 ff.; cf. now also R. C. Tucker, "The Theory of Charismatic Leadership," *Daedalus*, Summer 1968 (= Proceedings Amer. Acad. Arts and Sciences 97, No. 3), 731. ff., who stresses Weber's maxim that charismatic leadership arises "in times of psychic, physical, economic, ethical, religious, political distress" (p. 742).

[5] Cf. A. Klostermann, *Der Pentateuch*, II, 1907, pp. 418 ff.; A. Alt, *Kleine Schriften*, I, pp. 300 ff.; M. Noth, "Das Amt des Richters Israel," *Festschrift A. Bertholet*, Tübingen, 1950, pp. 404 ff.; H. W. Herzberg, "Die Kleinen Richter," *Beiträge zur Traditionsgeschichte und Theologie des AT.*, Göttingen, 1962, pp. 118 ff. Smend tried to see in the major and minor judges the representatives of the two central institutions of that period, which in his view were the Holy War and the amphictyonic tribal league; R. Smend, *Jahwekrieg und Stämmebund* (2nd edition), Göttingen, 1966, pp. 33 ff.

[6] Thus O. Grether, "Die Bezeichung 'Richter' für die charismatischen Helden der vorstaatlichen Zeit," *ZAW*, 57 (1939), 110 ff.; M. Noth, "*Überlieferungsgeschichtliche Studien*, Halle a/S, 1943, pp. 43 ff.; Beyerlin, *op. cit.*, p. 7; and now also I. L. Seeligman, in *Hebräische Wortforschung* (*VT*, Suppl. 16), Leiden, 1967, pp. 273 ff. Cf. Kaufmann's justified criticism of these assumptions in his commentary to Judges, pp. 46 ff.; and cf. also H. C. Thomson, "Shophet and Mishpat in the Book of Judges," *Transactions of the Glasgow University Oriental Society*, 19 (1961/62), 74 ff.; J. Dus, "Die Sufeten Israels," *Archiv Orientalni*, 31 (1963), 444 ff. The military aspect of the judge has been stressed in

particular by K. D. Schunck, *VT, Suppl.*
15 (1966), 252 ff.

7 On the biblical *shōfēṭ* in the light of
Mari and other external evidence, see A.
Malamat, *Encyclopaedia Biblica*, 4, s. v.
Mari, cols. 576/7 (Hebrew); *idem*, in
*Biblical Essays, Die Oud Test. Werkg. Suid
Afrika*, (1966), 45; F. C. Fensham, "The
Judges and Ancient Israelite Jurisprud-
ence," *ibid.*, 1959, 15 ff.; A. van Selms,
"The Title Judge," *ibid.*, 41 ff.; W. Richter,
"Zu den 'Richtern' Israels," *ZAW*, 77
(1965), 40 ff.; H. Cazelles, *VT, Suppl.* 15
(1966), 108 f. And cf. below, the chapter
"The Manner of the King," in this volume.

8 Cf. Noth, *op. cit.*, pp. 90 f.; *idem, Amt und
Berufung im AT.*, Bonn, 1958, pp. 21 f.

9 Alt, *Kleine Schriften*, II, pp. 190 f.

10 Y. Kaufmann, *The Book of Judges*,
Jerusalem, 1962, p. 48, (Hebrew); Kittel,
GVI, II (6/7th edition), p. 25.

11 See A. Malamat, "The Danite Migration and the Pan-Israelite Exodus-Conquest," *Biblica*, 41 (1970), 1 ff., and there
p. 14 note 1 on the dating of the conquest of
Laish.

12 Cf. Kittel, *op. cit.*, 19 f. (XI: "Unmög-
lichkeit einer zusammenhängenden Dar-
stellung").

13 Cf. Y. Yadin, *The Art of Warfare in
Biblical Lands*, Ramat Gan, 1963, pp. 261 f.
For the possibility of reading Tirzah
instead of Thebez see below, note 61.

14 See N. H. Tur-Sinai, *Lashon wa-Sefer*
(Hebrew), 2, Jerusalem, 1951, pp. 324 ff.

15 Various attempts have been made to
explain the name. The Sages interpreted
Bedan as *ben-Dan* [the son of Dan] i.e.,
Samson (Bab. Tal., Rosh Hashanah, 25a);
others identified him with the judge
'Abdon (omitting the initial 'ayin), or with
Barak (Septuagint); and cf. the commentaries. All these suggestions are unsatisfactory however; the reference is probably to a judge unknown from any other
source. Perhaps he is to be associated with
the name Bedan mentioned in the genealogical list of the "sons of Gilead, the son of
Machir, the son of Manasseh" (I Chr. 7:17).

16 Cf. M. D. Cassuto, *Tarbiz*, 12 (1941),
1 ff. (Hebrew); and in particular R.
Tournay, "Le Psaume LXVIII et le livre

des Juges," *RB*, 66 (1959), 358 ff.; E.
Lipinski, "Juges 5, 4–5 et Psaume 68,
8–11, *Biblica*, 48 (1967), 185 ff.

17 See in particular B. Maisler (Mazar),
Ycdiot, 4 (1936), 47 ff. (Hebrew); and S. I.
Feigin, *Missitrei Heavar*, New York, 1943,
pp. 31–33 (Hebrew), who attributes the
composition of the psalm to the period
immediately preceding Jephthah.

18 The toponym Gebal, which is doubtlessly the well-known town of Byblos on the
Phoenician coast (and not Gebalene in the
Arabah) does not fit into the context here
neither geographically, nor concerning the
structure of the hemistichs. Perhaps the
actual name twinned with it (Sidon?) has
dropped out and in the original version this
pair of names was coupled to the one
mentioning Tyre. Another instance of text
distortion is apparently that concerning the
second hemistich in v. 9: "[Ashur also is
joined with them] — they have helped the
children of Lot" (namely, Moab and
Ammon), which is out of place in the extant
text in combination with Assyria, but which
would apply to the eastern nomadic tribes
(Hagrites and Amalek) and Edom which
were mentioned earlier.

19 In this connection it is worth noting the
name of the King of Hazor in the Mari
Texts: Ibni-Adad, which is the Akkadian
form of a West Semitic name, Yabni-Addu.
Biblical Jabin could easily be a hypocoristic
form of the full theophoric name. Cf. W. F.
Albright, *The Biblical Period*, New York,
1963, p. 102 note 83, and A. Malamat, in
*Near Eastern Archaeology in the Twentieth
Century* (ed. by J. A. Sanders), New York,
1970, p. 168, p. 175 note 22.

20 Cf. Y. Yadin, "Hazor," in *Archaeology
and Old Testament Study* (ed. D. W. Thomas),
Oxford, 1967, pp. 245 ff.

21 This solution was first suggested by B.
Maisler (Mazar) *HUCA*, 24 (1952/3), 80 ff.,
and followed by Y. Aharoni, "The Battle
at the Waters of Merom and the Battle
with Sisera," in *The Military History of the
Land of Israel in Biblical Times*, Tel Aviv,
1964, pp. 91 ff. (Hebrew).

22 Cf. Y. Kaufmann, *Judges*, pp. 116–117;
W. Richter, *Bearbeitungen des Retterbuches*,
pp. 7 f.

23   Harosheth-goiim is generally identified with el-Ḥarithiyeh or with Tell el-'Amr, in the narrow pass between the Jezreel and the coastal plains. Mazar, however, considers it to be the name of a region, viz. the wooded mountainous area of Galilee; cf. his article mentioned above, note 21.

24   This suggestion goes back to W. F. Albright, "The Song of Deborah in the Light of Archaeology," *BASOR*, 62 (1936), 26 ff., while M. Engberg, *BASOR*, 78 (1940), 4 ff., would date the war to the gap between Megiddo strata VIA and V in the 11th century (opposing this now is Albright, *The Biblical Period*, p. 102 note 82). It is, however, untenable to accept such a late dating, which most recently was propagated by A. D. H. Mayes, "The Historical Context of the Battle against Sisera," *VT*, 19 (1969), 353 ff., who holds that Deborah's war was a prelude to the battle with the Philistines at Aphek in the late 11th century B.C.E. For the episodes of Deborah and Shamgar son of Anath in the light of the archeological evidence at Megiddo, cf. also Alt, "Megiddo im Übergang, etc." *Kleine Schriften* I, pp. 256 ff.

25   P. W. Lapp, "Taanach by the Waters of Megiddo," *BA*, 30 (1967), 8 ff., who, however, argues that Megiddo VII A was destroyed at the same time as Taanach. The last Canaanite stratum at Taanach produced a tablet in Ugaritic which proves that this script was used in Canaan a considerable time after the destruction of Ugarit itself; for the tablet see D. R. Hillers, *BASOR*, 173 (1964), 45 ff.; F. M. Cross. *ibid.*, 190 (1968), 41 ff.; A. F. Rainey, *Qadmoniot*, 2 (1969), 89 f. (Hebrew).

26   For a unit of 600 warriors in the Bible representing the force of a "brigade," cf. A. Malamat, *Biblica*, 51 (1970), 9 and note 3. Y. Aharoni considers the Philistines here as merely a mercenary force in the employ of the Egyptian garrison at Beth-shean; see in *Near Eastern Archaeology in the Twentieth Century*, New York, 1970, pp. 254 ff.

27   For a possible Hurrian etymology of the name Shamgar, cf. B. Maisler (Mazar), *PEQ*, 1934, 192 ff.; F. C. Fensham, *JNES*, 20 (1961), 197 ff.; and also E. Danelius,

JNES, 22 (1963), 191 ff. There is no doubt that his patronymic ben-'Anath, a name attested in the 13th–11th centuries in Ugaritic, Phoenician and Egyptian documents (also in the forms ben-'Ana, ben-'An) is Canaanite and related to the goddess Anath; cf. A. van Selms, "Judge Shamgar," *VT*, 14 (1964), 294 ff. It may even have been used as an epithet signifying a professional warrior; cf. O. Eissfeldt, *Festschrift W. Baetke*, Weimar, 1966, pp. 110 ff.

28   See W. F. Albright, *JPOS*, 1 (1921), 60 f. and now *idem, Yahve and the Gods of Canaan*, London, 1968, p. 218 (for a Luwian origin of the name); see also A. Alt, *Kleine Schriften* I, pp. 266 f., who attributes to the name an Illyrian origin. On the other hand, according to S. Yeivin, the name occurs as a component of a place name in the topographical lists of Ramses III (no. 103), and possibly also of Ramses II (no. 8), which he reads as Qaus-Sisera and locates it in Western Galilee; cf. *Atiqot*, 3 (1961), 176 ff.

29   Note in particular the Egyptian prose and poetical versions of the Battle of Kadesh; cf. A. H. Gardiner, *The Kadesh Inscriptions of Ramses II*, Oxford, 1960. On a comparison of Deborah's Song with other Ancient Near Eastern victory hymns, see now P. C. Craigie, "The Song of Deborah and the Epic of Tukulti-Ninurta," *JBL*, 88 (1969), 253 ff. On the poetical structure of the song, see in addition to the commentaries, W. F. Albright, *Yahwe and the Gods of Canaan*, pp. 11 ff.

30   See Kaufmann's attempt to smooth out all the discrepancies between the two chapters, in his *Judges*, pp. 113 ff.; and cf. for a detailed analysis of the divergencies W. Richter, *Traditionsgeschichtliche Untersuchungen zum Richterbuch*, Bonn, 1963, pp. 29 ff. However, Richter also considers these divergencies as resulting merely from the different literary composition and transmission of these two chapters, but not necessarily as derivations from different historical events.

31   For recent doubts concerning the idea of an "Israelite amphictyony," whose chief exponent is M. Noth, see H. M. Orlinsky, "The Tribal System of Israel and Related

Groups in the Period of the Judges," *Oriens Antiquus*, 1 (1962), 11 ff.; G. Fohrer, "Altes Testament — "Amphiktyonie" und "Bund"? *Studien zur alttest. Theologie und Geschichte*, Berlin, 1969, pp. 64 ff. An intermediate stand is taken by Smend, *Jahwekrieg und Stämmebund*, pp. 10 ff.; and now "Gehörte Juda zum vorstaatlichen Israel?" *Fourth World Congress of Jewish Studies*, I, Jerusalem, 1967, pp. 57 ff., who rightly criticises the assumption of an amphictyony inferred from the Song of Deborah alone; in any event he attributes to the amphictyonic league a secondary and minor importance in comparison to the institution of the Holy War. For the Israelite tribes in the Song of Deborah as compared to the descriptions thereof in Jacob's and Moses' blessings, see H. J. Zobel, *Stammesspruch und Geschichte*, Berlin, 1965.

32 For a military and topographical analysis of the war cf. A. Malamat, "Mount Tabor as a Battle Ground in Biblical Times," in *Remnants from the Past*, Tel Aviv, 1951, pp. 64 ff. (Hebrew).

33 On the Holy War characteristics to be found in the Israelite battles, cf. in particular G. von Rad, *Der Heilige Krieg im Alten Israel*, (2nd edition), Zürich, 1952; R. de Vaux, *Ancient Israel*, New York, 1961, pp. 258 ff.

34 For this location at Khirbet Qedish, where remains of an Early Iron Age settlement were found, see M. Kochavi, *Yediot*, 27 (1963), 165–173 (Hebrew); *idem, Doron–Hebraic Studies* (in honor of A. I. Katsh), New York, 1965, pp. 90 ff. This city must be distinguished from Kedesh in the northern part of Naphtali which is far from the scene of these events.

35 In addition to the poetical description in the Song of Deborah of the inundation caused by the swollen Kishon brook (Jud. 5:21), allusions to the heavy rains may be found in the description of the theophany at the beginning of the song (vv. 4–5), as well as in a relevant passage in Psalms (68:9: "A bounteous rain"). Josephus already remarked upon the special weather conditions prevailing at the outset of the war of Deborah (*Ant.* V, 4).

36 Cf. A. Malamat, *JAOS*, 82 (1962), 144 ff. Among the Mari documents adduced there on the West Semitic term *ḥibrum* Hebrew *ḥever*, designating a small tribal division, *ARM* VIII, No. 11, is especially illuminating. There reference is made to a *ḥibrum* which constitutes a nomadic unit within the clan of the "sons of Awin" of the Rabbean tribe, paralleling the context of Jud. 4:11, according to which Heber belonged to the clan of the "sons of Hobab" of the Kenite tribe.

37 On the charismatic character of Jael, see B. Mazar, *JNES*, 24 (1965), 301 f.; on the covenant between Israel and the Kenites, cf. F. C. Fensham, *BASOR*, 175 (1964), 51 ff.

38 On the Midianites, see J. Liver, *Encyclopaedia Biblica*, (Hebrew), 4, cols. 686–691, s.v. Midian and the bibliography there; to the latter, add O. Eissfeldt, "Protektorat der Midianiter über ihre Nachbarn" etc., *JBL*, 87 (1968), 383 ff.; and W. F. Albright in the next note.

39 The absence of any evidence for camel caravans before this time has repeatedly been emphasized by Albright; see his most recent statement "Midianite Donkey Caravans" in *Translating and Understanding the Old Testament* (ed. H. T. Frank and W. L. Reed), Nashville–New York, 1970, pp. 197 ff., where he points out the shift from the 13th century Midianite donkey nomadism (cf. Num. 31), to camel nomadism a century later. See also W. Dostal, "The Evolution of Bedouin Life," *L'antica società Beduina* (ed. F. Gabrielli), Rome, 1959, pp. 21 ff.; J. Henninger, "Zum frühsemitischen Nomadentum, "*Viehwirtschaft und Hirten-Kultur*," (ed. L. Földes), Budapest, 1969, pp. 38 ff.

40 Cf. A. Malamat, *JAOS* 82 (1962), 144. The specialized usage of *ummā*, denoting also the sub-tribes of the Ishmaelites (Gen. 25:16) most likely corresponds to the (West Semitic?) Mari term *ummatum*, as employed, e.g. in King Yahdun-lim's Foundation Inscription; see G. Dossin, *Syria*, 32 (1955), 1 ff. There it designates first an association of three rebellious sub-tribes of the nomadic Yaminites (col. III: 17, *ummat TUR-mi-im*; and see below notes

44 and 54), and later the tribal organization of Hana (l. 28: *ummat Ḥa-na*).

41   Such a date seems plausible since the Gideon episode post-dates that of Deborah, as pointed out above, and a similar date can be inferred from a possible, indirect synchronism referred to in Gen. 36:35. According to this passage an Edomite king, Haddad son of Bedad, who flourished five generations before Saul or David, i.e. ca. 1100 B.C.E., "smote Midian in the field of Moab." This clash may have been connected with the general Midianite retreat in Southern Transjordan after their defeat by Gideon. Cf. E. Meyer, *Die Israeliten und ihre Nachbarstämme*, Halle a/S, 1906, p. 381; and W. F. Albright, *Archaeology and the religion of Israel*, p. 206, note 58 (here however the date is lowered one generation).

42   Thus, e.g., Tell Beth Mirsim, stratum B of the Early Iron Age, has revealed a particularly large number of granaries within the city limits, indicating that crops stored outside the city boundaries were endangered by marauding groups such as the Midianites; and cf. W. F. Albright, *The Archaeology of Palestine and the Bible*, New York, 1935, pp. 107–8.

43   Cf. F. M. Abel, *Géographie de la Palestine* II, Paris, 1938, pp. 402 ff. Another possible identification for Ophrah with the ancient site at Afula has been suggested by Z. Kallai, *The Tribes of Israel*, Jerusalem, 1967, pp. 356 ff. (Hebrew). If so, Gideon's hometown was on Manasseh's borderland and is not to be considered as an enclave within another tribal area.

44   This alliance of several tribes seems authentic and should not be considered a later, tendentious enlargement, as held by some critics (see above, pp. oo), e.g. W. Beyerlin, *VT*, 13 (1963), 1 ff. Such multi-tribal alliances are well documented in the Mari texts, e.g. the joint rebellion of three tribes against King Yahdun-lim, as attested in his Foundation Inscription; see below note 54, and A. Malamat, *JAOS*, 28 (1962), 144.

45   This place should be identified with Khirbet eṣ-Ṣafṣafa, 1 km northeast of the Arab village Indur on the northern slope

of the hill of Moreh. See N. Zori, *PEQ*, 84 (1952), 114 ff.

46   See A. Malamat, "The War of Gideon and Midian — A Military Approach," *PEQ*, 85 (1953), 61 ff.; and in greater detail in the parallel chapter in *The Military History of the Land of Israel in Biblical Times*, pp. 110 ff. (Hebrew). For other and partly different analyses see Field-Marshall A. P. Wavell, "Night Attacks — Ancient and Modern," in his *The Good Soldier*, London, 1948, pp. 162 ff.; Y. Yadin, *The Art of Warfare in Biblical Lands*, pp. 256 ff.

47   Most likely to be identified with Tell Abu Ṣūṣ; see H. J. Zobel, *ZDVP*, 82, (1966), 83 ff.; N. Zori, *Yediot*, 31 (1967), 132 ff. (Hebrew).

48   Succoth has been located by various scholars at Tell Deir ʿĀlla, which was excavated in recent years by H. J. Franken, see *VT*, 10 (1960), 386 ff., 11 (1961), 361 ff.; 12 (1962), 378 ff.; however, more recently Franken has given up this identification; *ibid.*, 14 (1964), 422, and cf. now his *Excavations at Tell Deir ʿAlla*, Leiden, 1969, p. 5 ff. There is no certainty as to whether the inhabitants of Succoth and Penuel were Israelites, or Canaanites as in Shechem. A foreign population has recently been propagated by H. Reviv, *Tarbiz*, 38 (1969), 309 ff., (Hebrew).

49   See in particular Kaufmann, *Judges*, pp. 191 ff., who strongly rejects the view of the Wellhausen school that Gideon's answer expresses a Second Temple, theocratic concept, and that actually he accepted the people's offer (cf. the commentaries). On the other hand, the argument of M. Buber that Gideon's statement represents the one and only authoritative concept prevailing in Israel before the rise of the Monarchy is too extreme, see his *Königtum Gottes*, Berlin, 1932, pp. 1 ff.; and cf. now also J. A. Soggin, *Das Königtum in Israel* (*BZAW*, 104), Berlin, 1967, pp. 15 ff.; H. J. Boecker, *Die Beurteilung der Anfänge des Königtums in den deuteronomischen Abschnitten des I. Samuelbuches*, Neukirchen, 1969, pp. 20 ff.

50   On Jotham's parable, cf. in addition to the commentaries E. H. Maly, "The Jotham Fable-Antimonarchical?", *CBQ*, 22

(1960), 299 ff.; M. C. Astour, "The Amarna Age Forerunners of Biblical Anti-Royalism," *Max Weinreich Festschrift*, Hague, 1964, pp. 6 ff.; U. Simon, *Tarbiz*, 34 (1965), 1 ff. (Hebrew). The importance of the royal shadow in the Canaanite city-states (in this instance of the King of Byblos) is well reflected in the contemporary tale of Wen-Amon; cf. A. L. Oppenheim, *BASOR*, 107 (1947), 7 ff.

51 Several of the following points have been emphasized in the commentaries; and cf. also E. Nielsen, *Shechem*, Copenhagen, 1955, p. 143, note 1; B. Lindars, "Gideon and Kingship," *JThS* (N.S.), 16 (1965), 315 ff.; G. Wallis, "Die Anfänge des Königtums in Israel," *Geschichte und Überlieferung*, Berlin, 1965, pp. 51 ff.

52 Since it cannot be presumed that Gideon married into a noble Shechemite family before his act of deliverance, it must be assumed that his rule lasted a long time after, for Abimelech was already grown up when his father died. On the other hand, Gideon must have been middle aged at the time of his war with the Midianites since Jether, his first-born, already bore his own sword at that time (Jud. 8:20). This confirms the biblical statement that Gideon lived to a ripe old age (Jud. 8:32).

53 See H. Reviv, "The Government in Shechem in the El-Amarna Period and in the Days of Abimelech," *IEJ*, 16 (1966), 252 ff.; and cf. M. C. Astour *op. cit.*, p. 10 note 21. One cannot agree with Kaufmann that Shechem was an Israelite and not a Canaanite city and that the war with Abimelech was an internal Israelite conflict; cf. his commentary to *Judges*, pp. 195–196.

54 E. g. Yahdun-lim's Foundation Inscription — G. Dossin, *Syria*, 32 (1955), 14 (col. III: 4 ff.) "Laum, king of [the city of] Samanum and the country of [the tribe of] the Ubrabeans, Bahlukulim, king of Tuttul and the country of the Amnanum, Ayalum, king of Abattum and the country of the Rabbeans." Cf. also H. Klengel, *Saeculum*, 17 (1966), 211. Our instances would reflect M. Rowton's apt concept of a "dimorphic society" (category IV); see *XVe rencontre*

assyriologique internationale, Liège, 1967, pp. 109 ff.

55 For Baal-berith as a guarantor of a treaty, see recently R. E. Clements, *JSS*, 13 (1968), 21 ff.; and for the significance of *ḥᵃmōr*, i.e. donkey, in a treaty context, cf. W. F. Albright, *Archaeology and the Religion of Israel*, p. 113.

56 Arumah has to be located at Khirbet el-'Ormah on the summit of the imposing Jebel el-'Ormah, 10 km. south east of Shechem, an identification confirmed by a recent survey where, *inter alia*, Early Iron pottery was found; cf. E. F. Campbell, *BASOR*, 190 (1968), 38 ff. The obscure word *torma* in Jud. 9:31 may perhaps be emended to the place-name Arumah.

57 On the Gaal incident, cf. also R. G. Boling, "And who is *ŠKM*,"? *VT*, 13 (1963), 479 ff. The temporary rule of a band in a city and its expulsion by the local inhabitants is a frequent phenomenon. Cf. for example the episode of David and his band capturing Keilah whence they were expelled by the inhabitants upon pressure by Saul (I Sam. 23:1 ff.).

58 For a general discussion of the archeological finds in Shechem and their bearing upon the story of Abimelech, see G. E. Wright, *Shechem*, New York, 1965, pp. 80 ff.; pp. 123 ff.; and cf. pp. 126–127 for the term *zᵉrīaḥ* ("hold") which *here* means a tower or an upper storey of some structure rather than a crypt, as frequently held. The various attempts to reconcile the complex archeological and biblical data have recently been discussed by J. A. Soggin, "Bemerkungen zur alttest. Topographie Sichems mit besonderem Bezug auf Jdc. 9," *ZDPV*, 83 (1967), 183 ff. For the term *migdō/āl* as comprising both temple and fortress, cf. B. Mazar, *Encyclopaedia Biblica*, 4, col. 633 ff. (Hebrew), and G. R. H. Wright, *ZAW*, 80 (1968), 16 ff.

59 The location of the temple of El-berith on the slopes of Mount Gerizim is debated in the literature cited in the previous note. Recent archeological evidence refutes this view however, for the sanctuary brought to light there had already been destroyed early in the Late Bronze Period; see R. G.

Boling, *BA*, 32 (1969), 81 ff.; E. F. Campbell–G. E. Wright, *ibid.*, 104 ff.

60   For the different explanations, cf. S. Gevirtz, "Jericho and Shechem — A Religio-Literary Aspect of City Destruction," *VT*, 13 (1963), 52 ff.; and see the note there by J. Greenfield (*ibid.* p. 61, note 1).

61   The toponym Thebez is actually a *hapax legomenon* in Jud. 9:50 (this very passage being quoted in II Sam. 11:21; cf. above, p. 000). Its usual identification with the Arab village Ṭubas, 15 km northeast of Shechem, lacks both archeological and linguistic basis (only the letter *b* being held in common; could the modern village-name have possibly been derived from Tobias?). We assume that Thebez is merely a corrupted spelling, most likely of the place-name Tirzah; this has been accepted by Y. Aharoni, *The Land of the Bible*, London, 1967, p. 242. Such a textual corruption can easily be explained on the basis of an originally defective spelling of the name Tirzah (*trẓ* — without the final *h*), and on account of the similarity of the letters *r* and *b* in the palaeo-Hebrew script, particularly in cursive script, before the letter *ẓ*.

Indeed, the city of Tirzah fits perfectly into this context, historically, geographically and probably also archeologically. The site has been identified with Tell el-Far'ah, 10 km northeast of Shechem, and the excavations there have revealed an important fortified Canaanite town (cf. Josh. 12:24), but the precise dating of the destruction layer of the Late Bronze Age city is uncertain; see R. de Vaux, "Tirzah," *Archaeology and Old Testament Study*, p. 375, and the bibliography there on p. 383. It is quite surprising that this important center in the vicinity of Shechem should not appear in the story of Abimelech. It is further noteworthy that Jeroboam I, founder of the northern Israelite Kingdom, rebuilt Shechem and Penuel (I Kings 12:25), both of which were *migdāl*-type cities destroyed in the days of Gideon and Abimelech. The third town which Jeroboam appears to have rebuilt is Tirzah (I Kings 14:17), and if the identity with Thebez is

accepted, it also had such a Canaanite *migdāl*.

62   On the Israelite settlement in Transjordan and its relationship with the neighboring states, see the series of studies by M. Noth, *PJB*, 37 (1941), 50 ff.; *ZAW*, 60 (1944) 11 ff.; *ZDPV*, 68 (1946–51), 1 ff; 75 (1959), 14 ff.; and R. de Vaux," Note d'histoire et de topographie transjordaniennes," *Bible et Orient*, Paris, 1967, pp. 115 ff. See now also B. Oded, *Israelite Transjordan during the Period of the Monarchy*, (doctoral thesis), Jerusalem, 1968, (Hebrew).

63   For southern Transjordan in the Early Iron Age, see N. Glueck, "Explorations in Eastern Palestine, I–IV," *AASOR*, 14 (1933–34); 15 (1934–5); 18–19 (1937–9); 25–28 (1945–9); and his recent summary "Transjordan" in *Archaeology and Old Testament Study*, pp. 429 ff. On the establishment of about three hundred settlements between the Yarmuk and Arnon rivers in Iron Age I and II, see in particular *AASOR*, 25–28, 228 f., 285. Numerous additional settlements of the early Iron Age in the region between the Yarmuk and the Jabbok have been discovered recently by S. Mittmann, see his *Beiträge zur Siedlungs- und Territorial Geschichte des nördlichen Ostjordanlandes*, Wiesbaden, 1970.

64   For the time of Edom's war with the Midianites, cf. above, note 41. For the dating of the events related in the Book of Ruth, the lineage of David appended to this book (4:17 ff.) may be instructive. According to this list David was the fourth generation after Boaz and Ruth.

65   For this recently rediscovered and deciphered inscription, see K. A. Kitchen, *JEA* 50 (1964), 47 ff., who proposes dating this expedition early in Ramses' reign, before the area was conquered by Sihon. This newly attested Egyptian influence in that region may perhaps explain the discovery of the Balu'a stele in Moab, north of the Arnon, which bears a relief in distinct Egyptian style and an enigmatic inscription in characters apparently imitating hieroglyphic writing. The relief shows a god and goddess flanking a local ruler of characteristically Bedouin type (could it

portray the "first king of Moab" mentioned in Num. 21:26?). For the latest treatment of this stele, see W. A. Ward — M. F. Martin, *Annual of the Department of Antiquities of Jordan*, 8–9 (1964), 5 ff., pls. I–VI. In connection with Ramses' campaign to Moab, the recent discovery of an Egyptian mining center at Timna is of interest, the finds there including inscriptions of Ramses II. See above, the chapter on "The Egyptian Decline in Canaan," p. 000 and note 43.

66 See Glueck, *AASOR*, 18–19, 242 ff., who appropriately calls this extended area of Moab "Greater Moab." Cf. also A. H. van Zyl, *The Moabites*, Leiden, 1960, pp. 125 ff.

67 The "city of palm trees" certainly refers to Jericho in Deut. 34:3 and II Chr. 28:15 (but not necessarily in Jud. 1:16). This designation may have referred to the city of Jericho — which lay at that time in ruins — together with the fertile oasis surrounding it. Mention of the city of Gilgal later in the story also points to this area. One cannot accept the view of E. Auerbach, *Wüste und Gelobtes Land*, I, Berlin, 1932, pp. 100 f., who identifies the place with Tamar and transfers the geographical scene of Ehud's story to the region south of the Dead Sea.

68 Since the immediate continuation of the story (v. 27) places Ehud in the hill-country of Ephraim, the location of Seirath has usually been sought along the route from Jericho to the hills of Ephraim; see the latest discussion, J. Braslavi, "Ha-Seiratha and the Jordan Fords," *Beth-Mikra*, 34 (1968), 37 ff. (Hebrew). However, already some of the recensions of the Septuagint add, in v. 27, after the words "[and Ehud] escaped into Seirath. And it came to pass, when he was come'" the phrase: "to the land of the children of Israel," before mentioning the mountains of Ephraim. Hence, this version explicitly indicates that Ehud first fled to a place beyond Israel's borders — apparently to the land of Seir — and only thence did he return to Ephraim.

69 Cf. the commentaries; for an analysis of the story cf. also E. G. Kraeling, "Dif-

ficulties in the Story of Ehud," *JBL*, 54 (1935), 205 ff.; W. Richter, *Traditionsgesch. Untersuchungen*, pp. 1 ff.

70 The existence of an *'alliyyā*, "upper chamber", in palaces is attested both in II Kings 1:2 (the palace of Samaria) and in the Egyptian tale of Wen-Amon. Interestingly enough, the latter — as in the story of Ehud — relates that the (Egyptian) emissary was received by the King of Byblos in his upper chamber (the Egyptian text uses here the same word, borrowed from the Canaanite-Hebrew: *'lyt*); cf. *ANET*, p. 26b.

71 See Y. Yadin, *Art of Warfare*, pp. 254 f.

72 W. F. Albright, "Notes on Ammonite History," *Miscellanea Biblica B. Ubach*, Montserrat, 1953, pp. 131 ff.

73 See Glueck, *AASOR*, 18–19, 151 ff. and the later surveys of the Germans who located the continuation of the border line in the south as far as Rujm el-Fehud; H. Gese, *ZDPV*, 74 (1958), 55 ff.; R. Hentschke, *ibid.*, 76 (1960), 103 ff.; G. Fohrer, *ibid.*, 77 (1961), 56 ff.; H. Reventlow, *ibid.*, 79 (1963) 127 ff.; and H. J. Stoebe, *ibid.*, 82 (1966), 33 ff. and cf. also G. M. Landes, "The Material Civilisation of the *BAr*, 24 (1961), 65 ff.

74 S. Mittmann, "Aroer, Minnith und Abel-Keramim," *ZDPV*, 85 (1969), 63 ff., proposes, doubtfully, to locate all these sites to the northwest of Amman (nearer to Jephthah's starting-point); and see there for the usual identifications in the south-west.

75 As with several other toponyms (e.g. Shechem), the name Gilead came to designate both a city and a broader region; a land as well as a mountain range, and even a tribal unit. For the complex problems of the borders of the land of Gilead and the identification of the city of the same name, see M. Noth, *ZDPV*, 75 (1959), 14 ff.; and now M. Ottosson, *Gilead-Tradition and History*, Lund, 1969; Z. Kallai, *The Tribes of Israel*, index (p. 435), s. v. Gilead.

76 Cf. J. Mendelsohn, *IEJ*, 4 (1954), 116 ff., who discusses the legal aspect of Jephthah's expulsion, which he thinks could have been effected only by the intervention of the institution of the elders of Gilead.

77 The titles *rō'š* and *qāzīn* appear in parallel in Mic. 3:1, also as the nation's supreme leaders. For these terms cf. J. van der Ploeg, *RB*, 57 (1950), 52, 58 f. For the title *rō'š*, see now also J. R. Bartlett, *VT*, 19 (1969), 1 ff. These two terms occur also in external documents: *qāzīn* in the Ugarit documents and as a loanword from the Canaanite in Egyptian inscriptions (*kḏ/ṭn*), denoting a chariotry commander; and *rō'š* in Assyrian sources from the time of Tiglath-pileser III on, denoting the heads of nomadic tribes (*rēšu*, *rā'šāni*); cf. e.g. J. A. Brinkman, *A Political History of Post-Kassite Babylonia*, Rome, 1968, p. 265 and note 1705. For an even earlier extra-biblical attestation of *rō'š*, see *Archives Royales de Mari* I, Paris, 1950, No. 10:20 — "our lord is our sole chief (*rašani*)".

78 That is why the suggestion of Noth, *ZDPV*, 75 (1959), 36, to identify it with el-Mishrefe, 2 km north of Khirbet Jel'ad, seems correct, while others would identify it with the latter locality itself (e.g. R. de Vaux) or with Khirbet Umm ed-Danānīr, south of it; Glueck, *AASOR*, 18–19, 100 ff.

79 The exegetes generally considered this pericope a later composition, actually reflecting the relationship between the Israelites and *Moab*, which is interpolated into the Jephthah cycle. For recent discussions, see W. Richter, "Die Überlieferungen um Jephthah," *Biblica*, 47 (1966), 522 ff.; Ottosson, *op. cit.*, pp. 161 ff. The basic authenticity of this episode, however, has rightly been stressed by Kaufmann, *Judges*, pp. 219 ff.

80 According to Abel and Albright, while Glueck identifies this place with the town of Zarethan. The recent excavations of this site revealed an important cemetery from the 13th–12th centuries B.C.E.; cf. J. B. Pritchard, *BAr*, 28 (1965), 10 ff.; *idem*, in *The Role of the Phoenicians in the Interaction of Mediterranean Civilizations* (ed. by W. Ward), Beirut, 1968, pp. 99 ff.

81 See E. A. Speiser, "The Shibboleth Incident," *BASOR*, 85 (1942), 10 ff.; R. Marcus, *ibid.*, 87 (1942), 39. Cf. D. Leibel, "On the Linguistic Peculiarity of the Ephraimites," *Molad*, 23 (September 1965), 335 ff. (Hebrew); and see also the illuminating remarks by the medieval commentator Rabbi David Kimḥi (*ad loc.*). According to him the catchword "Shibboleth" seems to refer here to "the current of the river" rather than to the usual meaning: "ear of corn."

82 Meroz may be identified with Khirbet Mazar on one of the western summits of the Gilboa range, ca. 12 km east of Taanach. See *Encyclopaedia Biblica* 5, col. 451 (Hebrew). As with the people of Succoth and Penuel, it is not clear whether its inhabitants were Israelites (of the tribe of Manasseh) or rather Canaanites in treaty with the Israelites, as assumed by A. Alt, *Kleine Schriften*, I, pp. 274 ff. For the significance of the Hebrew verb '*rr* "to curse," see H. C. Brichto, *The Problem of "Curse" in the Hebrew Bible*, Philadelphia, 1963, pp. 77 ff. This cursing of a city may resemble the Egyptian Execration Texts, as might the proscription of the leaders of Succoth (R. Grafman's suggestion) mentioned above, p. 146. For the latter practice one may now refer to the recently found Canaanite ostraca from Kamid el-Loz, apparently bearing a malediction formula and personal names; see G. Mansfeld, *Kamid el-Loz-Kumidi*, Saarbrücker Beiträge für Altertumskunde, 7.

83 On this episode and its historical setting in the period of the judges, see J. Dus, "Die Lösung des Rätsels von Jos. 22," *ArOr* 32 (1964), 529 ff.

84 See in particular E. C. Kingsbury "He set Ephraim before Manasseh," *HUCA*, 38 (1967), 129 ff., who stresses, however, Ephraim's pre-eminence in the cultic rather than in the political sphere, as exemplified by the shift of the cult-center from Shechem to Beth-el and Shiloh.

85 The strong ties between the tribe of Benjamin and Gilead are indicated in several biblical sources, as has been pointed out by E. A. Melamed, *Tarbiz* 5 (1934) 121 ff. (Hebrew): (a) the genealogical lists — where the clans of Shuppim and Huppim are affiliated with both Benjamin and Machir the Gileadite (I Chr. 7:12 and 15); (b) the story of Gibeah — attesting to the marriage between the maidens of Jabesh-Gilead and the Benjaminites (cf. below),

of which Saul may even have been an offspring, which would in turn more definitely explain both the help he rendered to the besieged city and the conduct of its inhabitants in recovering the bodies of Saul and his sons from Beth-shean; (c) the reference in a much later period to such a connection by the prophet Obadiah (1:19).

86 For the authenticity and antiquity of the account, cf. Kaufmann, *Judges*, pp. 277 ff.; in contrast, see M. Güdemann, *MGWJ*, 18 (1869), 357 ff., followed by H. Graetz, who assumed that the story was composed as a piece of political polemics in the rivalry between the House of David and that of Saul (who lived in Gibeah), with the intention of denigrating the latter and his tribe.

87 The chronology of this story is disputed, as we have noted. At first sight the mention of the priest Phinehas the grandson of Aaron, in Jud. 20:28, may indicate a very early dating within the period of the judges, an opinion held already by Josephus. Yet his appearance is of no particular chronological significance, especially since he tends to figure in biblical tradition in connection with the Ark of the Covenant and pan-Israelite undertakings (cf. Num. 31:6; Josh.22), and may here be the result of later, tendentious recension (and cf. above, p.00).

88 This point has been emphasized by O. Eissfeldt, "Der geschichtliche Hintergrund der Erzählung von Gibeas Schandtat," *Festschrift G. Beer*, Stuttgart, 1935, pp. 19 ff. (= *Kleine Schriften*, II, Tübingen, 1963, pp. 64 ff.), who considers the pan-tribal portrayal as the result of a later recension. And cf. K. D. Schunck, *Benjamin*, Berlin, 1963, pp. 57 ff.

89 For the significance of Beth-el as amphictyonic center as deduced from this story, see M. Noth, *Geschichte Israels*, (3rd ed.), pp. 91 ff.; and cf. also W. F. Albright, *Archaeology and the Religion of Israel*, pp. 104 f.; J. Dus, *Oriens Antiquus*, 3 (1964), 227 ff.

90 On these institutions and their authority, see A. Malamat, "Organs of Statecraft in the Israelite Monarchy," *BAr*, 28 (1965), 34 ff. (slightly revised in *BAr* Reader, 3, New York, 1970, pp. 163 ff.); see on the slogan "We will not any of us go to his tent, neither will we any of us turn unto his house" (Jud. 20:8), *ibid.*, p. 40, (pp. 169 f. respectively), where it is regarded as a formula indicating a positive decision reached by the general assembly. Cf. also R. Gordis, "Democratic Origins in Ancient Israel — The Biblical 'Edah," *A. Marx Jubilee Volume*, New York, 1950, pp. 369 ff.; and now H. Tadmor, in *Cahiers d'Histoire Mondiale*, 11 (1968), 8.

91 For similar drastic means described in a Mari letter, see "Mari," *Encyclopaedia Biblica*, 4, col. 575 (Hebrew); G. Wallis, *ZAW*, 64 (1952), 57 ff.

92 The destruction of the city seems to be indicated by the end of stratum I (the pre-fortress city) at Tell el-Fūl; cf. L. A. Sinclair, "The Archaeological Study of Gibeah," *AASOR*, 34–35 (1960). For the military strategy, cf. Y. Yadin, *Art of Warfare*, pp. 262 f.; W. Roth, "Hinterhalt und Scheinflucht," *ZAW*, 75 (1963), 20 ff. As generally accepted, Roth also considers one of the two descriptions of the city's conquest as a mere literary replica of the other; in his case, the story of Ai was copied from the episode at Gibeah.

Yet it would rather seem that we have here a common stratagem, adopted by the Israelites in several instances. As a matter of fact, this tactic of ambush and deceptive flight is mentioned as a common practice by the Roman tactician Frontinus in his *Strategemata* (see e.g. Book II, 5, 1 and 8; Book III, 10, 1 ff.). Moreover, in some instances utter surprise was achieved by repeated feigning of flight (e.g. Book III, 5, 8), which may be compared to the initially real retreats of the Israelites (cf. immediately below).

93 This English version of the Hebrew original (published in 1967) has been revised and brought up to date in 1970.

CHAPTER VIII

THE PHILISTINES AND THEIR WARS WITH ISRAEL

1 See the view of J. M. Grintz in the *Moses Schorr Memorial Volume*, New York, 1945, pp. 96 ff.; and cf. C. H. Gordon, *The World of the Old Testament*, New York, 1960, pp. 121 ff.

2 Cf. B. Mazar "Caphtor," *Encyclopaedia Biblica* (Hebrew), 4, cols. 236 ff. and *ibid.* the bibliography.

3 Cf. J. Vercoutter, *L'Égypte et le monde Egéen Préhéllenique*, Paris, 1956, pp. 369 ff.; F. Schachermayer, *Die minoische Kultur des alten Kreta*, Stuttgart, 1964, pp. 109 ff.

4 Cf. W. F. Albright, *The Bible and the Ancient Near East*, New York, 1961, p. 359, note 79; O. Eissfeldt, *Philister und Phoenizier*, Leipzig, 1936.

5 Out of the large literature cf. M. L. and H. Erlenmeyer, "Über Philister und Kreter," *Orientalia*, (NS) 29–30 (1960–1961); 33 (1964); G. Bonfante, *American Journal of Archaeology*, 50 (1946), 251 ff.; M. Riemschneider, *Acta Antiqua*, 4 (1956), 17 ff.; G. A. Wainwright, *JEA*, 47 (1961), 71 ff.; *idem*, *VT*, 6 (1956), 199 ff. Cf. also W. Kimming, *Seevölkerbewegung und Urnenfelderkultur*, Bonn, 1964; P. Prignaud, *RB*, 71 (1964), pp. 215 ff.

6 See V. Georgiev, *Jahrbuch für Kleinas. Forschung*, 1 (1951), 136 ff.; and also F. Lochner-Hüttenbach, *Die Pelasger*, Vienna, 1960, pp. 141 ff.

7 Cf. W. F. Albright, "Syria, the Philistines and Phoenicia," *CAH*, II (rev. ed.), ch. XXXIII, (1966), p. 27.

8 On these events see H. Otten, *MDOG*, 94 (1962) 1 ff.

9 See in particular W. Helck, *Die Beziehungen Ägyptens zu Vorderasien im 3. und 2. Jahrt. v. Chr.*, Wiesbaden, 1962, pp. 240 ff.

10 Various suggestions were made for identifying these Sea-People, apart from the Philistines, with peoples known to us from other sources. It is generally accepted that the Tjeker (Tjekel) are none other than the Teukroi who, according to Greek legend, settled in Salamis, Cyprus; according to another view they are Homer's Sikeloi who apparently gave their name to Sicily, as the Sherden gave theirs to Sardinia. For the time being these and other such views still belong to the realm of conjecture. The Denyen certainly cannot be separated from the land of Danuna mentioned in a letter of the governor of Tyre and found in the Amarna archives (cf. G. A. Wainwright, *JEA*, 49 [1963], 175 f.). They are the Danaoi known as the inhabitants of Cilicia from the Karatepe inscriptions in Anatolia and their identification with the Danaioi, who originate from the East according to Greek tradition, seems certain. Cf. the recent article by Y. Yadin, in *Western Galilee and the Galilean Coast* (Hebrew), Jerusalem, 1965, pp. 49 ff.; H. Donner and W. Rollig, *Kanaanäische und aramäische Inschriften*, Wiesbaden, 1964, II, p. 39.

11 The inscriptions of Ramses III were published by W. F. Edgerton and J. A. Wilson, *Historical Records of Ramses III*, Chicago, 1936; *ANET*, pp. 262 ff.

12 Cf. H. H. Nelson, *Medinet Habu*, I–II, Chicago, 1039–32; W. Wreszinski, *Atlas zur altägypt. Kulturgeschichte*, II, Leipzig, 1932, fig. 110 ff.; Y. Yadin, *The Art of Warfare in the Land of the Bible* (Hebrew), Ramat Gan, 1963, pp. 252 ff., tabls. 254–259.

13 Cf. in particular T. Dothan, *Eretz Israel* (Hebrew) 5, (1959) 55 ff. and also G. E. Wright, *BAr*, 22 (1959), 54 ff. An anthropoid coffin was also found in Saḥab, east of Amman (W. F. Albright, *American Journal of Archaeology*, 36 [1932] 295 ff.). It might belong to a mercenary from among the Sea-People in the service of Ammon.

14 See *ANET*, p. 262.

15 On Philistine pottery cf. W. A. Heurtley *Quarterly of the Department of Antiquities in Palestine*, 5 (1936) 90 ff.; T. Dothan, *Antiquity and Survival*, II, 2/3, 1957, pp. 151 ff.; E. Saussey, *Syria*, 5 (1924), 169 ff.; V. D. d'A. Desborough, *The Last Mycenaeans*, Oxford, 1964, pp. 207 ff.

16 Cf. Alt, *Kleine Schriften*, I, pp. 261 ff. About the troubled conditions prevailing at the time of Shamgar son of Anath

we read in the Song of Deborah: "In the days of Shamgar the son of Anath, in the days of Jael, the highways ceased, and the travellers walked through byways" (Jud. 5:6); it cannot, however, be concluded from the text whether this situation was caused only by Canaanite oppression or also by the recruitment of Philistines.

17 For the identification of Gath, cf. Y. Aharoni, *The Land of Israel in Biblical Times* (Hebrew), Jerusalem, 1963, p. 234; and for the identification of Ekron, see Y. Naveh, *Yediot*, (Hebrew), 21 (1957), 178 ff.

18 See A. Gardiner, *Ancient Egyptian Onomastica*, Oxford, 1947, I, pp. 24 ff.; Alt, *op. cit.*, I, pp. 231 ff.

19 *ANET*, pp. 25 ff.; M. A. Korostovtzev, *Puteshestviye Un-Amuna v. Bibl.*, Moscowa, 1960, and W. F. Albright, *Studies Presented to D. M. Robinson*, St. Louis, 1951, pp. 223ff.

20 See B. Maisler (Mazar), *BASOR* 102, (1946), 9 ff., Albright, *The Bible and the Ancient Near East*, p. 383, note B.

21 Cf. B. Mazar, "The Philistines and the Establishment of the Kingdoms of Israel and Tyre," *Proceedings of the Israel Academy of Sciences* I, vii, (1964), pp. 3–4.

22 See R. D. Barnett, *Journal of Hellenistic Studies*, 73 (1953), 142 ff.; Yadin, *ibid.*, 51.

23 On the excavation in Tell Qasileh cf. B. Mazar, *IEJ*.

24 Cf. Mazar, "The Philistines and the Establishment of the Kingdoms of Israel and Tyre," p. 5 note 19, and *ibid.*, the bibliography.

25 Cf. Mazar, *ibid.*, p. 5, and on the epigraphical material as a whole — F. M. Cross, *BASOR* 134 (1954), 15 ff.; 168 (1962), 12 ff.

26 See H. Kjaer, *JPOS*, 10 (1930), 97 ff.

27 A problem all of its own arises concerning the stronghold at Gibeath Shaul (Tell el-Fūl) excavated by Albright; cf. M. F. Albright, *BASOR*, 52 (1933), 6 ff.; R. L. Cleveland, *AASOR*, 34/5 (1960), 10 ff. The assumption that it was defended by a casemate wall with towers at the corners has been lately challenged in the light of new examinations made at the site; and cf. P. Lapp, *BAr*, 27 (1964) 46. Concerning the problems of Geba (Gibeah) and *Gibeath Elohim*, see B. Maisler (Mazar) *Yediot*, (Hebrew), 10 (1943), 73; and K. D. Schunk, *Benjamin*, Berlin, 1963, pp. 90 ff., pp. 116 ff.

28 Cf. G. E. Wright, *BAr*, 6, 2 (1943) 33.

29 Cf. G. Loud, *Megiddo*, II, Chicago, 1948, 33 ff.; and for the dating of stratum VI A, see B. Maisler (Mazar), *BASOR*, 124 (1951), 21 f.; G. E. Wright, *BASOR*, 155 (1959), 13 f. It is worth noting that at Megiddo Philistine pottery appears already in stratum VII A, but is mainly found in stratum VI. The last stage of this layer (VI A) fits layer X in Tell Qasileh, when the tradition of Philistine pottery had already died out, and cf. above.

30 In Beth-shean, stratum VI definitely belongs to the time of Ramses III and his successors, and also the anthropoid coffins appear to belong to the same period, while the early stage of layer V doubtlessly represents the days of Philistine rule in the second half of the 11th century. Cf. W. F. Albright, *AASOR*, 17 (1936–7), 76 ff.; B. Mazar, *Yediot*, (Hebrew), 16 (1952), 14 ff. On the sanctuaries of stratum V cf. A. Rowe, *The Four Canaanite Temples of Beth-Shean*, I, Philadelphia, 1930, pp. 22 ff., pl. X–XIII; also S. Yeivin and M. Avi-Yonah, *Our Country's Antiquities* (Hebrew) I, Tel-Aviv, 1956, pp. 180 ff.

31 On Samuel and the beginning of the monarchy cf. also W. A. Irwin, *AJSL*, 58 (1941), 113 ff.; H. Wildberger, *Theologische Zeitschrift*, 13 (1957), 442 ff.; A. Weiser, *Samuel*, Göttingen, 1962; Schunk, *op. cit.*, pp. 80 ff. J. Liever "Melek" [3] *Encyclopaedia Biblica*, (Hebrew) 4, cols. 1085 ff.

32 For an interesting point of view, in direct contrast to that suggested here, cf. H. E. Kassis, *JBL*, 84 (1965), 259 ff.

CHAPTER IX

THE ISRAELITE TRIBES

1 In contrast to *shēveṭ* which is used to designate the Israelite tribes, the Bible employs for tribal units among other nations the term *ummōt,* as in the case of the sons of Ishmael (Gen. 25:16) and in that of Midian (Num. 25:15). This term (*ummātum*) appears in the Mari documents in the sense of a tribe or a tribal association. Other tribal units, smaller than the *ummātum*, are the *gāium* (cf. the biblical *goy*) and *ḥibrum* (cf. the biblical *ḥever*); see J. Bottéro, *ARM*, VII, pp. 223 ff.; E. A. Speiser, *JBL*, 79 (1960), 157–63; M. Noth, *Die Ursprünge des alten Israel im Lichte neuer Quellen*, Cologne and Opladen, 1961, pp. 15 ff.; A. Malamat, *JAOS* 82 (1962), 143–150; *idem*, Les congrès et colloques de l'Université de Liège 42, XVᵉ rencontre assyriologique internationale, *La civilization de Mari*, Liège, 1967, pp. 129–138.

2 The same flexibility in the use of the term *bītu* is to be found in the Mari documents, where it indicates both a father's house in its narrow sense and a family comprising many fathers' houses; see Bottéro, *op. cit., loc. cit.*

3 Several scholars maintain that the Bible and the traditions of ancient Semitic peoples contain evidence of the relics of a matriarchal regime in vogue among these peoples at the outset of their existence, that is, a regime in which family kinship, inheritance, and the entire social structure are based on the relationship to the mother and not to the father; thus, for example, G. A. Wilken, *Das Matriarchat bei den alten Arabern*, Leipzig, 1884; W. Robertson Smith, *Kinship and Marriage in Early Arabia* (2nd ed.), London, 1903, pp. 152 ff., 191 ff.; J. Morgenstern, *ZAW*, 47 (1929), 97–110; 49 (1931), 46–58; D. Jacobson, *The Social Background of the Old Testament*, Cincinnati, 1924, pp. 3–34; A. Lods, *Israel from its Beginnings to the Middle of the Eighth Century*, New York, 1932. But the social regime as reflected in the Bible (cf. A. S. Herschberg, *Ha-Tᵉqufa* [Hebrew], 28 [1936], 348 ff.; W. Plautz, *ZAW*, 74 [1962], 9–30), and as prevalent among the Semitic tribes during those periods for which there is evidence, was fundamentally patriarchal (on the status of the family among Arab tribes in pre-Islamic times, see J. Henninger, in *L'antica societa Beduina*, ed. by F. Gabrieli, Rome, 1959, pp. 86–93, and the extensive bibliography on the subject cited there). Not only are family relationships and the social structure based on descent from the father, but the father of the family enjoys almost unlimited authority and power of coercion over the members of his house (cf. Gen. 38:24; Ex. 21:7; Neh. 5:1–13). The question whether the Bible contains information on customs and forms of life explicable as relics of a matriarchal regime that existed among the ancient Semites, the forefathers of the Hebrew tribes, is irrelevant here. For the fratriarchal elements in the biblical patriarchal society, see C. H. Gordon, *JBL*, 54 (1935), 223–31; E. A. Speiser, *Biblical and Other Studies*, ed. by A. Altmann, Harvard, 1963, pp. 15–28.

4 Most scholars accept this connotation of the "thousand." Y. Yadin, *The Scroll of the War of the Sons of Light against the Sons of Darkness*, Oxford, 1962, pp. 49–53, holds that the "thousand" is a conscripted unit drawn from the father's house and not from the family, but it is difficult to accept his suggestion. Yadin contends that this is the meaning adduced from the biblical texts. But an examination of all the texts in which the "thousand" is clearly a tribal unit reveals that it is identical with the family or — a fact that militates against Yadin's suggestion — with the tribe. Moreover, even if Yadin's assumption were to some extent correct that the "myriad" in the figures of the musters in the Book of Numbers is the conscription unit of the family and the "thousand" that of the father's house, it has no basis in fact, its historical value being the same as that of the exaggerated numbers in the census lists in the Book of Numbers. On the basis of these same census lists, G. E. Mendenhall,

JBL, 77 (1958), 52–66, has lately suggested that the "thousand" numbered no more than a few men fit for military service, but this suggestion, too, is not supported by biblical sources.

5 Robertson Smith, *Kinship and Marriage in Early Arabia*, is still important for a study of the tribal regime among the ancient Arabs; for a more recent consideration of the subject, see *L'antica societa Beduina* which includes extensive bibliography on the subject. The ancient extra-biblical sources dealing with the tribes which wandered on the borders of the settled country, that is, tribes close to the Hebrews in origin and time, are usually written documents of kingdoms and nations with a developed urban culture. Nor do they treat sufficiently for present purposes of the life and social structure of these nomadic tribes. The position is somewhat different with regard to the Mari documents which deal with tribes in various transitional stages, from nomads on the borders of the settled land to permanent settlements subject to the authority of state; see, in particular, J.-R. Kupper, *Les nomades en Mésopotamie au temps des rois de Mari*, Paris, 1957; and the studies mentioned in note 1, above.

6 On the Arab nomadic tribes of this period and their regime, see C. M. Doughty, *Travels in Arabia Deserta* (2nd ed.), London, 1928; A. Musil, *Arabia Petraea* (3rd ed.), Vienna, 1908; *idem, The Manners and Customs of the Rwala Bedouins*, New York, 1928; Max von Oppenheim, *Die Beduinen*, I–III, Leipzig, 1939–1952.

7 For a discussion of the tribal genealogical lists in the traditions of the Arabs, see Robertson Smith, *op. cit.*, pp. 1 ff. On the lists themselves, see F. Wüstenfeld, *Genealogische Tabellen der arabischen Stämme und Familien*, Leipzig, 1852–1853.

8 See Robertson Smith, *op. cit.*, pp. 40 ff.; J. Pedersen, *Israel, Its Life and Culture*, I–II, London and Copenhagen, 1926, pp. 378–402; J. Scharbert, *Solidarität in Segen und Fluch im AT und seiner Umwelt*, Bonn, 1958, *passim*.

9 See section H, below.

10 Cf. the use of "my people ('*am*)" "his people" in expressions such as "...that soul shall be cut off from his people" (Gen. 17:14; etc.); "...and was gathered to his people" (Gen. 25:8; etc.); "There shall none defile himself for the dead among his people; except for his kin, that is near unto him" (Lev. 21:1–2); "I dwell among mine own people" (II Kings 4:13). And cf. also personal names such as Ammiel, Ammishaddai, or Jeroboam, Jokneam, etc., which may be connected with '*am* signifying a near member of the family, its avenger of blood, but not a nation. The Hebrew '*am* in the sense of a near member of the family may perhaps be connected with the Arabic denoting a paternal uncle. For a detailed discussion of the meaning of '*am* as a near member of the family, see M. Noth, *Die israelitischen Personennamen*, Stuttgart, 1928, pp. 76 ff.; L. Rost, "Die Bezeichnungen für Land und Volk im Alten Testament," *Festschrift O. Procksch*, Leipzig, 1935, pp. 142 ff.; Speiser, *JBL*, 79 (1960), 157–63. On *ḥay*, see Robertson Smith, *op. cit.*, pp. 41–6; J. Liver, *Encyclopaedia Biblica* (Hebrew), III, Jerusalem, 1958, col. 107.

11 In II Sam. 14:5–7 the woman of Tekoa tells King David about her two sons, one of whom killed the other in a field, and the whole family rose against her to kill her surviving son for the life of his brother whom he had slain. But, a) this is merely a parable, the purpose of which was to illustrate the harsh attitude adopted by the king toward Absalom his son, the situation described in the story being apparently in contradiction to the procedure customary in Israel; b) the woman of Tekoa hints that the members of the family are not prompted by a desire to avenge the blood that had been spilled but rather to inherit her property by killing the heir (verse 7).

12 The status of the elders in Israelite society after the Settlement may be compared to that of the elders (*šibūtum*) in the Mari documents; its society was also then in a transitional stage from a tribal to a monarchical regime; see J. Bottéro and A. Finet, *ARM*, XV (Répertoire analitique), p. 257, s. v. *šibum;* Bottéro, *ibid.*, VII, p. 242; and cf. also A. Malamat, *Encyclopaedia Biblica*, IV, Jerusalem, 1962, cols. 573–4, s.v. Mari. On the status of the

elders in Israelite tribal society, see also J. L. McKenzie, *Biblica*, 40 (1959), 522–40; J. van der Ploeg, *Festschrift H. Junker*, Trier, 1961, pp. 175–91.

13   Emphasis on the function and authority of the elders in maintaining law and order is characteristic of the Book of Deuteronomy. Its composition and especially the composition of its laws are not to be dated as late as the time of Josiah, in keeping with the view current in biblical research from the days of De Wette and Wellhausen. Objections to this view have been raised in several quarters (see M. D. [U.] Cassuto, *Encyclopaedia Biblica*, II, Jerusalem, 1954, cols. 607–19, s v. Deuteronomy). The code of laws in Deuteronomy most probably emanates from the early period of the Monarchy, or perhaps even before that. In any event, the way of life reflected in them dates from the days of the Judges when the family and the elders predominated in the social structure. See also S. Yeivin, *Sefer Dinaburg* (Hebrew), Jerusalem, 1949, pp. 31–48.

14   For a more detailed discussion of these points, see the chapter "Law," below.

15   Cf. Jud. 6:12; 11:1; I Sam. 9:1; Ruth 2:1. This term had a similar meaning in the period of the Monarchy; see II Kings 15:20; 24:14; etc. On the warriors, (*Gibbōrḥail*) see J. van der Ploeg, *RB*, 50 (1941), 120–5; W. McKane, *Transactions of the Glasgow University Oriental Society*, 17 (1959), 28–37.

16   According to a widespread view there were also judges of this sort, namely those termed Minor Judges (Jud. 10:1–5; 12:8–15); see A. Alt, *Kleine Schriften*, I, pp. 300–2; M. Noth, *Festschrift A. Bertholet*, Tübingen, 1950, pp. 404–17; and others. Noth contends that the title of Judge applied basically only to the Minor Judges whose main task was to administer the law, and that in the process of editing the Book of Judges the term Judge was transferred to the charismatic saviors. But Noth's suggestion lacks any real basis; see F. C. Fensham, "The Judges and Ancient Israelite Jurisprudence," *Die Ou Testamentiese Werkgemeenskap in Suid-Afrika, Papers Read at the Second Meeting*, Pretoria, 1959, pp. 15–22. Y. Kaufmann, *The Book*

of Judges (Hebrew), Jerusalem, 1962, pp. 46–8, maintains that there was no essential difference between the major Judges and those called minor, both having been saviors, both having been charismatic, both having made sporadic appearances, except that the narratives dealing with the minor Judges have not been preserved. In any event, the Book of Judges views the charismatic Judges who delivered Israel from the oppression of its enemies as characteristic of the image of the "Judge."

17   See the chapter "The Settlement of the Israelite Tribes," above.

18   See M. Noth, *Das System der Zwölf Stämme Israels*, Stuttgart, 1930, pp. 3 ff.

19   Cf. B. Maisler (Mazar), "The Genealogy of the sons of Nahor and the Historical Background of the Book of Job" (Hebrew), *Zion*, 11 (1946), 1–16; S. E. Loewenstamm, *Encyclopaedia Biblica*, I, Jerusalem, 1950, cols. 99–100, s. v. Edom; J. Liver, *ibid*, IV, cols. 762–3, s. v. Joktan. There may have been a somewhat similar tribal association among the peoples of Gashgash in Asia Minor, the twelve tribes of Gashgash, against whom Shuppiluliuma King of the Hittites (14th century B.C.E.) fought, being mentioned in a Hittite document. See H. G. Güterbock, *JCS*, 10 (1956), 67.

20   Noth, *op. cit.*, (following earlier scholars) has compared the league of the Israelite tribes with the classical *amphictyony* and has drawn far-reaching conclusions from it concerning the Conquest, the Settlement, and the religious and social regime of Israel in Canaan — even to the extent of regarding the Israelite tribal league as an actual *amphictyony* in every respect. By comparing it to an *amphictyony* which, as stated, is basically an association of tribes or peoples permanently settled around some sanctuary, Noth is obliged to assume that the Israelite tribal league was formed in Canaan, and that after the tribes had settled in the country they grouped themselves around some cultic center, which he holds was at Shechem. No actual data however support Noth's suggestion (for a view opposed to that of Noth, cf., in particular, H. M. Orlinsky, "The Tribal System of Israel and Related Groups in the Period of the Judges",

Oriens Antiquus, 1 [1962], 11–20). Against Noth's view stands the fact that the first two tribes enumerated — Reuben and Simeon — remained semi-nomads until the end of the monarchy, which reinforces the notion that originally it was a league of nomadic tribes, the foundation of which pre-dated the Settlement; see also J. Liver, *JSS* 8 (1963) 227 ff.

21 Some scholars hold that the ark was transferred from place to place until it found a permanent home at Shiloh. According to M. Noth, *Geschichte Israels* (2nd ed.), Göttingen, 1954, pp. 88–93, the ark was first at Shechem which was also at the beginning of the Conquest the center of the tribal league; it was then taken to Beth-el, and from there to Gilgal, and finally to Shiloh. For all this however there is no real evidence in the Bible. On the contrary, according to the Book of Joshua the ark was at Shiloh as early as the time of Joshua (Josh. 18:1–6). Nor does the account of the assembly of the tribes at Shechem (Josh. 24) contradict the assumption that the ark and the tent of meeting were already then at Shiloh. Theoretically they may first have been in various places and later at Shiloh, but there is no actual proof of this. In the story of the concubine at Gibeah the ark is mentioned as being at Beth-el (Jud. 20:26–27), where the Israelites also prayed to God before the battle and after their first defeat (Jud. 18; 21:1–2), but in this selfsame story Shiloh is mentioned as the place where the feast of the Lord was held from year to year (Jud. 21:19).

22 This story is apparently intended to reconcile the contradiction between the fact that the Israelites concluded a covenant with the Gibeonites, inhabitants of the country (cf. Josh. 10), at the beginning of the Settlement and the injunction of a total ban on the inhabitants of the land. The actual conditions of the covenant with the Gibeonites, that is, the covenant made with the entire congregation and the protection granted to them which was bound up with the obligation to serve the congregation (Josh. 9:27), fit in with the regime of the congregation (a great deal of comparative material is cited by J. M.

Grintz, "The Treaty with the Gibeonites" (Hebrew), *Zion*, 26 [1961], 69–84). For the story in general, see Liver, *JSS*, 8 (1963), 227–43.

23 Cf. Gen. 17:20; 25:16; Num. 25:18. On the other hand, the genealogical lists in the Book of Chronicles refer to princes of those border tribes among whom a tribal regime existed also after the Settlement — Reuben (I Chron. 5:6) and Simeon (I Chron. 4:38) — whereas the chief princes of the tribe of Asher, mentioned in the list of the military census (I Chron. 7:40), have no connection with the tribal regime. On these lists, see J. Liver, *'Oz le-Dawid (Ben-Gurion Volume)*, Jerusalem, 1964, pp. 493–9. On the term prince (*nāsik*) and his function and status, see E. A. Speiser, *CBQ*, 25 (1963), 111–117.

24 "The men of Israel ... numbered four hundred thousand men that drew sword" (Jud. 20:17); on the first day twenty-two thousand men of Israel were slain (verse 21); and there are other similarly exaggerated figures. The story of the concubine at Gibeah likewise tells of the complete devastation of the land of Benjamin, of the destruction of Jabesh-gilead, of the killing of the males in it (Jud. 21:10 ff.), and other such events. The account of the assembly of all the Israelite tribes to wage war against Gibeah is in the same spirit; and since it does not agree with what is known of the relations among the tribes in the days of the Judges, it is probably one of the fictitious elements in the story, which nonetheless contains an historical kernel. It was however not a war in which all the tribes took part, but rather a clash between Benjamite families and the tribe of Ephraim; cf. O. Eissfeldt, "Der geschichtliche Hintergrund der Erzählung von Gibeas Schandtat," *Festschrift G. Beer*, Stuttgart, 1935, pp. 19–40; K. D. Schunck, *BZAW*, 86 (1963), 57 ff.

25 See section C, above.

26 For a detailed discussion of studies on this subject, see W. F. Duffy, *The Tribal-Historical Theory on the Origin of the Hebrew People*, Washington D. C., 1944; and see also J. Liver, *Encyclopaedia Biblica*, III, cols. 663–71, s. v. *yaḥas*.

27 That there were family genealogies in the period of the First Temple can be seen from Ezra 2:62 concerning the priestly families which in the early days of the Restoration looked for their genealogical register but could not find it; cf. Neh 7:5 — "The book of the genealogy of them that came up at the first." Other indications that pedigrees existed in Israel are to be found in expressions such as: "And if not, blot me, I pray Thee, out of Thy book" (Ex. 32:32); "And in Thy book they were all written" (Ps. 139:16); "In the register of the house of Israel" (Ezek. 13:9).

28 Cf. I Chron. 5:17; 7:7, 40; etc.; see Liver, 'Oz l^e-Dawid, pp. 489–90.

29 The Book of Genesis enumerates ten generations of the fathers of mankind from Adam to Noah (Gen. 5), and another ten from Shem the son of Noah to Abraham (Gen. 11:10–26). This list corresponds in structure to the Sumerian-Babylonian king list (see T. Jacobsen, Sumerian King List, Chicago, 1939; ANET, pp. 265 ff.), which first enumerates the kings who reigned until the Flood and then those who reigned after it. The Sumerian king list is associated with mythological motifs; according to it all the kings before and some after the Flood were deities or semi-deities. Similar traditions, also basically mythological, are given in the Bible in the form of a genealogical schema — father, son, grandson, etc. — adjusted to the thought-patterns of the Israelite tribes; see also M. D. (U.) Cassuto, A Commentary on the Book of Genesis, Part I: From Adam to Noah (engl. trans. by I. Abrahams), Jerusalem, 1961, pp. 249 ff. A. Malamat, "King Lists of the Old Babylonian Period and biblical Genealogies," BIES (Hebrew) 31 (1967), 9–28.

30 See note 26, above.

31 For examples, see section H, below.

32 In the history of the sons of Jacob (Gen. 29–35) and in the list of the sons of Jacob, in the catalogue of those who went to Egypt (Gen. 46:8 ff.; Ex. 1:1 ff.), the census lists in the Book of Numbers (Num. 1; 26), and the order in which the tribes camped and wandered in the wilderness (Num. 2), in the list of the spies (Num. 13:1 ff.), the blessing cf Jacob (Gen. 49) and that of Moses (Deut. 33), the lists of the tribal territories (Josh. 13–19), etc. For a detailed discussion of the order of the tribes in these lists and their historical significance, see Noth, Das System der Zwölf Stämme Israels. For an extensive study of the early history of the Israelite tribes, see Duffy, op. cit.; H. H. Rowley, From Joseph to Joshua, London, 1950, passim; and the detailed bibliographies cited in them.

33 Some scholars contend that Levi was never a tribe such as the others were, and that from the outset the name indicated the status of priests and attendants of the sanctuary who were made into a fictitious tribe. They find support for their view in the name lw', lw't which occurs in Minean inscriptions from Dedan (now al-'Ulā) in northern Arabia dating from the 5th or 4th century B.C.E. These belonged to the temple and, as the name suggests, were apparently dedicated to the sanctuary in fulfilment of a vow or even in repayment of a debt (see H. Grimme, Muséon, 37 [1924], 169–99; W. F. Albright, Archaeology and the Religion of Israel, Baltimore, 1953, pp. 109 ff., 204). The attempt to draw a parallel between the tribe of Levi and the lw' in the Minoan inscriptions is far-fetched, especially since they are mentioned in only a few inscriptions which are much later than the beginnings of the Israelite tribes. It is however impossible to reconcile the assumption that the Levites were from the beginning a class of priests engaged in divine service with the early tradition of the part played by Simeon and Levi against the men of Shechem (Gen. 34), and in particular with the harsh statements made about these tribes in Jacob's blessing in Gen. 49:5–7. Cf. Y. Kaufmann, A History of the Israelite Faith (Hebrew), Tel-Aviv, I, 1937, pp. 173 ff.: Rowley, op. cit., pp. 8 ff.

34 On the lists of the tribes, including those not mentioned here, see Noth. op. cit. Most of the tribes are referred to also in the Song of Deborah (Jud. 5), and some maintain that the Song mentions all those that then belonged to the tribal league. Since the names of Simeon and Judah are omitted there, it is contended that at an early stage only ten tribes belonged to the

tribal league, Judah having been an independent people, genealogically related to Israel (thus E. Meyer, *Die Israeliten und Ihre Nachbarstämme*, Halle a/S, 1906, pp. 232 ff.; S. Mowinckel, *Zur Frage nach dokumentarischen Quellen in Josua* 13–19, Oslo, 1946, pp. 21 ff.; idem, *BZAW*, 77 [1958], 137–42; and others). There is however no substance in this view that denies Judah a place in the league of the Israelite tribes from its beginning merely on the basis of the Song of Deborah which, dealing with one specific battle in the north of the country, was not concerned to enumerate all the Israelite tribes.

35 Nor indeed does this fact corroborate the theory that the sons of Joseph entered Canaan before the tribes of Leah.

36 According to Josh. 7:1 Carmi was the father of Achan who committed an offence by breaking the ban, but in I Chron. 4:1 Carmi is included together with Hur and Shobal, among the chief families of Judah; Carmi, that is the family of the Carmites, one of whose offspring was Achan (here disparagingly called Achar), is also mentioned in I Chron. 2:7.

37 The sons of Jair may have originated from the early nomadic tribes in Gilead, related by origin to Israel and identified with the Ya'uri mentioned among the nomadic tribes in the Syrian desert in Assyrian documents of the 13th century B.C.E. See B. Maisler (Mazar), *Tarbiz* (Hebrew), 15 (1944), 63–4; D. D. Luckenbill, *Ancient Records of Assyria and Babylonia*, I, Chicago, 1926, pp. 28, 57, 60.

38 Jashub is a place mentioned on Samaria ostracon no. 48 and is apparently Khirbet Kafr Sib to the north of Tul Karm; see B. Maisler (Mazar), *JPOS*, 14 (1934), 96 ff. The family of Shimron is most probably connected with Shemer the owner of the hill Samaria (I Kings 16:24), on which the town of Samaria was later founded. See Y. Kutscher, *Tarbiz*, 11 (1940), 17–22. The connections between Manasseh, Asher, and

Issachar are also indicated in the obscure verse in Josh. 17:11 — "And Manasseh had in Issachar and in Asher...," which apparently refers to the expansion of the families of Manasseh towards the Valley of Jezreel.

39 See also E. Z. Melamed, *Tarbiz*, 5 (1934), 121–6.

40 Num. 26:28–34; Josh. 17:1–3; I Chron. 7:14–19; and see on these lists also A. Bergman, "The Israelite Tribe of Half Manasseh," *JPOS*, 16 (1936), 224 ff.

41 The geographical name Hoglah is mentioned on the Samaria ostraca nos. 45 and 47, and the name Noah on ostracon no. 50.

42 For a discussion of these genealogical lists see S. Klein, *Zion* (Hebrew), 3 (1929), 1–16; Meyer, *op. cit.*, pp. 400 ff.; M. Noth, "Eine siedlungsgeographische Liste in 1 Chr. 2 und 4," *ZDPV*, 55 (1932), 97–124.

43 According to I Chron. 7–16 the name of Machir's wife was Maacah, while in verse 15 she is mentioned as the sister or wife of Machir. On Maacah in the Bible and in ancient Near Eastern sources, and on the connections of Maacah with Israel, see B. Mazar, "Geshur and Ma'cah" *JBL* 80 (1961), 16–28.

44 See H. L. Ginsberg and B. Maisler (Mazar), "Semitized Hurrians in Syria and Palestine," *JPOS*, 14 (1934), 234–67; cf. also B. Maisler (Mazar), *BIES* (Hebrew), 13 (1947), 106–7, 110–4.

45 For Hurrian elements in northern Judah, see also S. Kallai, *The Northern Boundaries of Judah* (Hebrew), Jerusalem, 1960, pp. 35 ff.

46 On Caleb and Jerahmeel in the involved genealogical lists of Judah in I Chron. 2; 4, and on the areas of Caleb and Jerahmeel's settlement, see J. Liver, *Encyclopaedia Biblica*, III, cols. 861–3, s.v. Jerahmeel; *ibid.*, IV, cols. 106–10, s. v. Caleb, and the bibliography cited there.

47 See S. Klein, *Zion*, 4 (1930), 14 ff.; Noth, *op. cit.*, pp. 112 ff.

332

CHAPTER X

THE RELIGIOUS CULTURE OF THE JEWISH PEOPLE
IN BEGINNINGS: THE FAITH AND THE CULT

1 J. Wellhausen, *Prolegomena zur Geschichte Israels*, Berlin, 1886, p. 440.

2 Various attempts have been made lately to find the origin of the name of the deity יהו or יי in ancient Western Semitic names, or in Ugarit documents (De Langhe, "Un dieu Jahwe à Ras Shamra?"; *Bull. voor Geschiedeniss en Exegese von OT*, 14 (1942), 91–101, and also in the name of a place in the Negev which is mentioned in an Egyptian document from the time of Ramses II (B. Grdseloff, *Revue de l'histoire juive en Egypte*, 1 [1947], 79–82). But these hypotheses are doubtful.

3 It is worth noting that the very concept "Sefer Torah" — Book of the Law — is late in biblical literature, and in this respect it is instructive to compare Joshua 1:7, which mentions inquiring of God before going into battle, with the verse following (8), which was added by a deuteronomist scribe and which speaks of "this book of the law." The primary meaning of the root ירה is "to throw"; hence yᵉriat ḥiẓim and avanim and also yᵉriāt gōrāl (Joshua 18:6). And hence the connection between the priest who casts the Urim and Thummim so as to discern between the evil man (the accursed) and the righteous (the pure). This apparently is the primary use of the mantic instrument, which in the course of time also assumed the task of foretelling the future by means of alternative asking (see in particular I Sam. 23:2, 4, 11:12). And see S. Iwry, *JAOS*, 81 (1961), 27–34; and Deut. 33:8–11; where the giving of the Urim to Levi — who does not acknowledge his relatives when dispensing justice — is juxtaposed to the teaching of the ordinances and the Law of God.

4 Wellhausen points out the existence of the theophoric name "Yᵉhoshua" in Ephraim; but the story of the changing of the name of Hosea son of Nun to Joshua (Num. 13:16) in effect points to a conclusion opposite to that of Wellhausen's, namely, the acception of the name of JHWH by the House of Joseph.

5 It is glaringly clear that what is said in Exodus 20:4–6 is simply an explanatory addition to "Thou shalt have no other gods before Me." The deuteronomist scribe sensed the monolatrous character of the verse, which rejects the assumption of monotheism, and deliberately changed its import by an addition. Anyone who interprets "Thou shalt have no other" and "Thou shalt not make" separately, and nevertheless maintains that these words are written in the spirit of monotheism, is truly pious.

6 The identification of morality with universality has been an impediment to Wellhausen's whole theory (see the continuation). This identification was indeed one of the glorious creations of human thought in Wellhausen's day, but it is refuted by facts: The Egyptian "Book of the Dead," which contains lofty rules of ethics on the order of the Decalogue, is a blatantly polytheistic creation, with no universalist tendencies whatsoever. At the same time, there is no proof that the last five commandments were included in the tablets of the Decalogue; but Wellhausen sees no reason to contradict this.

7 See note 6, above. Against this ideational speculation — which also expresses the feeling that there must have been one essential thing in the religion of Moses that could be developed — there is this to be said: a) In no pantheon do we find the phenomenon of a god of morality being turned into a supreme god. b) JHWH does not become a god of justice by virtue of His national role, but by virtue of the fact that He knows what is hidden, teaches justice and righteousness, and answers those who seek Him.

8 Because it was founded by Engnell of Sweden and Nyberg and Nielsen of Denmark. The appearance of H. S. Nyberg's *Studien zum Hoseabuche*, Uppsala, 1935,

marks the beginning of the school; a summary and explanation of its view is given in E. Nielsen, *Oral Tradition*, London, 1954.

9   J. Pedersen, *Israel, Its Life and Culture*, vol. II, London, 1926; pp. 18 f.

10   Paul Volz, *Moses*, Tübingen, 1932.

11   This is not to be understood as referring to phenomenological research, or a philosophical essay on the phenomenon of the divine call.

12   M. Buber, *Moses*, Jerusalem and Tel Aviv, 1946, V.

13   Emissary prophecy does not in any sense appear to derive from the fact that God is one. It is connected with the idea of the covenant, which makes God the King of the Israelites, which is not necessarily a monotheistic idea. (The rest of Kaufmann's views on the nature of monotheism stands fast, but not all Bible scholars agree with his assumption that the absence of magic and the appreciation of the traditional-symbolic role of worship apply to the entire Scriptures).

14   A. Alt, *Der Gott der Väter*, Stuttgart, 1929.

15   The conception of the religion of Moses as a continuation and development of the special concepts of the Hebrew religion of the Patriarchs begins with M. Buber's *Moses*, but the assumptions in our survey deviate from Buber's theory on a number of points.

16   There are, of course, those who reject the historical reliability of the pragmatic framework of the Book of Judges. Possibly the pragmatic adapter of the episode was confronted with a story about the house of Baal-berith, and imagined that the Israelites "made Baal-berith their god" (Jud. 8:33). But the very "making of Baal-berith their god" reflects such a paucity of knowledge of the Canaanite religion and its concepts, that we are constrained to doubt that the pragmatic editor had a clear idea of that Baal-berith. Scholars who advocate the version of Canaanite Shechem do not pay attention to the fact that Baal-berith is not a Canaanite concept, though it fits in very well with the Israelite view that God is the ally (*ba'al berit*) of the people.

334

CHAPTER XI

LAW

1 *ANET*, p. 220.
2 *ANET*, pp. 219 f.
3 For these documents and additional parallel Nuzi laws cf. C. H. Gordon, *BAr*, 3 (1940), 1–2, R. T. O'Callaghan, *CBQ*, 6 (1944), 398–404.
4 Cf. for example the Code of Hammurabi p. Ia, lines 32–39; p. XXIV b, lines 59–62; The Epos of Keret, *KRT* C VI, lines 31–49.
5 Gaius, *Institutiones* IV, 11.
6 These are the laws of Eshnunna, cf. A. Goetze, *The Laws of Eshnunna*, New Haven, 1956; The Law of Lipith-Ishtar, cf. S. N. Kramer, *ANET*, pp. 159–161; the law of Ur-Namu, cf. S. N. Kramer, *Orientalia*, (NS) 23 (1954), 40–51.
7 The Code of Hammurabi, p. XXV b. lines 40–43.
8 B. Landsberger, "Die babylonischen Termini fuer Gesetz und Recht", *Symbolae*, Leiden, 1939, 219–234.
9 II Sam. 15:2.
10 The Assyrian Law tablet A, §§ 7, 18, 19, 21, 40; tablet B §§ 7–9, 15, 18; tablet C §§ 3, 8, 11; and cf. also the Code of Hammurabi, § 202.
11 Cf. the profound discussion of Deut. 25:1 by Maimonides which begins with the words: "It is accepted by tradition that the stripes are given to those who have violated one of the negative commandments; why then are they mentioned in connection with a civil matter?"
12 G. Bergsträsser, *Grundzüge des islamischen Rechts*, edited and revised by J. Schacht, Berlin, 1935.
13 The Code of Hammurabi, p. XXVI b. lines 95–98.
14 The Code of Hammurabi, p. V a. lines 14–24, and cf. H. Cazelles, *Etudes sur le Code de l'Alliance*, Paris, 1946, pp. 186–188; J. van der Ploeg, *CBQ*, 13 (1951), 297.
15 M. Noth, *Die Gesetze im Pentateuch*, Halle, a/S, 1940, 78–82; G. E. Mendenhall, *BAr*, 17 (1954), 28–31, 50, 76, who emphasizes the parallels between the Sinaitic and Shechem

Covenants and the Hittite Covenant Treaties.
16 Landsberger, "Die babylonischen Termini etc.," *ibid.*, 223, compares the civil and criminal laws with the Akkadian term *dīnu*, the accepted rules for social behavior with *kibṣu*, the laws of a purely religious nature with *parsu*, though it must be pointed out that the law books restrict themselves to the *dīnu*, and that a clear distinction is made between the three subjects, which is not the case with biblical and Muslim law.
17 W. Rudolph, *Ruth*, Leipzig, 1939, p. 37–41; M. Burrows, *JBL*, 59 (1940), 445–454; M. Z. Segal, *Golak and Klein Memorial Volume*, (Hebrew), Jerusalem, (1942), 124–132; Th. C. Vriezen, *OTS*, 5 (1948), 80–88.
18 For the time of the Book of the Covenant cf. Cazelles, *op. cit.*, pp. 11–37, 169–189. For the Law of Holiness cf. L. E. Elliot-Binns, *ZAW*, 67 (1955), 26–40.
19 A. Jirku, *Das weltliche Recht im Alten Testament*, Gütersloh, 1927.
20 Landberger, "Die babylonischen Termini etc.,", *ibid*, 223, note 19.
21 A. Alt, "Die Ursprünge des israelitischen Rechts," *Kleine Schriften*, I, pp. 278–332.
22 Mendenhall, *BAr*, 17 (1954), 36 ff., Cazelles, *op. cit.*, p. 169.
23 Mendenhall, *ibid.*, 30.
24 Th. J. Meek, *ANET*, p. 218, note 24.
25 J. van der Ploeg, *CBQ*, 12 (1950), 422, ff., deals with the formulation of the Eshnunna laws in general. Cf. his discussion of the types of formulation in the laws of the Ancient East, *ibid.*, 416–427.
26 W. F. Albright, *A. Marx Jubilee Volume*, New York, 1950, 74–82, suggested that this law reflects the reforms of Jehoshaphat King of Judah, which are described in II Chr. 19:4–11.
27 Goetze, *op. cit.*, p. 32.
28 S. E. Loewenstamm, *IEJ*, 7 (1957), 193 ff.
29 The absence of laws of tenancy has its parallel in the absence of the type of loan which the borrower repays "to the barn,"

that is to say, when the crop is in the barn. The social basis of this type of loan, current in the whole of the Ancient East, belongs to the institution of land tenancy which does not exist in the Pentateuch, and cf. Loewenstamm, *ibid.*, 197 ff. In the Pentateuch the place of the laws of land tenancy is taken by the laws of the Jubilee, which turn every land sale into a kind of tenancy.

30 A. van Praag, *Droit Matrimonial assyro-babylonien*, Amsterdam, 1945, p. 208.

31 Most scholars are of the opinion that the reason for the levirate marriage given in the pentateuchal law is late (and cf. also Gen. 38:8), and in different ways try to discover the original reason. On these attempts and on the question whether the biblical law of levirate marriage has its parallels in the rest of Ancient Eastern laws, cf. S. E. Lowenstamm, "Levirate Marriage," *Encyclopaedia Biblica*, (Hebrew), III, cols. 444–447.

32 Gordon, *UM*, text 77, line 19.

33 G. R. Driver—J. C. Miles, *Babylonian Laws*, I, Oxford, 1956, pp. 271–275.

34 Talmudic law does not compel the father to give a dowry to his daughter, but it is considered meritorious for the father to give his daughter a dowry in accordance with his means. Cf. for example B. T. Keth, 52*b*; B. T. Ta'an. 24*a*.

35 Cf. note 32 above.

36 C. H. Gordon, *JBL*, 54 (1935), 231–233.

37 See Segal, *ibid.*, pp. 125–126, who considers the possibility that also other passages reflect the law of a widow's inheritance.

38 H. S. Maine, *Ancient Law*, London, 1930, p. 164.

39 *Idem*, op. cit., 162 ff.

40 Some scholars claim that "a double portion" (*pi sh*e*nāyim*) everywhere means two thirds, i.e., the first-born takes two thirds of the inheritance even if he has many brothers, and as evidence these scholars quote Zech. 13:8 where the same words mean two thirds, as well as the Akkadian word *šine/ipiāṭum* or *šine/ipu* — two thirds. But in Ben Sira 12:5; 18:32, according to all opinions "*pi sh*e*nāyim*" means "double", we need not, however, be surprised at the ambiguousity of the expression "*pi sh*e*nāyim*,"

since we similarly find "four parts" ("*Ar-ba'ha-yādoth*") (Gen. 47:24) — four fifth as against "five times" ("*ḥāmēsh yādoth*") — five (unlike the Akkadian where combinations with *qātāti* always indicate a fraction, e.g. *ḥamiš qātāti* — five sixth). We therefore accept the tradition which explains "*pi sh*e*nāyim*" in Deut 21:17 as a "double portion" (cf. the LXX and in the Barayta, B.T.B.Bathra, 122b; 123a). And if this is so then the law of the first-born in the Bible has its parallel in the Mesopotamian law, and cf. R.T. O'Callaghan, *JCS*, 8 (1954), 139 ff.

41 R. North, *Sociology of the Biblical Jubilee*, Rome, 1954, claims that according to the law of the Jubilee all land that had been sold returned to its owners forty-nine (or fifty) years after its sale. Against this view cf. S. E. Loewenstamm, *Beit Miqra* (Hebrew), (1956) 8–27.

42 This is how these verses have to be explained according to the Jewish tradition as handed down by Josephus, *Antiq.* IV, viii, 26; as well as in B.T.Mez. 113a–b, and the reference is not to a pledge given at the time when the loan was made as a few modern scholars think, e.g. Cazelles, *op. cit.* p. 80. Against this cf. M. David, *OTS*, 2 (1943), 79–86.

43 The prohibition of taking interest was differently explained by E. Neufeld, *HUCA*, 26 (1955), 355–403, Neufeld deduced from the prohibition of taking interest from the poor (Ex. 22:24; Lev. 25:35–37) permission for taking interest from those who are not poor. The law in Deut. 23:20 which prohibits the taking of interest from any Israelite, he considers a Second Temple period innovation; but all this is rather farfetched.

44 For the decrees of Mesopotamian kings who cancelled all debts, cf. J. B. Alexander, *JBL*, 57 (1938), 75–79, there is no mention, however, of the automatic cancellation of debts at dates fixed in advance.

45 Cf. J. Rabinowitz "Loans," *Encyclopaedia Biblica* (Hebrew), II, cols. 813–816.

6 According to many scholars the original reason for leaving the forgotten sheaf and the poor man's tithe was based on a magic belief that a little of the crop must be left

in the field to insure the fertility of the earth, and that the Pentateuch changed this ancient magic custom into a social law. Cf. for example A. Causse, *Du groupe ethnique à la communauté religieuse*, Paris, 1937, 140 ff.

47   S. Klein, "The Cities of the Priests and Levites and the Cities of Refuge, "*Meḥqarim Eretz Yisraeliyim* (Hebrew), Vol. 3 note 4, Jerusalem–Tel Aviv, (1934). W. F. Albright, *L. Ginzberg Jubilee Volume*, New-York, pp. 49–73; B. Mazar, *OTS*, 7 (1960), 193–205; M. Haran, *JBL*, 80 (1961), 45–54.

48   G. E. Wright, *VT* 4 (1954), 325–330.

49   J. Wellhausen, *Prolegomena zur Geschichte Israels*, Berlin, 1905, pp. 132 f.

50   According to many scholars the sojourners originated from the Canaanites whom the Israelites did not kill, and cf. for example, I. L. Seeligman, "Sojourner," *Encyclopaedia Biblica* (Hebrew), II, cols 546–549. This view is mainly based on a comparison of the text in I Kings, 5:29 with the passage in II Chr. 2:16–17, which explicitly calls the Canaanite population subject to Solomon, sojourners. It is doubtful though, if one may here explain the language of the Pentateuch on the basis of a linguistic usage in Chronicles. It is difficult to imagine that, on the one hand, the Pentateuch commanded the expulsion, and destruction of this population (Ex. 22:23–33; Num. 33: 50–56; Deut. 7:1–6), and on the other hand, requested them to be loved. Neither can this problem be solved by separating sources. Lev. 18:24–28, also commands the sojourner not to become contaminated by the abomination of the nations who were in the country before the Israelites; and Deuteronomy, which is greatly concerned with the sojourner, commands putting the former inhabitants under the ban.

51   For an attempt of fitting this obscure law into the historical framework, cf. K. Galling, *Festschrift A. Bertholet*, Tübingen, 1950, pp. 176–191.

52   M. Noth, *Festschrift O. Procksch*, Leipzig, 1940, pp. 101–112; A. Alt, *op. cit.*, pp. 20 ff. who thinks that the name Hebrew here denotes a class. As against this cf. M. Greenberg, *Tarbiz* (Hebrew), 24 (1955), 369, 370, 377.

53   Causse, *op. cit.*, 173; and cf. also North,

op. cit., pp. 153–157, who emphasizes the doubtful benefit of freeing the slave in the seventh year, when he has no certainty of being able to earn an independent living.

54   V. Korošec, *Hethitische Staatsvertrage*, Leipzig, 1931, pp. 56 ff., 80 ff.; J. Nougayrol, *PRU* IV, (1965), 105 ff.

55   That is how the plain meaning of this law appears. Cf. I. P. Teicher, *VT*, I (1951), 125–129 ff.; P. E. Kahle, *The Cairo Geniza*, London, 1947, pp. 122 ff.

56   For a summary of the exegesis on this law cf. Cazelles, *op. cit.* p. 73.

57   The conflict between the principle of individual responsibility and collective responsibility is known also from the history of the Hittite law, and cf. V. Korošec, *Archiv Orientální*, 18/3 (1950), 187–209.

58   B. Baentsch, *Exodus, Leviticus and Numeri*, Göttingen, 1903, pp. 58, 340; G. Beer, *Exodus*, Tübingen, 1939, 64.

59   H. Gunkel, *Genesis*, Göttingen, 1910, p. 270.

60   The early formulation of the law, in contrast to the formulation in Num. 35:12, 15, had not as yet reached the abstract definition of "unintentionally" and they allude to this concept in casuistic terminology.

61   For example, N. M. Nicolsky, *ZAW*, 48 (1930), 146–175; M. David, *OTS*, 9 (1951) 30–48.

62   Cf. note 47 above.

63   According to Nicolsky and David (note 61) the law of the refuge cities has its origin in the special protection granted the murderer who fled to the altar, and also the "place" mentioned here is simply a holy place; but this is not convincing.

64   The closest parallel to the laws of the cities of refuge are found in the laws of Athens, legislated by Dracon around the year 622 B.C.E. On the subject of these laws and their influence on late Hebrew law cf. J. Baer, *Zion*, (Hebrew), 17 (1952), 23–27, concerning the plain meaning of the biblical passage, see his important observation that the return of the unintentional murderer to his town involved religious ceremonies of atonement, there is therefore no reason to be surprised at the law in Num. 35:25 which makes the murderer's return to his

people dependent on the death of the high priest, since this atones for his transgression.

65   Cf. the Laws of Eshnunna, § 12.

66   For the extent of similarity between the laws of the goring ox in Mesopotamia and the pentateuchal laws cf. on the one hand, A. van Selms, *Archiv Orientální*, 18/4 (1950), 312–330, who questions the assumption of this proximity, and on the other, S. E. Loewenstamm, *ibid.*, (note 28 above), 196 ff.

67   The principle of an eye for an eye is counted among the innovations of the Code of Hammurabi; ancient Sumerian law only knows a monetary fine. And cf. A. S. Diamond, *Iraq*, 19 (1957), 161–155, who claims that in ancient law there only existed monetary punishment and that corporal punishment belongs to a later stage of the history of law.

68   And cf. also C. H. Gordon, *JPOS*, 15 (1935), 29 ff.

69   Cf. in the Law of Eshnunna § 26; in the Code of Hammurabi § 130.

70   M. David, *VT*, 1 (1951), 219–221; A. Alt, *VT*, 2 (1952), 153–159; M. V. Bravmann, *JCS*, 7 (1953), 27.

71   Cf. D. Daube, *Studies in Biblical Law*, Cambridge, 1947, p. 95. As against this cf. the article "Kidnapping" in the *Encyclo-paedia Biblica*, II, col. 538, where the law in Ex. 21:16 is explained as if it read: "And if a man be found stealing any of his breathern, and sell him . . .".

72   The formulation "A person shall be put to death only on the testimony of two or more witnesses; he must not be put to death on the testimony of a single witness" (Deut. 17:6) is unintelligible. And cf. H. Z. Reines, *Sinai*, (Hebrew), 42 (1958), 248–252, who explains that even though a court can punish the accused on the evidence of only two witnesses, it must also take evidence from a third witness (and similarly from additional witnesses) if there is any.

73   *ANET*, pp. 216 ff.

74   C. H. Gordon, *JBL*, 54 (1935), 139–144; G. R. Driver–J. C. Milles, *Iraq*, 7 (1940), 132–138; E. Speiser, *Orientalia;* (NS) 25 (1956), 15–23; A. E. Draffkorn, *JBL*, 76 (1957), 216–224.

75   Cazelles, *op. cit.* p. 67.

76   *Idem, op. cit.*, pp. 68 ff. Cf. also Draffkorn, *ibid.*, 222, who assumes that both the plaintiff and the defendant had to swear, and that only after they were both under oath did God make His decision. There is, however, no evidence to support this assumption.

CHAPTER XII

THE SEER-PRIEST

* This subject has been dealt with by me at greater length in "The Seer in Ancient Israel," *Oriens Antiquus*, 4 (1965), 153–74.

1 J. A. Wilson, *The Burden of Egypt*, Chicago, 1951, p. 243 (subsequently published as a Phoenix Paperback under the title *The Culture of Egypt*).

2 There is a very considerable bibliography on our subject generally for the ancient Near East; but it is important to warn the reader that there is an urgent need of a detailed comparative account and analysis of the many forms of divination as they were practiced — or if they were not, why not — in Sumer, Babylonia, Assyria, the territory of the Hittites, Canaan, etc. Thus A. L. Oppenheim, *Ancient Mesopotamia : Portrait of a Dead Civilization*, Chicago, 1964, while noting that "the royal art of astrology is the method of divination for which Mesopotamia is famed," has observed that "study of the rise of astrology in Mesopotamian civilization has hardly begun" (p. 224). For literature on the subject, see the bibliography on this chapter, below.

3 The term "seer-priest" is employed in this chapter as a general expression covering the four terms used in the Bible for those endowed with uncommon powers in the earlier, pre-prophetic period: visionary, seer, man of God, prophet. The expression "diviner" would have been better, except that this term would recall — unnecessarily and misleadingly — too many of the practices of the ancient Near Eastern diviner (the Canaanite not least among them) to which the Israelite seer did not resort (see Excursus II, below); such terms as "diviner-priest" and "oracle-priest," though accurate, are perhaps somewhat clumsy for regular usage.

4 It is unfortunate that scholars have permitted themselves to be misled by and to place such great emphasis upon the element of ecstasy. This was true even before — as well as in consequence of — the appearance of G. Hölscher, *Die Profeten*, Leipzig, 1914, chaps. I–III, as though ecstasy, or a special, frenzied brand of it, marked an essential difference between seer and prophet, or as though it was a special type of ecstasy that rendered the biblical prophet *sui generis* in all history. Thus J. Lindblom's *Prophecy in Ancient Israel*, Oxford, 1962, would have been a better work had it not been burdened with the "Supernormal Experiences" in chaps. I–III. Cf. the survey by H. H. Rowley, *The Servant of the Lord and other Essays on the Old Testament*, London, 1952, chap. III, pp. 91 ff., and *passim*: "The Nature of Old Testament Prophecy in the Light of Recent Study." The chapter appeared originally in *HTR*, 38 (1945), 1–38. See also on Wen-Amon, below (Section G, end).

5 See W. F. Albright, *Archaeology and the Religion of Israel*, Baltimore, 1942, pp.125–9.

6 The "prophets" in A. R. Johnson, *The Cultic Prophet in Ancient Israel*, Cardiff, 1944, pp. 59 ff., are really "seers." It would seem that Lindblom, *op. cit.*, would have been much clearer and more useful had he used the term "seer" (or diviner) and "prophet" with greater discrimination. On W. F. Albright, *Samuel and the Beginnings of the Prophetic Movement*, Cincinnati, 1961, see my comments on pp. 93–4 of the chapter on "Old Testament Studies" in *Religion*, ed. by P. Ramsey, Englewood Cliffs, N. J., 1965; M. A. Cohen, "The Role of the Shilonite Priesthood in the United Monarchy of Ancient Israel," *HUCA*, 36 (1965), 65 ff., and notes 20–1.

7 On *limmudai* "pupils, disciples" in Isa. 8:16, see Orlinsky, "The Seer in Ancient Israel," *loc. cit.*, 156 note 7.

8 Cf. A. Haldar, *Associations of Cult Prophets among the ancient Semites*, Uppsala, 1945, pp. 34 ff.; I. Mendelsohn, "Guilds in Ancient Palestine," *BASOR*, 80 (1940), 17–21 (especially note 29); *idem*, "Guilds in Babylonia and Assyria," *JAOS*, 60 (1940), 68–72. Oded, the father of Azariah the prophet, who is mentioned in II Chron. 15:1 ff., may himself also have been a prophet; unfortunately, verse 8 is corrupt at this point. The only other person in the Bible with the name Oded is likewise a

prophet (of Samaria) in the days of Pekah (II Chron. 28:9).

9   It is thus clear that Jesus as a miracle-worker is not to be associated with the classical prophets. In general, there was a resurgence in the belief and practice of magic and miracle-working, as well as the rise of an elaborate angelology, in the later part of the Second Jewish Commonwealth (cf., for example, the Book of Daniel; the Apocryphal literature). This was due chiefly not to the influence of any holdover from the ancient, pre-prophetic past but to that of the new Persian-Hellenistic culture all about Judea; however, this is outside our present period of study.

10   For some passages that would seem to indicate the contrary (Isa. 23:15-17; Jer. 25:11-12; 29:10), see Orlinsky, "The Seer in Ancient Israel," loc. cit., note 10. Such passages (on Isa. 7:8, see, for example, Lindblom, op. cit., p. 290, and note 116), where they are not ex eventu, are merely generalizations.

11   M. Jastrow, Jr. put it very well in "Rô'ēh and Ḥōzēh in the Old Testament," JBL, 28 (1909), 56: "His [that is, the prophet's] main purpose is to speak out in the name of a Deity, to speak forth rather than to foretell. It is therefore a mistaken view of the later tradition which regarded the רֹאֶה as the prototype of the נָבִיא. The rô'ēh is a diviner as is the ḥōzēh . . ." In time a number of scholars, such as R. H. Charles, A Critical and Exegetical Commentary on the Book of Daniel, Oxford, 1929, will call the diviner a "foreteller" and the prophet a "forthteller." It might also be said that the prophet represented a high-cultural tradition, as against the low-cultural tradition represented by the seer-priest (oral communication from M. A. Cohen).

12   On the seer's intervention in the affairs of non-Israelites on foreign soil (for example, Elijah, Elisha) — an activity unknown to the prophet — see Orlinsky, "The Seer in Ancient Israel," loc. cit., 159-60, and notes 16-8 (the last with reference to Jonah).

13   Jastrow, "Rô'ēh and Ḥōzēh in the Old Testament," loc. cit., 43 ff.

14   Note that the term "Levi(te)" has nothing to do here with the tribe "Levi" that allegedly existed along with eleven other tribes from the time that the Israelites settled in Canaan — "allegedly" because throughout the account in Jud. 17-18 the term "Levi(te)" breathes no hint of anything tribal. The opposite is the effect one gets; cf., for example, Jud. 17:7 — "There was a young man from Bethlehem of Judah, from the clanseat of Judah; he was a levite and had lived there as a sojourner." It will be noted that Judah, too, does not constitute a tribe in these chapters, but rather a geographical designation. See Cohen's acute analysis of "The Role of the Shilonite Priesthood," loc. cit., 59 ff. — one of the exceedingly few that comprehends the social forces that shaped Israel's early history — as well as his "Excursus on the Origin of the Tribe of Judah," HUCA, 36 (1965), 94-8.

Neither do the Danites constitute a tribe in Jud. 18; they are a petty clan of sorts. It is a pity that Israel's history in the period of the Judges has been terribly distorted by scholars who have uncritically accepted the later biblical statement that Israel then consisted of twelve tribes and who have even created for the non-existing twelve tribes an amphictyonic society; cf. H. M. Orlinsky, "The Tribal System of Israel and Related Groups in the Period of the Judges," Oriens Antiquus, 1 (1962), 11-20 (= Studies and Essays in Honor of Abraham A. Neuman, Philadelphia, 1962, pp. 375-87).

15   The text (Jud. 17:10) reads: "And Micah said to him, 'Remain with me, and be a father and a priest to me.'" Whether the term אב "father" is to be understood here honorifically, or as a formula of adoption, or as a corruption of an original א/ב, a diviner of sorts, is immaterial for our purpose; verse 11 favors the first (and commonly accepted) interpretation: "So the levite agreed to remain with the man; and the young man became to him like one of his own sons."

16   Cf. Jud. 17:13 — "Then said Micah, 'Now I know that the Lord will prosper me, for the levite has become my priest.'"

17   It may be noted that if any sacrifice was involved here, it was of too little significance to the biblical writer to merit attention.

18 Cohen, "The Role of the Shilonite Priesthood," *loc. cit.*, 65.

19 See, in this connection, the much-overlooked discussion by O. H. Gates, "The Relation of Priests to Sacrifice before the Exile," *JBL*, 27 (1908), 67–92. A good idea of the confusion in which our subject finds itself may be gained from the article by R. Rabba, "Priests and Levites," *The Interpreter's Dictionary of the Bible*, New York, 1962, III, pp. 876b–89b; and cf. E. Nielsen, "The Levites in Ancient Israel," *Annual of the Swedish Theological Institute*, 3 (1964), 16–27.

20 Cf., for example, A. L. Oppenheim, *The Interpretation of Dreams in the Ancient Near East*, Philadelphia, 1956, § 5 : "Interpretation and Interpreters," pp. 217 ff.; also his interesting chapter (III), "A Bird's-Eye View of Mesopotamian Economic History," in *Trade and Market in the Early Empires; Economies in History and Theory*, ed. by K. Polanyi, C. M. Arensberg, and H. W. Pearson, Glencoe, 1957, pp. 27–37; *idem*, *Ancient Mesopotamia*, chap. II, § "The Great Organizations," pp. 95–109; Wilson, *op. cit.*, Index, s.v. Priest, Priesthood, Priests; Haldar, *op. cit.*, chap. II, "Associations of Priests and Prophets in the O.T.," pp. 90 ff. — where, however, no distinction is made between the earlier seer and later prophet, and where conclusions are frequently reached too hastily; T. J. Meek, *Hebrew Origins* (rev. ed.), New York, 1950 chaps. IV, "The Origin of the Hebrew Priesthood," and V, "The Origin of Hebrew Prophecy," pp. 119 ff., 148 ff.

I do not include here such biblical figures as Joseph, Moses, and Joshua, not merely because they antedate Israel's settlement and consolidation in Canaan but because they were not professional seers. In their earlier period, the leading representatives of the Hebrews were believed to be able — with the direct intervention of God — to duplicate and even surpass the "superhuman" qualities of their non-Hebraic counterparts. Thus Jacob, in his famous blessing (Gen. 49), could tell his sons what shall befall them in days to come. His son Joseph had previously interpreted the dreams of Pharaoh's chief cup-bearer and chief baker, and then the monarch's own two-in-one dream (Gen. 40–41. On the term for "interpret," *ptr*, Akkadian *pašāru*, see Oppenheim, *The Interpretation of Dreams*, pp. 217–22). Moses and Aaron could duplicate, and more, the wizardry of Pharaoh's magicians; indeed, Moses brought on Ten Plagues, he sweetened bitter waters by casting a log into them, he brought forth water from a rock by striking it, and he had cooperated with God in His dividing the waters of the Sea of Reeds (Ex. 7–17). Joshua caused the walls of Jericho to come tumbling down by magical rites that included the blowing of the shofar and various acts involving the potent number "seven"; and he later caused the sun and the moon to stop in their natural courses (Josh. 6:10).

In later times, in referring to Moses, Israel's outstanding founder of its nationality and its lawgiver, it was but natural to refer to him as "prophet" and "the man of God"; on the latter term, see — though with some reserve — R. Hallevy, "Man of God," *JNES*, 17 (1958), 237–44.

21 Cf. H. Junker, *Prophet und Seher in Israel. Eine Untersuchung über die ältesten Erscheinungen des israelitischen Prophetentums insbesondere Prophetenvereine*, Trier, 1927; and see note 8, above.

22 Amaziah, priest at Beth-el, called Amos a "visionary." But the priest applied this term scornfully (Amos 7:12): "Visionary, go, flee away to the land of Judah, and eat bread [i.e. earn your living] there by prophesying there" — to which Amos retorted (verse 14): "I am neither a [professional] prophet nor a member of a prophets' guild" (*lo navi anoki wᵉ-lo ben navi anoki*).

23 The account of Eli in the Book of Samuel is very prejudiced. Thus the introduction to Eli's career is *via* the pre-natal career of Samuel; and the first reference to Eli is by way of his two wicked sons (I Sam. 1:3; this is so even if "Eli" stood in our text originally; cf. S.R. Driver, *Notes on ... Samuel* [2nd ed.], Oxford, 1913, *ad loc.*). Samuel is made to be the "minister" (*mᵉsharet*) not of Eli — as, for example, Joshua was of Moses — but of God directly (I Sam. 2:11; 3:1), and he is said to have received the dream-call directly from Him. Again, Eli deserved to die as he did because

of his two sinful sons; but Samuel died nicely at a ripe old age — even though he was also the father of two sinful sons — and he was never repudiated by Israel; it was God who was repudiated (I Sam. 2:27–36; 8: 1–9; I Kings 2:26–27).

24 On a later occasion, when David took refuge from Saul at Samuel's permanent shrine in Ramah (I Sam. 19:18–24) and Saul sent messengers to take David, they saw "the company (lahaqat) of prophets prophesying, while Samuel was standing as head (nizzav) over them." (On lahaqat, cf. J. C. Greenfield, HUCA, 29 [1958], 212–4; on nizzav, see Driver, op. cit., ad loc.) This so affected the three successive groups of messengers which the monarch had sent to take David that "the spirit of God came upon the messengers of Saul, and they also prophesied." And when Saul himself came to effect the capture, "the spirit of God came upon him also, and he went along prophesying... And he too stripped off his clothes ..." This second event was then made to share with the first occasion for the origin of the proverb, "Is Saul also among the prophets?"

25 See J. A. Montgomery, A Critical and Exegetical Commentary on the Books of Kings, Edinburgh, 1951, p. 350.

26 See ibid., loc. cit., on this "garb ... of professional austerity."

27 See note 23, above, on how God was made to replace Eli in this connection.

28 See Orlinsky, "The Seer in Ancient Israel," loc. cit., 166.

29 For additional data and references, involving Nathan the prophet and David in relation to Solomon, Ahijah and Jeroboam and "the man of God" from Judah, Shemaiah and Rehoboam, Azariah and Asa, etc., see ibid., 165–6.

30 The idea that the Israelite tribes in this period constituted an amphictyony is one of the scholarly fictions of our own making; see note 14 (end), above, for reference to my article on this. Cohen, "The Role of the Shilonite Priesthood," loc. cit., 63, put it this way: "If an amphictyony existed, what kind of organization would it be if it possessed no effective military power?"

31 Ibid., 63–4, 69–70.

32 For additional data, see Orlinsky, "The Seer in Ancient Israel," loc. cit., 168, and notes 32–5.

33 On the incubation dream of Solomon at Gibeon (I Kings 3:5 ff.// II Chron. 1: 7 ff.), as well as the dream subsequent to the completion of the Temple (I Kings 9:1–9 // II Chron. 7:12 ff.), see Oppenheim, op. cit., pp. 187 ff.; on other aspects, cf. ibid., pp. 191, 193 (on how David "transmitted" to Solomon the pattern of the Temple). It is probably no mere coincidence that it is precisely from this period that reference in the Bible to the ark, the Urim and Thummim, and the ephod virtually ceases.

34 The latest reference to diviners in our period (thus excluding the Book of Daniel) — after the lapse of over one hundred and fifty years — deals with King Manasseh of Judah (II Chron. 33:18): "Now the rest of the acts of Manasseh, and his prayer to his God, and the words of the visionaries who spoke to him [divrei ha-hozim ha-medabberim elaw] in the name of the Lord, the God of Israel, they are to be found in the Chronicles of the kings of Israel." The reference to divrei hozai (Septuagint: hozim) in verse 19 is obscure.

35 From a private communication from Prof. Ellis Rivkin.

36 Cf., for example, M. Noth, "History and the Word of God in the Old Testament," Bulletin of the John Rylands Library, 32 (1950), 194–206; W. von Soden, "Verkündung des Gotteswillens durch prophetisches Wort in den altbabylonischen Briefen aus Mâri," Die Welt des Orients, 1 (1947–1952), 397–403. On these, see, however, H. M. Orlinsky, Ancient Israel, Ithaca, 1954, p. 144, note 4: "These articles have erred in connecting the Mari text with the later, uniquely Israelite phase of prophecy." See also H. H. Rowley, Prophecy and Religion in Ancient China and Israel, London, 1956, pp. 16 f., and note 4 (with references also to F. M. Th. de Liagre Böhl and H. Schmökel).

37 A. Lods, "Une tablette intéressante pour l'histoire ancienne du prophétisme sémitique," in Studies in Old Testament Prophecy Presented to ... T. H. Robinson, ed. by H. H. Rowley, Edinburgh, 1950, pp. 103–10

(translation and transcription of the text by G. Dossin). For a more recent analysis of this text, see A. Malamat, "History and Prophetic Vision in a Mari Letter" (Hebrew), *Eretz-Israel*, 5 (1958), 67–73 (English summary, pp. 86* f.); cf. *idem, VTS*, 15 (1966), 207 ff.

38 Lods, *op. cit.*, pp. 108 f.

39 See also the earlier study of this letter by A. Malamat, "'Prophecy' in the Mari Documents" (Hebrew), *Eretz Israel*, 4 (1956), 74–84. The first four Letters discussed by Malamat (*loc. cit.*, 75–81), selected from *ARM*, II, III, VI (from among the correspondence of Kibri-Dagan and Bahdi-lim) make reference to the *muḫḫûm* (Letters 1–3) and *muḫḫûtum* (Letter 4), which are there rendered *navi* and *nᵉvi'a*. But this Hebrew term is misleading here; as noted by the author himself (*loc. cit.*, 75), *mᵉshugga'* "frenzied" would be a more appropriate correspondent (cf. the state of the "possessed" boy in the tale of Wen-Amon, below). It is the Israelite seer and his role, not the classical prophet, who corresponds to the *muḫḫûm* here.

40 This letter is No. 5 in Malamat, *loc. cit.*,

81 ff. (For an English translation of the Letter, see Oppenheim, *op. cit.*, p. 195.) Note how Zechariah the son of Jehoiada the priest, in the role of seer ("And the spirit of God clothed [*lavᵉsha* = took possession of] Zechariah"), exhorts the people, who had gone to worship at other shrines, not to abandon "the house of the Lord" (II Chron. 24:17–22).

41 See the translation by J. A. Wilson, *ANET*, p. 26; see also *idem, The Burden of Egypt*, pp. 289 ff.; and cf., for example, Meek, *op. cit.*, pp. 155 f.

42 On this word, Wilson has noted (*ANET*, p. 26 note 13): "The determinative [sign] of the word '[prophetically] possessed' shows a human figure in violent motion of epileptic convulsion."

43 In his later discussion of "Prophetic Revelations in New Documents from Mari and the Bible," *VTS*, 15 (1966; Geneva Congress Volume), 207–27 (in Hebrew, *Eretz Israel*, 8 [1967], 231–40), A. Malamat has continued to overlook the basic differences between the seer-priest of ancient Israel and the Near East and the Israelite prophet.

EXCURSUS I: ON THE TERMINOLOGY FOR "SEER-PRIEST"

The terms *ḥoze* and *ro'e* can hardly be differentiated in their biblical usage. One opinion[1] that the former was of Aramaic usage has now been upset by its use in Ugaritic-Phoenician. An earlier suggestion by Jastrow[2] had it that "רֹאֶה is the 'inspector' [cf. Bab. *bārû*] who looks for a sign and interprets it, the חֹזֶה is the one to whom a sign appears, and who recognizes its meaning when it manifests itself."

Nor is it possible to determine precisely the original meaning and usage of the term *navi*. It would seem that *navi* in the Bible meant approximately "spokesman," as when the Lord told Moses, "your brother Aaron shall serve you as spokesman "(*navi:* Ex. 7:1; with which should be compared the term *pe* "mouth, spokesman" in Ex. 4:16). This is how the Jews themselves translated *navi* in the Septuagint ca. 200 B.C.E.; the Greek word which was there employed, προφήτης, "declarer; inter-

preter," is the source of the English word "prophet."[3] Scholars generally are inclined to the view that the term *navi*, when employed for Abraham (Gen. 20:7; note the use of the verb *ra'a* in verse 10), or Moses (Deut. 34:10; cf. Hos. 12:14; and cf. Num. 11:25–29 for Eldad and Medad), or Samuel (II Chron. 35:18; cf. I Sam. 3:20), or Nathan (II Sam. 7:2; 12:25; etc.), or an unnamed person (for example, Jud. 6:8 — *ish navi*) is the product of later usage, as is similarly the term *nᵉvi'a* "prophetess," when employed for Miriam (Ex. 15:20) and Deborah (Jud. 4:4 — *isha nᵉvi'a*).[4] This accords with the editorial statement in I Sam. 9:9 — "Formerly in Israel, when a person went to inquire of God, thus he said, 'Come let us go to the seer'; for he who is now called a prophet was formerly called a seer."[5]

It is likewise the consensus of scholarly opinion that the term "(the) man of God,"[6] when associated with such early figures as Moses (Deut. 33:1; Josh. 14:6; Ps. 90:1; Ezra 3:2; I Chron. 23:14; II Chron. 30:16) and David (Neh. 12:24, 36; II Chron. 8:14), is the product of a later age.[7]

In the Book of Chronicles, as in the Septuagint and Targum, the terms *ḥoze* and *ro'e* are sometimes interchanged with "prophet" : 1) *Ro'e* is usually rendered by ὁ βλέπων (but ὁ προφήτης in I Chron. 26 : 28 — Samuel; II Chron. 16 : 7, 10 — Hanani) and *ḥezwayya* (but the Targum has, for example, *nᵉvu'at* for *ḥazut* in Isa. 29:11). 2) *Ḥoze* is usually reproduced by ὁ ὁρῶν (ὁ βλέπων in II Chron. 19:2 — Hanani; II Chron. 29:30 — Assaph; II Chron. 35:15 — Asaph, Heman, and Jeduthun; in I Chron. 25:1 they are described as *ha-nibbᵉ'im bᵉ-ḳinnorot*, and hence ὁ ἀνακρουόμενος for Heman as *ḥoze ha-melek* in verse 5) and *ḥezwayya* (but *nᵉviyaya* in Isa. 30:10). For *ḥazon* the Septuagint will employ both προφητεία (used also for *nᵉvu'a*) and ὅρασις (used also for *massa*).

This usage in the Septuagint and Targum

is natural enough, when in the Bible itself reference is made, for example, to Gad as both prophet and seer (II Sam. 24:11 — *Gad ha-navi ḥoze David*); to Asaph, Heman, and Jeduthun as "seers" and "who prophesy" (I Chron. 25:1, 5; II Chron. 35:15); to Shemaiah as "the man of God" (I Kings 12:22; II Chron. 11:2) and "prophet" (II Chron. 12:5); to Samuel as all three: seer, man of God, and prophet. And so on.

If one must hazard an opinion, it would appear that the use of *ḥoze*, *ro'e*, and *navi* depends upon chronological-regional factors. Thus Samuel is called *ro'e*, but never *ḥoze*. And Hanani is the only other one to be called *ro'e* (II Chron. 16:7, 10). Again, neither Elijah nor Elisha is ever referred to as *ḥoze* or *ro'e;* the former is either "the Tishbite" (*ha-Tishbi*) or *navi*, and the latter is either *navi* or (more commonly) *ish ha-Elohim*. Several persons are referred to as the *ḥoze* of a king (for example, Gad, Heman, Jeduthun); but no one is either the *ro'e* of a king or his *navi* — except for Aaron as the *navi* or *pe* of Moses, the *navi* can be only God's.[8]

---

[1] M. A. van den Oudenrijn, "De vocabulis quibusdam termino נביא synonimis," *Biblica*, 6 (1925), 304 f. A. R. Johnson, *The Cultic Prophet in Ancient Israel*, Cardiff, 1944, *passim*, discusses the etymology and usage of these and related terms. L. Koehler, *Lexicon in V. T. Libros*, Leiden, 1949, p. 284b, s.v. חזה, in recording "ug. *ḥdy*" as a cognate, proceeds to assert, "*the Aramaic word for Hebrew* ראה, *early used by the Hebrew*"; the justification for this assertion is not apparent.

[2] M. Jastrow, Jr., "Rô'ēh and Ḥōzēh in the Old Testament," *JBL*, 28 (1909), 53.

[3] Cf. T. J. Meek, *Hebrew Origins* (rev. ed.), New York, 1950, pp. 150 f.

[4] *Ḥoze* and *ro'e* as technical terms do not occur in biblical Hebrew in the feminine form, singular or plural. Women do not seem to have taken a direct part in the cult worship in ancient Israel (pending determination of the exact meaning of *ha-zovᵉ'ot* in Ex. 38:8; I Sam. 2:22); but they were seers and prophetesses, for example, the woman of En-dor who divined by a ghost (I Sam. 28:3 ff.), Huldah (II Kings 22:14 ff. // II Chron. 34:22 ff.), and Noadiah (Neh. 6:14 — a "false" prophetess). The "prophetess" mentioned in Isa. 8:3 refers apparently to the prophet's wife.

[5] Most scholars would transpose this gloss to the word "seer" in verse 11. Yet note "the man of God" in verse 8, at which point the gloss is really just as pertinent.

[6] The term *ish (ha-)Elohim* (never *ish Yahweh;* or the plural *anshei (ha-)Elohim* or *Yahweh*) is to be dis-

tinguished clearly from *mal'ak Elohim* or *Yahweh* "messenger of God/the Lord; angel." If the being in human form (*ish*) is believed to be superhuman, he is then a *mal'ak Elohim* or *Yahweh*. This is clear from the story of Gideon (Jud. 6), where Gideon realizes that it was a divine being rather than a mortal, that he saw face to face; and from the story of Manoah's wife (Jud. 13; where cf. the use of *mal'ak Elohim* or *Yahweh* and *ish ha-Elohim*, and the dialogue in verses 22–23). A. Haldar, *Associations of Cult Prophets among the Ancient Semites*, Uppsala, 1945, pp. 129 f. (in the section " 'Man of god' and 'messenger' "), has missed this completely, and has made the *mal'ak* a cult functionary. R. Hallevy, "Man of God," *JNES*, 17 (1958), 238 f., and note 7, is not clear in this distinction.

[7] Cf. *ibid.*, 243–4.

[8] When "seers" and "visionaries" (and "prophets" too) have ceased to flourish except in the memory of the people, it is easy to designate Hanani as *ro'e* but his son Jehu as *ḥoze* (II Chron. 16:7; 19:2); where Jehu is designated *navi* (I Kings 16:7, 12), it may well be that this term was added later (cf. J. A. Montgomery, *A Critical and Exegetical Commentary on the Books of Kings*, Edinburgh, 1951, *ad loc.*, pp. 282–3, 289) to distinguish our Jehu from King Jehu. The term *navi* was bandied about freely; in the case of Elijah, the Septuagint added in I Kings 17:1 "the reverential title 'the prophet' which he was not technically" (Montgomery, *op. cit.*, pp. 292–3); other uses of *navi* for Elijah are suspect (cf. *ibid.*, p. 311, on I Kings 18:36).

EXCURSUS II: THE ISRAELITE SEER-PRIEST AND ANCIENT NEAR EASTERN DIVINATION

To what extent the Israelite seer practiced the same occult arts as his non-Israelite colleague is not certain. The Bible makes no mention of the seer, visionary, man of God, or prophet (the earlier, let alone the later) resorting to lecanomancy, libanomancy, necromancy, extispicy, bird-omina, stargazing, hepatoscopy, and the like, to determine the future.[1] Indeed, it would appear that the injunction to burn the *lobus caudatus* of the liver prevented its use in divination.[2] And it may well be that various forms of divination were banned simply because they were practiced in foreign modes of worship. Thus Y. Kaufmann would regard all forms of divination as foreign to, and, when in some periods imported from the outside (for example, Canaan-Phoenicia), incompatible with Israel's monotheism.[3]

It is clear that the Israelite seer-priest, who was believed to have direct and exclusive access to the Lord through an oracle — the ark, the ephod, and the Urim and Thummim come to mind at once — would oppose non-Yahwistic diviners and their means of divination. In any case, for whatever reasons, Saul had forbidden the use of necromancy in Israel on pain of death. But when Saul himself, in the midst

of a crucial battle with the Philistines, had failed to receive any reply from God, "either by dreams, or by Urim, or by prophets," he ordered his aides to find him a necromancer. And thus came about the dramatic event involving Saul, the woman of En-Dor, and Samuel's ghost (I Sam. 28:3 ff. Interestingly, Samuel rebuked Saul not for resorting to necromancy but for disturbing him by bringing him up; cf. verse 15). In the days of Elijah, Israelite kings (for example, Ahab) resorted to the divination of "the prophets of Baal," and King Ahaziah of Judah attempted to inquire of Baal-zebub at Ekron.[4] So that in whatever period divination was banned, segments of the Israelite population occasionally made use of it and were vigorously denounced by the prophets for doing so.

Yet it should be noted that this practice of divination did not necessarily entail transgression of monotheism, for the Lord could as readily be the Deity involved. Hence divination in Israel did not necessarily coincide with idolatry.

The Balaam oracles (Num. 22–24) need not be taken up here, for they are an example not of Israelite but of non-Israelite divination, involving a foreign (probably Mesopotamian) diviner.[5]

[1] A number of terms are found in the Bible for those who practiced forms of divination — though it is not yet possible to determine the precise meaning of most of the terms here listed, and several of the meanings given are but convenient guesses: *menaḥesh* "diviner"; *mekashef* "sorcerer"; *meʻonen* "soothsayer"; *qosem* "augur"; *eshet baʻalat-ov* "necromancer"; *yiddeʻoni* "wizard"; *melaḥesh* "charmer"; *hover haver* "enchanter"; *holem* "dreamer"; *ḥartom* "magician" (on which, see A. L. Oppenheim, *The Interpretation of Dreams in the Ancient Near East*, Philadelphia, 1956, p. 238b), and the like. Cf. I. Mendelsohn, "Magic," *Interpreter's Dictionary of the Bible*, New York, 1962, III, pp. 223b–5a.
[2] M. Jastrow, Jr., "Rôʼēh and Ḥôzēh in the Old Testament," *JBL*, 28 (1909), 48, has argued that this "points to the knowledge of this form of divination among the Hebrews." Yet two significant facts stand out: a) In the list of various kinds of diviners in Deut. 18:10–11, there is no mention of hepatoscopy; b) clay models of livers have been found in Canaan (as in Mesopotamia), but this does not hold

true for Israel. See also Jastrow, *ibid.*, for the possible significance of "on the roof ... at sunrise" in I Sam. 9:25–26.

Y. Kaufmann, *History of the Israelite Religion*, (Hebrew), Tel-Aviv, 1937–1956, II, pp. 282 ff., 458 ff.; III, pp. 659 ff., 709 ff.; see M. Greenberg's abridgment and translation, *The Religion of Israel*, Chicago, 1960, chap. II, "Pagan Religion" (especially pp. 40 ff.). And see I. Mendelsohn, "Divination," *Interpreter's Dictionary of the Bible*, New York, 1962, I, pp. 856b–8b.

[4] At the end of his long reign (about 870 B.C.E.), in the midst of his serious illness, King Asa of Judah (II Chron. 16:12) "did not inquire of the Lord, but of the physicians" (*rofeʼim*), where *refaʼim*, traditional "shades," may well have stood originally.

[5] See W. F. Albright, *JBL*, 63 (1944), 207–33, with special reference to S. Daiches, "Balaam — a Babylonian *bārū*," *H. Hilprecht Anniversary Volume*, Leipzig, 1909, pp. 60–70 (= *Daiches' collected Bible Studies*, London, 1950, pp. 110–9).

CHAPTER XIII

THE MANNER OF THE KING

1 On this subject in general, see the paper under this title by S. Talmon in the *Biram Volume* (Hebrew), Jerusalem, 1956, pp. 45–56. While our respective accounts differ considerably in scope, emphasis, and not a few of the results, Talmon's article merits careful attention on the part of all students of the Bible.

2 For the Mari parallels, see J. Bottéro and A. Finet, *ARM*, XV (Répertoire analytique), pp. 264–5; and cf. above the chapter on "The period of the Judges," A.

3 Cf. G. Dossin, "L'inscription de fondation de Jaḫdun-Lim, roi de Mari," *Syria*, 32 (1955), 4, lines 3, 9.

4 For the text which best illustrates this particular character of the *šipṭum* and contains the complete wording of the reprimand involved, see *ARM*, II, 92.

5 See, especially, Ex. 6:6; 7:4.

6 Wiseman, *Alalakh*, no. 17. For Sumerian *m e*, cf. E. A. Speiser in *The Idea of History in the Ancient Near East*, ed. by R. C. Dentan, New Haven, 1955, p 37.

7 See Talmon, *loc. cit.*, *p.* 47.

8 The remarks which follow have been further developed in my essay "Mesopotamia — Evolution of an Integrated Civilization," chap. 4c: "Mesopotomia and the World of the Bible," in Vol. I (*The Dawn of Civilization*) of the present series, pp. 255–65, as well as in a separate article in *IEJ*, 7 (1957), 201–16.

9 Cf. M. Noth, "Gott, König, Volk im Alten Testament," *Zeitschrift für Theologie und Kirche*, 47 (1950), 157–91 (*Gesammelte Studien zum Alten Testament*, Munich, 1960, pp. 188–229).

10 See E. A. Speiser, "Of Shoes and Shekels " *BASOR*, 77 (1940), 18–20.

11 On this subject, see M. Noth, *Das System der Zwölf Stämme Israels*, Stuttgart, 1930. pp. 151–62.

12 How far taxation was actually carried can be seen from the evidence of Ugarit. See J. Nougayrol, *PRU*, III, 1955, pp. 225, 226–7. There was even a levy on serving as best man (*kasap susabīnūti*) and on the removal of refuse.

BIBLIOGRAPHY

CHAPTER I

THE HISTORICAL DEVELOPMENT

Aharoni, Y., *The land of Israel in Biblical Times ; A Historical Geography*, (transl. from the Hebrew), Westminster Press, Philadelphia, 1967.

Albright, W. F., "The Excavations of Tell Beit Mirsim", *AASOR*, 12–13, 17 (1932–1938).

"Syrien, Phönizien und Palästina", *Historia Mundi*, II, Bern 1953, 331 ff.

"The Role of the Canaanites in the History of Civilization", *The Bible and the Ancient Near East* (Essays in honor of W. F. Albright, ed. by G. E. Wright), New York 1961, 328–362 (= *Studies in the History of Culture* [Waldo H. Leland Volume], Menasha, Wis. 1942, 11–50).

"Syria, the Philistines and Phoenicia", *CAH*, II (rev. ed.) (ch. XXXIII).

Alt, A., *Kleine Schriften zur Geschichte des Volkes Israel*, I, III, München 1953, 1959.

Amiran, R., *Ancient Pottery of the Holy Land*, (transl. from the Hebrew), Ramat Gan, 1969.

Campbell, E. F., *The Chronology of the Amarna Letters*, Baltimore 1964.

Faulkner, R. O., "Egypt from the Inception of the 19th Dynasty to the Death of Ramesses III", *CAH*, II (rev. ed.) (chap. XXIII).

Gardiner, A., *The Kadesh Inscriptions of Ramesses II*, Oxford 1960.

Goetze, A., "The Struggle for the Domination of Syria", *CAH*, II (rev. ed.) (chap. XVII).

"Anatolia from Shuppiluliumash etc.", *ibid.* (chap. XXI).

"The Hittites and Syria (1300–1200 B.C.)", *ibid.* (chap. XXIV).

Gordon, C. H., *Ugaritic Textbook*, Roma 1965.

Gray, J., *The Legacy of Canaan, etc.*, Leiden 1957.

Helck, H. W., *Die Beziehungen Ägyptens zu Vorderasien, etc.*, Wiesbaden 1962.

Hornung, E., *Untersuchungen zur Chronologie und Geschichte des Neuen Reiches*, Wiesbaden 1964.

Kantor, H. J., *The Aegean and the Orient in the Second Millenium B.C.*, Bloomington 1947 (= *American Journal of Archaeology* 51 [1947], 1–103).

Kitchen, K. A., *Suppiluliuma and the Amarna Pharaohs*, Liverpool 1962.

Knudtzon, J. A., *Die El-Amarna Tafeln*, I–II, Leipzig 1907–1915.

Loud, G., *The Megiddo Ivories*, Chicago 1939, *Megiddo*, II, Chicago 1948.

Maisler (Mazar), B., *A History of Eretz Israel*, I, (Hebrew), Tel Aviv 1938.

Malamat, A., "Syrien-Palästina in der 2. Hälfte des 2. Jahrtausends", *Fischer Weltgeschichte*, III, Frankfurt a/M 1966, 177–221, 347–352.

Nougayrol, J., *Le Palais royal d'Ugarit*, III–IV, Paris 1955–1956.

Otten, H., "Hethiter, Hurriter und Mitanni", *Fischer Weltgeschichte*, III, Frankfurt a/M 1966, 102–176.

Rowe, A., *The Topography and History of Beth-Shan*, Philadelphia 1930.

The Four Canaanite Temples of Beth-Shan, Philadelphia 1940.

Schaeffer, C. F. A., *Ugaritica*, I-IV, Paris 1939–65.

Simons, J., *Handbook for the Study of the Egyptian Topographical Lists Relating to Western Asia*, Leiden 1937.

Stubbings, F. H., *Mycenaean Pottery from the Levant*, Cambridge 1951.

The military History of the Land of Israel in Biblical Times (ed. J. Liver) (Hebrew), Jerusalem, 1964.

Tufnell, O., et alii, *Lachish*, II: *The Fosse Temple*, London 1940.

Virolleaud, Ch., *Le Palais royal d'Ugarit*, II, V, Paris 1957, 1965.

Wisemann, D. J., *The Alalakh Tablets*, London 1953.

Yadin, Y., et alii, *Hazor* I-IV, (Hebrew), Jerusalem 1958–1961.

Yeivin, S., *Studies in the History of the Israelites and their Land*, (Hebrew), Tel Aviv and Jerusalem 1960.

CHAPTER II

THE EGYPTIAN DECLINE IN CANAAN AND THE SEA-PEOPLES

Albright, W. F., "Syria, the Philistines and Phoenicia", *CAH*, II (rev. ed.) (chap. XXXIII).
Yahwe and the Gods of Canaan, London 1968.

Alt, A., *Kleine Schriften zur Geschichte des Volkes Israel* I, München, 1953.

Barnett, R. D., "The Sea Peoples" *CAH* II (rev. ed.) (chap. XXVIII).

Bilabel, F., *Geschichte Vorderasiens*, etc., I, Heidelberg 1927.

Černý, J., "Egypt from the Death of Ramesses III etc.", *CAH*, II (rev. ed.) (chap. XXXV).

Drioton, É. — Vandier, J., *L'Égipte*[4], Paris, 1962.

Edgerton, W. F. — Wilson, J. A., *Historical Records of Ramses III*, Chicago 1936.

Faulkner, R. O., "Egypt from the Inception of the 19th Dynasty to the Death of Ramesses III", *CAH*, II (rev. ed.) (chap. XXIII).
Fischer Weltgeschichte, III: Die Altorientalischen Reiche; II, Das Ende des 2. Jahrtausends, Frankfurt a/M 1966 (chapters by H. Otten and A. Malamat).

Goetze, A., "The Hittites and Syria (1300–1200 B.C.)", *CAH*, II (rev. ed.) (chap. XXIV).

Helck, H. W., *Die Beziehungen Ägyptens zu Vorderasien im 3. und 2 Jahrtausend v. Chr.*, Wiesbaden 1962.

Klengel, H., *Geschichte Syriens im 2. Jahrtausend v.u.Zeit*, II, Berlin, 1969.

Liverani, M., "*Storia di Ugarit*," Roma 1962.

Malamat, A., "Cushan Rishathaim and the Decline of the Near East around 1200 B.C.," *JNES*, 13 (1954), 231–242.

Meyer, E. *Geschichte des Altertums*[2], II, 1–2, Stuttgart and Berlin, 1928–1931.

Otten, H., "Neue Quellen zum Ausklang des Hethitischen Reiches", *MDOG*, 94 (1963), 1–23.

Schaeffer, C. F. A., Nougayrol, J. et alii, *Ugaritica V*, Paris, 1968.

Virolleaud, Ch., *Le Palais Royal d'Ugarit*, Paris 1965.

Wainwright, G. A., "Some Sea-Peoples", *JEA*, 47 (1961), 71–90.

CHAPTER III

SOCIETY AND ECONOMIC CONDITIONS

Albright, W. F., "The Role of the Canaanites in the History of Civilization", *The Bible and the Ancient Near East* (Essays in honor of W. F. Albright, ed. by G. E. Wright), New York 1961, 328–362 (= *Studies in the History of Culture* [Waldo H. Leland Volume], Menasha, Wis. 1942, 11–50).

Breasted, J. H., *Ancient Records of Egypt*, I–V, Chicago 1906–1907.

Contenau, G., *La Civilization Phénicienne*, Paris 1949.

Kantor, H. G., *The Aegean and the Orient in the Second Millennium B.C.*, Bloomington 1947 (= *American Journal of Archaeology*, 51 [1947], 1–103).

Knudtzon, J. A., *Die El-Amarna Taffeln*, I–II, Leipzig 1907–1915.

Langhe, R. de, *Les textes de Ras Shamra-Ugarit et leurs rapports avec le Milieu Biblique de l'Ancien Testament*, I–II, Gembloux 1945.

Maisler (Mazar), B., *A History of Eretz Israel*, I, (Hebrew), Tel Aviv, 1938.

Nougayrol, J., *Le Palais royal d'Ugarit*, III, Paris 1955.

Schaeffer, C. F. A., *The Cuneiform Texts of Ras Shamra-Ugarit*, London 1939.

Wisemann, D. J., *The Alalakh Tablets*, London 1953.

Yeivin, S., (ed.) *Trade, Industry and Crafts in Ancient Palestine* (Library of Palestinology, IX–X) (Hebrew), Jerusalem, 1937.

CHAPTER IV

CULTURAL AND RELIGIOUS LIFE

Gordon, C. H., *The Common Background of Greek and Hebrew Civilizations*, New York 1965.
The ancient Near East, New York 1965.
Ugaritic Textbook, Roma 1965.
Ugarit and Minoan Crete, New York 1966.
Evidence for the Minoan Language, Ventnor, N.J. 1966.

Knudtzon, J. A., *Die El-Amarna Tafeln*, I–II, Leipzig 1907–15.

Lefebvre, G., *Romans et contes Égyptiens de l'époque pharaonique*, Paris 1949.

Mercer, S. A. B., *The Tell el-Amarna Tablets*, I–II, Toronto 1939.

Meyer, E., *Geschichte des Altertums*[2], I–III, Stuttgart 1907–37.

Nougayrol, J., *Le Palais royal d'Ugarit*, III–IV, Paris 1955–1956.

Pritchard, J. B. (ed.), *Ancient Near Eastern Texts Relating to the Old Testament*, Princeton 1955.

Virolleaud, Ch., *Le Palais royal d'Ugarit*, II, V, Paris 1957, 1965.

CHAPTER V

THE EXODUS AND THE CONQUEST

Aharoni, Y., *The Land of Israel in Biblical Times; A Historical Geography*, (transl. from the Hebrew), Westminster Press, Philadelphia, 1967.

Alt, A., *Kleine Schriften zur Geschichte des Volkes Israel*, I–III, München 1953–59.

Beyerlin, W., *Herkunft und Geschichte der ältesten Sinaitraditionen*, Tübingen 1961.

Burney, C. F., *Israel's Settlement in Canaan*, London 1919.

Cazelles, H. — Gellin, A., *Moses in Schrift und Überlieferung*, Düsseldorf 1963.

Duffy, W. F., *The Tribal-Historical Theory on the Origin of the Hebrew People*, Washington D.C. 1944.

Eissfeldt, O., *Baal Zaphon, Zeus Kasios und der Durchzug der Israeliten durchs Meer*, Halle a/S 1932.

Garstang, J., *Joshua-Judges*, London 1931.

Glueck, N., "Explorations in Eastern Palestine", *AASOR*, 25–28 (1945–1949).

Gressmann, H., *Mose und seine Zeit*, Göttingen 1913.

Kaufmann, Y., *A History of the Israelite*

Religion, IV, (Hebrew), Jerusalem and Tel Aviv 1954–1957.

The Narrative of the Conquest of the Land of Israel in the Bible (Hebrew), Jerusalem, 1955.

The Book of Joshua (Hebrew), Jerusalem, 1962.

Kitchen, K. A., "Some New Light on the Asiatic Wars of Ramesses II", *JEA*, 50 (1964), 47–70.

Loewenstamm, S. E., *The Tradition of the Exodus in its Development* (Hebrew), Jerusalem 1965.

Lubsczyk, H., *Der Auszug aus Ägypten*, Leipzig 1963.

Maisler (Mazar), B., *A History of Eretz Israel* I, (Hebrew), Tel Aviv 1938.

Meek, T. J., *Hebrew Origins* (rev. ed.), New York 1950.

Noth, M., *Das System der Zwölf Stämme*

Israels, Stuttgart 1930.

Josua², Tübingen 1953.

Rowley, H. H., *From Joseph to Joshua*, London 1950.

Schunck, K. D., *Benjamin*, Berlin 1963.

Simpson, C. A., *The Early Traditions of Israel*, Oxford 1948.

Smend, R., *Jahwekrieg und Stämmebund*, Göttingen 1963.

The Military History of the Land of Israel in Biblical Times (ed. J. Liver) (Hebrew), Jerusalem 1964.

Tufnell, O., *Lachish*, IV, London 1958.

Winnett, F. V., *The Mosaic Tradition*, Toronto 1949.

Yeivin, S., *Studies in the History of the Israelites and their Land* (Hebrew), Tel Aviv and Jerusalem, 1960.

Zyl, A. H. van, *The Moabites*, Leiden 1960.

CHAPTER VI

THE SETTLEMENT OF CANAAN

Aharoni, Y., *The Settlement of the Israelite Tribes in Upper Galilee* (Hebrew), Jerusalem, 1957.

Albright, W. F., "Excavations and Results at Tell El-Fûl (Gibeah of Saul)", *AASOR*, 4 (1924).

Alt, A., *Die Landnahme der Israeliten in Palästina*, Leipzig 1925 (= *Kleine Schriften*, I, München 1953, 89–125).

"Erwägungen über die Landnahme der Israeliten in Palästina", *PJB*, 35 (1939), 8–63 (= *Kleine Schriften*, I, 126–175).

Bergman, A., "The Israelite Occupation of Eastern Palestine in the Light of Territorial History", *JAOS*, 54 (1934), 169 ff.

"The Israelite Tribe of Half-Manasseh", *JPOS*, 16 (1936), 233 ff.

Burney, C. F., *Israel's Settlement in Canaan*, London 1919.

Garstang, J., *Joshua–Judges*, London 1931.

Glueck, N., *The Other Side of the Jordan*, New Haven, 1945.

Klein, S., *Studies of the Genealogical chapters in*

Chronicles, (Hebrew), Jerusalem, 1930 (= *Zion* 2 [1927], 1–16; 3 [1929], 1–16; 4 [1930], 14–30).

Maisler (Mazar), B., *A History of Eretz Israel*, I, (Hebrew), Tel Aviv 1938.

Meyer, E., *Die Israeliten und ihre Nachbarstämme*, Halle a/S 1906.

Noth, M., "Die Ansiedlung des Stammes Juda auf dem Boden Palästinas", *PJB*, 30 (1934), 31–47.

"Eine Siedlungsgeographische Liste in 1. Chr. 2 und 4", *ZDPV*, 55 (1932), 97–124.

"Studien zu den historisch-geographischen Dokumente des Josuabuches", chap. IV: Die israelitischen Siedlungsgebiete im Ostjordanland, *ibid.*, 58 (1935), 230–255.

Saarisalo, A., *The Boundary between Issachar and Naphtali*, Helsinki 1927.

Schmidtke, F., *Die Einwanderung Israels in Kanaan*, Breslau 1933.

Steuernagel, K., *Die Einwanderung der Israelitischen Stämme in Kanaan*, Berlin 1901.

CHAPTER VII

THE PERIOD OF THE JUDGES

Albright, W. F., *Archaeology and the Religion of Israel*, Baltimore 1942 (2nd ed. 1946).

Auerbach, E., *Wüste und Gelobtes Land*, I², Berlin 1938, 95–124.

Bright, J., *A History of Israel*, London 1960, 142–160.

Burney, C. F., *The Book of Judges*, London 1920 (reprinted with *Prolegomenon* by W. F. Albright, New York 1970).

Cundall, A. E., *Judges*, London 1968.

Desnoyers, L., *Histoire du peuple Hebreu*, I: La période des Judges, Paris 1966.

Die Ou Testamentiese Werkgemeenskab in Suid Africa, Papers read at the 2nd Meeting, 1959.

Eissfeldt, O., "The Hebrew Kingdom", *CAH* II (rev. ed.) (chap. XXXIV), 1965.

Garstang, J., *Joshua-Judges*, London 1931.

Glueck, N., *The other Side of the Jordan*, New Haven 1945.

Kaufmann, Y., *The Book of Judges* (Hebrew), Jerusalem 1962.

Kittel, R., *Geschichte des Volkes Israel*, II (sixth and seventh ed.), Stuttgart 1925.

Lagrange, M. J., *Le livre des Judges*, Paris 1903.

Maisler (Mazar), B., *A History of Eretz Israel*, I, (Hebrew), Tel-Aviv 1938.

Malamat, A., "Syrien-Palästina in der 2. Hälfte des 2. Jahrtausends" *Fischer Weltgeschichte*, III, Frankfurt a/M 1966, 177–221, 347–352.

Noth, M., *Geschichte Israels*,(2nd ed.) Göttingen 1956, 131–151.

Olmstead, A. T., *History of Palestine and Syria*, New York–London 1931, 270–293.

Richter, W., *Traditionsgeschichtliche Untersuchungen zum Richterbuch*, Bonn 1963.
Die Bearbeitungen des "Retterbuches", etc., Bonn 1964.

Smend, R., *Jahwekrieg und Stämmebund*, (2nd ed.), Göttingen, 1966.

Studies in the Book of Judges (Collection of lectures), (Hebrew), Jerusalem 1966.

Täubler, E., *Biblische Studien — Die Epoche der Richter*, Tübingen 1968.

The Military History of the Land of Israel in Biblical Times, (ed. J. Liver) (Hebrew), Jerusalem 1964.

Wright, G. E., *Biblical Archaeology* (2nd ed.), Philadelphia–London 1962, 86 ff.

Yadin, Y., *The Art of Warfare in Biblical Lands*, Ramat Gan 1963.

Zapietal, V., *Das Buch der Richter*, Münster 1923.

CHAPTER VIII

THE PHILISTINES AND THEIR WARS WITH ISRAEL

Albright, W. F., "The Eastern Mediterranean about 1060 B.C.", *Studies Presented to D. M. Robinson*, I, St. Louis 1951.
"Syria, the Philistines and Phoenicia", *CAH*, II (rev. ed.) (chap. XXXIII).

Alt, A., *Kleine Schriften*, I, München 1953.

Bonfante, G., "Who were the Philistines?", *American Journal of Archaeology*, 50 (1946), 251 ff.

Burn, A. R., *Minoans, Philistines, and Greeks*, London 1930.

Desborough, V. R. d'A., *The Last Mycenaeans and their Successors*, Oxford 1964.

Dothan, T., "Studies in Philistine Culture," *Eretz Israel* 5 (Hebrew), (1959), 55–66.
The Philistines and their Material Culture (Hebrew), Jerusalem 1967.

Edgerton, W. F. — Willson, J. A., *Historical Records of Ramses III*, Chicago 1936.

Eissfeldt, O., "Palestine in the time of the Nineteenth Century: (a) The Exodus and the Wanderings", *CAH*, II, (rev. ed.) (chap. XXVI).

Erlenmeyer, H. and M. L., "Über Philister und Kreter", *Orientalia* (N.S.), 29 (1960), 121–150, 241–272; 30 (1961), 269–293; 33 (1964), 199–237.

Gardiner, A. H., *Ancient Egyptian Onomastica*, I–III, Oxford 1947.

Grant, E. — Wright, G. E., *Ain Shems Excavations*, V, Haverford 1939.

Loud, G., *Megiddo*, II, Chicago 1948.

Macalister, R. A. S., *The Philistines*, London, 1914.

Maisler (Mazar), B., "Excavations at Tell Qasileh," *Eretz Israel* I (Hebrew), (1951), 45–71.

"The Philistines and the Establishment of the Kingdoms of Israel and Tyre, "*Pro-ceedings of the Israel Academy of Sciences* I, vii, (1964).

Petrie, F., et alii, *Beth Pelet*, I–II, London 1930–1932.

Wainwright, G. A., "Some Early Philistine History", *VT*, 9 (1959), 73 ff.

Weiser, A., *Samuel*, Göttingen 1962.

Wreszinski, W., *Atlas zur altägyptischen Kulturgeschichte*, II, Leipzig 1932.

Yadin, Y., *The Art of Warfare in Biblical Lands*, Ramat Gan, 1963.

"And why did Dan remain in ships" in *Western Galilee and the Coast of Galilee*, (Collection of articles) (Hebrew), Jerusalem 1965, 42–55.

CHAPTER IX

THE ISRAELITE TRIBES

Alt, A., *Die Staatenbildung der Israeliten in Palästina*, Leipzig 1930 (= *Kleine Schriften*, II, München 1953, 1–65),

Barrois, A., *Manuel d'archéologie biblique*, II, Paris 1953.

Benzinger, I., *Hebraeische Archeologie³*, Leipzig 1927.

Bright, J., *A History of Israel*, London 1960.

Causse, A., *Du groupe ethnique à la communauté réligieuse*, Paris 1937.

Duffy, W., *The Tribal-Historical Theory on the Origin of the Hebrew People*, Washington D.C. 1944.

Flight, W. J., "The Nomadic Idea and Ideal in the Old Testament", *JBL*, 42 (1923), 152–226.

Gabrieli, F., *L'antica societa Beduina*, Roma 1959.

Jacobson, D., *The Social Background of the Old Testament*, Cincinnati 1942.

Kaufmann, Y., *A History of the Israelite Religion*, IV, (Hebrew), Jerusalem and Tel Aviv 1954–1957.

Klein, S., *Studies of the Genealogical Chapters in Chronicles*, (Hebrew), Jerusalem 1930 (= *Zion* 2 [1927], 1–16; 3 [1929], 1–16; 4 [1930], 14–30).

Lods, A., *Israël, des origines au milieu du VIIIe siècle*, Paris 1930.

Luther, B., "Die Israelitischen Stämme", *ZAW*, 21 (1901), 1–76.

Maisler (Mazar), B., *A History of Eretz Israel*, I, (Hebrew), Tel Aviv 1938.

"The Genealogy of the Sons of Nahor and the Historical Background of the Book of Job, *Zion* 11 (Hebrew), (1946), 1–16.

Meyer, E., *Die Israeliten und ihre Nachbarstämme*, Halle a/S 1906.

Noth, M., *Das System der Zwölf Stämme Israels*, Stuttgart 1930.

Geschichte Israels (2nd ed.), Göttingen 1954.

Pedersen, J., *Israel, Its Life and Culture*, I–II, London-Copenhagen 1926.

Ploeg, J. van der, "Les chefs du peuple d'Israël et leurs titres", *RB*, 57 (1950), 40–61.

Scharbert, J., *Solidarität in Segen und Fluch im Alten Testament und in seiner Umwelt*, Bonn 1958.

Smend, R., *Jahwekrieg und Stämmebund*, Göttingen 1963.

Robertson Smith, W., *Kinship and Marriage in Early Arabia²*, London 1903.

Vaux, R. de, *Les institutions de l'Ancien Testament*, I, Paris 1958.

Weber, M., *Das antike Judentum* (= *Gesammelte Aufsätze zur Religionssoziologie*, III), Tübingen 1921.

Wolf, C. U., "Terminology of Israel's Tribal Organization", *JBL*, 65 (1946), 45–49.

"Traces of Primitive Democracy in Ancient Israel", *JNES*, 6 (1947), 98–108.

CHAPTER X

THE RELIGIOUS CULTURE OF THE JEWISH PEOPLE IN ITS BEGINNINGS: THE FAITH AND THE CULT

Albright, W. F., *From the Stone Age to Christianity*, Baltimore 1940, 189–220.

Auerbach, E., *Moses*, Amsterdam 1953.

Buber, M., *Moses*, Jerusalem and Tel Aviv 1946.

Cazelles, H., Gelin, A., et alii, *Moïse, l'homme de l'alliance*, Paris 1955.

Gressmann, H., *Mose und seine Zeit*, Göttingen 1913.

Kaufmann, Y., *A History of the Israelite Religion*, IV, (Hebrew), Jerusalem and Tel Aviv 1954–1957.

Rowley, H. H., "Moses und der Monotheismus", *ZAW*, 69 (1957), 1–21.

Men of God, London 1963, 1–36.

Smend, R., *Das Mosebild von H. Ewald bis M. Noth*, Tübingen 1959.

Volz, P., *Mose und sein Werk*, Tübingen 1932.

CHAPTER XI

LAW

Alt, A., *Die Ursprünge des israelitischen Rechts*, Leipzig 1934 (= *Kleine Schriften*, I, München 1953, 278–332).

Cazelles, H., *Études sur le Code de l'Alliance*, Paris 1946.

Daube, D., *Studies in Biblical Law*, Cambridge 1947.

David, M., "The Codex Hammurabbi and its Relation to the Provisions of Law in Exodus", *OTS*, 7 (1950), 148–178.

Falk, Z. W., *Hebrew Law in Biblical Times*, Jerusalem 1964.

Greenberg, M., "Some Postulates of Biblical Criminal Law", *Y. Kaufmann Jubilee*

Volume, Jerusalem 1960, 5–28.

Jirku, A., *Das weltliche Recht im alten Testament*, Gütersloh 1927.

Kaufmann, Y., *A History of the Israelite Religion*, IV, (Hebrew), Jerusalem and Tel Aviv 1954–1957.

Mendenhall, G., *Law and Covenant in Israel and the Ancient Near East*, Pittsburgh 1955.

Noth, M., *Die Gesetze im Pentateuch*, Halle a/S 1940.

Ploeg, J. van der, "Studies in Hebrew Law", *CBQ*, 12 (1950), 248–259, 416–427; 13 (1951), 164–171.

CHAPTER XII

THE SEER-PRIEST

Cohen, M. A., "The Role of the Shilonite Priesthood in the United Monarchy of Ancient Israel", *HUCA* 36 (1965), 59–98.

Contenau, G., *La divination chez les Assyriens et les Babyloniens*, Paris 1940.
La Magie chez les Assyriens et les Babyloniens, Paris 1947.

Daiches, S., "Balaam — a Babylonian *bārū*. The Episode of Num. XXIII, 2 — XXIV, 24 and some Babylonian Parallels", *Assyriologische und archeologische Studien. Herman v. Hilprecht ... gewidmet*, Leipzig 1909, 60–70 (= S. Daiches, *Bible Studies*, London 1950, 110–119).

Gaster, T. H., *Thespis; Ritual, Myth and Drama in the Ancient Near East* (rev. ed.), New York 1961.

Gates, O. H., "The Relation of Priests to Sacrifice before the Exile", *JBL*, 27 (1928), 67–92.

Haldar, A., *Associations of Cult Prophets among the Ancient Semites*, Uppsala 1945.

Hölscher, G., *Die Profeten. Untersuchungen zur Religionsgeschichte Israels*, Leipzig 1914.

Jastrow, M., Jr., "Rô'ēh and Ḥôzēh in the Old Testament", *JBL*, 28 (1909), 42–56.
Aspects of Religious Belief and Practice in Babylonia and Assyria, New York 1911 (especially pp. 143–264).

Johnson, A. R., *The Cultic Prophet in Ancient Israel*, Cardiff 1944.

Junker, H., *Prophet und Seher in Israel. Eine Untersuchung über die ältesten Erscheinungen des israelitischen Prophetentums insbesondere Prophetenvereine*, Trier 1927.

Lexa, F., *La Magie dans l'Égypte antique etc.*, 3 vols., Paris 1925.

Lindblom, J., *Prophecy in Ancient Israel*, Oxford 1962.

Meek, T. J., *Hebrew Origins* (rev. ed.), New York 1950; chaps. IV ("The Origin of the Hebrew Priesthood"), V ("The Origin of Hebrew Prophecy").

Mendelsohn, I., "Divination", *The Interpreter's Dictionary of the Bible*, I, 1962, 856b–858b.
"Magic(ian)", *ibid.*, III, 1962, 223b–225a.

Oppenheim, A. L., *The Interpretation of Dreams in the Ancient Near East*, Philadelphia 1956 (= *Transactions of the American Philosophical Society*, New Series, XLVI, 3).
Ancient Mesopotamia: Portrait of a Dead Civilization, Chicago 1964, 171–227, 364–369, 385–386.

Orlinsky, H. M., *Ancient Israel*[2], Ithaca 1960, chap. VIII ("The Hebraic Spirit: The Prophetic Movement and Social Justice", 142–168).
"The Seer in Ancient Israel", *Oriens Antiquus*, 4 (1965), 153–174.

Rowley, H. H., *The Servant of the Lord and Other Essays on the Old Testament*, London 1952, chap. III ("The Nature of Old Testament Prophecy in the Light of Recent Study") (= *Harvard Theological Review*, 38 [1945], 1–38).

Thompson, R. C., *Reports of the Magicians and Astrologers of Nineveh and Babylon in the British Museum*, 2 vols., London 1900.
The Devils and Evil Spirits of Babylonia etc., 2 vols., London 1903–1904.
Semitic Magic: Its Origin and Development, London 1908.

Vaux, R. de, *Ancient Israel: Its Life and Institutions*, New York 1961: Part IV, "Religious Institutions," pp. 271–517 (and the bibliography there, pp. 537–552).

INDEX OF NAMES AND PLACES

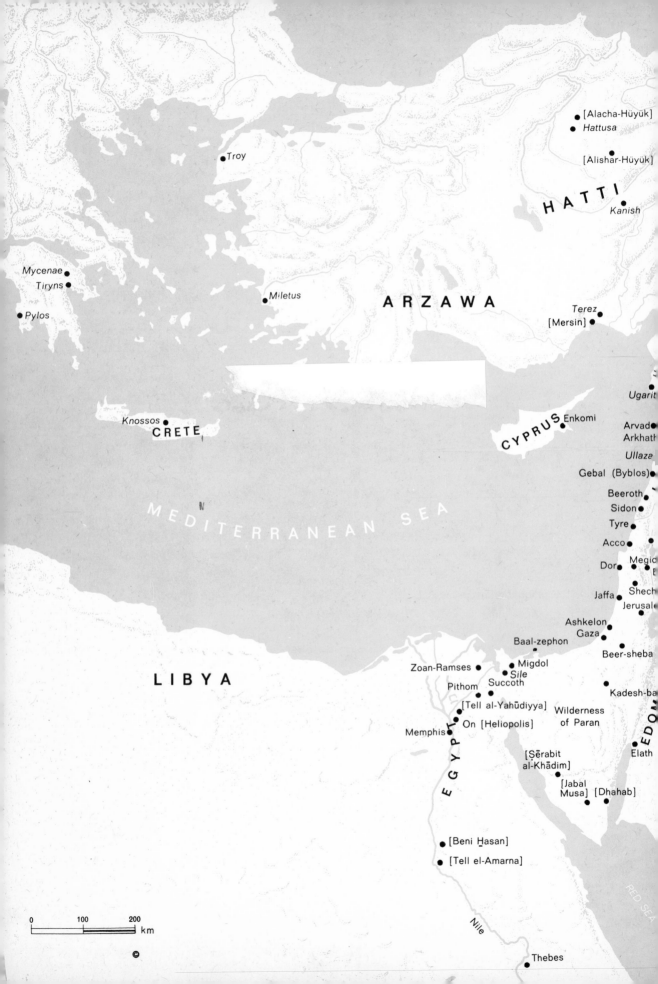

Troy

[Alacha-Hüyük]
Hattusa
[Alishar-Hüyük]

HATTI

Kanish

Mycenae
Tiryns

Pylos

Miletus

ARZAWA

Terez
[Mersin]

Ugarit

Knossos
CRETE

CYPRUS

Enkomi

Arvad
Arkhath

Ullaza

Gebal (Byblos)

MEDITERRANEAN SEA

Beeroth
Sidon
Tyre
Acco
Dor   Megid
Jaffa   Shech
             Jerusale
Ashkelon
Gaza
Beer-sheba

Baal-zephon

LIBYA

Zoan-Ramses
Pithom
[Tell al-Yahūdiyya]
On [Heliopolis]
Memphis

E
G
Y
P
T

Migdol
Sile
Succoth

Wilderness
of Paran

Kadesh-ba

E
D
O
M

Elath

[Sěrabit
al-Khādim]

[Jabal
Musa]   [Dhahab]

[Beni Hasan]

[Tell el-Amarna]

Nile

RED SEA

0   100   200
                    km

Thebes